Society of the Query Reader

Reflections on Web Search

Society of the Query Reader
Reflections on Web Search

Editors: René König and Miriam Rasch
Copyediting: Morgan Currie
Design: Katja van Stiphout
Cover design: Studio Inherent
Printer: Drukkerij Tuijtel, Hardinxveld-Giessendam
Publisher: Institute of Network Cultures, Amsterdam, 2014
ISBN: 978-90-818575-8-1

Contact
Institute of Network Cultures
phone: +31205951865
email: info@networkcultures.org
web: www.networkcultures.org

Order a copy or download this publication freely at:
www.networkcultures.org/publications.

Visit the blog and join the mailinglist about online search at:
http://networkcultures.org/query.

Supported by: Create-IT, Amsterdam University of Applied Sciences (Hogeschool van Amsterdam), Amsterdam Creative Industries Publishing, and Stichting Democratie en Media.

Thanks to everyone at INC, to all of the authors for their contributions, Morgan Currie for her copyediting, and to Stichting Democratie en Media and Amsterdam Creative Industries Publishing for their financial support.

This publication is licensed under Creative Commons Attribution ⓘ NonCommercial Ⓢ ShareAlike ⓞ 3.0 Unported (CC BY-NC-SA 3.0). To view a copy of this license, visit http://creativecommons.org/licenses/by-nc-sa/3.0/.

Society of the Query Reader

Reflections on Web Search

EDITED BY
RENÉ KÖNIG
AND **MIRIAM RASCH**
INC READER #9

Previously published INC Readers:
The INC Reader series is derived from conference contributions and produced by the Institute of Network Cultures. They are available in print and PDF form. The *Society of the Query Reader* is the ninth publication in the series.

INC Reader #8: Geert Lovink and Miriam Rasch (eds),
Unlike Us Reader: Social Media Monopolies and Their Alternatives, 2013.

INC Reader #7: Geert Lovink and Nathaniel Tkacz (eds),
Critical Point of View: A Wikipedia Reader, 2011.

INC Reader #6: Geert Lovink and Rachel Somers Miles (eds),
Video Vortex Reader II: Moving Images Beyond Youtube, 2011.

INC Reader #5: Scott McQuire, Meredith Martin and Sabine Niederer (eds),
Urban Screens Reader, 2009.

INC Reader #4: Geert Lovink and Sabine Niederer (eds),
Video Vortex Reader: Responses to YouTube, 2008.

INC Reader #3: Geert Lovink and Ned Rossiter (eds),
MyCreativity Reader: A Critique of Creative Industries, 2007.

INC Reader #2: Katrien Jacobs, Marije Janssen and Matteo Pasquinelli (eds),
C'LICK ME: A Netporn Studies Reader, 2007.

INC Reader #1: Geert Lovink and Soenke Zehle (eds),
Incommunicado Reader, 2005.

All INC Readers, and other publications like the *Network Notebooks Series* and *Theory on Demand*, can be downloaded and read for free.
See www.networkcultures.org/publications.

CONTENTS

René König and Miriam Rasch
Reflect and Act! Introduction to the Society of the Query Reader   9

THEORIZING WEB SEARCH

Kylie Jarrett
A Database of Intention?   16

Andrea Miconi
Dialectic of Google   30

Vito Campanelli
Frictionless Sharing: The Rise of Automatic Criticism   41

POLITICS OF SEARCH ENGINES

Dirk Lewandowski
Why We Need an Independent Index of the Web   49

Astrid Mager
Is Small Really Beautiful? Big Search and Its Alternatives   59

Ippolita
The Dark Side of Google: Pre-Afterword – Social Media Times   73

Angela Daly
Dominating Search: Google Before the Law   86

THE HISTORY OF SEARCH

Richard Graham
A 'History' of Search Engines: Mapping Technologies of Memory,
Learning and Discovery   105

Anton Tanter
Before Google: A Pre-History of Search Engines in Analogue Times   121

BETWEEN GLOBALIZATION AND LOCALIZATION

Min Jiang and Vicenţiu Dîngă
Search Control in China   139

Anna Jobin and Olivier Glassey
'I Am not a Web Search Result! I Am a Free Word.' The Categorization
and Commodification of 'Switzerland' by Google   149

Amanda Scardamaglia
Keywords, Trademarks, and Search Engine Liability   163

Martin Reiche and Ulrich Gehmann
Towards an Anthropology of Location-Based Recommendation and Search   180

_____ **RESEARCH AND EDUCATION** _____

Jacob Ørmen
Historicizing Google Search: A Discussion of the Challenges Related
to Archiving Search Results   188

Martin Feuz
Exploratory Search and Extended Cognition in Health Information Interaction 203

Dave Crusoe
Educating for Search: Understanding the Past and Present Search
Technology to Teach for Future Resilience   216

Simon Knight
Finding Knowledge: What Is It To 'Know' When We Search?   227

_____ **CREATIVE REFLECTIONS** _____

M.E. Luka and Mél Hogan
Polluted and Predictive, in 133 Words   239

Martina Mahnke and Emma Uprichard
Algorithming the Algorithm   256

Phil Jones and Aharon Amir
Search-Art: The Narcissus Search Engine, Skateboarding, and Oranges   271

_____ **APPENDICES** _____

Society of the Query Conferences
Society of the Query I in Amsterdam   286
Society of the Query II in Amsterdam   287

Author Biographies   288

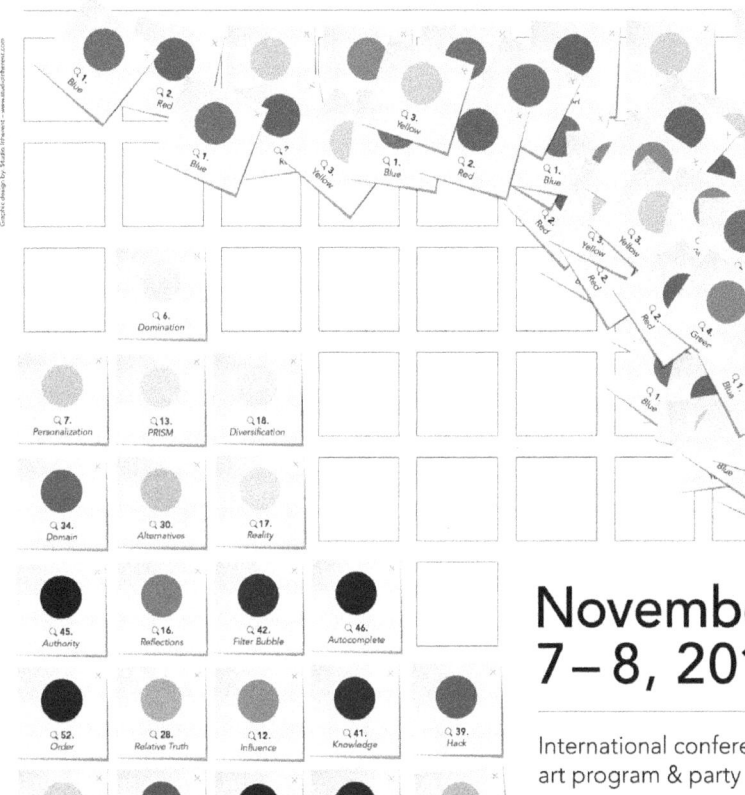

Reflect and Act!

Introduction to the Society of the Query Reader

Reflect and Act!

¬

Introduction to the Society of the Query Reader

In the span of only a few years, search engines such as Google and Bing have become central infrastructure-like elements of the web. Within milliseconds they offer answers to pretty much all of our questions, providing a remarkably effective access point to the ever-growing ocean of information online. As usual for infrastructures, there is a harsh contrast between the importance they have in our daily lives and the attention we pay them. Just as we expect water running from the tap, electricity coming from the plug, and roads to drive on, we take for granted that there are search engines to give us the information we need.

However, search engines are becoming invisible, thereby increasing their implicit power. To counter this tendency, we need to design visibility campaigns to make their influence apparent. This is the main aim of Society of Query and similar initiatives such as Deep Search.[1] Integrated in smart phone interfaces, browsers, apps, and platforms such as YouTube, we take for granted that there is a search bar in close range. Within a remarkably short time range we have familiarized ourselves with the search logic: type, select, click, and move on. The ever-increasing speed we use to search has created a collective 'techno-unconsciousness' from which we have to wake up. This INC Reader is a modest step in this direction.

The rise of mobile devices and connections has increased the infrastructural significance of search engines even further, with a deep impact on our cultures and societies. We carry search technology with us all the time; we use it like an extended memory for factual questions (what was the name again of the author playing Julian Assange in that 2013 biopic? And while we're at it, what year did Wikileaks start again?); we feed them with our existential fears and doubts ('my daughter is overweight, my son is a genius – what should I do?'[2]). But we do not grasp their workings or question the answers they give. We're not in control of our search practices – search engines are in

---

1. See Society of the Query project page: http://networkcultures.org/query/; the Deep Search conference page http://world-information.org/wii/deep_search/en and book: Konrad Becker and Felix Stalder (eds) *Deep Search: The Politics of Search beyond Google*. Innsbruck: Studienverlag, 2009.
2. Amanda Marcotte, 'Parents Ask Google If Their Sons Are Geniuses and If Their Daughters Are Fat', *Slate*, 21 January 2014, http://www.slate.com/blogs/xx_factor/2014/01/21/parents_ask_google_is_my_son_gifted_and_is_my_daughter_overweight.html.

control of us and we readily agree, though mostly unconsciously, to this domination. 'We're citizens, but without rights'[3] in the Society of the Query.

It is of the greatest importance to understand critically that search engine infrastructures are mostly commercial operations, in contrast to the state-owned or at least state-regulated electricity and water infrastructures or road systems. Web search is not just about providing users with the information they are looking for in the most efficient way possible; search engine companies are also driven by the desire to make a profit, and to increase this profit by penetrating ever more areas of our lives and social relationships, predicting our behavior and (information) needs.

With revelations about how user data flow almost directly from companies such as Google to the NSA we seem to be at a crossroads. These insights raise public awareness, leading to a demand for insightful and critical information about the workings of digital technologies such as web search. At the same time there is a growing interest in this subject in fields outside of traditional computer studies – in humanities, history, social sciences, legal sciences, and so on. The time is right to tear apart our common sense of search engines; how to do that exactly remains difficult, however. Just as we don't really know where the water from our taps and the electricity from our plugs come from, and hardly notice the street until it is cut off, we usually do not have much insight into the functionality of web search. It is a black-boxed technology, which means operating a search engine doesn't really require any further knowledge of the technology itself. While previous information systems often demanded a certain level of expertise, modern search engines rather follow the Silicon Valley mantra 'the user is always right'. Since most search engine-providing companies are led by commercial interests, they aim to attract as many users as possible by keeping the entry barriers low. Everyone must be able to use the technology, and when the technology fails to meet the demands of the user, then it must be amended.

In practice, this leads to user interfaces such as Google's, which is as 'neutral' and clean as possible. The user still is required to enter a query in the search bar – at the moment this remains the core interaction between users and search engines. But already today, autocomplete features try to predict what users want to know before they actually formulate their queries. Services such as Google Now even bypass user queries by giving information before you've asked for it: 'From knowing the weather before you start your day, to planning the best route to avoid traffic, or even checking your favorite team's score while they're playing' as the website asserts.[4] Increasing localization and personalization, with the help of encompassing data gained from mobile devices, allow and speed up this development.

---

3. William Gibson, 'Google's Earth', *The New York Times,* 31 August 2010, http://www.nytimes.com/2010/09/01/opinion/01gibson.html?ref=todayspaper&_r=0. The quote begins with: 'In Google, we are at once the surveilled and the individual retinal cells of the surveillant, however many millions of us, constantly if unconsciously participatory. We are part of a post-geographical, post-national super-state, one that handily says no to China. Or yes, depending on profit considerations and strategy. But we do not participate in Google on that level. We're citizens, but without rights.'
4. See, http://www.google.com/landing/now/#whatisit.

The website lmgtfy.com ('Let me google that for you') performs searches on Google in a video sequence that can be sent to others. The idea: 'LMGTFY is for all those people who find it more convenient to bother you with their question rather than google it for themselves.'[5] Googling is not only a word that made it to a number of dictionaries, it has become a social norm. We are not simply enabled but also *expected* to use the search engine, in school, at home, and at social gatherings. Search engines are more and more intertwined in our lives, while the control we have over them doesn't increase accordingly – rather the opposite. At the same time, much of the internet-related public interest has concentrated on social media. Only with the revelations by Edward Snowden can we see a heightened awareness of the power of media monopolies including Google. However, we also seem to be lost and tired; where can we turn without these platforms? How to find our way on the net (or on the streets without Google Maps, for that matter)? Isn't it too late to change these infrastructures, which seem as solid as a brick road?

Ironically, the impact of search engines seems underestimated. Whether Facebook and Twitter are believed to fuel revolutions or are accused of supporting state surveillance and oppression, hardly anyone will deny their massive societal impact. But search engines – let's face it – are unsexy. They are old (in the pace of internet technology); their appearance is unremarkable; their core is inaccessible and they are taken for granted. But the same characteristics can be taken as arguments for why search engines *should be* at the center of our attention: their age and the fact that they survived all other short-term internet trends proves their significance, while the bland surface and hidden complexity evoke important questions about the problem of their lack of transparency. Because search engines are so taken for granted that we never question them in our daily routines, it is even more important to have a deeper understanding of their functionality and their impact.

Social media, most notably Facebook, have only partly overtaken the predominance of search engines as the 'Age of Internet Empires' map provided by Mark Graham and Stefano De Sabbata shows.[6] The map pictures the world's top sites (based on the rankings by Alexa.com in August 2013) in different countries. While Facebook has gained a considerable share especially in the Arab world, Google still clearly dominates the West. Graham and De Sabbata explain:

> The countries where Google is the most visited website account for half of the entire Internet population, with over one billion people [...] Thanks to the large Internet population of China and South Korea, Baidu is second in this rank, as these two countries account for more than half a billion Internet users, whereas the 50 countries where Facebook is the most visited website account for only about 280 million users, placing the social network website in third position.

Search engines not only remain a backbone of the present internet, but equating of search engines with Google is common and justified in most parts of the world – with striking regional exceptions.

---

5. See, http://en.lmgtfy.com.
6. See Mark Graham and Stefano De Sabbata, 'Age of Internet Empires' Map, http://geography.oii.ox.ac.uk/#age-of-internet-empires.

Obviously, that does not mean that we should agree with this equation on any other level than this banal acknowledgement of the factual status quo. 'Search engine' does not equal 'Google', not in the past, and probably – or hopefully – not in the future. Alternatives are possible and must be pursued. A crucial dilemma that any critical analysis of the current situation of web search has to face is the balance between acknowledging the reality of Google's predominance and at the same time not focusing on it too much, because that would miss all opportunities for alternative and fresh thinking, while re-enforcing the criticized situation by reproducing its logic. Fortunately, we are not starting at zero. There have been a number of intellectually stimulating debates that reveal crucial problems of the Society of the Query. It seems necessary and fruitful to sum up some of the central findings in this field of the last decade or two:

1. *Search engines are not neutral:* Although search engine developers often insist that they only provide a neutral tool, it is obvious by now that their products are much more than that. Search engines function as gatekeepers, channeling information by exclusion and inclusion as well as hierarchization. Their algorithms determine what part of the web we get to see and their omnipresence fundamentally shapes our thinking and access to the world. Whatever their bias may look like, it is obvious that man-made decisions are inscribed into the algorithms, leading unavoidably to favoring certain types of information while discriminating against others. Eli Pariser's depiction of the 'filter bubble'[7] is slowly becoming part of our common knowledge and is now being experimentally tested in different academic environments. Whether the filter bubble is as closed and personalized a bubble as Pariser argues, remains to be seen.[8] However, it is clear by now that search results are to some degree subject to personalization, localization, and selection, which makes neutrality or objectivity an illusion.

2. *Googlization is real, and it is a problem:* The highly concentrated (and often even monopoly-like) search engine market intensifies the already significant societal and cultural impact of search technology. The field is in the barely regulated hands of one of the most powerful corporations in the world and its few competitors can hardly challenge Google's overarching supremacy. The tempting offer of seemingly gratis services has apparently led to a point of no return: Google effectively controls access to an unthinkable ocean of data (way beyond its original core competence of search) which is to a good extent crucial for all kinds of aspects of our lives. While we shouldn't forget the pains of searching the web before Google, it is yet another thing to trade our private data for the wealth of this treasure without really thinking about it. As Siva Vaidhyanathan, author of *The Googlization of Everything (and Why We Should Worry)* stated: 'For the last decade we have systematically outsourced our sense of judgment to this one company, we've let this company decide for us what's important and what's true for a large number of questions in our lives.'[9]

---

7. Eli Pariser, *The Filter Bubble: What the Internet Is Hiding from You*, New York: Penguin, 2011.
8. See for example Pascal Jürgens' talk 'Measuring Personalization: An Experimental Framework for Testing Technological Black Boxes' in which he claims that 'the filter bubble does not exist', Society of the Query #2, Institute of Network Cultures, 12 November 2013, http://networkcultures.org/wpmu/query/2013/11/12/measuring-personalization-an-experimental-framework-for-testing-technological-black-boxes-pascal-jurgens/.
9. 'Short interview with Siva Vaidhyanathan', recorded at Society of the Query #2, 8 November 2013, http://vimeo.com/82099408.

3. *Search engines pose a serious threat to our privacy:* Unavoidably, every query we type into a search engine reveals something about ourselves. In contrast to the mostly intentionally shared information on social media platforms, the data gained from search provides a much more comprehensive profile of its users, including what they don't want to share with anyone. Even the queries typed in the search bar and then deleted again without actually hitting enter are recorded (as is the case on Facebook, too). Modern search engines are multi-purpose rather than specific, so they may gain insights into anything from embarrassing knowledge gaps to secret sexual desires and diseases we may fear to have. Now that the Snowden revelations have shown that this confidential data is not safe in the hands of search engine providers, the threat of it being passed on and misused is all too real – for example to insurance companies or law enforcement.

4. *We don't know how to handle search engines:* While most users feel confident with search engines (simply because they use them every day), they usually don't know much about how they actually function and how to operate them efficiently. There are also rarely any attempts to educate users about this specific form of information retrieval in schools or higher education. Teachers refer to Google as an educational tool without having control over the information their students find and use. Even on a procedural level a certain helplessness in the face of search technology is observable: judges struggle to apply often outdated and unsuitable laws on various legal issues, from copyright and personal rights to competition law. Governmental control is difficult, given the international character of the search market. Political attempts to build a search engine have all failed accordingly.

5. *Search engines are a boost to creative energy and responses*: Let's face it, search engines may not be sexy, but they do give us a lot of joy and knowledge, and spark ideas, research, and great art that wouldn't have been possible just ten or fifteen years ago. Despite the pressing problems, it is clear that search engines enrich our lives and only few of us want to go back to the world before digital search.

Although a number of these findings have been intensively discussed, countless open questions on web search and its impact remain. We hope the Society of the Query Reader will shed light on some of them. This volume of essays follows the successful event held in Amsterdam on 7-8 November 2013. The Society of the Query #2 conference brought together an international group of researchers and artists to reflect on web search and discuss alternatives, art, activism, and to interact with the public.[10] Many of the speakers are represented in this collection and the themes roughly follow those of the event.

Starting with theorizing web search, the foundations of this technology are critically analyzed: How can the dialectic of standardization and individualization be understood? What are the implications of gathering personal information in an attempt to assess our intentions? This foreshadows the politics of search which are addressed in the next section, focusing on Google's domination and potential ways out of it. Here, not only

---

10. The conference program can be found as an appendix from page 285 onwards. All talks and blog posts are available through http://networkcultures.org/query.

the omnipresent issues of Googlization are spelled out but also problems of alternative providers are discussed – from technical and economical questions to their underlying ideologies and the challenges of legal regulation. In the third section we take a step back to look at the often neglected history of search. Already centuries ago people used 'search engines' – be they human, a tool, or made of paper. Not only historically speaking is there a world beyond Google, but also geographically. Globalization goes hand in hand with localization, as we can see in the fourth section. We look into the situation in China, where the search engine Baidu provides a whole other picture; the attempts of creating locally adapted search results are critically examined; and the tensions of globally operating search engine providers under national laws are portrayed. The Society of the Query Reader also wants to bring awareness to the epistemological workings of web search engines and the challenges and opportunities they pose for research and education, which are addressed in the fifth section: How can we analyze and archive search engine results for research purposes? What does it actually mean to find knowledge online and how can it be taught? We close this collection with three examples of artistic and associative reflections, which take search as an inspiration and thus reveal the unprecedented wealth and treasure lying at our fingertips.

Our intention is less to find final answers to the overarching challenges imposed by search technology but rather to continue and stimulate a critical debate. The Society of the Query needs to get out of its passive role, and reflect, discuss, and shape the present and future landscape of search. Visit the Society of the Query blog on networkcultures.org/query to watch videos, read articles, and join the mailinglist. Feel free to contact us and we hope to see you in the near future on a next Society of the Query event.

René König and Miriam Rasch
Karlsruhe and Amsterdam, March 2014

References

Becker, Konrad and Felix Stalder (eds). *Deep Search: The Politics of Search beyond Google*. Innsbruck: Studienverlag, 2009.

Gibson, William. 'Google's Earth', *The New York Times,* 31 August 2010, http://www.nytimes.com/2010/09/01/opinion/01gibson.html?ref=todayspaper&_r=0.

Graham, Mark and Stefano De Sabbata. 'Age of Internet Empires' Map, http://geography.oii.ox.ac.uk/#age-of-internet-empires.

Jürgens, Pascal. 'Measuring Personalization: An Experimental Framework for Testing Technological Black Boxes', Society of the Query #2, 12 November 2013, http://networkcultures.org/wpmu/query/2013/11/12/measuring-personalization-an-experimental-framework-for-testing-technological-black-boxes-pascal-jurgens/.

Marcotte, Amanda. 'Parents Ask Google If Their Sons Are Geniuses and If Their Daughters Are Fat', Slate, 21 January 2014, http://www.slate.com/blogs/xx_factor/2014/01/21/parents_ask_google_is_my_son_gifted_and_is_my_daughter_overweight.html.

Pariser, Eli. *The Filter Bubble: What the Internet Is Hiding from You*, New York: Penguin, 2011.

'Short interview with Siva Vaidhyanathan', recorded at Society of the Query #2, 8 November 2013, http://vimeo.com/82099408.

A Database of Intention?

Kylie Jarrett

A Database of Intention?

¬

Kylie Jarrett

In his 2005 study of Google, industry analyst John Battelle describes the company's technology as a 'database of intentions', 'a massive clickstream database of desires, needs, wants, and preferences that can be discovered, subpoenaed, archived, tracked, and exploited for all sorts of ends'.[1] This database is a collation of each search term entered by a user and various other kinds of data, such as the geographic location of the computer's IP address, the time spent on particular sites, and user preferences gleaned from profiles on various related sites such as YouTube, Google Books, Gmail, or Google+. These data are re-integrated into the Google infrastructure in various forms: as market demographic information, as personalization algorithms that refine search parameters, as mechanisms for algorithms to 'learn' natural language use, or as evidence of collective wisdom in 'trending' statistics, to name but a few instances of re-purposing. This vast archive is Google Inc.'s key monetizable resource, as its contents are sold to advertisers to generate the bulk of the company's revenues. It is also a worrying feature of the cultural surveillance machinery of the contemporary geopolitical moment and its ongoing 'war on terror'. As John Battelle says of Google's database, this 'living artifact of immense power [...] is holding the world by its thoughts'.[2]

But defining Google as a 'database of intention' raises a series of questions. What is 'intention' as a lived, embodied experience and can that really be captured by Google's systems? What transformations occur in that capture, and are these the same across the broad range of systems and processes associated with Google's database? What are the ideological, economic, and social implications of this capture? Ultimately, how may we understand Google's relationship to our intentions? What follows is a series of reflections attempting to unravel some of the complexity suggested by describing Google as a database of intention. The interrelated vignettes seek to explore some of the tensions of Google's data-mapping in order to complicate our picture of the political economy of search.

Vignette One: Intention and Alienation
When U.S. National Security Agency employee Edward Snowden bravely released information about the U.S. government clandestine surveillance operation codenamed

---

1. John Battelle, *The Search: How Google and Its Rivals Rewrote the Rules of Business and Transformed Our Culture*, New York: Penguin, p. 6.
2. Battelle, *The Search*, pp. 2-3.

PRISM, attention quickly turned to major internet sites such as Facebook and Google. It was claimed that not only was Google providing consumer records upon legally certified request, but also that the company had provided a 'back door' to its databases, allowing carte blanche access to unmediated user data. Senior executives made robust denials. Google CEO Larry Page and Chief Legal Officer David Drummond posted on the company's official blog, 'First, we have not joined any program that would give the U.S. government – or any other government – direct access to our servers. Indeed, the U.S. government does not have direct access or a "back door" to the information stored in our data centers. We had not heard of a program called PRISM until yesterday.'[3] With a variety of other high technology companies including Facebook, Apple, and Microsoft, and in alliance with non-profit and trade organizations such as Human Rights Watch and the American Civil Liberties Union, Google subsequently drafted a letter to legislators demanding more transparency in the surveillance operations of the U.S. government.[4]

The anxiety experienced by these companies and their users about the security of these data reflects the implicit concern in Battelle's understanding of Google as a database of intention that can be 'discovered, subpoenaed, archived, tracked, and exploited for *all sorts of ends*' (my emphasis). It is the ambiguity of these ends that worries many about the intentional capture of every entered search term. On one hand, the use of these data to personalize search and generate results pertinent to each individual are typically of little concern to the average user, and may indeed be considered a valuable facility. Similarly, the use of this broad-ranging data collection to enable 'academic inquiry' into usage practices, the original stated intention in building data capture into the system's infrastructure,[5] is considered a fairly trouble-free, if not admirable, aspect of Google's systems. These useful or mostly benign ends are one facet of Google's gathering of intention.

On the other hand, 'ends' such as the wide-spread clandestine monitoring of user activity by more or less hostile state or corporate agencies exemplified by PRISM are conceived as a problem and a threat to privacy and the liberties that privacy assures.[6] These are serious and important concerns. If Google really is a database of our intentions for action or engagement in life, then access to that information breaches long held assumptions about the private possession of our own thoughts and desires. But it is not only privacy that is at stake in the possession of intention by commercial search sites such as Google.

The gathering of user information is the backbone of digital media economics. Typically based in advertising revenue models, the costs of using a 'free' site are the data each user actively or passively inputs, which become consumer traffic and demo-

---

3. Larry Page and David Drummond, 'What the...?', Google Official blog, 7 June 2013, http://googleblog.blogspot.ie/2013/06/what.html.
4. John Koetsier, 'The Full PRISM Letter Google, Yahoo, Apple, Facebook, and Microsoft Are Sending Congress', *Venture Beat*, 18 July 2013, http://venturebeat.com/2013/07/18/the-full-prism-letter-google-yahoo-apple-facebook-and-microsoft-are-sending-congress/.
5. Sergey Brin and Larry Page, 'The Anatomy of a Large-Scale Hypertextual Web Search Engine', *Computer Networks and ISDN Systems* 30 (1998): 107-117, http://ilpubs.stanford.edu:8090/361/.
6. Daniel J. Solove, *The Digital Person: Technology and Privacy in the Information Age*, New York: New York University Press, 2004.

graphic information that is sold to advertisers and marketers, often in real time. This economic model reconstitutes user activity into demographic and taste-identifying statistics, thereby transforming it into a commodity with economic exchange-value in the advertising marketplace. In doing so, it privatizes the energies of individuals and groups, effectively expropriating those resources from the subjective lived experience of each user, typically without fiscal compensation equal to the value of the economic surplus generated through this transformation. Such logic forms the basis of the capitalist economics of most of commercial search and the consumer web and has been explored extensively elsewhere.[7] What I wish to emphasize about this process though is not the exploitation that occurs because user inputs are not adequately compensated, but how the banking of intention by Google exemplifies and articulates the process of alienation inherent to the capitalist system.

Value is generated in capitalism when a worker's possession of physical and intellectual energies is transferred to the capitalist, denying that laborer control over both the products of his or her labor as well as organization of the labor process. Activity and goods are no longer defined by their utility to the worker – use-value – who might use them to enrich their own lives, but in terms of the monetized value they can generate for the capitalist. This alienation of the worker from the products of their time and energy, and so from their own agency, is at the core of capitalism and at the core of search economics, where user data become commodities in an advertising market. Yet my intentions are meaningful only to me; they have an inalienable use-value for me in my lived existence. For this value to be transformed into a commodified object with exchange-value, over which I have no control and no right to claim sovereignty, is a powerful act of symbolic violence. In the process of reification and alienation of user activity inherent to the database of intention, my thoughts and activities are transformed into an alienated object that is no longer part of me, is not in my possession, and has agency that is not linked to my concerns. Once alienated, my intentions have the power to act upon me, autonomously of my desires, meanings, or interests.

In search contexts, our user data become the economic surplus that allows Google to continue to grow, build more server farms, and engage in research and development to identify new tools or systems to further capture our user data. It becomes that which allows Google Inc. to continue to be a capitalist enterprise and a 'buyer of people' as employees and as users.[8] In commercial contexts, where users have little to no capacity to influence the form of these technologies or industries, the user becomes affected from the outside by the forces released by their living labor (intention) transformed into the dead labor of capital (advertising data). The alienated commodity of each user's data thus feeds back into the very same capitalist process that subjugates that user. But it is more than merely Google's particular domination of the user that is perpetu-

---

7. For instance, Christian Fuchs, *Internet and Society: Social Theory in the Information Age*, Oxfordshire: Routledge, 2008; Matteo Pasquinelli, 'Google's PageRank: Diagram of the Collective Capitalism and Rentier of the Common Intellect', in Konrad Becker and Felix Stalder (eds) *Deep Search: The Politics of Search Beyond Google*, Innsbruck: Studienverlag, 2009, pp. 152-162; Elizabeth Van Couvering, 'The History of the Internet Search Engine: Navigational Media and the Traffic Commodity', in Amanda Spink and Michael Zimmer (eds) *Web Search: Multidisciplinary Perspectives*, Berlin: Springer-Verlag, 2008, pp. 177-206.
8. Karl Marx, *Capital: A New Abridgement*, ed. David McLellan, Oxford: Oxford University Press, 2008, p. 384.

ated in the way commodified user behavior acts upon us. As Astrid Mager describes, the 'capitalist spirit gets embedded in search algorithms' by way of the impetus users give to the continuation of search and its advertising-based metrics.[9] More than this, though, the penetration of commercial search through the fabric of our daily life perpetuates the social relationship of alienation inherent to capitalism itself in everyday activity, reiterating and normalizing a context where our desires and knowledge 'naturally' become the property of others and, as such, taken from our control. This phenomenon is certainly not isolated to search or commercial digital media, for it is the logic of the entire consumer complex. But whenever I instinctively reach for my phone to 'ask Mr. Google' that nagging question to which I do not know the answer, I participate in yet another perpetuation of that capitalist rationality. While our everyday uses of search may be in themselves benign, what the economics of Google's database do is bind those intentions to the self-perpetuating circuits of capitalist production. At a global, systemic level, this is anything but a benign consequence of the database of intention.

If Google, both as a corporation and as a data structure, is primarily a web of user intentions, then this Marxist reading has serious implications for lives increasingly mediated by search. First, it asserts Google's role in increasing estrangement from our lived experience, implying a further diminution of rich sociality. Second, it also implicates search in the perpetuation of capitalist relations, not simply because it is dominated by commercial entities, but because it helps to normalize and perpetuate the system's underlying logic of expropriation and alienation. Revelations about PRISM and the potential for our intentions to act against us in state surveillance should be of concern. But these are merely extraordinary uses of Google's database of intention. Its quotidian functioning as a mechanism for generating and perpetuating alienation is no less ideological and is as implicated in inequitable power dynamics, and it should concern us just as much.

Vignette Two: The Intentional Fallacy
As part of a discussion on issues of censorship and in an attempt to demonstrate the capacities of algorithms to dictate information retrieval, I recently conducted a search for the term 'abortion' using search engines from three countries with differing social and legal contexts for abortion: Australia, Ireland, and the U.S.. The study was not in any way systematic, and the results were fundamentally skewed by the search term being entered from particular geographically located IP addresses. Nevertheless, the results usefully demonstrated for a diverse, generally non-technical audience how different versions of the same story appear for the same search term when different algorithmic parameters are applied.

While the data generated in this experiment was not valid, what did emerge of real interest was the subsequent display of advertising related to this search term in my Gmail account. For months, appearing in the sidebars of my email account were ads for Marie Stopes International, the U.K. women's health service provider that many Irish women rely on when seeking a termination. This advertising appeared despite my never being logged into my Gmail account at the same time as I was conducting

---

9. Astrid Mager, 'Algorithmic Ideology', *Information, Communication & Society* 15:5 (2012), p. 779.

searches and gathering data for this project. This research was also conducted using different computers distributed between my work and home offices. My interest was piqued by this clear demonstration of how Google's algorithmic surveillance links activity from each of my IP addresses, compiling activity across those addresses into an intentional logic that it then attributes to a singular umbrella profile spanning its many online properties.

Of greater interest though was how this also revealed the search engine's inability to meaningfully understand the intentional logic of my searching. Evident in this persistent advertising of abortion services was the assumption that in entering the term 'abortion', I wanted to secure this procedure. In actuality I had no intention of seeking a termination, but every intention to research Google itself. Even with the aggregated activity of my IP address to inform its interpretation of these data, Google got it wrong. The purpose ascribed to me, and distributed across my digital identity, was not mine. While Google had a very clear idea of what I had searched for, my *intention* in conducting these searches was precisely what it didn't, and perhaps couldn't, adequately know. This leads to some important questions. Is it actually 'intention' that is captured by Google's systems? Can intention be abstracted meaningfully into search terms? What is intention anyway?

Most dictionary, legal, and literary definitions associate intention with purposive action. However this frame doesn't seem to capture what we pragmatically understand as intention. For instance, we may not intend to cause offense – our motivation may be humorous – but offense may still be found in our words. There is a disconnect between our actions, their effects, and our desires. What animates behavior is not necessarily co-extensive with its manifestation, shaped as the latter is by intervening social, cultural, and technological factors. The underlying drives, the rich tapestry of cognitions, experiences, embodied desires that shape any person's goals, cannot be read directly off externalized activity. Google, therefore, can read and capture the extensive output of my search terms, but this is merely the mapping of my behavior rather than real insight into its motivational logic. My purpose may have been to search for 'abortion', but what animated that search was not contained in the term itself. Google was committing the intentional fallacy in assuming it could read my intentional logic from my output or in ascribing motivation to the range of behavioral traces I leave across my search activity, Gmail, Google+ profile, or YouTube viewing.

Further, what animates intention *prior to* its manifestation as purposive behavior is not necessarily transparent, even to the actor. This action may be shaped by non-purposive, non-rational, even non-cognitive drives. Embodied desire and affect move us in more or less conscious ways, fundamentally shaping our activities, including our search behaviors and the terms through which these manifest. Read this way, intention can be understood as involving both the purposive behavior manifest in search terms, but also an underlying affect. Drawing on the work of Brian Massumi, affect can be understood as those sensory practices of movement and feeling that function beyond the directly signifying properties of discourse, but which nevertheless constitute some of the lived existence – the cultural and social psychology – of all individuals. Affect is differentiated from emotion, for it is an intensity that is outside conscious articulation. Emotion, on the other hand, is 'the sociolinguistic fixing of the quality of an experience',[10] the resolution of affect into something we recognize and can articulate. This resolution qualifies the intensity of the experience, inserting it into knowable, narrativizable meaning. Emotion is 'intensity owned and recognized [while] affect is unqualified. As such, it is not ownable or recognizable.'[11] Affect is the autonomous energy that motivates and non-rationally shapes our practices and intentions. It is a state of potential that cannot be captured or confined within a body, perception, or cognition without undergoing a fundamental transformation.

Intention, as extensively manifested as a search term, is similar to emotion in that it is a qualification of the non-rational motivating force of affect. The conceptualizing of a search goal transforms an autonomous moment of potential, the animating energy of a search, into an abstract and reductive 'intention', which does not directly correspond with the embodied, pre-conscious animating logics that give this intention its inherent meaning. The moment of chaos associated with affect when 'a system enters a peculiar state of indecision, where what its next state will be turns entirely unpredictable' is excessive and beyond the capture of any of our cultural, psychological, and technological mechanisms.[12] It certainly exceeds the value-making systems of Google's database of intention because they cannot capture libidinal, affective energy. Shaped by the hyper-rationality of its engineering culture and the ultimate genericism of its algorithmic logic, Google's technology is not well attuned to understand or engage with these elusive forces.

The intentions that constitute Google's database must therefore be understood only as *ascriptions* of a limited conceptualization of intention and not as meaningful manifestations of the embodied affective logics of those intentions. The keywords and clickstream data it collects are reductive products of the full richness of our motivating energies. Certainly, they tell something about us, but they cannot ever reflect the panoply of desiring intentionality inherent to those searches. If Google can still be called a database of intentions, it is only of extensive manifestations – the textual, cognitive, discursive traces of digital activities. The affective, embodied use-values of these activities are simply not available to its algorithms and its data capture systems, no matter how sophisticated. Google cannot in actuality capture the meaningful, inalienable aspects of my intention. These cannot be alienated from me. They cannot be expropriated from me. And that is a source of comfort.

Vignette Three: Preempting Intention
The austerity of Google's home search page is often commended. The simplicity of the page speaks to the infinite potential of the web and of search as a cultural activity. But when entering a search term, the complexity of the database that exists under that apparently transparent surface becomes manifest. Entering the term 'intention' into the empty search box invokes a range of Autocomplete suggestions, twisting through various permutations in time with the keystrokes of my typing. I journey from 'i', suggesting my often used sites *'Irish Times'* or 'Irish Rail', to 'in', indicating 'instagram' or 'indeed.ie' (two sites I have barely and never used respectively), through various

---

10. Brian Massumi, *Parables for the Virtual: Movement, Affect, Sensation*, Durham and London: Duke University Press, 2002, p. 28.
11. Massumi, *Parables for the Virtual*, p. 28.
12. Massumi, *Parables for the Virtual*, p. 109.

permutations until I enter 'intention' which suggests the term itself along with 'intention to treat', 'intention tremor', and 'intention to create legal relations'. Whenever Google makes these helpful suggestions using Autocomplete or Knowledge Graph, or corrects spelling through Autocorrect, the lie is given to the concept of search as a transparent mediator of information on the web. The underlying data structures become too apparent to sustain that mythology.

But they also indicate a key aspect of Google's data capture systems – they work through pre-emption. Knowing my intention is important for Google so it can anticipate my future search desires and propose helpful suggestions to make search 'faster', perpetuating its own dominance in a context where speed is valued. Pre-emption is the essence of the push mobile technology Google Now that, unbidden, offers users web services such as weather and traffic reports, news items, or information pertinent to appointments at times when their calendars and prior activity predict this information will be useful. The model of relevance Google uses in this technology and its search functions draws on data of each user's past behavior along with aggregated generic data to propose a future model. This is then mobilized to propose personalized and yet generic search results and search suggestions shaped for that user. Thus, the intentions ascribed to each individual, constituted by an amalgam of that user's search practices and the intentional logic ascribed to users as a mass, are deployed to guess the desires and orientations of each user and use and preemptively structure the search experience. When I enter 'i' it is assumed to mean '*Irish Times*' and not the '*Irish Independent*', 'izakaya', 'iPhone', or 'igloo', based on the intentions Google has associated with my profile and with similar users in my geographic and demographic areas. In these mechanisms, the intentions ascribed to me are fed back to me, working to inform my ongoing search articulations. A feedback loop emerges in which presumptions about activity, based on Google's assumptions about users' intentions, go on to inform a user's experience of, although not necessarily engagement with, the web.

The implications of this preemptive capture are broader than the display of easily ignored search options. Not only may search results be shaped by these expectations – search intentions themselves may become caught in the self-informing loops of what Tarleton Gillespie calls 'public relevance algorithms'.[13] According to Massumi, during the transformation of affect into emotion, the unknowable potential of affect – its futurity – is folded back on itself, capturing that potential in the repetition and regularity of forms recognizable from previous states of resolution.[14] Similarly, the extensive manifestations of intention that are our search terms draw upon assumptions of valuable and effective keywords that we assume will find the search target. This occurs not only mechanically in the offerings of Autocomplete but in our own cognitive practices as searchers. Drawing upon our previous experiences, we search using terms we know or assume will get optimal results. For instance, I know that information about train timetables in Ireland is more likely to manifest using searches for 'Irish Rail', 'Iarn-

---

13. Tarleton Gillespie, 'The Relevance of Algorithms', in Tarleton Gillespie, Pablo Boczkowski and Kirsten Foot (eds) *Media Technologies*, Cambridge, MA: MIT Press, forthcoming. http://www.academia.edu/2257984/The_Relevance_of_Algorithms_forthcoming_in_Tarleton_Gillespie_Pablo_Boczkowski_Kirsten_Foot_eds._Media_Technologies_MIT_Press_2013_.
14. Massumi, *Parables for the Virtual*.

ród Éireann', or 'trains Ireland' than the more whimsical term 'choo-choos Emerald Isle'. Appropriate search terms, or search strategies, are effectively bookmarked in my head. The moment of articulating keywords – of articulating my intention – is thus already marked with infolded expectations of how Google's mechanisms and algorithms will function. The potentiality of the embodied affective self is channeled in directions recognizable to and recognizable from the database of intention in order to achieve expected results.

The intention we articulate in search is thus previously shaped by the intentions we, and others, have already articulated into the database. In this recursive logic, the potential of futurity becomes limited by past resolutions. Embedding the output of search into the logics of search in this way can be understood as a form of control. It 'forecloses the creative mutation' of the affective potential of the search subject, instead channeling that potential into pre-ordained forms.[15] This preemptive shaping of our searching is momentous because we are adapting our knowledge logic to that of the commercially produced algorithm, generating a 'calculated public'.[16] It enables the preemptive capture of our intentions, generating normative frameworks for 'how we may think', if I may upend Vannevar Bush's seminal description of hypertextual environments.[17] When we articulate our desire into the forms of searchable intention, we are made over in the image of the algorithmic logic of search. Google's database of intention may not capture the affective desires that animate our searches, but the logic of its algorithms can become so entwined with how we articulate those into intentions that the distinction becomes null and void.

Vignette Four: Intentional Subjects
In the vast architecture of Google's collection of data is an ever-changing entity that is effectively 'Me'. This is the version of Kylie Jarrett that Google has created and which it mobilizes in its personalization algorithms, in its various automated suggestions, in the advertising options it so helpfully displays for me, and in the lists of search results it provides as answers to my searches. This digital proxy, ascribed an intentionality that is not necessarily that of the biological 'Me', for all intents and purposes functions as 'Me' within the vast universe penetrated by Google. This 'algorithmic identity' grows and adapts with each instance of data, entered either actively or passively, that is attributed to the IP addresses and profiles that constitute the entity Google recognizes as Kylie Jarrett.[18]

This is the database subject that in 1995 Mark Poster warned would come to dominate in the *Second Media Age*. Long before the ascendancy of search and the emergence of the social media network sites into which we pour various kinds of personal information, Poster raised concerns about the digital profiles being built from credit card use, marketing surveys, insurance information, electoral registers, and government in-

---

15. Patricia Ticiento Clough, Greg Goldberg, Rachel Schiff, Aaron Weeks and Craig Willse, 'Notes Towards a Theory of Affect Itself', *Ephemera* 7.1 (2007): 70.
16. Gillespie, 'Relevance of Algorithms'.
17. Vannevar Bush, 'As We May Think', *Atlantic Monthly,* July 1945, http://www.theatlantic.com/magazine/archive/1945/07/as-we-may-think/303881/.
18. John Cheney-Lippold, 'A New Algorithmic Identity: Soft Biopolitics and the Modulation of Control', *Theory, Culture and Society* 28.6 (2011): 164-181.

stitutional systems. He argued that the portraits of consumers built up in the relational databases of these institutions

> become additional social identities as each individual is constituted for the computer, depending on the database in question, as a social agent. Without referring the database back to its owner and his or her interests or forward to the individual in question as a model of its adequacy or accuracy, we comprehend the database as a discursive production which inscribes positionalities of subjects according to its rules of formation.[19]

Like Poster's database subjectivities, the person Google believes me to be lacks subtlety and is reductive and incomplete, and the intentions that Google attributes to me are shaped by the limitations of its data capture systems. However, that these intentions are not 'really' mine becomes irrelevant. Ascribed (fallacious) intentions that are then inscribed into my digital identity, my online existence becomes that which is constituted by the database's expectations.[20] This ascribed and inscribed identity goes on to serve as the subject for whom personalization systems are built, for whom suggestions are made in Autocomplete, and it is the traces of this subject that advertisers and PRISM pick over to identify my role in the economy and the polity. With this agency, the database subject assumes a capacity to act upon me and to potentially act against me.

In recognizing this subject, we return to the alienation inherent in the economic logic of Google's database of intention. But we are here not under the assumption that something intrinsic – our intentionality – has 'really' been captured and that this is the key cause for concern. In the ascriptive and inscriptive processes of the database, whether these are 'my' intentions or not does not alter their ability to represent 'Me'. I am functionally and practically the subject cached in Google's database for anyone who draws on these resources. If my Google traces show that I have searched for 'abortion', according to advertisers I have an interest in securing this procedure. In a state where abortion on demand is illegal, and where new legislation offers a jail term of up to 14 years for acquiring or assisting a termination, the potential for this subject to act against my interests is great. And if my experience of being online, including the preemptive structuring of my searches, is profoundly shaped by assumptions that I am this subject, how much does it matter that the affective logic of my searching escapes capture, remains inalienable and immanently resistant? In the brutal logic of an algorithmic world, how do I elude the shadow of my digital doppelgänger? What will it mean if I cannot?

In mobilizing a subject marked with ascribed and inscribed intent, Google is exerting what Parisi and Goodman describe as preemptive power.[21] Predicting behavior is a means of managing risk. It works by generating temporary normalizing categories through which future behavior is assessed and imbued with intelligibility. But it is a performative logic, bringing into existence the activity it proposes in the form of

---

19. Mark Poster, *The Second Media Age*, Cambridge: Polity Press, 1995, pp. 87-88.
20. Poster, *The Second Media Age*.
21. Luciana Parisi and Steve Goodman, 'The Affect of Nanoterror', *Culture Machine* 7 (2005), http://www.culturemachine.net/index.php/cm/article/viewArticle/29/36.

a response to that activity. This logic can be seen in the contemporary preemptive drone attacks across the Middle East and South Asia where calculations of the future serve as the basis for action in the present. An assumed threat of terrorism is acted upon in a preemptive drone strike as if it were already manifest, and in doing so the effects of the (non-existent) threat, which would be a retaliatory assault, are actualized. Preemption thus creates the future it proposes and also controls its effects prior to their manifestation. Such preemption is ultimately about, as Parisi and Goodman describe, intervening and engineering reality. As a governance system, preemptive power allows a State to be ready with policing and management processes that systematically modulate behavior based on calculations of likely behavior. This assures the continuation of a normative reality based on activities assessed by their presumed value.

Similarly, by ascribing intentions inferred from past behavior and then acting upon the anticipated, categorized, labeled, and valorized activity projected from these data, Google goes on to configure the future, shaping what becomes the (likely) search experience for each user. As Cheney-Lippold argues, the linking of 'potential for alternative futures to our previous actions as users based on consumption and research for consumption' generates a regulatory framework for activity.[22] When my search results are tailored only to the inferred intentions of the Kylie Jarrett in Google's database, my access to information is effectively and opaquely marshaled. The path-dependency this creates ensures search activity increasingly understood through and regulated by the intentions ascribed to my database identity.[23] By assuming activity based on previously determined knowledge categorizations, the database of intention renders the searcher – as a mass, a more or less finely grained demographic, or as a particular user profile – a predictable and consequently manageable entity, while also securing the future by ensuring that appropriate predicted behavior is realized through mechanisms that structure the search experience. Google controls its subjects by preemptively ascribing and preparing for particular intentional subjects. To read intention from search terms, and to feed that intention back into the system in the form of technical (Autocomplete) or psychical mechanisms (the infolding of algorithmic logic into the articulation of intention) is thus an act of preemptive power.

At the level of the individual, this is never a totalizing, fully normalizing regulatory framework due to the ability of the database to absorb new data and reconstitute parameters accordingly. Nor are Google's search predictions about imposing singular behavioral norms on individual users – these capacities have more to do 'with capturing [users'] actions within a controllable framework', providing control at a group or social level.[24] Google's database identities thus have a role in biopolitics, in that they 'give meaning to the categorizations that make up populations' which are then used to 'softly suggest' particular avenues of activity to those categories of

---

22. Cheney-Lippold, 'Algorithmic Identity', p. 169.
23. Felix Stalder and Christine Mayer, 'The Second Index: Search Engines, Personalisation and Surveillance', in Konrad Becker and Felix Stalder (eds) *Deep Search: The Politics of Search Beyond Google*, Innsbruck: Studienverlag, 2009, pp. 98-115.
24. Theo Röhle, 'Dissecting the Gatekeepers: Relational Perspectives on the Power of Search Engines', in Konrad Becker and Felix Stalder (eds) *Deep Search: The Politics of Search Beyond Google*, Innsbruck: Studienverlag, 2009, pp. 117-132.

people.²⁵ The effects of this control are overtly demonstrated in the diverging search results generated for individual users whose profiles fall into differing class, racial, economic, gender, sexual, or geographic categories. The performativity of these constructed identities – that they bring about the behavior they are attributing to users – perpetuate these categorizations, feeding, and feeding into, assumptions about taste, ideology, and politics. These assumptions can then be mobilized at the level of the individual, sustaining social inequality through the ways information resources are delivered, or in macro-level governance systems, especially those of electioneering and market-driven state policy development that organize resources based on these assumptions. Offered as calculated insight, what emerges from the algorithms' preemptive assessment of the intentions of constructed segments of the population can become the future.

That the identities at the base of this control are based on merely inferred and ascribed intentions makes their inscription into popular information systems such as Google a crucial political problem. This inscription by inference makes the question of the database of intention not only about economics or individual access to transparent and unbiased information sources, nor merely about the post-facto surveillance of any individual user's database identity. It is the widespread mode of control 'situated at a distance from traditional liberal politics, removed from civil discourse via the proprietary nature of many algorithms' that these database subjects exemplify that should perhaps be giving us greatest pause.²⁶

A Database in Tension
To pull the various threads of these reflections together is not simple. Each vignette informs the other, but there is an inherent contradiction within them. The emphasis on the affective impetus behind search and its inherent unknowability and chaos outlined in the second vignette suggests possibilities to escape the control of the search algorithm. Contrarily, the constant return to questions of alienation, and the potential for the alienated subject generated by increasingly complex forms of preemptive capture to act upon us, suggests a mire from which there is no meaningful return. I am not convinced that Google is a database of intention, particularly not in the rich sense of intention as meaningfully resonant energy used here. I am equally sure, however, that it functions as if it were such, and that this reality assumes significance far beyond the delivery of irrelevant or inapt advertising. By way of summary then, I want to emphasize how in this dissonance lies possibility.

Google's database – of search terms, of user behavior, of intention – is vast and pervasive. It has an ability to relate disparate traces of data and transform those data into, effectively, a subject with significance for us personally and politically – the searcher. But this data can never be absolute, for the searcher is excessive. The database subject is too reductive to capture the affective and libidinal subjectivity of the individual involved in the search. In her or his insistent potentiality, the searcher generates a futurity that must lie beyond the logic of this database, despite attempts to preempt that subjectivity. Consequently the subjectivity Google Search actually

---

25. Cheney-Lippold, 'Algorithmic Identity', p. 173.
26. Cheney-Lippold, 'Algorithmic Identity', p. 165.

encounters always potentially slips beyond the knowable and explicable logic of the search algorithm and the advertising database. The searcher can thus never fully be captured by the economic system, even while remaining its product. To search then is to occupy this tenuous position both inside and potentially always outside its systemic logic.

Consequently, between the constantly mapping geography of the database of intentions and the terrain of everyday, embodied use is an inherent tension, but a tension from which the impetus for change can be built. In the disquieting and dissatisfying gaps between the desires that move us, that we intrinsically feel, and the tools through which we are able to manifest them as intentions is the potential to recognize the machinery of our digital mediators, to see through their apparently seamless integration into our lives. As Gillespie says in his call for greater public debate and engagement with algorithmic logics:

> It is important that we conceive of this entanglement not as a one-directional influence, but as a recursive loop between the calculations of the algorithm and the "calculations" of people.[27]

The tension at the heart of Google's database opens a space not only for the passive resistance produced by affective excessiveness, but for mobilization and organization to ensure these databases and their algorithms are serving meaningful ends. While we may never want, or be capable of producing, a database that can actually capture intention and thus allow us better representation in technologically mediated systems, we may be able to work towards technological, social, and economic models that reduce the capacity of the reductive subjects of search to become alienated from our control and to work outside our interests. It is within the tension associated with intention that we can locate and promote struggle to better understand, to make transparent, and to reform the algorithmic logic of powerful mediators such as Google. This type of intervention should be an intentional goal of our interrogation of search.

---

27. Gillespie, 'Relevance of Algorithms'.

References

Battelle, John. *The Search: How Google and Its Rivals Rewrote the Rules of Business and Transformed Our Culture*, New York: Penguin, 2005.

Brin, Sergey, and Larry Page. 'The Anatomy of a Large-Scale Hypertextual Web Search Engine', *Computer Networks and ISDN Systems* 30 (1998): 107-117. http://ilpubs.stanford.edu:8090/361/.

Bush, Vannevar. 'As We May Think', *Atlantic Monthly,* July 1945, http://www.theatlantic.com/magazine/archive/1945/07/as-we-may-think/303881/.

Cheney-Lippold, John. 'A New Algorithmic Identity: Soft Biopolitics and the Modulation of Control', *Theory, Culture and Society* 28.6 (2011): 164-181.

Clough, Patricia Ticiento, Greg Goldberg, Rachel Schiff, Aaron Weeks and Craig Willse. 'Notes Towards a Theory of Affect Itself', *Ephemera* 7.1 (2007): 60-77.

Fuchs, Christian. *Internet and Society: Social Theory in the Information Age*, Oxfordshire: Routledge, 2008.

Gillespie, Tarleton. 'The Relevance of Algorithms', in Tarleton Gillespie, Pablo Boczkowski, and Kirsten Foot (eds) *Media Technologies*, Cambridge, MA: MIT Press, forthcoming, http://www.academia.edu/2257984/The_Relevance_of_Algorithms_forthcoming_in_Tarleton_Gillespie_Pablo_Boczkowski_Kirsten_Foot_eds._Media_Technologies_MIT_Press_2013_.

Koetsier, John. 'The Full PRISM Letter Google, Yahoo, Apple, Facebook, and Microsoft Are Sending Congress', *Venture Beat*, 18 July 2013, http://venturebeat.com/2013/07/18/the-full-prism-letter-google-yahoo-apple-facebook-and-microsoft-are-sending-congress/.

Mager, Astrid. 'Algorithmic Ideology', *Information, Communication & Society* 15.5 (2012): 769-787.

Marx, Karl. *Capital: A New Abridgement*, ed. David McLellan, Oxford: Oxford University Press, 2008.

Massumi, Brian. *Parables for the Virtual: Movement, Affect, Sensation*, Durham and London: Duke University Press, 2002.

Page, Larry and David Drummond. 'What the...?' Google Official blog, 7 June 2013, http://googleblog.blogspot.ie/2013/06/what.html.

Parisi, Luciana and Steve Goodman. 'The Affect of Nanoterror', *Culture Machine* 7 (2005), http://www.culturemachine.net/index.php/cm/article/viewArticle/29/36.

Pasquinelli, Matteo. 'Google's PageRank: Diagram of the Collective Capitalism and Rentier of the Common Intellect', in Konrad Becker and Felix Stalder (eds) *Deep Search: The Politics of Search Beyond Google*, Innsbruck: Studienverlag, 2009, pp. 152-162.

Poster, Mark. *The Second Media Age*, Cambridge: Polity Press, 1995.

Röhle, Theo. 'Dissecting the Gatekeepers: Relational Perspectives on the Power of Search Engines', in Konrad Becker and Felix Stalder (eds) *Deep Search: The Politics of Search Beyond Google*, Innsbruck: Studienverlag, 2009, pp. 117-132.

Solove, Daniel J. *The Digital Person: Technology and Privacy in the Information Age*, New York: New York University Press, 2004.

Stalder, Felix and Christine Mayer. 'The Second Index: Search engines, personalisation and surveillance', in Konrad Becker and Felix Stalder (eds) *Deep Search: The Politics of Search Beyond Google*, Innsbruck: Studienverlag, 2009, pp. 98-115.

Van Couvering, Elizabeth. 'The History of the Internet Search Engine: Navigational Media and the Traffic Commodity', in Amanda Spink and Michael Zimmer (ed.) *Web Search: Multidisciplinary Perspectives*. Berlin: Springer-Verlag, 2008, pp. 177-206.

Dialectic of Google

Andrea Miconi

Dialectic of Google

Andrea Miconi

Premise

Let's be honest: we don't know exactly how Google works. However, we all use Google to get information, probably because everybody else does. And although available data is quite ambiguous and inconsistent, *everybody* means almost literally everybody: at the beginning of this decade, 65 percent of daily online searches in the United States were made through Google,[1] while in Italy the percentage of people who declared using Google had grown to 92 percent.[2] To be more precise, though, some local markets show significant differences: Google's algorithm is mostly supposed to be suitable for the Latin alphabet, and in all likelihood this is why some geo-cultural systems such as Russia or China are resistant to its hegemony.[3] In any case, generally speaking, Google's growing influence is exactly the first problem we have to face: in the last 15 years, the 'big G' has become the most powerful company in the history of cultural industries, and here it will be considered as such. A very simple fact, which nonetheless raises a radical question: how could such a monopoly emerge from the decentralized project of the World Wide Web?

And to be honest, I *do* use Google, but I am worried about the way it is shaping our culture. The interesting problem to tackle is that Google's power is not about *censorship*. Such cases as the well-discussed deal between Google and the Chinese government or Google's likely adherence to the Digital Millennium Copyright Act are indeed borderline cases; they are very telling but at the same time quite easy to detect. On the contrary, the main problem is ultimately Google's ordinary strategies: the 'Big Firewall' working daily behind the scenes, the biased representation of reality proposed by an agency that pretends to be neutral even though it obviously is not. For this same reason, a critical analysis of Google's power is seriously limited by two opposing things: one, the object to be analyzed also belongs to our daily experience, as often happens in social sciences, and two, we then have to take into account a device whose technical rules *we hardly understand*, as is common in the narrower field of platform studies or software studies. The two problems become one effect: the current paradigm in the organization of culture, which is universally affecting everyday practices, ultimately relies on a technological secret (to some extent, we could even consider Google's algorithm as the digital version of the Coca-Cola recipe: everybody likes it, while no-

---

1. Data available at www.comscore.com.
2. Data available at www.fullplan.it.
3. Siva Vaidhyanathan, *The Googlization of Everything (And Why We Should Worry)*, Berkeley and Los Angeles: University of California Press, 2011, p. 144.

body knows why or how it is actually made). Furthermore, awareness of this problem is nearly non-existent because of the perception of Google as a neutral and user-friendly (or even friendly) interface, and even as a beautiful, free of charge tool, likely to enable people to look for almost everything they want. But what is the secret of Google's success, information for information's sake, or something more complicated?

The Kingdom of (Apparent) Neutrality
Apparent neutrality: this could be a good definition for this search engine's industrial strategies. In other words, Google's lack of neutrality does not raise any problems; mass media and cultural agencies are never neutral, nor even expected to be. The problem with Google is that it is *perceived* as a neutral tool, rather than as an active gatekeeping function, while search engines, as Karine Barzilai-Nahon points out, play exactly the same part as human gatekeepers in traditional media.[4] Nonetheless, while the role of traditional gatekeepers has been gradually brought to light, many surveys show how search engines are contrarily considered to be very reliable information sources. As for Google, we might wonder, to what extent is its white interface passing off as a neutral tool even though of course it is not? We could say that the stylistic choice of a plain white interface puts accent on neutrality, despite the information reduction and hierarchization through its algorithms. Google's maybe not hiding all its filtering operations, but in a sense provides the user with the 'promise of objectivity', as Gillespie recently put it.[5] It is no accident that the search result page – designed to be visibly free from any imposed frame – is visually very different from Google News, which on the contrary shows a very crowded page, full of information, images, and so forth.[6] According to a Pew survey, 68 percent of users consider search engines as an 'unbiased source of information', and 62 percent of them are not capable of distinguishing between 'paid and unpaid results': for some reasons, people simply tend to 'trust search engines'[7] while no longer trusting traditional news media, and this attitude is arguably destined to give Google particular strength.

Does the problem ultimately rely on the software, or the people using it? According to the surveys focused on search engines, the web user – far from being *engaged*, as she is too often supposed to be – assumes a very *lazy* attitude. Most users, for example, only type a *one-word* query,[8] and very rarely combine more than three words,[9] in this way reducing complexity and limiting themselves to the minimum cognitive ef-

---

4. Karine Barzilai-Nahon, 'Toward a Theory of Network Gatekeeping: A Framework for Exploring Information Control', *Journal of the American Society for Information, Science and Technology* 59.9 (2008): 1493-1512.
5. Tarleton Gillespie, 'The Relevance of Algorithms', in Tarleton Gillespie, Pablo Boczkowski, and Kirsten Foot (eds) *Media Technologies*, Cambridge, MA: MIT Press, forthcoming.
6. See David Vise and Mark Malseed, *The Google Story*, New York: Random House, 2005.
7. Deborah Fallows, 'Search Engine Users. Internet Users are Confident, Satisfied and Trusting – but They Are Also Unaware and Naïve', Pew Internet & American Life Project, 2005, p 15.
8. Bernard Jansen and Amanda Spink, 'How We Are Searching the World Wide Web? A Comparison of Nine Search Engine Transaction Logs', *Information Processing and Management* 42 (2006): 252-256; see also Peiling Wang, Michael Berry, and Yiheng Yang, 'Mining Longitudinal Web Queries: Trends and Patterns', *Journal of the American Society for Information Science and Technology* 54.8 (2003): 743-758.
9. Bernard Jansen, Amanda Spink, and Tefko Saracevic, 'Real Life, Real Users, and Real Needs: A Study and Analysis of User Queries on the Web', *Information Processing and Management* 36.3 (2000): 216.

fort. Confirming other studies, Jansen, Spink, and Pedersen showed that most people usually dedicate no more than five minutes to a web search and, in so doing, tend to select nothing but the most common tools.[10] In other words, if search engines are, as stated years ago by Paul di Maggio et al., 'biased in their identification and, especially, ranking of sites, the effects of this bias are compounded by the tendency of engine users to employ simple search terms and to satisfice by terminating searches at the first acceptable site'.[11]

Further, surveys show a more relevant tendency dealing with the way people normally receive and filter information. Between 60 and 80 percent of users read only the first ten results proposed by the search engine, and data vary marginally between surveys, making their general meaning clear. Those surveys are focused on the general use of search engines rather than on Google as a specific service, however they tell us something very important: people choose between *the first five or ten links* selected by the algorithm, which are, according to the original project, the most linked rather than the most reliable. Consider Larry Page and Sergey Brin's 1998 presentation of Google:

> Academic citation literature has been applied to the web, largely by counting citations or backlinks to a given page. This gives some approximation of a page's importance or quality. PageRank extends the idea by not counting links from all pages equally, and by normalizing by the number of links on a page.

And the following 'justification' is that,

> Intuitively, pages that are well cited from many places around the web are worth looking at. If a page was not high quality, [...] it is quite likely that Yahoo's homepage would not link to it. PageRank handles both these cases and everything in between by recursively propagating weights through the link structure of the web.[12]

Some approximation, *intuitively*, *quite likely:* PageRank can possibly work as an indicator of quality – *possibly*, but this is not its main goal. PageRank's quantitative bias is not a well-kept secret; this is generally the way Google works, and there is nothing bad in quantitative methodology as such. The problem is not that Google arbitrarily selects information, in this way establishing a cultural (and hence political) hierarchy. The problem is that this ranking is not perceived as arbitrary as it is, and has recently become a kind of universal and well-established hierarchy. The most striking aspect of the problem is that users only read the first results page,[13] therefore basically *validating* without question the hierarchy arbitrarily established by the algorithm. Consequently, PageRank is 'recursively propagating' its bias and leading people to conform to what

---

10. Bernard Jansen, Amanda Spink, and Jan Pedersen, 'A Temporal Comparison of AltaVista Web Searching', *Journal of the American Society for Information, Science and Technology* 56.6 (2005): 564.
11. Paul Di Maggio, Eszter Hargittai, W. Russell Neuman, and John P. Robinson, 'Social Implications of the Internet', *Annual Review of Sociology* 27 (2001): 314.
12. Sergey Brin and Larry Page, 'The Anatomy of a Large-Scale Hypertextual Web Search Engine', Seventh International World Wide Conference, Brisbane, 1998, http://ilpubs.stanforde.edu:8090/361/.
13. See Craig Silverstein, Monica Henzinger, Hannes Marais, and Michael Moricz, 'Analysis of a Very Large AltaVista Query Log', *Newsletter ACM SIGIR Forum* 33.1 (1999): 6-12.

all the others are reading and (arguably) to take this as a given. As for the exact percentage of people who only read the first results page, data are not entirely consistent but are enough to allow some confidence in the findings: 70 percent in a 1999 study,[14] 58 percent in a 2000 survey focused on Excite,[15] 73 percent in a 2002 survey dedicated to nine different search engines,[16] more than 72 percent in a 2005 research on AltaVista.[17] Though clearly data vary, they account for the large majority of web users. If we look at more recent surveys, we can find some partial confirmations of previous tendencies. According to Jansen and Spink, web users are 'unwilling to invest additional effort to locate' relevant contents, and still show a 'low tolerance of viewing any results past the first page'.[18] Statistical data released by Bing in 2013 show that 50 percent of users simply click the top result, while only '4-6 percent click the third result'.[19] On the other hand, Keane, O'Brien and Smyth provided an empirical test by simulating a Google interface able to reverse the order of results, thus showing how people's search is 'partially biased', even though users are sometimes able to detect the most relevant page even at the bottom of the list.[20] In other words, the degree to which the use of search engines is biased is still to be proved. The bias, however, exists, since users are barely aware of the way algorithms filter data and direct operations.

Unfortunately, the most part of available data reported in this article are too old to provide a clear understanding of the current use of search engines; however, they can help us raise some questions. What do they suggest? Simply and sadly, that often people do not see any reason to challenge search engines, or question their reliability and transparency. If we consider that people now limit their consumption to *one* search engine, the problem suddenly becomes evident.

Google as Social Pattern
I said earlier that people use only Google and so do I, but is this happening by accident or design? The reason why everybody uses Google could actually be simple: Google provides the most reliable results. We may however wonder to what extent such a universal usage ultimately depends on a clear understanding of technical performances – which should be based on a systematic comparison between *different* search engines – or rather on the pressure of current cultural frames. In this respect, we may wonder whether Google has been achieving dominance over its competitors through a two-step process. At a first level, quality arguably played a part: Google is considered to provide more complete and spam-free results than its competitors, and people prefer it over other search engines because of its accuracy and overall quality.[21] What is more, the fact that Google is set as a default home page in some popular browsers has probably contributed to its universal adoption, or at it least to the consolidation of its lead-

---

14. Amanda Spink and Bernard Jansen, 'A Study of Web Search Trends', *Webology* 1 (2004), www.webology.ir.
15. Jansen, Spink, and Saracevic, 'Real Life, Real Users, and Real Needs', p. 215.
16. Jansen and Spink, 'How We Are Searching the World Wide Web?', pp. 257-258.
17. Jansen, Spink, and Pedersen, 'A Temporal Comparison of AltaVista Web Searching', p. 563.
18. Jansen and Spink, 'How Are We Searching the World Wide Web?' p. 260.
19. Data available at http://www.bing.com/blogs/site_blogs/b/searchquality/archive/2013/04/24/ten-blue-links-no-more-dynamic-page-sizing.aspx.
20. Mark Keane, Maeve O' Brien, and Barry Smyth, 'Are People Biased in Their Use of Search Engines?' *Communications of the ACM* 51.2 (2008): 49-52.
21. Fellows, *Search Engine Users*, p. 14.

ership. For these reasons, it is actually difficult to distinguish between technical and social factors when it comes to analyzing their consequences on daily life practices. A social pattern, wrote Pierre Bourdieu, is basically a form of 'habitus':

> a system of durable, transposable dispositions, structured structures predisposed to function as structuring structures, that is, as principles of the generation and structuring of practices [...] which can be adapted to their goals without presupposing a conscious aiming at ends or an express mastery of the operations necessary to attain them [...].[22]

Could things have gone differently? Obviously yes, but this is how social habitus works: as a piece of 'history turned into nature', explains Bourdieu, by which the class structure governs real practices through the mediation of a cultural scheme, able to engender 'all the thoughts, all the conditions, all the actions consistent with those conditions, and no others'. As a consequence, people are forced to make a virtue out of necessity, 'at the cost of double negation', that is, 'to refuse what is anyway refused and to love the inevitable'.[23] Was Google necessary? I do not know. Could people even *imagine* a Google-free life? Arguably no, or at least I don't think so. *Double negation*, in Bourdieu's explanation, means that you cannot desire something different from what the system wants you to desire, and now you cannot perceive as real something which is not included in Google. It seems that search engines eventually pass the test of an ontological proof.

In the end, the main difference between traditional and algorithm-driven media is this: all traditional media are each obviously biased, and this is arguably why audiences no longer trust them. As Manuel Castells pointed out, all recent international polls have been showing a very similar trend, according to which people barely believe in political parties, newspapers, and broadcasting media, all reported to be part of the same influential lobby. According to Castells, this dissatisfaction with traditional media is a first step toward discovering 'mass self communication': people *have* to get rid of TV, so as to explore the new possibilities opened up by the web.[24] But this time Castells is simply wrong, in my opinion. People do not believe in TV anymore, but they *do trust* Google, and his almost naïve distinction between 'vertical' and 'horizontal' media does not provide a serious understanding of power as it is now taking place within the new digital platforms.

The Bubble Will Have You
PageRank is simply the first stage in Google's strategy. The second is characterized by the customization strategies through the use of cookies, most likely launched in 2007 after the acquisition of digital marketing company DoubleClick. The reasons behind this new strategy are difficult to discern: arguably, the limits of the traditional business model, which were only based on advertising revenues, played a part. In fact, for some time and especially before its stock went public, market conditions allowed Google to gather wealth by simply exploiting advertising links; however, a new problem arose when technological innovation finally promised web users the ability to skip the ad links.[25]

---

22. Pierre Bourdieu, *Outline of a Theory of Practice*, Cambridge: Cambridge University Press, 1977 (1972), p. 78.
23. Bourdieu, *Outline of a Theory of Practice*, p. 77.
24. Manuel Castells, *Communication Power*, Oxford: Oxford University Press, 2009.
25. See Vise and Malseed, *The Google Story*.

In this sense, the massive use of cookies can be intended as a more narrow strategy to occupy the market: according to Eli Pariser, cookies allow Google to 'extrapolate what you like', and shape the search results according to your individual traffic history. More importantly, Google is now 'filtering out' all the information that is not supposed to be relevant for the target. Better yet, it is filtering out the information that is not relevant according to what the user has done *in the past*, in this way giving shape to an inherently static and *conservative* culture. The result of this customization practice is a 'bubble', a kind of *cage*, in which individuals experience a particular version of reality, different from that perceived by others.[26]

To some extent, one could say, we have always been living in a 'bubble'. Any mass medium – newspaper, television, etc. – provides a biased representation of reality, and thus in turn builds a kind of bubble, preventing its users from reading or watching all dissonant content. This is of course true, even though Google's bubble is more dangerous, according to Eli Pariser, because it takes place at a very deep and hidden level, characterized by three main differences: it is narrow, invisible, and, what is more, almost impossible to avoid. 'You are alone in the bubble', he writes, it being built upon individual rather than collective preferences, and dedicated to a single consumption history rather than to a community, such as the audience of a TV channel. On the other hand, the new bubble is invisible: the framing operated by traditional media can be ambiguous, but at its first level you obviously *know* that you are accessing a given information environment, ruled by a given gatekeeper. Conversely, in the new bubble the user is no longer aware, for the cookies act at a very hidden level, such that you do not even know that cookies *exist*. For the very same reason, in the end the web user cannot decide to 'enter the bubble', as we do when choosing a magazine, radio station, or a movie. The bubble is choosing the user and surrounding his or her daily practices.[27]

Both PageRank and cookies reveal that Google *does* indeed filter information, in this way falsifying the 'filter failure' thesis suggested by David Weinberger[28] (and, in different words, by Clay Shirky[29]). According to Weinberger, the web is not properly affected by a serious overload, but rather a weakening of filters. It is this weakness of filters – which no longer filter out, according to his optimistic idea – that is simply showing the long forgotten state of our culture, that is, a disproportion between individual comprehension, on the one hand, and knowledge as a whole, on the other. Things are too big to know, Weinberger suggests, and the web simply reveals this well-kept secret; but in any case the idea that the new platforms simply filter forward and do not filter out is hardly suitable for the way algorithm works, and it is entirely wrong if we consider the deep effects of customization practices.

After PageRank and cookies, the next level is constituted, not by accident, by a kind of hybrid form likely to implement social network functions (Google+) in the search engine system. From the web at large to the personal network: this narrowing of cul-

---

26. Eli Pariser, *The Filter Bubble. What the Internet is Hiding from You*, New York: Penguin, 2011.
27. Pariser, *The Filter Bubble*, pp. 9-10.
28. David Weinberger, *Too Big to Know*, New York: Basic Books, 2011.
29. Clay Shirky, *Cognitive Surplus. Creativity and Generosity in a Connected Age*, New York: Penguin, 2010.

tural horizons can come as a surprise, but it is hardly unexpected if we consider that Google *does not trade information*, as it claims it does, but something very different. In a complex cultural system, as Tiziana Terranova recently noted, the true traded value is no longer information, but *attention*. While in fact the first is too widely available, the latter is under a scarcity regime, and is the ideal 'condition that can give rise to a proper economy'.[30] Therefore, 'technology of attention' is a good definition for what Google, along with other players, is now doing – gathering and trading people's attention, and even reducing its information flow (to a great extent, attention for attention's sake: the use of personal data is actually not as important as its control and storage). Or, as Rachael – *Blade Runner*'s most controversial replicant – famously said: I am not in the business; I *am* the business.

Page and Brin's famous paper only describes the first stage in the evolution of Google, but we know that its functioning cannot be reduced to PageRank: its algorithms are actually based 'on more than 200 unique signals', including 'the freshness of content' and the user's region.[31] In the last years, Google has released many new features, such as 'social search', designed to 'understand not only content but also people', and allow users to find information directly related to them;[32] 'knowledge search', which introduces some elements of the so-called 'semantic web';[33] and Google Now, a service expected to provide you with the right information 'before you even ask', through the implementation of geo-locative technologies.[34] In short, Google combines many different services and tools, but I here consider only two of them – PageRank and the use of cookies – which seem to produce the most interesting effects. While the PageRank algorithm tends to favor the most linked pages, thus building a kind of homogenized agenda of knowledge and information, the use of cookies on the contrary leads to a very specific customization, likely to provide any user with a sort of individual 'bubble'. So cookies oppose the tendency of PageRank, insofar as cookies model search results after the user's individual tastes and preferences, which can be automatically detected. Google's action is therefore splitting into two different and almost opposite tendencies: the maximum degrees of standardization and individualization, which becomes quite a challenge for social studies.

Dialectic of Google
I've said the maximum degrees of standardization and individualization coexist in the same device. This seems to confirm Geert Lovink's idea that in the stage of mass web diffusion there would no longer be a dominant tendency, whether we look for positive or negative effects of the internet.[35] But there is something more here. What emerges is in fact a new technical version of the most traditional sociological problem, the tension between individual and structure, and the rise of a new order, regulating the relationship between the two.

---

30. Tiziana Terranova, 'Attention, Economy and the Brain', *Culture Machine* 13 (2012): 2.
31. See, http://www.google.com/intl/en/insidesearch/howsearchworks/algorithms.html.
32. See, http://googleblog.blogspot.it/2012/01/search-plus-your-world.html.
33. See, http://www.google.com/insidesearch/features/search/knowledge.html.
34. See, http://www.google.com/landing/now/.
35. Geert Lovink, *Zero Comments: Blogging and Critical Internet Theory*, New York: Routledge, 2007.

The role played by media and cultural industries in maintaining this balance has been widely investigated. In particular, Adorno and Horkheimer made a critical analysis in their *Dialectic of Enlightenment*:

> The sociological theory that the loss of the support of objectively established religion, the dissolution of the last remnants of precapitalism, together with technological and social differentiation or specialization, have led to cultural chaos is disproved every day; for culture now impresses the same stamp on everything.[36]

Even 70 years after Adorno and Horkheimer's masterwork, this point remains: the idea according to which the evolution of our societies will eventually destroy all solid structures and lead to a kind of cultural chaos is simply 'disproved' by fact. According to Adorno, capitalist culture is stable (the 'rhythm of the iron system') rather than fluid, or, as we would say in present terms, post-modern or liquid. As Franco Moretti recently pointed out, Western bourgeoisie has actually been historically functioning as a conservative *force*, so as to normalize social turbulence, and build up a predictable pattern of everyday life – and 'all that was solid' eventually 'became more so'.[37] At the same historical end, it seems that Google is stressing this tendency to its limits, 'now impressing the same stamp on everything' – *everything*: news and general contents, books and geographical maps, social circles and e-mail services, and so on. Two opposite and *dynamic* tendencies that nonetheless cooperate to produce a *static* result: the 'inherently conservative' nature of Google's cultural processes by which, as discussed by Eli Pariser and Siva Vaidhyanathan, anyone will basically find what he or she is inclined to look for, and will eventually know what he or she already knows. The bubble, in this sense, is the ultimate technical version of a long-term process by which the individual has become a predictable part of a predictable statistical pattern:

> Everybody must behave (as if spontaneously) in accordance with his determined and indexed level, and choose the category of mass product turned out for his type. Consumers appear as statistics on research organization charts [...]. The technique is that used for any type of propaganda.[38]

Therefore, the individual bubble, the homogeneous global agenda, and the tension between the two factors can be regarded, to a considerable extent, as a tension of opposites. But do we really need such a complicated explanation as a *dialectic* of Google? More consideration needs to be given to three aspects of Google's hegemony: the search algorithm, the contradiction between PageRank and the customization strategies, and finally the dynamic evolution of both tools.

PageRank obviously relies on *quantity*: the more links you have, the higher you will rank according to the algorithm's hierarchies. We know what logically follows is the power law nature of the web: links, as almost any other resource, tend to cluster around a handful of sites, following the '80/20 rule' of the Pareto principle.[39] In this sense,

---

36. Theodor Adorno and Max Horkheimer, *Dialectic of Enlightenment*, London: Verso, 1997 (1944), p. 120.
37. Franco Moretti, *The Bourgeois Between History and Literature*, London: Verso, 2013, p. 15.
38. Adorno and Horkheimer, *Dialectic of Enlightenment*, p. 123.
39. Albert-Laszlo Barabási, *Linked: The New Science of Networks*, New York: Perseus, 2002.

PageRank is neither establishing nor questioning a ranking, while the algorithm simply reproduces a previous hierarchy. This is why, following Vaidhyanathan, Google's power has less to do with cultural than 'infrastructural' imperialism – the production of ideological content, or public opinion shaping, versus the control of the communication *process* as such.[40] However, during this process, something is happening: quantity is definitely turning into *quality*, and for the very same reason – content does not matter, only links do. This tendency can be labeled simply as 'the transformation of quantity into quality and vice versa'.

We've seen that this standardization tendency is counter-balanced by a different process, enabled by the use of cookies: a very narrow customization strategy, likely to build up a bubble around any individual profile. But the point I am most interested in is that Google's inner process is not exhausted by either tendency, but is made of both, however contradictory they may be. Search results are organized according to the individual footprints detected by cookies, but ultimately rely on the same, common, *sterilized* cultural universe. Two opposite forces in the very same device – in other words, a kind of 'interpenetration of opposites'.

However, this is not a static contradiction but a mobile tension, wherein any innovation is not just an advancement of a previous technology, but its overcoming through the exploration of a new evolutionary path. The PageRank algorithm, for example, is said to make the world too homogenous, with cookies now providing the opposite effect. Though Google can be blamed for destroying the copyright system and even the humanistic heritage as a whole, Google Books will eventually save it. We must still keep in mind all the polemics of the 'virtual' world and its likely effects on the representation of reality, as when Google Maps suddenly provides a hybrid representation of the planet, half 'real' and half 'virtual'. Any process is a negation of the previous one, leading the system to a temporary equilibrium, destined in turn to give new transformation a place. Perhaps we could define this phenomenon with Hegel's words: the 'negation of negation'.

I will stop here, as I have attempted, in a half serious way, to apply Friedrich Engels' laws of dialectics to Google's cultural system.[41] *Serious*, because I think that current technological innovation does require a strong theoretical investigation rather than a merely quantitative analysis usually operated through crawlers (which, in a sort of vicious circle, provide a further legitimation of commercial software as the only valuable cultural platform, and so on). *Half* not serious, because I am not actually sure that the traditional forms of thought – such as Engels' dialectics, or Bourdieu's view of social practice – are the most suitable ones for the current needs of critical theory.

Absolutely, though, the two forces acting behind Google reproduce the basic tension between individualization and standardization that any social system is made of, while, at the same time, they move it to a next evolutionary level. What kind of sovereignty are we talking about with the homogenization of global knowledge and the 'micro-physical' customization of digital marketing? Put in different terms: cookies collect data in a

---

40. Vaidhyanathan, *The Googlization of Everything*, pp. 110-114.
41. See Friedrich Engels, *Dialectics of Nature*, Minneapolis and St. Paul: Wellred, 2012 (1883).

cultural ecosystem where, for good or for bad, such things as violence, pornography, multiple names, anonymity (in a word, *dissonance*) have been banned. In this context, the individual is a consumer, tracked with any move he or she makes, and living in a digital market where there is no room for conflict. What a powerful device, and what an ideal habitus for the world order of late capitalism.

References
Adorno, Theodor and Max Horkheimer. *Dialectic of Enlightenment* (1944), London: Verso, 1997.
Barabási, Albert-Laszlo. *Linked: The New Science of Networks*, New York: Perseus, 2002.
Barzilai-Nahon, Karine. 'Toward a Theory of Network Gatekeeping: A Framework for Exploring Information Control', *Journal of the American Society for Information, Science and Technology* 59.9 (2008): 1493-1512.
Bourdieu, Pierre. *Outline of a Theory of Practice*, Cambridge: Cambridge University Press, 1977 (1972).
Brin, Sergey, and Larry Page. 'The Anatomy of a Large-Scale Hypertextual Web Search Engine', Seventh International World Wide Conference, Brisbane, 1998, http://ilpubs.stanforde.edu:8090/361/.
Castells, Manuel. *Communication Power*, Oxford: Oxford University Press, 2009.
Di Maggio, Paul, Eszter Hargittai, W. Russell Neuman, and John P. Robinson. 'Social Implications of the Internet', *Annual Review of Sociology* 27 (2001): 307-336.
Engels, Friedrich. *Dialectics of Nature*, Minneapolis and St. Paul: Wellred, 2012 (1883).
Fallows, Deborah. 'Search Engine Users. Internet Users are Confident, Satisfied and Trusting – but They Are also Unaware and Naïve', Pew Internet & American Life Project, 2005.
Gillespie, Tarleton. 'The Relevance of Algorithms', in Tarleton Gillespie, Pablo Boczkowski, and Kirsten Foot (eds), *Media Technologies*, Cambridge, MA: MIT Press, forthcoming.
Jansen, Bernard, and Amanda Spink. 'How We Are Searching the World Wide Web? A Comparison of Nine Search Engine Transaction Logs', *Information Processing and Management* 42 (2006): 252-256.
Jansen, Bernard, Amanda Spink, and Jan Pedersen. 'A Temporal Comparison of AltaVista Web Searching', *Journal of the American Society for Information, Science and Technology* 56.6 (2005): 559-570.
Jansen, Bernard, Amanda Spink, and Tefko Saracevic. 'Real Life, Real Users, and Real Needs: A Study and Analysis of User Queries on the Web', *Information Processing and Management* 36.3 (2000): 207-227.
Keane, Mark, Maeve O'Brien, and Barry Smyth. 'Are People Biased in Their Use of Search Engines?', *Communications of the ACM* 51.2 (2008): 49-52.
Lovink, Geert. *Zero Comments: Blogging and Critical Internet Theory*, New York: Routledge, 2007.
Moretti, Franco. *The Bourgeois between History and Literature*, London: Verso, 2013.
Pariser, Eli. *The Filter Bubble. What the Internet Is Hiding from You*, New York: Penguin, 2011.
Shirky, Clay. *Cognitive Surplus. Creativity and Generosity in a Connected Age*, New York: Penguin, 2010.
Silverstein, Craig, Monica Henzinger, Hannes Marais, and Michael Moricz. 'Analysis of a Very Large AltaVista Query Log', Newsletter ACM SIGIR Forum, 33.1 (1999): 6-12.
Spink, Amanda and Bernard Jansen. 'A Study of Web Search Trends', *Webology* 1 (2004), www.webology.ir.
Terranova, Tiziana. 'Attention, Economy and the Brain', *Culture Machine* 13 (2012): 1-19.
Vaidhyanathan, Siva. *The Googlization of Everything (And Why We Should Worry)*, Berkeley and Los Angeles: University of California Press, 2011.
Vise, David, and Mark Malseed. *The Google Story*, New York: Random House, 2005.
Wang, Peiling, Michael Berry, and Yiheng Yang. 'Mining Longitudinal Web Queries: Trends and Patterns', *Journal of the American Society for Information Science and Technology* 54.8 (2003): 743-758.
Weinberger, David. *Too Big to Know*, New York: Basic Books, 2011.

Frictionless Sharing: The Rise of Automatic Criticism

Vito Campanelli

Frictionless Sharing: The Rise of Automatic Criticism

Vito Campanelli

In recent months, revelations about the existence of the surveillance program called PRISM and the consequent scandal (the 'datagate') that has troubled the administration of U.S. President Obama has caused an outbreak of public debate on the internet. Our awareness of programs that allow some U.S. and European intelligence agencies to spy on communications on the web (in addition to telephonic ones) has been increasing. However, it should be noted that very often the worst risks to the privacy of netizens do not come from the uncertain and contradictory policies of Western governments, but rather from some unexpected protagonists: the web companies that manage and organize the online spaces within which we spend an increasingly significant part of our days, transmitting huge amounts of data related to our personal spheres. The most famous and popular social network, Facebook, whose founder, Mark Zuckerberg, announced in the fall of 2011 the launch of a new sharing philosophy called 'frictionless sharing', provides an emblematic example of this.

The event was celebrated at Facebook F8, a conference organized by Facebook in a rather irregular fashion (no conferences were held in 2009, 2012, and 2013) to bring together developers and companies that make products and services that have been integrated into the social network. During these meetings, Facebook has frequently introduced new features. At the 2011 conference the most important novelty was the so-called 'timeline', a reorganization of the interface so that the history of users' activity is shown on their profile. Compared to such an authentic revolution in user experience, Zuckerberg's reference to frictionless sharing slipped into the background.[1] Indeed, only the most attentive participants caught the important implications of the approach underlying this conception.

The premise of this new philosophy of sharing is that one will no longer need to do the work of sharing tastes and preferences. Facebook, in fact, will register tastes automatically, thus making them available to the contacts (friends) of each user. This spur to conformism would be limited for the time being to media objects (movies, music, books, etc.) published in the most popular walled garden, but clearly, in the

---

1. Zuckerberg's expression was the following: 'real-time serendipity in a friction-less experience'. See Sheila Shayon, 'Facebook Unveils Timeline for "Friction-less" Serendipity', 22 September 2011, http://www.brandchannel.com/home/post/2011/09/22/Facebook-f8-Timeline-Announcement.aspx.

near future, nothing could stop Facebook from also recording consumption choices and preferences relative to all the other places visited by a user on the internet (and available technologies already allow such monitoring).[2] Evgeny Morozov is among those who noticed this claim by Facebook's founder. Never tired of emphasizing the weaknesses of internet culture, he perfectly captured that the most interesting aspect of this feature is the ideological one: Facebook's propaganda efforts aim to present an extreme form of sharing as something normal and even desirable. However, it is precisely this *sharing totalitarianism* that 'is killing *cyberflânerie*', because 'the whole point of the *flâneur*'s wanderings' is that one does not know what he or she cares about.[3]

On closer inspection, the functioning of Facebook's timeline is similar to Google Now (the 'intelligent and personal' information service that supposedly predicts what you want to know), and in fact it uses the potentialities of the most popular search engine, along with localization and access to personal user data, to automatically offer information and news about the context in which one is situated. The idea in this case is that such tools, which automatically organize the information we need, 'free' us, as they allow us to focus 'on what's important' to us.[4] Such a view implies that, according to Google, information selection should not be considered a core activity in the lives of human beings, but a burden that one may well leave to machines and their algorithms.

By crossing seemingly trivial data – for example, books or records purchased online – Facebook's tools can help determine, quite precisely, a profile of the observed user and then establish their political orientation, gender, religion, etc.[5] Beyond legitimate concerns for this additional threat to privacy (already severely under attack in social networks), perhaps an even greater danger should be considered: frictionless sharing. In fact, companies that have interests in common with Facebook could restrict their offer to those cultural products that are among the favorites of the standard category to which the user and their contacts/friends have been assigned. The risk is therefore that individual intellectual horizons will progressively narrow. If people in social networks encounter only cultural products that reflect the preferences of the ideal type to which one belongs according to contemporary marketing, the more predictable result would be a gradual desertification of the cultural life of individuals no longer able to encounter what is unusual, unexpected, and surprising.[6]

Some of the dynamics behind these narrowing horizons, however, are typical of social networks based on 'small worlds' – for example, those networks which consist of small groups densely connected to each other. (The model of the 'small world network' was

---

2. Vito Campanelli, *InfoWar: La battaglia per il controllo e la liberta della rete*, Milano: Egea, 2013, p. 115.
3. Evgeny Morozov, 'The Death of the Cyberflâneur', *The New York Times*, 5 February 2012, p. 6.
4. On the project's page is written: 'organizing the things you need to know and freeing you up to focus on what's important to you'. Retrieved at: http://www.google.it/landing/now.
5. On the state of art of profiling systems, see Claude Castelluccia, 'Behavioural Tracking on the Internet: A Technical Perspective', in Serge Gutwirth, Ronald Leenes, Paul De Hert, Yves Poullet (eds) *European Data Protection: In Good Health?*, London and New York: Springer, 2012, pp. 21-35.
6. Campanelli, *InfoWar*, pp. 115-116.

introduced in 1988 by Duncan Watts and Steve Strogatz.)[7] As explained by Clay Shirky, these networks act as amplifiers and filters of information.[8] In other words, because the information is spread from friends (or contacts) to *friends of friends*, one ends up stagnating in a flow of information filtered and amplified by one's contacts. With a closer look, everything that is not checked and highlighted in one's own small world is destined to go unnoticed.

To sum up, the ideology underlying frictionless sharing is based on the suppression of all criticism (whether aesthetic, social, or political) and the consequent reduction of users into 'robots without a soul' who have the unique function of consuming and therefore producing statistics, which are in turn fed to software algorithms capable of transforming them into new stereotypes and abstract consumption models.[9]

Similar concerns animate Eli Pariser's reflections on 'filter bubbles', a concept which represents the universe of information that Google, Facebook, etc. specifically prearrange for each of us. This U.S. activist effectively explains how the algorithms underlying the new conception of the net are increasingly tightening the circle around our preferences and our desires, to the point that when browsing the internet, it is unlikely that we will encounter something that has not been specifically designed for us. This trend provokes great alarm, because it ends up affecting our ability to choose how we want to spend our life.[10]

Right to Say No
From the perspective of cultural critique, the problematic relationship of humans with machines that have the capacity to filter cultural objects has been extensively addressed in the past century and is at the center of deep reflections on freedom by Vilém Flusser. The Bohemian thinker (whose horizon of observation is the diffusion of the first personal computers in the 80s) observes with great concern the consolidation of a tendency to escape the responsibility of critical consciousness and instead delegate every decision-making process to machines. This passage threatens to deprive humans of the critical role of *essences who make decisions*,[11] which spells 'the end of freedom'.[12] It is also not possible to consider it an expression of freedom when deciding whether to press one key or another; instead, the decision is based on prescripts and, ultimately, is a 'programmed freedom' (a choice between prescribed possibilities).[13] The

---

7. See Duncan Watts, *Small Worlds: The Dynamics of Networks between Order and Randomness*, Princeton: Princeton University Press, 1999. See also: Duncan Watts, *Six Degrees: The Science of a Connected Age*, New York: Norton, 2003.
8. Clay Shirky, *Here Comes Everybody: How Change Happens when People Come Together*, London and New York: Penguin, 2008.
9. Campanelli, *InfoWar*, p. 117.
10. Eli Pariser, *The Filter Bubble: What The Internet Is Hiding From You*, London and New York: Penguin, 2011.
11. It's useful to remember that for Flusser 'freedom is essentially the difference between that which is redundant and that which is actually information, and the free person is the one who is competent to decide'. Vilém Flusser, *Ins Universum der technischen Bilder*, Göttingen: European Photography, 1985, trans. *Into the Universe of Technical Images*, Minneapolis and London: University of Minnesota Press, 2011, p. 111.
12. Flusser, *Into the Universe of Technical Images*, p. 119.
13. Vilém Flusser, *The Shape of Things: A Philosophy of Design*, trans. Carl Hans, London: Reaktion, 1999 (1993), pp. 92-93.

escape offered by Flusser is a utopian telematic society in which it becomes possible to delegate the production of information to apparatuses in order to be free to devote oneself to the criticism of the information automatically produced by them.

Flusser perfectly anticipated the current scenario when he imagined that in the near future, machines would be calibrated according to informatic criteria (algorithms) to perform (automatically) the function of criticism as well. However, it should be underscored that according to Flusser, the apparatuses – which become 'critical machines' – assume the function of determining which redundant information (kitsch, gossip, etc.) requires filtering (discarding) and which informative data to *let go*, while it is clear that the kinds of experience that prelude the frictionless sharing philosophy are quite the opposite: redundant information is not discarded but heavily transmitted over digital networks. The Facebook timeline, for example, proposes the experience of continuously redundant content, that is, content that is endlessly repeated to induce users to conform to them. Moreover, as noted by Bob Hanke, '[s]ince Flusser's time, we have seen the rise of a myth of user agency and interactivity, the digital lock-down of culture, and the enclosure of the information commons.'[14]

Beyond this aspect, Flusser believes that even in the case of automatic apparatuses (which have become automatic critics), human beings retain a 'veto right'. The right to say 'no' (*Recht zum Neinsagen*) represents, in the Flusserian view, the negative decision (*negative Entscheidung*) that we call 'freedom'. Ultimately, for Flusser, telematics is a technology of freedom because, while it frees us from having to make decisions, at the same time it opens the doors to the fundamental freedom whereby we can say no to telematics itself.[15]

Freedom to Program

Flusser's interrogation into the opportunity to reject telematics and reassert human intelligence over artificial ones is particularly challenging in an era such as the present one, in which we are all struggling to affirm our freedom ('positive freedom') to control the fate of information (especially information about ourselves), while our agency is restricted by 'the "black boxing" of technologies, their networks, and intellectual property regimes'.[16] For Flusser, to avoid being programmed by the apparatuses, it is necessary to devote oneself to their reconfiguration and programming. In other words it is necessary to say, 'I want to have my program so that I won't be subject to anyone else's'. In a society dominated by 'unidirectional media' (TV, radio, etc.), senders (broadcasters) possess the programs, and we are possessed by them; hence, the need to dispossess and socialize programs emerges. However, in a fully realized information society, that is, a society in which centralized senders have been overcome, it would no longer make sense to speak in terms of dispossession but rather in terms of dialogical programming. Therefore, beyond using 'one's own program', it would be more appropriate to apply the formula 'programs of others'. In a telematic society, as Flusser points out, there is no longer the need to possess

---

14. Bob Hanke, 'Vilém Flusser's Digital Galaxy', *International Journal of Communication* (January, 2012): 25.
15. Flusser, *Into the Universe*, p. 122.
16. Hanke, 'Vilém Flusser's Digital Galaxy': 25.

one's own program to reduce the fear of succumbing to someone else's program. What is more fundamental is having the 'programs of others' in order to edit (remix) them and subsequently offer them back.[17]

In this regard, the popular media theorist Douglas Rushkoff, in his decalogue *Program or Be Programmed*, writes that '[p]rogramming is the sweet spot, the high leverage point in a digital society. If we don't learn to program, we risk being programmed ourselves.'[18] The media theorist notes that if in an earlier time there were no differences between using a computer and programming it, today we are confronted with a totally different scenario, and the goal of those who determine the development of software and hardware seems to be making interfaces increasingly stratified (below a 'user friendly' interface, the logic of functioning is made inaccessible and is in fact hidden under different levels of complexity). 'The easy command-line interface (where you just type a word telling the machine what you want it to do) was replaced with clicking and dragging and pointing and watching.'[19] Put simply, the computational *medium* has been made more opaque, thus more similar to television. Interfaces are becoming 'user friendly', but the internal functioning of machines is hidden in the background.[20] The most noteworthy examples are search engines, which billions of people use to filter information and access news. These are interfaces with the highest degree of opacity – indeed no one is able to determine exactly what algorithms they use to function.[21] This fact does not diminish their popularity, thanks to the misperception that the results they offer are 'objective' and not determined by user profiling, geographical position, interests of advertisers, etc., and they are growing at accelerated rates.[22]

The most immediate consequence of the tendency to blur interfaces is that we are learning the features that our computers offer us but not the operations that we *could* make them perform.[23] In other words, we are satisfied with following the paths drawn for us by others and do not try to forge our own way.

According to Rushkoff, despite the programming tools at our disposal, we continue to think in terms of the writing potential of the *medium*. Therefore we feel proud and satisfied enough by making a web page or filling in our profile information page on some social network site. We continue to be unaware of the biases of the programs we use, as well as of the ways in which they circumscribe our 'newfound authorship'

---

17. Flusser, *Into the Universe*, p. 155.
18. Douglas Rushkoff, *Program or Be Programmed: Ten Commands for a Digital Age*, New York: ORbooks, 2010, p. 133.
19. Rushkoff, *Program or Be Programmed*, p. 135.
20. On the unworkable nature of all interfaces (windows, doors, screens, etc.), see Alexander R. Galloway, *The Interface Effect*, Cambridge: Polity, 2012.
21. For a critical analysis of the role of search engines in current society and, in particular, of their ability to affect access to culture and information, see Konrad Becker and Felix Stalder (eds) *Deep Search: The Politics of Search beyond Google*, Innsbruck: Studienverlag, 2009, and Siva Vaidhyanathan, *The Googlization of Everything (And Why We Should Worry)*, Los Angeles: University of California Press, 2011.
22. The statistical analysis company comScore recently documented the breaking of the 20 billion searches per month roof, which happened in the U.S. market in March 2013. The research is available online at http://www.comscore.com/Insights/Press_Releases/2013/4/comScore_Releases_March_2013_U.S._Search_Engine_Rankings.
23. Rushkoff, *Program or Be Programmed*, p. 138.

within their predetermined agendas.[24] Our interactivity is clearly limited when the modalities of interaction have been planned in advance. Machines are then animated, as Flusser would describe it, by technologies that represent 'black boxes' known only to those who program (and whose good faith we are forced to accept on trust).[25] As Rushkoff writes:

> Digital technologies are [...] not just objects, but systems embedded with purpose. They act with intention. If we don't know how they work, we won't even know what they want. The less involved and aware we are of the way our technologies are programmed and program themselves, the more narrow our choices will become.[26]

Ruskoff arrives at a place similar to Flusser's: for both is it clear that 'the less we will be able to envision alternatives to the pathways described by our programs [...] the more our lives and experiences will be dictated by their biases'.[27] Moreover, as emphasized by Manovich, in a world dominated by software, it is not our skills alone that have a decisive influence – it is important also to take into consideration what software tools are used. In fact, what we can do with a single digital file changes dramatically depending on the software we have access to.[28]

Flusser believed that the individual human being can do nothing to reverse a situation in which we all risk being programmed by apparatuses. However, 'society as a whole' or as a 'collective brain' has for Flusser a greater competence than apparatuses that, though boasting great speed and infallible memories, remain 'idiotic'. The media philosopher assumed therefore that it is not individual 'functionaries'[29] and receivers, but *society as collective brain* that has the capacity to regain control of apparatuses and make judgments about when desirable (informative) situations have been created.

To avoid being programmed by apparatuses it is necessary that society as a whole is dedicated to the dialogic reconfiguration and programming of apparatuses.[30] But one should never forget, as Flusser warns, that this is not solely a technical but also a political question,[31] and therefore a general agreement about reconfiguration and programming must become widespread. In particular, users should be given the opportunity to personally intervene in the configuration of software platforms they interact with, so that they can decide for themselves what to share and possibly with whom; on which information they want software to make suggestions; and for which cultural objects the filters' operation is considered useful and which they would prefer to rely on serendipity, that is, random and unexpected encounters. Ultimately, the rise of a strong political

---

24. Rushkoff, *Program or Be Programmed*, pp. 139-140.
25. Rushkoff, *Program or Be Programmed*, p. 141.
26. Rushkoff, *Program or Be Programmed*, pp. 142-143.
27. Rushkoff, *Program or Be Programmed*, p. 143.
28. Lev Manovich, 'There is Only Software', 28 April 2011, http://www.manovich.net/DOCS/Manovich.there_is_only_software.pdf.
29. Flusser writes: 'most apparatuses are not so completely automatic that they can get along without human intervention. They need functionaries. In this way, the original terms human and apparatus are reversed, and human beings operate as a function of the apparatus.' Flusser, *Into the Universe*, p. 74.
30. Flusser, *Into the Universe*, pp. 73-77.
31. Flusser, *Into the Universe*, p. 76.

consensus regarding the inviolability of the right of users is necessary in order to decide (and to be able to modify at any time the decisions previously taken) whether and to what extent users want to rely on the automatic criticism of machines, and whether and to what extent they want to act as critics, thus as information selectors, instead.

It is also clear that in order for these freedoms to be effective, it is essential to overcome and leave behind the black box model that makes companies such as Google and Facebook prosper. The main condition for the development of a collective dialogue on reconfiguration and programming is in fact the transparency of the apparatuses with which one interacts. Therefore any idea of re-appropriating the role of the critic is condemned to remain an illusion until it is possible again to look inside our apparatuses, to understand how they work, and to share such knowledge.[32]

References

Becker, Konrad and Felix Stalder (eds). *Deep Search: The Politics of Search beyond Google,* Innsbruck: Studienverlag, 2009.
Campanelli, Vito. *InfoWar: La battaglia per il controllo e la libertà della rete*, Milano: Egea, 2013.
Castelluccia, Claude. 'Behavioural Tracking on the Internet: A Technical Perspective', in Serge Gutwirth, Ronald Leenes, Paul De Hert, and Yves Poullet (eds) *European Data Protection: In Good Health?*, London and New York: Springer, 2012: pp. 21-35.
Doctorow, Cory. 'The Coming Civil War over General Purpose Computing', *BoingBoing*, August 2012, http://boingboing.net/2012/08/23/civilwar.html.
Flusser, Vilém. *Into the Universe of Technical Images*, trans. Nancy Ann Roth, intro. Mark Poster, Minneapolis and London: University of Minnesota Press, 2011 (1985).
_____. *The Shape of Things: A Philosophy of Design*, trans. Carl Hanser, London: Reaktion, 1999 (1993).
Galloway, Alexander R. *The Interface Effect*, Cambridge: Polity, 2012.
Hanke, Bob. 'Vilém Flusser's Digital Galaxy', *International Journal of Communication* (January, 2012): 25-35.
Manovich, Lev. 'There is Only Software', 28 April 2011, http://www.manovich.net/DOCS/Manovich.there_is_only_software.pdf.
Morozov, Evgeny. 'The Death of the Cyberflâneur', *The New York Times*, 5 February 2012.
Pariser, Eli. *The Filter Bubble: What The Internet Is Hiding From You*, London and New York: Penguin, 2011.
Rushkoff, Douglas. *Program Or be Programmed: Ten Commands for a Digital Age*, New York: ORbooks, 2010.
Shayon, Sheila. 'Facebook Unveils Timeline for 'Friction-less' Serendipity', 22 September 2011, http://www.brandchannel.com/home/post/2011/09/22/Facebook-f8-Timeline-Announcement.aspx.
Shirky, Clay. *Here Comes Everybody: How Change Happens when People Come Together,* London and New York: Penguin, 2008.
Vaidhyanathan, Siva. *The Googlization of Everything (And Why We Should Worry)*, Los Angeles: University of California Press, 2011.
Watts, Duncan. *Small Worlds: The Dynamics of Networks between Order and Randomness*, Princeton: Princeton University Press, 1999.
_____. *Six Degrees: The Science of a Connected Age*, New York: Norton, 2003.

---

32. These considerations point to the more general issue of general purpose computers, a complex subject that has many criticalities addressed by the digital rights activist Cory Doctorow, see Cory Doctorow, 'The Coming Civil War over General Purpose Computing', *BoingBoing*, August 2012, http://boingboing.net/2012/08/23/civilwar.html.

Why We Need an Independent Index of the Web

¬

Dirk Lewandowski

Why We Need an Independent Index of the Web

¬

Dirk Lewandowski

Search engine indexes function as a 'local copy of the web'[1], forming the foundation of every search engine. Search engines need to look for new documents constantly, detect changes made to existing documents, and remove documents from the index when they are no longer available on the web. When one considers that the web comprises many billions of documents that are constantly changing, the challenge search engines face becomes clear. It is impossible to maintain a perfectly complete and current index.[2] The pool of data changes thousands of times each second. No search engine can keep up with this rapid pace of change.[3] The 'local copy of the web' can thus be viewed as the Holy Grail of web indexing at best – in practice, different search engines will always attain a varied degree of success in pursuing this goal.[4]

Search engines do not merely capture the text of the documents they find (as is often falsely assumed). They also generate complex replicas of the documents. These representations include, for instance, information on the popularity of the document (measured by the number of times it is accessed or how many links to the document exist on the web), information extracted from the documents (for example the name of the author or the date the document was created), and an alternative text-based

---

1. Knut Magne Risvik and Rolfe Michelsen, 'Search Engines and Web Dynamics', *Computer Networks* 39.3 (2002): 289-302.
2. Risvik and Michelsen, 'Search Engines and Web Dynamics'; Dirk Lewandowski, 'Suchmaschinen', in *Grundlagen der praktischen Information und Dokumentation*, 6, Ausgabe. Berlin: De Gruyter, 2013, pp. 495-508.
3. Dirk Lewandowski, 'A Three-Year Study on the Freshness of Web Search Engine Databases', *Journal of Information Science*, 34 (2008): 817-831; Alexander Ntoulas, Junghoo Cho, and Christopher Olston, 'What's New on the Web?: The Evolution of the Web from a Search Engine Perspective', *Proceedings of the 13th International Conference on World Wide Web*, 2004, pp. 1-12.
4. Studies show that search engines do not come close to achieving a comprehensive index and that different search engines do not always find the same documents. Although there is no current research on the comprehensiveness of search engines, from older research (Krishna Bharat and Andrei Broder, 'A Technique for Measuring the Relative Size and Overlap of Public Web Search Engines', *Computer Networks and ISDN Systems* 30.1-7 (1998): 379-388; Steve Lawrence and C. Lee Giles, 'Searching the World Wide Web', *Science* 280 (3 April 1998): 98-100; Steve Lawrence and C. Lee Giles, 'Accessibility of Information on the Web' *Nature* 400 (8 July 1998): 107-109; Antonio Gulli and Alessio Signorini, 'The Indexable Web is More Than 11.5 Billion Pages', *14th International Conference on World Wide Web*, 2005, pp. 902-903) we can however assume that even when taking into consideration recent technological advances, the coverage of the web is likely to be far from complete.

version of the document comprising the anchor texts from other documents that link to it. It is important to distinguish between simply finding and saving documents and performing the additional work involved in processing and preparing the documents for search engine use.

Another factor to consider is the user's perspective. Everyone uses web search. Using a search engine to look things up on the web is the most popular activity on the internet, ranking higher even than email.[5] Search engines are used for all types of research, everything from simply finding a previously visited website to trivia and complex queries, such as planning a vacation or treatment options for illnesses.

One amazing aspect of search is that users rely predominantly on one particular search engine, Google. Google has a near monopoly in European countries, where it commands a market share of over 90 percent.[6] Search engine users therefore must not only rely on Google as a search engine and its unique method of ordering results; they are also confined by the limitations of Google's collection of data. If Google hasn't seen it – and indexed it – or kept it up-to-date, it can't be found with a search query.

But what about the alternatives? If Google is handling over 90 percent of search requests, then at least the remaining 10 percent are going to other search engines. Here it is important to note that many providers of what may appear to be a search engine are simply services that access the data of another search engine, representing nothing more than an alternative user interface to one of the more well-known engines, and in many cases, that turns out to be Google.

The larger internet portals have not run their own search engines for quite some time. Instead, they rely on their services partners. If we take Germany as an example, we can see that the major internet portals T-Online, GMX, AOL, and web.de all display results obtained from Google. Consequently, Google's market share continues to grow. A significant proportion of those who believe they are using an alternative search engine are accessing Google's data whether they know it or not. True alternatives, which do exist, only play a very minor role in the German search engine market. The main contenders here are Bing, Ask.com, and Metager. But of these, only Bing can claim a significant share of search requests. Interestingly one of these alternatives is a meta-search engine that does not have its own index. Instead, Metager accesses the databases of several other search engines. The search engine market in other European countries is similar to Germany's. Google dominates, and other search engines can only achieve minimal market share or else don't represent a true alternative since they cannot display their own search engine results, only Google's.

---

5. Kristen Purcell, Joanna Brenner, and Lee Raine, *Search Engine Use 2012,* Pew Internet & American Life Project, 2012, http://pewinternet.org/~/media/Files/Reports/2012/PIP_Search_Engine_Use_2012.pdf; Birgit van Eimeren and Beate Frees, 'ARD/ZDF-Onlinestudie 2012: 76 Prozent der Deutschen online – neue Nutzungssituationen durch mobile Endgeräte', *Media Perspektiven* 7-8 (2012): 362-379.
6. Lunapark, 'Suchmaschinen-Marktanteile', Lunapark, 2013, retrieved from http://www.luna-park.de/blog/1175-suchmaschinen-marktanteile/; Holger Schmidt, 'Googles Marktanteil steigt auf 96 Prozent in Deutschland', *Focus Online*, 12 March 2012, http://www.focus.de/digital/internet/netzoekonomie-blog/suchmaschinen-googles-marktanteil-steigt-auf-96-prozent-in-deutschland_aid_723240.html.

One can of course view the decision to use the Google search engine as a personal choice and ask what's so bad about the fact that one search engine is used almost exclusively. The simple answer is that, much in the same way we require more than just a single newspaper to ensure a diverse range of opinions is represented in the media, we need more than one search engine to ensure that a broad range of opinions is represented in the search market.

The comparison with the media becomes somewhat less applicable when one considers that search engines do not play the role of gatekeepers quite the same way as media outlets do when they select a relatively small number of items from a large quantity of existing content. With search, every request generates a new collection of documents from which users can then make their selection. So what we end up with is a double or, more precisely, a two-stage selection process: the selection made by entering a search request as well as the selection of one or several of the results which are presented. Diversity in the search engine marketplace would be desirable to ensure that the selection does not always occur according to the same criteria and that users have the choice between different worldviews originating as a product of algorithm-based search result generation.

This argument is not to say that search engines are promoting any specific worldviews, consciously or otherwise. But the decisions required to implement algorithms for ranking documents are influenced by factors that go far behind purely technical considerations. Consequently, an ideology-free ranking algorithm is not possible and would also not be desirable. In its place, we should strive for diversity achieved through multiple ranking algorithms competing against one another. In the following, I will attempt to illuminate the critical role indexes play in the diversity of the search landscape. I argue for the merits of an independent index that is accessible to everyone and show that the lack of such an index can be viewed as a disincentive for investing in search.

Alternative Search Engine Indexes
There are only a handful of search engines that operate their own indexes. Particularly among new search engine startups, it can frequently be observed that they either prefer to rely on an existing external index, or limit themselves to a very specialized topic (which frequently requires only a very small index), or else they aggregate data from a number of different search engines to offer what is known as a meta search engine.

Meta search engines don't directly access the indexes of the search engines they collect their data from. Instead, they receive only a certain number of high-ranking results from each of their source search engines, which are then assembled to form a new ranking. Consequently, a meta-search engine that aggregates the results of five other search engines, receiving 20 items each from them, will have a maximum of 100 documents listed in its own ranking. It's easy to see how meta search engines are relatively limited; in addition, they don't have access to the documents themselves. Rather, meta search engines only have the URLs that are provided with the descriptions in the results lists of the source search engines together with the ranking information from the source search engines (i.e. how high the respective document ranked).

In addition to meta-search engines and specialized search engines,[7] there have been a few actual search engine startups in recent years. Providers such as Blekko and DuckDuckGo operate their own indexes. No information is available, however, on the amount of data these search engines have or how frequently they are updated, and they are more the exception than the rule in any case. Creating and operating a competitive independent web index is simply too expensive (at least for now) to be profitable.[8]

Above I mentioned that some portals and services that appear to be search engines are actually piggybacking on results from 'real' search engines. 'Real' search engine providers such as Google and Bing operate their own search engines but also provide their search results to partners. Yahoo, for instance, has been displaying results from Bing for years now. On the surface, Yahoo appears to be a search engine (it has its own layout and a somewhat different format for the results than Bing at first glance). The results themselves, however, are identical with those obtained from Bing.

All the major web portals that offer search as just one service among many have now embraced this model. The key component to this type of constellation is what is known as the partner index (the index the search engine provides its partners). Income is earned when the ads accompanying the search results are clicked on, and this revenue is split between the search engine provider and its partner. This model is attractive for both sides since the search engine provider encounters only minimal costs in giving the search results to its partners,[9] and the operator of the portal no longer needs to go to the great expense of running its own search engine. All that is required is enough traffic on their portal – very little effort is needed to earn a profit with this model. So it's no wonder that there are hardly any alternative search engines around anymore, and portals no longer operate their own indexes. The partner index model is simply too lucrative for an alternative solution to be feasible, and it has served to thin out the competition in the search industry.[10] The lack of diversity in the search engine market can be attributed at least in part to the success of this model. After all, the profits from the partner index model are higher the more search result page ads are served. Consequently, large search engines with a comprehensive advertising network have an inherent advantage.[11]

---

7. Specialized search engines can be defined as 'those which are limited to a specific subject matter or document property (such as file type)'. Dirk Lewandowski, 'Spezialsuchmaschinen', in Dirk Lewandowski (ed.) *Handbuch Internet-Suchmaschinen,* Heidelberg: AKA, 2009, p. 57.
8. It can be assumed that the indexes of the search engines mentioned here are comparably small. Bing, the only real competition for Google, has, since it was founded, incurred heavy losses, which can only be justified by strategic considerations for owning a proprietary web index, see: Dirk Lewandowski, 'Bing macht Milliardenverluste – wie lange wird Microsoft durchhalten?' *Password* 11 (2011): 26.
9. The largest share of the costs involved in providing a search engine service goes towards deploying the search engine (development costs and building and maintaining the index). The costs involved in processing the individual search requests play only a very minor role.
10. Dirk Lewandowski, 'Suchmaschinenindices', in Dirk Lewandowski (ed.) *Handbuch Internet-Suchmaschinen 3: Suchmaschinen zwischen Technik und Gesellschaft,* Berlin: Akademische Verlagsgesellschaft AKA, 2013, pp. 143-161.
11. It is assumed here that the search results and the ads are obtained from the same provider. This is the most common scenario but doesn't always have to be the case. Regardless, the search engine that's able to provide the widest range of results from the web would offer the best monetization for the portal operator (assuming the margin for the portal operator remains equal).

Access to Search Engine Indexes

The large search engine indexes can be accessed by means of what are known as application programming interfaces (APIs). The API allows partners to automatically obtain search results they can then use for their own purposes. This business model generally allows a certain quantity of free search requests per day, with payment required only after a certain limit is reached. So wouldn't that make it possible to operate a search engine without incurring the cost of creating and maintaining a separate index?

The problem is that even with APIs, there is no direct access to the search engine index. Instead, what is provided is merely a limited number of top results which have already been ranked by the search engine provider. In this way, access via APIs is similar to what is occurring at the meta-search engines (which in some cases also use the APIs), with the difference being that in this case, only one search engine is being used as a source.

For each search result, the API also provides the URL and the description as it is displayed on the results page of the search engine. The document itself, however, is not provided (this would need to be requested separately using the URL). Even more interestingly, the *representation* of the document in the source search engine is also not included. Additionally, the price is determined not only by the number of search requests made, but also by the number of results requested. For example, the Bing API normally provides the top 50 results. Bing charges for additional results beyond the first 50. The total number of results is also limited to 1000, which is frequently insufficient for the purpose of analysis. Other search engines (such as Google) offer only a free version of their API which, however, is limited regarding the search request volume available per day. It's nearly impossible to build a commercial service on this type of limited API.

Indexes that offer complete access do, however, exist. At the top of this list is Common Crawl,[12] a nonprofit project that aims to provide a web index for anyone who's interested. The Blekko search engine contributes to this index by donating its own web crawling results to the foundation. There are also a number of web crawling services that make their results available for research purposes, such as the Lemur project.[13] In both cases, the services are merely static crawls that are not updated on a regular basis. Due to this limitation, they are not suitable for use with a commercial search engine. Common Crawl represents an important development. The project has done groundbreaking work in making web indices widely available. The significance of the service should be determined less by whether or not it is actually successful in providing a comprehensive index for the purpose of internet searching and analysis and more by whether or not it succeeds in generating awareness for the topic of publicly available web indexes.

Alternative Search Engines

There have been efforts in the past to establish alternative search engines. But consensus is lacking on what constitutes an 'alternative'. One might consider all search

---

12. See, http://commoncrawl.org/our-work/.
13. See, http://lemurproject.org/clueweb12/specs.php.

engines that are not Google as alternatives. This would include all the search engines that have been heralded as the next 'Google killer', but never manage to succeed over the long run. The list of failed attempts is long. Cuil certainly counts as one of the higher-profile failures. The launch was preceded by grand claims and great anticipation, but after just a few years, the service was discontinued. Then there are the search engine alternatives that are not perceived as such because they are considered to be simply the same as Google. This type is mainly Bing, but also other providers such as Yahoo, back in the days when it still operated its own search engine. These search engines have in common that, although they are perhaps perceived as being independent providers, users do not see them as offering something that goes significantly beyond what Google can provide. They don't offer anything that would make switching search engines worthwhile.

And then there are search engines that explicitly position themselves as an alternative to Google by emphasizing their superior ability to deal with local or European languages and to control the quality of the search results through their enhanced knowledge of local matters. One such service was the 'European search engine' Seekport, which operated between 2004 and 2008.[14] These types of search engines thus do not differentiate themselves by providing a fundamentally different technical approach compared to the dominant search engines; instead, they focus on a regional approach.

We should also note attempts to provide public support for search engine technology in an effort to promote the creation of one or several alternative search engines. One example is the joint German-French project Quaero. After the French and German sides were not able to come to agreement, however, the project was split into two parts, Quaero (the French part) and Theseus (the German part). The French team developed technologies for multimedia searching. Theseus concentrated on semantic technologies for business-to-business applications (without focusing exclusively on search). 'Real alternatives', on the other hand, would be defined as search engines that pursue a different approach than the conventional web search engines. Conceivable services might include semantic search engines and alternative approaches to gathering web content and making it accessible, such as web catalogs, social bookmarking services, and collaborative question-answering services. What these projects all have in common, however, is that their market share is insignificant. The common thread here is that all of these models and alternatives have failed *as search tools*, even though they may have a role to play as their own genre on the web.

The proposal to provide government funding for search engine technology has been subject to intense criticism in the past. But it's not necessarily a bad idea. This type of support is not appropriate, however, when the objective is to establish only a single alternative. Even if this new alternative were to be of high quality, there would still be a number of factors that would cause it to fail, and they wouldn't even need to have anything to do with search itself. The problem could be poor marketing or the graphic design of the user interface. Regardless of the reason, a failure of the new search engine would result in the entire publicly funded initiative's failure.

---

14. Thomas Dominikowski, 'Zur Geschichte der Websuchmaschinen in Deutschland', in Dirk Lewandowski (ed.) *Handbuch Internet-Suchmaschinen 3*, pp. 3-34.

At this point I would like to revisit the concept of the search engine index. If we were to fund a search engine index and make it available to other providers, it would then be possible to create not just one alternative search engine, but a number of them instead. The failure of one of these search engines would not impact the others. In addition, even if the program is successful, the addition of just a single alternative search engine is not enough – only a critical mass of options (and of course the *actual use* of the new search engines) can truly establish diversity.

If one considers the topic of search engine indexes from an economic perspective, it becomes clear that only the largest internet companies are able to afford large indexes. As I explained above, Microsoft is the only company besides Google to possess a comprehensive search engine index. Yahoo gave up on its own index several years ago, choosing the familiar route of the web portal by sourcing its search results from other providers. It appears as though operating a dedicated index is attractive to practically no one – and there are hardly any candidates with the necessary financial resources in any case. Even if one of the occasional rumors that some company with deep pockets such as Apple is preparing to launch its own index were to come true, who would benefit? I am of the opinion that it makes practically no difference whether or not the search engine market is shared by two, three, or four participants. Only by establishing a considerable number of search engines can true diversity be achieved.

The Solution
The path to greater diversity, as we have seen, cannot be achieved by merely hoping for a new search engine (a Google killer), nor will government support for a single alternative achieve this goal. What is instead required is to create the conditions that will make establishing such a search engine possible in the first place. I have described how building and maintaining a proprietary index is the greatest deterrent to such an undertaking. We must first overcome this obstacle. Doing so will still not solve the problem of the lack of diversity in the search engine marketplace, but it may establish the conditions necessary to achieve that desired end. We cannot predict who will use the data from this index or for what purposes it will be used. But we can expect that the possibilities it presents would benefit a number of different companies, individuals, and institutions. The result will be fair competition to develop the best concepts for using the data provided by the index.

The vision behind this proposal is one that ensures an index of the web can be accessed with fair conditions for everyone.
- 'Everyone' means that anyone who is interested can access the index.
- 'Fair conditions' does not mean that access to the index must be free of charge for everyone. I assume that the index will be a government-funded initiative provided as infrastructure that should attempt to recoup at least part of the costs involved by charging usage fees. Analogous to the popular API business model described above, a certain number of document requests per day would be available at no cost in order to promote non-profit projects.
- 'Access' to the index can be defined as the ability to automatically query the index with ease. Furthermore, it should actually be easy to obtain all the information contained within the index. In contrast to the APIs of the current commercial search engines described above, the complete document representation including the full text of the document should be available. Additionally, there should be no limit with respect to

the number of documents or document representations, so users of the index can actually create a good ranking based on a large pool of documents. Nevertheless, basic ranking capabilities for querying the index should be provided so that the quantity of documents requested can also be limited in an appropriate manner.[15]
- The concept of 'index of the web' is intended to cover as much of the web as possible. That means that the index should contain all the common content types currently available from search engines today, including news, images, videos, etc. Additional content types that are not currently being indexed by search engines are, however, also a possibility. Bodies of information that pose no interest to consumers but are useful for researchers and developers also exist. Such information includes metadata derived from documents such as frequency distributions of words, information on spam, etc.

This type of project will require a considerable investment of funds. The total cost cannot be precisely forecast here. Several hundred million euros will likely be needed, however, when one considers the anecdotal reports provided by search engine operators. The losses Bing has reported on its search activities are one example. This may appear prohibitively expensive until one considers, for instance, that the German government invested roughly 100 million euros in the semantic technology developed as part of the Theseus program. Nevertheless, it is still clear that any one country alone cannot support this type of project. The only feasible option is a pan-European initiative.

Not only would the issue of financing need to be settled, the question of who would operate the index must also be considered. An existing research institution or newly founded institution is one possibility. The institute might operate and maintain the index while also conducting its own research based on the resulting pool of data. The most important thing is that the operator of the index does not obtain the exclusive right to determine the way in which the documents are used or made available. Instead, a board of trustees consisting of (potential) users of the index should participate in the decision-making process regarding document representations and the availability of the data.

In closing, I would like to reiterate the advantages of this type of search engine index. An index of the type described here would motivate companies, institutions, and developers pursuing personal projects to create their own search applications. The data available on the web is so boundless that it lends itself to countless applications in a broad range of fields. A new search engine index would not only make it possible to operate comprehensive web search engines that seek to include practically everything available on the web, it would also enable specialized search engines covering a broad range of subjects. The index would thus be useful not only for entities seeking to operate a general-purpose search engine, but also for libraries, museums, and other institutions seeking to supplement their own data with data from the web. The index would also be useful for applications completely unrelated to search. One example might be analyses based on data from the web, for instance to assess public interest in certain topics or the sentiment of users about certain issues over time.

---

15. This should be sufficient in the vast majority of cases. What is important, however, is that the quantity of documents can be determined by users themselves, not by the operator of the index.

Such an index would also enable applications we are not yet capable of even imagining. An open structure, transparency with respect to access, and the assurance of permanent availability thanks to state sponsorship would lay the groundwork for innovation, even innovation that requires larger investments. An index of this nature would allow anyone to invent new search technology and, more importantly, to test it. Building and operating a search engine index can thus be seen as part of government's role to provide public infrastructure. The state finances highways used by everyone, ensures that the electrical grid is available to all, and generates and disseminates geodata. Making web data available is no different from these other public services.

References

Bharat, Krishna and Andrei Broder. 'A Technique For Measuring the Relative Size and Overlap of Public Web Search Engines', *Computer Networks and ISDN Systems* 30.1-7 (1998): 379-388.

Dominikowski, Thomas. 'Zur Geschichte der Websuchmaschinen in Deutschland' in Dirk Lewandowski (ed.) *Handbuch Internet-Suchmaschinen 3: Suchmaschinen zwischen Technik und Gesellschaft*, Berlin: Akademische Verlagsgesellschaft AKA, 2013, pp. 3-34.

Eimeren, Birgit van and Beate Frees. 'ARD/ZDF-Onlinestudie 2012: 76 Prozent der Deutschen online – neue Nutzungssituationen durch mobile Endgeräte', *Media Perspektiven* 7-8 (2012): 362-379.

Gulli, Antonio and Alessio Signorini. 'The Indexable Web is More Than 11.5 Billion Pages', *14th International Conference on World Wide Web*, 2005, pp. 902-903.

Lawrence, Steve and C. Lee Giles. 'Accessibility of Information on the Web', *Nature* 400 (8 July 1998): 107-109.

_____. 'Searching the World Wide Web' *Science* 280 (3 April 1998): 98-100.

Lewandowski, Dirk. 'Bing macht Milliardenverluste - wie lange wird Microsoft durchhalten?' *Password* 11 (2011): 26.

_____. 'Spezialsuchmaschinen', in Dirk Lewandowski (ed.) *Handbuch Internet-Suchmaschinen*, Heidelberg: AKA, 2009.

_____. 'Suchmaschinen' in: *Grundlagen der praktischen Information und Dokumentation*, 6, Ausgabe. Berlin: De Gruyter, 2013, pp. 495-508.

_____. 'Suchmaschinenindices' in Dirk Lewandowski (ed.) *Handbuch Internet-Suchmaschinen 3: Suchmaschinen zwischen Technik und Gesellschaft*, Berlin: Akademische Verlagsgesellschaft AKA, 2013.

_____. 'A Three-Year Study on the Freshness of Web Search Engine Databases', *Journal of Information Science*, 34 (2008): 817-831.

Lunapark. 'Suchmaschinen-Marktanteile', Lunapark, 2013, retrieved from http://www.luna-park.de/blog/1175-suchmaschinen-marktanteile/.

Ntoulas, Alexander, Junghoo Cho, and Christopher Olston. 'What's New on the Web?: The Evolution of the Web from a Search Engine Perspective', *Proceedings of the 13th International Conference on World Wide Web* 2004, pp. 1-12.

Purcell, Kristen, Joanna Brenner, and Lee Raine. *Search Engine Use 2012*, Pew Internet & American Life Project, 2012, http://pewinternet.org/~/media/Files/Reports/2012/PIP_Search_Engine_Use_2012.pdf.

Risvik, Knut Magne and Rolfe Michelsen. 'Search Engines and Web Dynamics', *Computer Networks* 39.3 (2002): 289-302.

Schmidt, Holger. 'Googles Marktanteil steigt auf 96 Prozent in Deutschland', *Focus Online*, 12 March 2012, http://www.focus.de/digital/internet/netzoekonomie-blog/suchmaschinen-googles-marktanteil-steigt-auf-96-prozent-in-deutschland_aid_723240.html.

Is Small Really Beautiful? Big Search and Its Alternatives

Astrid Mager

Is Small Really Beautiful?
Big Search and Its Alternatives

Astrid Mager

Google is big in many ways. The company offers a myriad of services and products ranging from basic keyword search to futuristic glass technology. It possesses the most comprehensive index of the web and the most extensive database of user data, and its ranking algorithm is state of the art. Google figures as search engine number one, at least in the Western world, and is also the leader in online advertising. Just recently, it has been accused of collaborating with the U.S. National Security Agency (NSA), exemplifying its powerful role in collecting and profiling personal data.[1] In debates on big data, the conventional argument is that big data needs big methods to be mined and made productive for users. In light of big data, Google may be seen as *the* biggest method applied when trying to bring order to the web, to find answers to questions, to sift through the sea of information.

It is thus not surprising that Google is a flourishing company, and its algorithm incorporates and strengthens the capitalist ideology. Rather than blaming Google for doing evil, however, I suggest thinking of Google as being shaped by society. Google shows us the face of capitalism because it was born and raised in a capitalist society. 'Technology is society made durable', as Bruno Latour put it.[2] Accordingly, Google is not the only actor to blame. Quite on the contrary, actors such as policy makers, jurists, journalists, search engine optimizers, website providers, and, last but not least, users are part of the game too. If users would turn away from Google, the whole business model, including its sophisticated algorithm and database of personal data, would fall apart. But where can people turn to? Are there true alternatives to Google and their algorithmic ideology?

The goal of this article is to examine and discuss critically a selection of so-called alternative search engines and their ideological underpinnings. If Google embodies the capitalist ideology, what ideology do alternative search engines incorporate? What values do privacy-concerned search tools such as DuckDuckGo carry? What is green about green search engines? Can peer-to-peer search engines such as YaCy be inter-

---

1. For more information on accused collaborations between the NSA and IT companies leaked by Edward Snowden see, for example: Glenn Greenwald and Ewen MacAskill, 'NSA Prism Program Taps into User Data of Apple, Google and Others', *The Guardian*, 6 June 2013, http://www.theguardian.com/world/2013/jun/06/us-tech-giants-nsa-data.
2. Bruno Latour, 'Technology Is Society Made Durable', in John Law (ed.) *A Sociology of Monsters: Essays on Power, Technology and Domination*, New York and London: Routledge, 1991, pp. 103-131.

preted as communist search engines? Could search be seen as a scientific endeavor as WolframIAlpha suggests?

Big Search and Its Algorithmic Ideology

In my previous work,[3] I argue that algorithms, like all other technologies, should not be understood as merely technical, mathematical, or 'objective' tools, even though Google and its competitors try to establish them as exactly that. Rather, they should be seen as socially constructed entities mirroring and solidifying socio-political norms and values. Drawing on interviews with search engine experts,[4] I show how ideologies become inscribed in search algorithms by way of social practices. Following Luc Boltanski and Ève Chiapello,[5] I interpret ideology not only as a moralizing discourse, but as a set of shared beliefs, which are inscribed in institutions, embedded in actual practices, and hence anchored in reality. Along this line of thought, I show how ideology becomes manifested in search technology, Google in particular.

Google's success is built on flat hierarchies, a flexible work force, and a global scale, which are central characteristics of 'the new spirit of capitalism'.[6] Furthermore, Google corresponds well to new modes of exploitation that rose with this capitalist spirit. '*A form of exploitation that develops in a connexionist world* – that is to say, a world where the realization of profit occurs through organizing economic operations in networks.'[7] Scholars such as Matteo Pasquinelli and Christian Fuchs explain how Google extracts value from networks. Pasquinelli argues that Google's PageRank algorithm exploits the collective intelligence of the web since Google uses links from other websites to measure a websites' value. These links may be seen as a concretion of intelligence that is used by Google to create surplus value.[8] Fuchs further hints at the importance of including users' activities to understand Google's capital accumulation cycle. Google not only exploits website providers' content, but also users' practices and data. Fuchs thus concludes that 'Google is the ultimate economic surveillance machine and the ultimate user-exploitation machine'.[9] My colleague Jenny Eklöf and I additionally show that the capitalist spirit Google carries contributes to a commercialization of search results and has thus wider implications on the way we approach information and make sense of the world we live in.[10]

---

3. Astrid Mager, 'Algorithmic Ideology: How Capitalist Society Shapes Search Engines', *Information, Communication & Society* 15.5 (2012a): 1-19.
4. Between October 2010 and February 2011 I conducted 17 expert interviews, both personally and via Skype. My interview partners included computer scientists, programmers, software developers, and people working in information retrieval (mainly from big, universal search engines). Furthermore, I talked to one search engine optimization expert, one economic journalist, one net activist, one jurist, and two policy-makers concerned with search technology, as well as multiple search engine scholars from the social sciences (all from the U.S. and Germany, one from Ireland). This research was supported by HUMlab, Umeå University (Sweden), where I worked as a post-doctoral fellow from 2010-2012.
5. Luc Boltanski and Ève Chiapello, *The New Spirit of Capitalism*, London: Verso, 2007.
6. Boltanski and Chiapello, *The New Spirit of Capitalism*.
7. Boltanski and Chiapello, *The New Spirit of Capitalism*, p. 355 (italics in original).
8. Matteo Pasquinelli, 'Google's PageRank algorithm: A Diagram of Cognitive Capitalism and the Rentier of the Common Intellect', in Konrad Becker and Felix Stalder (eds) *Deep Search: The Politics of Search Engines Beyond Google*, Innsbruck: Studienverlag, 2009, pp. 152-162.
9. Christian Fuchs, 'A Contribution to the Critique of the Political Economy of Google', *Fast Capitalism* 8.1 (2011), http://www.uta.edu/huma/agger/fastcapitalism/8_1/fuchs8_1.html.
10. Jenny Eklöf and Astrid Mager, 'Technoscientific Promotion and Biofuel Policy: How the Press and Search Engines Stage the Biofuel Controversy', *Media, Culture & Society 35.4 (2013)*: 454-471.

But criticizing Google and its business model is not enough. It is essential to understand power relations and social practices involved in the construction and solidification of search algorithms. Website providers and users are not simply exploited by Google (and others); their desire for attention and information, but also for consumer goods, is perfectly served by companies such as Google. Accordingly, users and providers actively stabilize the technology by using it to reach their own goals of gaining visibility and finding answers to their questions. Also, services such as Google AdWords and Google AdSense would not work if people would not advertise with or click on Google ads. Furthermore, broader socio-political frameworks strengthen corporate actors like Google. The politics of privatization of the last decades put search on the free market. Despite past efforts, European policy makers have not succeeded in establishing a non-corporate search engine. Consequently, Google has become a powerful player challenging politics, law, and economics in Europe and beyond. Whether lack of technical expertise and carelessness have led to policy's loss of control over search technology, or whether governments actively decided to outsource search and related tasks of data collection and citizen surveillance to big companies to profit from their databases in post-9/11 societies, cannot be answered here. What is certain, however, is that politics and also mass media strongly participate in the stabilization of big players, the latter by constantly featuring new services, products and, ultimately, IT companies. This techno-euphoric breeding ground is about to change now that more and more data protection violations and scandals such as the NSA affair are critically discussed in the public domain. This shows that search engines such as Google are not external to society, but rather enacted and negotiated within society. Website providers, users, marketers, journalists, policy makers, and jurists are all part of the actor-network strengthening Google and its capitalist ideology.

This situation gives us the chance to opt out of Google's accumulation cycle, if we want to. If website providers and users broke out of the network dynamic, Google's power and its scheme of exploitation would fall apart. If mass media and activists continue a critical debate about search engines and the myriad of data they collect, store, and process, big players would be destabilized. If politics and law took on a stronger role in the regulation of search technology, limits would be set regarding the collection and use of personal data, and also business practices and advertising schemes. First steps towards a renegotiation of search engines are seen on various levels. A new data protection law is currently being negotiated in the E.U. More critical media debates on Google, Facebook, Amazon, and other IT companies are seen due to the increase of tracking methods, privacy violations, illicit practices of scraping WiFi data, and possible collaborations with secret services.

So the question is, why are users still not turning away from Google and other big players? Why do they not leave big search and move towards smaller search engines? The common answer, even amongst search engine experts, is because there are no real alternatives. But is that actually the case? What about all the other search projects trying to challenge Google and provide an alternative style of search?

Small Search and Its Ideological Inner Life
There are a number of so-called alternative search engines that are not as big as Google, Bing, or Yahoo! and that lead their lives at the margins of the search market.

Of course, Bing could be conceptualized as an alternative to Google in terms of its index and algorithm. However, Bing may also be considered yet another for-profit search engine that is no true alternative from an ideological standpoint. In line with the purpose of this article I conceptualize alternative search engines as search tools that claim to have a particular ideological agenda that clearly distinguishes them from big, corporate search tools.[11] Accordingly, all search engines included in this analysis explicitly devote themselves to a particular ideological framework. Further, all of them are general-purpose search engines with no particular topical focus, even though knowledge engines such as WolframIAlpha are specialized in answering factual questions rather than cultural, social scientific, or commercial ones, as I will exemplify later.

The central aim of this article is to discuss whether these chosen search engines may be seen as true alternatives in terms of their ideological stance and what norms, values, and ideas they carry. Further, their self-descriptions will be juxtaposed with their actual practices. Whether these search tools could be true alternatives on a technical level or whether their search results are better than those of their bigger relatives can only partly be answered since this would go beyond the scope of this article.

Privacy First
The first search engine in the analysis is DuckDuckGo, because it claims to be a privacy-concerned search engine. DuckDuckGo was founded by the entrepreneur Gabriel Weinberg, and its developers 'believe in better search and real privacy at the same time'.[12] Its website further explains that DuckDuckGo does not track, filter bubble, or share data with third parties, and it goes on with a lengthy discussion of privacy issues and a visual explanation of what it actually means to be tracked, collected, and shared with third parties when using larger search engines such as Google. So the company clearly tries to provide an alternative to major search engines in terms of data protection and anonymous search. Their default settings protect privacy rather than collecting and offering personal data to third parties (which big search engines usually do). They incorporate privacy in their technical Gestalt and may hence be interpreted as following the principle of 'Privacy by Design'. Privacy by Design builds on the idea of integrating privacy-relevant features into the design process of IT technologies to enable 'value-sensitive innovation'.[13] But can privacy be seen as their ideological framework?

Privacy is a moral concept, no doubt, and a central component of human rights, one codified in international agreements and law including the U.N.'s Universal Declaration of Human Rights and the E.U.'s Charter of Fundamental Rights. More specifically, privacy is regulated in recommendations and legal norms in the context of information technologies, such as the OECD Privacy Guidelines and the E.U. Data Protection Directive

---

11. Social search or social bookmarking techniques such as Delicious may also be seen as alternatives to big search. Since their search services are limited to a certain platform or user-generated indexes they will not be included in the analysis.
12. See, https://duckduckgo.com/about.
13. Doris Allhutter and Roswitha Hoffmann, 'Deconstructive Design as an Approach for Opening Trading Zones', in Jordi Vallverdú (ed.) *Thinking Machines in the Philosophy of Computer Science: Concepts and Principles*, Hershey: IGI Global, 2010, pp. 175-192.

95/46/EC.[14] The latter is currently under negotiation, since the European Commission plans to unify data protection within the E.U. with a single, binding law, the General Data Protection Regulation. But privacy is not only about rights; it comes with ideas about autonomy and freedom, and it is an essential prerequisite for democratic societies.[15] Privacy can be seen as something stronger than law and regulations; it may be interpreted as an ideological tool to tame the free market, to set boundaries where boundaries are missing, and to provide technological alternatives that enable individual choice. DuckDuckGo may hence indeed be seen as positioning itself as an ideological counterpart to Google with its practice of user profiling. This tactic seems to work in times of increasing privacy violations and scandals, as shown by the record traffic on DuckDuckGo following the news coverage of Google's possible collaboration with the NSA.[16]

So can this become a success story of David against Goliath? In terms of data protection it probably can. When looked at more closely, however, DuckDuckGo is troubled with cosmetic flaws. Even though it does not sell personal data to gain profit it does provide contextual advertising on its site. Its ads are provided by Bing Ads and should adhere to their privacy policy, as its website claims. But DuckDuckGo does not only use Bing Ads; it also uses Bing's search results. Although DuckDuckGo operates its own web crawler, the DuckDuckBot, it is also dependent on results from other search engines and sources. According to its community platform it obtains its results from over 100 sources including crowd-sourced sites such as Wikipedia and also for-profit search tools, including Yandex, WolframlAlpha, Bing, and Yahoo! (the latter also displaying Bing results).[17] Maintaining its own web crawler and building a comprehensive web index is a very expensive endeavor.[18] Consequently, most search engines either partner with one search engine or use results from multiple sources. Since DuckDuckGo uses both commercial and non-commercial sources, it partly depends on for-profit search engines such as Bing, which does track users and sells personal data to third parties.

So even if DuckDuckGo provides encrypted search and does not sell user data to third parties itself, it does make use of big players and their business practices. That DuckDuckGo is in alliance with commercial players and their tracking methods, I would say, casts a shadow over the company's belief in privacy and fundamental rights. In fact, the company needs big search in order to keep its small search engine running. This situation similarly applies to other privacy-concerned search engines including

---

14. For a detailed discussion of privacy guidelines and regulations see, for example, Johann Čas, 'Ubiquitous Computing, Privacy and Data Protection: Options and Limitations to Reconcile the Unprecedented Contradictions', in Serge Gutwirth, Yves Poullet, Paul De Hert, Ronald Leenes (eds) *Computers, Privacy and Data Protection: An Element of Choice*, Dordrecht, Heidelberg, London, New York: Springer, 2011, pp. 139-171.
15. Walter Peissl, 'Information Privacy in Europe from a TA Perspective', Serge Gutwirth, Yves Poullet and Paul De Hert (eds.) *Data Protection in a Profiled World*, Dordrecht, Heidelberg, London, New York: Springer, 2010, pp. 247-257.
16. Jennifer Slegg, 'DuckDuckGo Sees Record Traffic After NSA Prism Scandal', Search Engine Watch, 18 June 2013, http://searchenginewatch.com/article/2275867/DuckDuckGo-Sees-Record-Traffic-After-NSA-PRISM-Scandal.
17. See, DuckDuckGo, 'Sources', https://dukgo.com/help/en_US/results/sources.
18. See also Dirk Lewandowski's contribution in this volume: 'Why We Need an Independent Index of the Web', pp. 49-58.

Ixquick[19] and MetaGer,[20] which also use results from bigger search engines. While such companies fetch results from these other search engines without saving users' IP addresses or passing on personal information, they still would not be able to exist without their data-collecting counterparts.

Green Search
Another model of ideological search is green search. Green search engines offer the possibility to support ecological projects financially by using their search services. Ecosia, for instance, helps plant trees, as it states most prominently on its homepage.[21] The company describes itself as a 'social business' based in Berlin, and its basic idea is to donate 80 percent of its advertising revenue to the Nature Conservancy, which helps to afforest the Brazilian rainforest. The ads it displays on its site are served by Yahoo!, which pays Ecosia a share of revenue generated from these ads. Ecosia's own servers run on green power. However, Ecosia's search results come from Bing, which does not use green energy. This is an example of what Dirk Lewandowski coins the 'partner index model'.[22] Ecosia uses Bing's partner index, and, in turn, the advertising revenue is split between Yahoo! (partnering with Bing) and Ecosia (donating 80 percent to the rain forest). Since online searches are co-produced by computers, computer networks, and servers, a great deal of CO_2 emission are produced during each search (up to seven grams of CO_2 in the case of Google, according to a Harvard physicist).[23] To compensate for the CO_2 emission generated by the Bing searches, Ecosia supports a project in Madagascar.[24]

When looking at its initiatives, Ecosia clearly follows a green agenda. Contrary to search engines such as the Green Planet Search that help find ecological information,[25] Ecosia enables users to take action. Since environmentalism is increasingly embedded in everyday routines and situated in objects,[26] green search engines can function as a vehicle to engage in environment protection. Similar to the recycling bin and other objects, green search engines can be seen as a materialization of civic engagement and political action. According to Noortje Marres such objects '[...] have the capacity to turn everyday material activities into forms of engagement with the environment [...]'[27]. Green search engines may hence be interpreted as 'technologies of participa-

---

19. See, https://www.ixquick.com/eng/.
20. See, http://metager.de/en/.
21. See, http://www.ecosia.org/.
22. Lewandowski, 'Why We Need an Independent Index of the Web', p. 53.
23. Jon Swaine, 'Two Google Searches "Produce Same CO2 as Boiling a Kettle"', *The Telegraph*, 11 January 2009, http://www.telegraph.co.uk/technology/google/4217055/Two-Google-searches-produce-same-CO2-as-boiling-a-kettle.html.
24. In 2010 Google launched its green initiative with the main purpose of cutting down its environmental impact (e.g. by reducing their data center energy use) and investing in environmentally conscious technology. Jack McGrath, 'Google's Green Initiative: Environmentally Conscious Technology', TechnoBuffalo, 18 May 2012, http://www.technobuffalo.com/2011/05/18/googles-green-initiative-environmentally-conscious-technology.
25. See, http://www.greenplanetsearch.com.
26. Jutta Haider, 'The Environment on Holidays or How a Recycling Bin Informs Us on the Environment', *Journal of Documentation* 67.5 (2011): 823-839.
27. Noortje Marres, 'The Costs of Public Involvement: Everyday Devices of Carbon Accounting and the Materialization of Participation', *Economy and Society* 40.4 (2011): 515.

tion'[28] that make involvement easy since they do not require any significant change in the practice itself (compared to green devices that would require crucial material, social, and technical transformations).[29]

Similar to privacy-concerned search engines, Ecosia's green ideology is endangered by its dependence on big search for both search results and advertising revenue – a threat not only in an ideological but also a very practical sense if we look at the history of green search projects. There have been multiple green search engines in the past. Except from Znout,[30] which compensates Google searches with renewable energy certificates, all of these companies have closed down. Businesses that used Google search as their back-end, such as Ecocho, are no longer supported by Google because they 'jibe with Google's AdSense policy, which prohibits the compensation of third parties through the promise of performed searches'.[31]

Their fate hence exemplifies the difficulty that comes with depending on a single search engine. Big players simply can stop supporting small projects if they no longer harmonize with their own advertising policy. Besides, green search engines actively support big search in terms of their revenue model; they not only use big search tools for their own results, they even support advertising practices of corporate search tools since they use (need) them for their own (green) purposes. It is a collaboration that serves both parties. Green search engines may be seen as surfing on the capitalist wave towards more ecological technology. However, their journey can be abruptly stopped at any time if big search tools decide to opt out of green projects, as we have seen in the past. 'Informational capitalism'[32] is the captain steering the green ship through the rough sea of online search after all.

The Commons
Aside from search engines with a centralized web index, there are projects that try to provide decentralized search, following the principle of file-sharing networks such as the Pirate Bay. The most popular proponent of such decentralized search projects is the peer-to-peer network YaCy, created by the German free software enthusiast Michael Christen. While reading through the YaCy website, the major goal and ideological ambition of the search engine jumps out at you right away: 'We want to achieve freedom of information through a free, distributed web search which is powered by the world's users.'[33] The image that is displayed in their 'About Us' section clearly shows that the search engine characterizes itself as a true alternative to centralized search engines such as Google or Bing and their capitalist ideology:

---

28. Nigel Thrift, *Non-Representational Theory. Space, Politics, Affect*, London: Routledge, 2008.
29. Marres, 'The Costs of Public Involvement'.
30. See, http://us.znout.org/.
31. Nathania Johnson, 'Google Says "No" to Ecocho', Search Engine Watch, 23 April 2008, http://searchenginewatch.com/article/2054343/Google-Says-No-to-Ecocho.
32. Manuel Castells, *The Rise of the Network Society. The Information Age: Economy, Society and Culture, Volume 1*, Malden: Blackwell, 2000.
33. See, http://yacy.net/en/index.html.

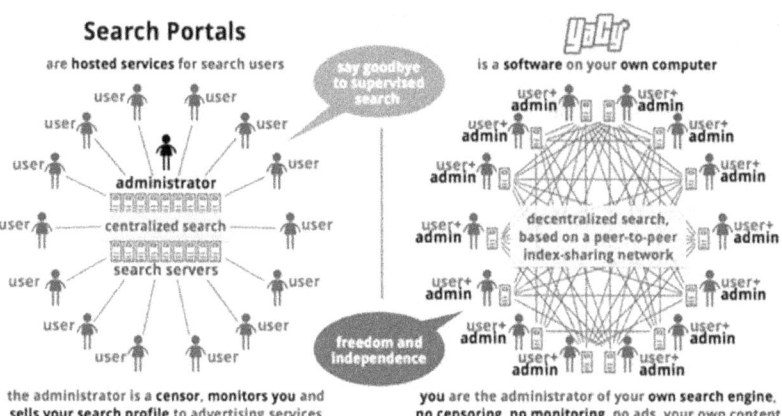

Fig. 1. YaCy homepage, about YaCy.

Freedom and independence are put first. Rather than relying on big search engines, YaCy provides users with the possibility to run a search technology on their own computers and/or participate in a private computer network that is not controlled by a single company or individual. This basically means that there is no central index of the web, such as Google's. Rather, there is an index that each user builds by searching the web through the YaCy Proxy (that one needs to install first). This index is then shared with other peers in the network so that a global index comes into being. Furthermore, a web crawler expands the index, which has gained more and more importance over the last years. When users do a global search, the index of all peers that are currently online is searched.

This means that everyone can see how information is obtained by the search engine and displayed to the user. YaCy is open-source, free software that is completely transparent, as its website claims. No collaboration with big search engines is needed.[34] Quite on the contrary, YaCy wants to make free content accessible through free software so that users do not have to go through proprietary search engines 'in an increasingly monopolistic internet infrastructure because then the monopoly holders decide what information is visible'.[35] Moreover, YaCy protects privacy since there is no central evaluation or monitoring of search queries and helps to green the web because only users' computers are needed and no additional data centers with enormous power consumption are required.

From an ideological standpoint YaCy may be interpreted as devoting itself to 'commons-based peer production', a term coined by Yochai Benkler. 'The salient charac-

---

34. In contrast to the peer-to-peer search project Seeks, which aims to be a free software/open source project, but uses commercial search engines to generate its index too: http://www.seeks-project.info.
35. YaCy, 'Philosophy', http://yacy.net/en/Philosophy.html.

teristic of commons, as opposed to property, is that no single person has exclusive control over the use and disposition of any particular resource in the commons.'[36] Michael Hardt even goes further by arguing that the commons are able to create not only new goods, but also new humanity:

> Communism should be defined not only by the abolition of property but also by the affirmation of the common – the affirmation of open and autonomous production of subjectivity, social relations, and the forms of life; the self-governed continuous creation of new humanity.[37]

The communist manifesto is not on the list of references that YaCy provides on its website. It does, however, reference and support manifestos by the Free Software Foundation Europe, the Chaos Computer Club, the German Pirate Party, and the Charter of Civil Rights for a Sustainable Knowledge Society. This alliance shows that the free software movement and commons-based peer production are central pillars of YaCy's ideological framework. Following Hardt's argumentation YaCy may even be seen as closer to the communist spirit than to capitalist ideology.

Knowledge Engines
Finally, to round off the picture, knowledge engines are worth mentioning in terms of alternative search projects. Knowledge engines claim to provide users with new knowledge. Rather than pointing users to information available already, they aim at providing users with new answers to their questions. Wolfram|Alpha is well-known for this style of search. Wolfram|Alpha is a search tool, or rather software, developed by Stephen Wolfram, a British physicist and mathematician. Wolfram built the software Mathematica, which integrates computer algebra, symbolic and numerical computation, visualization, and statistics. Wolfram's profession tells us a lot about the ideological underpinning of his software product. On its website, Wolfram|Alpha is described as a scientific tool that provides answers to factual queries by computing materials from external sources: 'Our goal is to build on the achievements of science and other systematizations of knowledge to provide a single source that can be relied on by everyone for definitive answers to factual queries.'[38] Rather than offering users sources and websites that may contain answers to their questions, Wolfram|Alpha wants to provide users with straight answers in a scientific manner. The software favors 'expert-level knowledge', facts, and figures and hence clearly dedicates itself to the scientific paradigm. The attempt to offer knowledge rather than information mirrors the idea of enlightening citizens. In contrast to conventional search engines providing users with heterogeneous, often contradictory information that needs to be actively transformed into knowledge by the individual user,[39] Wolfram|Alpha promotes reason and scientific thought and aims to provide users with straight knowledge. Technically it contains a

---

36. Yochai Benkler, *The Wealth of Networks: How Social Production Transforms Markets and Freedom,* New Haven, Connecticut: Yale University Press, 2006, p. 61.
37. Michael Hardt, 'Reclaim the Common in Communism', *The Guardian,* 3 February 2011, http://www.theguardian.com/commentisfree/2011/feb/03/communism-capitalism-socialism-property.
38. See, http://www.wolframalpha.com/about.html.
39. Astrid Mager, 'Search Engines Matter: From Educating Users Towards Engaging with Online Health Information Practices', *Policy & Internet* 4.2 (2012b): pp. 1-21.

natural language interpreter at the front-end and a number of key data sources, which have been captured and standardized by Wolfram staff, at the back-end (e.g. Wikipedia, Encyclopædia Britannica, and newspapers).

Another, yet more metaphysical knowledge engine is YossarianLives!. Its algorithm uses metaphors to return image results that are conceptually related to search terms. These results should enable users to see problems in a new way rather than provide users with more of the same information;[40] they should further help to circumvent the filter bubble.[41] Even though YossarianLives! is constituted as a company, it does not seem to have a proper business model yet. In contrast, Wolfram|Alpha has developed a sophisticated business strategy.

Similar to Google, Wolfram|Alpha incorporated the capitalist ideology into its scientific endeavor. Unlike big search, though, the company does not only count on advertising. Besides its free, advertising-based search tool, Wolfram|Alpha offers a Pro version that includes additional features for a monthly subscription fee of $5 and that does not display advertising. It further makes money with sponsoring contracts and licensing partnerships. This underlines the fact that Wolfram|Alpha is a software product rather than a search tool. The Infoworld journalist Neil McAllister argues that Wolfram|Alpha even goes beyond conventional software companies in terms of copyright questions.[42] When reading through Wolfram|Alpha's terms of use, one can see that the software does not only claim ownership for the software itself, but also for its output. This is the exact phrasing:

> In many cases the data you are shown never existed before in exactly that way until you asked for it, so its provenance traces back both to underlying data sources and to the algorithms and knowledge built into the Wolfram|Alpha computational system. As such, the results you get from Wolfram|Alpha are correctly attributed to Wolfram|Alpha itself.[43]

Taking this seriously would mean that Wolfram|Alpha holds a copyright of all users' search queries. Moreover, open data are closed down when being processed by the software that aims to 'bring broad, deep, expert-level knowledge to everyone', as it claims on its homepage. This crucially runs counter to the ideal of both free software and freedom of information. In contrast to YaCy, Wolfram|Alpha contributes to closing down web information that is freely available by simply processing it. Serious trouble with copyright law may follow from this policy since computers should not be entitled to credit for their calculations, as the free software activist Richard Stallman argues.[44]

---

40. See, http://about.yossarianlives.com/index.html.
41. Frederiek Pennink, 'Rethinking Search: YossarianLives!', Institute of Network Cultures, 16 May 2013, http://networkcultures.org/wpmu/query/2013/05/16/rethinking-search-yossarianlives.
42. Neil McAllister, 'How Wolfram Alpha Could Change Software', InfoWorld, 29 July 2009, http://www.infoworld.com/d/developer-world/how-wolfram-alpha-could-change-software-248?page=0,0.
43. See, http://www.wolframalpha.com/termsofuse/.
44. Richard Stallman, 'Re: How Wolfram Alpha's Copyright Claims Could Change Software', A2K Listserve, 4 August 2009, http://lists.essential.org/pipermail/a2k/2009-August/004865.html.

Conclusions

When considering alternative search projects in the limelight of ideology, we can see that the capitalist spirit is by far not the only ideology shaping contemporary search engines. Quite on the contrary, there are multiple algorithmic ideologies at work. There are search engines that carry democratic values, those that incorporate the green ideology, some that believe in the commons, and others that subject themselves to the scientific paradigm. This means that we can set an ideological example by choosing one search engine over the other.

In daily practice, however, the capitalist ideology appears to be hegemonic since not all ideologies are equal in terms of exercising their power. The majority of users turns to big search engines and hence solidifies the capitalist spirit more than any other ideology.[45] Moreover, most alternative search engines are subordinate to 'informational capitalism'. DuckDuckGo and Ecosia both entered alliances with big search engines by using their search results and advertising methods. They assimilate the capitalist spirit by relying on big search and its capital accumulation cycle. Their ideological agendas are not deeply embedded in technical layers and algorithmic logics because both the index and the algorithms they use are borrowed from other search engines. Their ideology is only carried out on the surface; e.g. their user interfaces, encryption techniques, and donation models. In contrast, WolframIAlpha chose to be independent on an algorithmic level, but ended up as a commercial product too. The only exception is YaCy. The peer-to-peer network is the only search tool discussed that provides a true alternative to corporate search engines; it is the most radical alternative to proprietary search and expresses its values on the level of infrastructure, software, and content. YaCy's ideology is deeply woven into its technical Gestalt and computational logics and hence embedded in actual practices. All other search tools absorb the capitalist spirit.

This indicates that opting out of big search and its capitalist underpinnings is not as easy as it may seem at first sight. Everyone is free to choose alternatives, of course. But selecting a true alternative, both in terms of technology and ideology, would require not only awareness and a certain amount of technical know-how, but also effort and patience. The latter has become a rare good in our fast moving, comfortable consumer culture. Using YaCy to its full extent, for example, requires installing YaCy first, accessing the global index, and being patient in case the desired information does not appear immediately. It probably also involves missing some pieces of information other search engines would provide, for better or worse. The network is only as good as its participants, after all. This indicates that the farther you move away from big search engines towards smaller ones, the more beautiful their technical and ideological Gestalt become. Such a move however reveals that the beauty of search comes at a cost. True alternatives can only be reached with a critical mass of users who are willing to sacrifice bits of their convenience in return for a search tool that is created and owned in the public domain.

---

45. Google has a market share of more than 90 percent in most European countries according to the website SEO Chief: Mobaruk Hussain, 'The Market Share of Google in Various Countries', SEO Chief, 6 July 2010, http://www.seo-chief.com/5950/the-market-share-of-google-in-various-countries.

Whether a peer-to-peer search engine like YaCy will ever be able to compete with Google in regards to the scope and quality of its results will ultimately depend on the number of users participating. But time and money is needed too. Crawling and indexing the web has become a time-consuming and very expensive undertaking that involves sophisticated technology and highly skilled engineers. In the case of centralized search, it further needs large data centers around the globe. Big search engines such as Google possess years of experience with handling big data, an enormously skilled workforce, and large-scale infrastructure. Small search engines, such as the ones discussed in the article, just started out with taming big data and the challenges that come along with it. Whether they will succeed in providing a true ideological alternative to corporate search tools such as Google will depend on the human resources and funding they are able to acquire in the end. Dirk Lewandowski suggests providing public funding to create a public index of the web that would enable programmers to build various search engines on top of it and, as a result, to achieve greater diversity on the search engine market.[46] Whatever the incentives and specific actions will be to strengthen non-corporate search engines in the future, this article has shown that there are still certain barriers to be conquered on the road towards alternative search both in terms of technology and ideology.

Acknowledgements

The analysis of alternative search engines was conducted as part of the research project 'GLOCAL SEARCH. Search technology at the intersection of global capitalism and local socio-political cultures' (funded by the Jubiläumsfonds of the Oesterreichische Nationalbank (OeNB), project number 14702). I would like to thank the Society of the Query #2 conference participants and the editors of this volume for their helpful comments and feedback.

References

Allhutter, Doris and Roswitha Hoffmann. 'Deconstructive Design as an Approach for Opening Trading Zones', in Jordi Vallverdú (ed.) *Thinking Machines in the Philosophy of Computer Science: Concepts and Principles*, Hershey: IGI Global, 2010, pp. 175-192.

Benkler, Yochai. *The Wealth of Networks: How Social Production Transforms Markets and Freedom.* New Haven, Connecticut: Yale University Press, 2006.

Boltanski, Luc and Ève Chiapello. *The New Spirit of Capitalism*, London: Verso, 2007.

Cas, Johann. 'Ubiquitous Computing, Privacy and Data Protection: Options and Limitations to Reconcile the Unprecedented Contradictions', in Serge Gutwirth, Yves Poullet, Paul De Hert, Ronald Leenes (eds) *Computers, Privacy and Data Protection: An Element of Choice*, Dordrecht, Heidelberg, London, New York: Springer, 2011, pp. 139-171.

Castells, Manuel. *The Rise of the Network Society. The Information Age: Economy, Society and Culture*, Volume 1, Malden: Blackwell, 2000.

DuckDuckGo. 'Sources', https://dukgo.com/help/en_US/results/sources.

Eklöf, Jenny and Astrid Mager. 'Technoscientific Promotion and Biofuel Policy: How the Press and Search Engines Stage the Biofuel Controversy', Media, Culture & Society 35.4 (2013): 454-471.

Fuchs, Christian. 'A Contribution to the Critique of the Political Economy of Google', *Fast Capitalism* 8.1 (2011), http://www.uta.edu/huma/agger/fastcapitalism/8_1/fuchs8_1.html.

Haider, Jutta. 'The Environment on Holidays or How a Recycling Bin Informs Us on the Environment',

---

46. Lewandowski, 'Why We Need an Independent Index of the Web'.

Journal of Documentation 67.5 (2011): 823-839.

Hardt, Michael. 'Reclaim the Common in Communism', *The Guardian*, 3 February 2011, http://www.theguardian.com/commentisfree/2011/feb/03/communism-capitalism-socialism-property.

Hussain, Mobaruk. 'The Market Share of Google in Various Countries', SEO Chief, 6 July 2010, http://www.seo-chief.com/5950/the-market-share-of-google-in-various-countries.

Johnson, Nathania. 'Google Says "No" to Ecocho', Search Engine Watch, 23 April 2008, http://searchenginewatch.com/article/2054343/Google-Says-No-to-Ecocho.

Latour, Bruno. 'Technology Is Society Made Durable', in John Law (ed.) *A Sociology of Monsters: Essays on Power, Technology and Domination*, New York and London: Routledge, 1991, pp. 103-131.

Lewandowski, Dirk. 'Why We Need an Independent Index of the Web', in René König and Miriam Rasch (eds) *Society of the Query Reader: Reflections on Web Search*, Amsterdam: Institute of Network Cultures. 2014, pp. 50-58.

Mager, Astrid. 'Algorithmic Ideology: How Capitalist Society Shapes Search Engines', Information, Communication & Society 15.5 (2012a): 1-19.

Mager, Astrid. 'Search Engines Matter: From Educating Users Towards Engaging with Online Health Information Practices', *Policy & Internet* 4.2 (2012b): 1-21.

Marres, Noortje. 'The Costs of Public Involvement: Everyday Devices of Carbon Accounting and the Materialization of Participation', *Economy and Society*, 40.4 (2011): 510-533.

McAllister, Neil. 'How Wolfram Alpha Could Change Software', InfoWorld, 29 July 2009, http://www.infoworld.com/d/developer-world/how-wolfram-alpha-could-change-software-248?page=0,0.

McGrath, Jack. 'Google's Green Initiative: Environmentally Conscious Technology', TechnoBuffalo, 18 May 2012, http://www.technobuffalo.com/2011/05/18/googles-green-initiative-environmentally-conscious-technology.

Pasquinelli, Matteo. 'Google's PageRank Algorithm: a Diagram of Cognitive Capitalism and the Rentier of the Common Intellect', in Konrad Becker and Felix Stalder (eds) *Deep Search: The Politics of Search Engines Beyond Google*, Innsbruck: Studienverlag, 2009, pp. 152–162.

Peissl, Walter. 'Information Privacy in Europe from a TA Perspective', in Serge Gutwirth, Yves Poullet and Paul De Hert (eds) *Data Protection in a Profiled World*, Dordrecht, Heidelberg, London, New York: Springer, 2010, pp. 247-257.

Pennink, Frederiek. 'Rethinking Search: YossarianLives!', Institute of Network Cultures, 16 May 2013, http://networkcultures.org/wpmu/query/2013/05/16/rethinking-search-yossarianlives.

Slegg, Jennifer. 'DuckDuckGo Sees Record Traffic After NSA Prism Scandal', Search Engine Watch, 18 June 2013, http://searchenginewatch.com/article/2275867/DuckDuckGo-Sees-Record-Traffic-After-NSA-PRISM-Scandal.

Stallman, Richard. 'Re: How Wolfram Alpha's Copyright Claims Could Change Software', A2K Listserve, 4 August 2009, http://lists.essential.org/pipermail/a2k/2009-August/004865.html.

Swaine, Jon. 'Two Google Searches "Produce Same CO2 as Boiling a Kettle"', *The Telegraph*, 11 January 2009, http://www.telegraph.co.uk/technology/google/4217055/Two-Google-searches-produce-same-CO2-as-boiling-a-kettle.html.

Thrift, Nigel. *Non-Representational Theory. Space, Politics, Affect*, London: Routledge, 2008.

The Dark Side of Google: Pre-Afterword – Social Media Times

¬

Ippolita

The Dark Side of Google:
Pre-Afterword – Social Media Times

Theory on Demand #13, 2007/2013
Ippolita[1]

Performance Societies in the Clouds

Many years have passed since Ippolita first addressed the need to distinguish between the Free Software movement and the Open Source movement.[2] Although both movements are associated with a certain 'freedom', the 'freedom' proposed by the Free Software movement is very different in nature from the one proposed by the Open Source movement. The former is more ideological, whereas the latter focuses on defining the best way of promoting a product in an open manner. In other words, it completely follows a market logic. The Open Source movement has adopted the playful attitude of hacker peer sharing and uses it in a profit-oriented logic of work and exploitation. In so doing the movement has neutralized peer sharing's originally revolutionary potential.

The subsequent analysis will show that Google, which is a hegemonic attempt to organize 'all the world's information', progressed in a similar fashion. This argument will address how the logic of open source, in combination with the Californian philosophy of academic excellence found in Google's motto 'Don't be evil', is merely an excuse to place itself under the banner of capitalist abundance, turbo-capitalism's illusion of unlimited growth and extremist anarcho-capitalism. Google sells the myth that *more, bigger, and faster* always equates with *better* and that the 'I'm feeling lucky button' will immediately and effortlessly satisfy all our desires with a simple click of the mouse. In other words, the company creates the comfortable illusion that you will be taken care of if you create a Google account, that there's nothing else you need.

Unfortunately, claims about informational totalitarianism are not as ridiculous as they may sound. Although it has been established many times that there is nothing *more* to produce and, more importantly, that unlimited growth is a chimera (even in the digital world), run-ups to the next useless and shiny gadget continue to appear. Our weary world could use the blow that comes with the uncomfortable acknowledgement of

---

1. The following text is the new forword to the translation by Patrice Riemens of Ippolita's *The Dark Side of Google*, Amsterdam: Institute of Network Cultures, 2013.
2. Ippolita, *Open Non è Free: Comunità Digitali tra Etica Hacker e Mercato Global,* Milano: Elèuthera, 2005.

limited growth. We must start looking around, looking at each other, and exchanging what we need. We must imagine and build something meaningful together.

We also need to understand that IT is not merely a technique to manage information in an automatic way. IT is increasingly seen as a panacea for solving social problems (from delinquency to the crisis of traditional politics). In fact, *automation* easily degenerates with this delegation, sliding very quickly from a technical register to a social register. Instead of offering precise tools to solve specific problems, automation becomes a universal medicine that presents itself as working regardless of human intervention and will. However, society and sociability, such as politics and power management, are not problems to be solved once and for all: they are constitutive elements to face and deal with as part of a meaningful existence. Yet this shift from the utilitarian to the social occurs because IT's inherent logic, cybernetics, is based on a system of retroactive adjustments: the effects generated by the adoption of a particular technological tool directly influence the very perception of the surrounding environment – physical, social, psychological. The cybernetic IT systems continuously reshape their very foundations by being transformed into ideology, which is actually an output of these technological beginnings.[3] To illustrate this, think of how Google uses this recursive logic as an extraordinary machine, constituted through its own use by users. In this sense IT can be seen as an 'autopoietic' complex of machines that accumulate all the basic information entered on the web by millions of users every day. And it is not only Google that applies this recursive logic; Facebook, Amazon, and Apple also exploit these same processes.

When these 'mega machines' – consisting of a datacenter and the very best coders – had only just started to emerge, after being safely locked up by a NDA (Non-Disclosure Agreement), one of the first problems they encountered was that they had to be filled with something. The content did not matter much, as long as the costs remained low and, if possible, free. A new and relatively cheap type of industrial production was born, yet the question had become, how could these databases actually return fabulous profits for their owners?

By this time the net had emerged. Slowly, broadband connections were becoming less asymmetrical (mainly due to investments and the incentive to connect and bridge the digital divide, which meant a loss of the public sector), rates were down (although remaining unjustifiably high), and the upload capacity had significantly increased. Consequently, it was at this point in time that the solution to the mega-machines' problems was revealed: the data centers could be filled by pouring into them the online contents of users – all of the data they had assembled via their computers, smartphones, and cameras. This solution meant that the 'free market' was introduced: everyone would finally be able to publish! This development led to the birth of a new myth: the false promise of unlimited growth in the Era of User Generated Content. The ideology of this era proposes that the margins are huge, that the process of the 'webification and cloudification of everything' has only just started, and that its prospects are fabulous. The 'cloud' of cloud computing can increase by many orders of magnitude.

---

3. This description is a very brief summary of Humberto R. Maturana and Francisco J. Varela's idea of autopoiesis (from *Autopoiesis and Cognition: The Realization of the Living*, Boston Studies in the Philosophy of Science, Vol. 42, Dordrecht: D. Reidel Publishing Company, 1980). Here, we can imagine the 'internet' like a 'living organism' in Maturana's terms.

As a result, what we now face is one of the most effective Weapons of Democratic DistrAttention that has ever been developed: the administering of gratification for users who cannot wait to post, tag, comment, and link, not only to their own photos, videos, tweets, and texts, but also to those of their friends in the great *mare nostrum* of social networks. However, what is often forgotten is that this sea is actually not at all *nostrum* ('ours'), since it is almost always someone else's space, whether that of Facebook, Flickr, Twitter, or the next digital aquarium to entertain and nurture net-fish. We are happy as long as we possess the latest expensive tool for self-denunciation and as long as we can always be online and connected. Soon we will all make our purchases with some 'smart-stuff' – thereby forgetting credit cards – because we always want to know what we are interested in, what we like, what we think, where we are, what we do and with whom. And since the devices are getting smaller and less capacious, it is easy to predict that an explosion of the storage of online personal data will soon take place.

From the File to the Cloud

> If we want things to stay as they are, things will have to change.
> – Tomasi di Lampedusa[4]

Today web applications are able to replace almost all software created for the computer. The very idea of a personal computer has ceased to exist now that everyone is able to have his or her own personal web space. Ten years ago users were still struggling to understand how to manage file systems. Today, users are completely unaware that they are under the thumb of the dispersion of their online content.

Hardware devices now almost exclusively serve to provide access to the web and its services. As users we do not 'own' anything, because everything is shared with the large corporations that provide us with services free of charge. For the common user, the computer as a physical entity has faded into the impalpability of cloud computing. Like Olympic gods, the informatics of domination that rule our lives stay in the clouds. This 'evolution' reflects a precise technical and economic goal, namely, that the web must become the main environment for IT development. Key elements of this evolution are cloud computing, the smartphone, tablet, e-reader (or mobile devices in general), browsers, HTML5, and social networks.

One of the most interesting innovations associated with mobile devices and the web in general is the disappearance of the concept of files and file systems. On desktop systems we have grown accustomed to working with folder and files. Our documents are files, images are files, and all of these files are organized in folders. Often the links between different types of files and applications are very clear: a word processor creates, displays, or edits textual files, while an image viewer handles image files.

However, for mobile devices with access to content on the web, this organization into files and folders is close to meaningless. Instead of files and folder, these devices

---

4. Giuseppe Tomasi di Lampedusa, *Il Gattopardo*, trans. Archibald Colquihoun, New York: Alfred A. Knopf, Everyman's Library, 1998, p. 22.

speak of services or features. This development is undoubtedly interesting and not devoid of a dark side. What happened to music files is perhaps most evocative. In a desktop environment – before the birth of applications such as iTunes – audio files (often with confusing names) were typically placed in folders or collected in a playlist. Music programs read these audio files or playlists and so allowed us to listen to the music. However with the birth of programs (capable of self-generating playlists and music libraries, and of categorizing audio files into virtual folders, collecting them by author, year, and album), the 'file' for music has disappeared. Once uploaded on the device, music ceases to exist as a file (for the user at least) and ends up inside the mysterious cloud of music libraries from programs such as iTunes.

The next step was the online audio library, from which it is no longer necessary to download audio files through P2P networks (thereby avoiding 'cybercrime'), because applications now offer us everything we want to listen to directly on the internet. Libraries and their content are all available without many limits, so there is no need anymore for files that are actually stored and cataloged on your device. Examples of these online audio libraries are Spotify and Grooveshark.

This loss of 'stored' files in online audio libraries also extends to other types of files. Pictures and videos are immediately uploaded onto social platforms, and textual documents are stored in office suites and made accessible online by different services for which you no longer have to install any programs. The cloud offers services, space, sync, the myth of the 99.99 percent uptime – basically everything that our devices cannot 'physically' have, unlimited and almost always for free.

Cloud computing is trivialized in a series of buzzwords, such as SaaS (Software as a Service), DaaS (Data as a Service) and so on. The cloud has in fact become the very virtualization of a 'feature' offered as an online service. Everything is up and running somewhere in the clouds of the web, ready to be used. Everything changes so that nothing changes. While the way in which we make use of data has changed drastically (think of the amount of data we handle, its quality, and the devices we use to access big data), the main managers of these clouds are still the usual suspects: Google first and foremost, and also Amazon.

However, besides making use of cloud computing, Google has also entered competition with mobile devices. The advent of smartphones and tablets with internet access has revolutionized the mobile market, and it gave birth to a new mass ritual, namely, 'Connectivity Everywhere', and the mantra 'Always On!' The smartphone has become a status symbol to the point of unleashing wars for the hegemony of the market. Together with iOS, Google's Android has emerged as one of the major competitors.

Android is an operating system built on a Linux kernel and distributed under the open source Apache license. Note how we use 'open' and not 'free', because the Free Software Foundation GNU's components and libraries used by GNU/Linux OSs have actually been replaced by BSD-based ones. Android has been chosen by several hardware manufacturers and is therefore available on different models that often compete with each other. It could thus be argued that Android has become a *de facto* standard, in a similar way to how the Windows operating system for desktop became a standard. The only basic difference is that, thanks to the open source license, manufacturers can create custom flavors of Android for their hardware. Along with the Android operating system – and in addition to having acquired the manufacturer Motorola – another important element of Google's entrance in the mobile market is its own specific smartphone, the Nexus. In contrast to Android, iOS forms a proprietary and closed operating system, specifically designed by Apple for its mobile products, iPhone, iPad, and iPod.

Besides numerous and frequent legal battles over patents, the scenario in the mobile market is further complicated by the joint venture Nokia-Microsoft with Windows Mobile, and also by the former leader of the mobile market RIM, which continues to plod along with Blackberry. One of the most representative examples of a gigantic, Asiatic corporative capitalist is the aggressive Samsung. This Korean company has begun the most profitable electronic conglomerate in the world, which in large part can be attributed to their tablet and smartphones using Android. Finally, Chinese players such as ZTE and Huawei are also gaining a foothold in the war for hegemony of the mobile market.

Bearing in mind the strong competition that surrounds the mobile market, it is easy to understand the browser instrument's importance as an environment for development. Google released the first version of its Chrome browser in 2008 and was early enough to catch the trend that would soon become dominant: web services. Once again, Google found itself in the lead position.

Unlike Mozilla Firefox, whose innovations are for a large part linked to the methodological structure of work and cultural heritage of open source, Chrome contains only technical innovations. As sons of Californian turbo-capitalism, Page and Brin staked everything on speed. The result with Chrome is a phenomenal JavaScript engine and the division of each web page loaded as a single running process. In contrast to other web languages, JavaScript describes the 'logic' of sites and applications. The better its performance, the greater the speed of execution of the service we are using.

HTML5, W3C: Standards, Architectural Dominance, and Control Methods

In the highly complex world that is the internet, some elements need to be shared in as universal a manner as possible. In order to make computer processes communicable, common rules, conventions, and alphabets are necessary. This is why standards have been established over the course of years. Think of the HTTP protocol born at the end of the 80s, which enabled machines and humans to access the web. Without HTTP, the World Wide Web would not exist and – although many are eager to innovate – no one has the slightest intention of changing it. Not even the nerd supremacists of Silicon Valley, who are on the payroll of the most visionary anarcho-capitalists.

This is in sharp contrast to the changes that have been made in HTML (essential for web pages) and which have become ground for some of the most important battles for architectural dominance the computer world has ever fought (but not won). The evolution of HTML is managed, along with other basic standards, by the W3 Consortium, one of the supranational institutions responsible for making suggestions and recommendations on what the web should be.

The W3C tasks are organized into different working groups. Each group makes drafts of specifications and recommendations for each individual project. To become a recommendation, a draft must have at least two independent implementations (meaning no code is shared) that are meaningful, fully functional, and already used by a considerable number of users. It therefore depends for a large part on Google whether HTML5 or other specific recommendations become W3C standard. However, it should be noted that Google develops its Chrome browsers on the same WebKit rendering engine that is used by Safari, Apple's proprietary browser. Google is also the main funder of the Mozilla Software Foundation, which develops Firefox, based on the Gecko rendering engine. Now that the Opera browser has switched to WebKit, Gecko-Mozilla remains the only alternative, together with Microsoft's Internet Explorer, to implement new standards.

This quick rise behind the scenes of the web is a brief example of what Ippolita means by analyzing the technocratic systems on which the informatics of domination are based. From the moment that (mobile) devices began multiplying, laptops have been emptied of software and data, and now that the craze of everything 'social' has exploded, it is easy to understand how browsers and HTML are of primary importance for building a worldwide computing hegemony – both from an economic and political point of view.

Open Is Not Free, and Published Is Not Public
And here we are today. Unlike the times in which Ippolita was one of the few shouting about how we don't have to put everything on Google – because the delegation of our data and trust (even if semi-unconscious) marks the beginning of domination (in this case, technocratic) – today many voices have been raised against the social networks and the whole Web 2.0 tale, accusing them of violating the privacy of users.[5]

The techno-enthusiasm is dismissed as a false revolutionary ideology, because however social the internet as a movement may appear, this is overshadowed by its elitism: how contradictory and fideistic! Commentators such as danah boyd point out that Facebook in particular is a project based on the ideology of *radical transparency,* because it is in its nature to strive for publishing everything indiscriminately.[6] It should not be forgotten, however, that Facebook's first venture capital financier, who came from the Paypal mafia, was intertwined with military and civilian intelligence services, offering political support to U.S. right-wing libertarians (e.g. people who believed Bush Sr. to be a 'moderate'). As Tom Hodgkinson already commented in *The Guardian,* these are people who define themselves as 'anarcho-capitalists'.[7] Umair Haque even dares to notice, from the privileged surroundings of Harvard, that perhaps the 'bubble' of social media also exists from an economic point of view: so far no one has shown that social media have contributed to selling customized products through personal advertising.[8] In the meantime, various scholars have accomplished more extensive pieces of analysis and criticism. We remember Siva Vaidhyanathan's thorough *The*

---

5. Giles Slade, *The Big Disconnect: The Story of Technology and Loneliness*, New York, Prometheus Book, 2012. See chapter three in *The Dark Side of Google*: 'Trusting Machines'.
6. danah boyd, 'Facebook and Radical Transparency: A Rant', 14 May 2011, http://www.zephoria.org/thoughts/archives/2010/05/14/facebook-and-radical-transparency-a-rant.html.
7. Tom Hodkinson, 'With Friends Like These', *The Guardian*, 14 and 16 February 2008, http://www.theguardian.com/technology/2008/jan/14/facebook.
8. Umair Haque, 'The Social Media Bubble', Harvard Business Review blog, 23 March 2010, http://blogs.hbr.org/2010/03/the-social-media-bubble/.

*Googlization of Everything (And Why We Should Worry).*⁹ Evgeny Morozov's *To Save Everything, Click Here* has rightly focused the debate on solutionism and internet-centrism, fideistic acceptances of the so-called inevitable 'technological revolutions' taking place.¹⁰ These attitudes described by Morozov claim to be scientific and objective, but instead are highly ideological, endemically spreading now in too many private and public speeches. But Morozov lacks a broader theoretical discourse on power, based on the practices of technocratic delegation that users perform in everyday life.

Beyond both concrete and rather unrealistic proposals for fighting this social media bubble (e.g. mass 'suicide' on Facebook, the failed Diaspora project to rebuild a social network for free, complaints and petitions to various authority figures and guarantors who are unable to even supervise themselves), it is actually someone such as the techno-enthusiast Jeff Jarvis who puts his finger on the problem: the public. Similar to how 'opening code' does not equate to 'making it free', 'publishing content' does not equate to 'making it public'. On the contrary, with Facebook (although G+ or other social platforms work in the same way) it becomes clear that things actually work in the opposite way. Everything that is posted becomes the non-exclusive property of the company and can be resold to third parties, as can be (re)read in the TOS (Terms of Service). In the clouds of social networks, then, publishing does not mean public. For almost all web 2.0 applications, publishing means 'private' – a corporation or a private company owns the content. Every time we access our online profiles (our digital alter egos), we work for these corporations for free. By serving us with increasingly invasive and targeted advertisements, the sites' algorithms try to make money on our backs – on our digital bodies.

Ippolita's harsh concerns about Google's totalizing ambitions seem all the more urgent when we consider the case of Facebook. Yesterday's champion in 'invasiveness', Google, almost pales in comparison to the champion of social control today. The way that Gmail uses advertising, the power of geolocation in Google Maps, the successes of Chrome as a browser and of the Android OS, or even the most controversial projects, such as Google Books, which has stunned the entire publishing market, seem almost harmless when compared to the capacity of Facebook to expand a consensual method of social control. After all, Google is an Enlightenment dream; a dream of global knowledge characterized politically more by liberal than conservative tendencies. Facebook, on the other hand, which we expect to deliver consistently despite a lot of interplanetary gossip, has a political connotation that is clearly reactionary. Facebook works because more than a billion people are on it, an incredible power, but to do what? We still don't really know. (Ippolita wrote extensively about Facebook in *Nell'acquario di Facebook,* to be translated and published in English as *In the Facebook Aquarium.*)¹¹

Of course we should not forget that networks have played an important role in the 2008

---

9. Siva Vaidhyanathan, *The Googlization of Everything (And Why We Should Worry),* Berkeley: University of California Press, 2011.
10. Evgeny Morozov, *To Save Everything, Click Here,* New York: Public Affairs, 2013.
11. Ippolita, *Nell'acquario di Facebook*, Milano: Ledizioni, 2012. Spanish translation: *En el acuario de Facebook*, Madrid: Enclave de Libros, 2012. French translation: *J'aime pas Facebook*, Paris: Payot & Rivages, 2012.

revolt in Iran and in the uprisings of most countries in North Africa, as well as in Asian dictatorships and the Arab world in general. Facebook has been very helpful for the Indignados, and Twitter and Foursquare for Occupy Wall Street. These and other private instruments will probably be used again in revolts for freedom that are yet to come, and we hope that these will be more and more numerous. However, this is not a good reason to link social networks to democracy, freedom, and equality. Social networks do not make revolutions – it is people who make them. As the controversial WikiLeaks and Anonymous cases have clearly shown, if they want, governments and established powers may stifle any initiative branded as subversive, especially when it comes to matters of direct action that strongly depend on digital technologies.

Social networks are not necessarily free, autonomous, and self-managed. We use them and create them to try to expand the possibilities of autonomy, but we cannot truly think that for-profit companies provide free of charge tools to access a world of freedom and equality. The use of technologies depends on the people. In itself, no technology guarantees anything. The methodological approach that we have practiced so far suggests that we should evaluate not the 'what' but the 'how' – that is, the way in which technological tools are created and modified through use and the methods by which individuals and groups adapt and change their behavior. It seems clear, then, that the same reasoning applies to social networks as to any other social value: the necessary consistency between means and ends. We are facing an anthropo-technical turning point.

The situation is critical. However, this story is not a new one, and we are not at a hazardous point in this situation. While following discussions on any technological buzz, from the iPhone to iPad, Android to Windows 8, Facebook to Twitter, we have to laugh at the ingenuity of gurus, enthusiasts, and ordinary users – a bitter laugh, from Italy. In this country it has always been clear that it will not be the so-called democratic institutions that will guarantee our rights. Nor will it be the machines of this or that multinational company with the consecrated status of Goodness and Progress for All that will give us, free of charge, a world of freedoms. Italy continues to be the political laboratory of the future; it is the only Mediterranean country in the G8. Here in Italy, a movement that started online on a private blog has won a quarter of the electorate in 2013, and it now proposes itself as a force for renewal, much in line with the new digital movements whose major vocation is claiming to represent the 99 percent (Indignados, Occupy Wall Street, Pirates). Politics are already a technocracy, and proposals for technological democracy, web 2.0, or what have you, are increasingly enmeshed within this technocracy. Who creates and manages these tools of democracy? Are they the nerd supremacists on the payroll of anarcho-capitalists? How can repentant soldiers, technocratic geeks, or whistleblowers constantly on the run inspire the struggle for freedom? The sad stories of oppression suffered by Manning, Assange, Snowden, and many others, otherwise similar, are only the first chapters in a saga that promises to be detrimental to civil liberties. The technical skills and the geeks' enthusiasm by themselves are not enough to 'do the right thing', because deliberation, morality, and aesthetics are not technical matters: the better algorithms will not automagically create better societies, and radical transparency is a totalitarian nightmare.

Participation Myth Corollaries: We Are the 99 Percent
Digital activism could be framed as an interesting corollary to the online mass par-

ticipation myth, and the claim that 'social networks fueled revolutions' is part of that same narrative. Of course people use what is available to them to communicate, and Facebook, Twitter, and Foursquare have been very important tools for movements as diverse as the Arab Springs (Egypt above all), the Indignados (Spain), and Occupy Wall Street (U.S. and elsewhere). However, we would like to emphasize an aspect of these movements that relies more on ancient rituals than on the 'digital networks connected us' rhetoric.

Ippolita shares the idea that

> [s]ocial media have been chiefly responsible for the construction of a *choreography of assembly* as a process of symbolic construction of public space which facilitates and guides the physical *assembling* of a highly dispersed and individualized constituency.[12]

The key question is how these media were used to 'get physical'. How, in the modern theater of the social internet, do various technical layers contribute to social performance? How do so-called leaderless movements distribute power by channeling individual emotions in a collective emotional choreography? These self-named leaderless movements hide the importance of organization and have increasingly become emotional management. However, the true leaders of social networks are the technical managers, because they can control the information flow. Technocracy is here. The choice for a specific communication platform is not neutral either. The main communication platform of the aforementioned Italian 'Five Star Movement' is hosted on the private, individual blog Beppegrillo.it. Technical procedures to be posted and shared are the key to power articulation in these kinds of digital movements, as was shown by the insistence of the German Pirate movement on Liquid Feedback tools of interaction.

We are certainly not the only ones to proclaim the notion that 'what is true today, was true yesterday'. You must be able to imagine your future in order to understand the present. We need to be more contemporary to our times, that is to say *untimely,* or in the words of Agamben, 'contemporary is the one whose eyes are struck by the beam of darkness that comes from his own time'.[13] By recalling the past and creating a collective story (since memory is a collective tool), nothing is ever repeated. However, the differences are similar, and the insipid soup of yesterday, a little pimped up, may be dished out as the radical innovation of tomorrow.

For this reason, we leave intact the escape routes identified in *The Dark Side of Google*.[14] Although things have changed, we want to remind ourselves about what has happened. For example, the logic of the trusted network that we identified in FOAF (Friend of a Friend) was realized in a different manner and eventually publicized by Facebook. Indymedia has run its course, and the dreams of digital democracy are embodied in new movements. If what we 'imagine' is reflected by the advertising on TV or on other

---

12. Paolo Gerbaudo, *Tweets and the Streets*, London: Pluto Press, 2012.
13. Giorgio Agamben, 'What Is the Contemporary', in *What Is an Apparatus? And Other Essays*, Stanford: Stanford University Press, 2009, p. 45.
14. Ippolita, *The Dark Side of Google,* Amsterdam: Institute of Network Cultures, 2013 (2007). See chapter seven, 'Technocracy, Algocracy'.

devices, or by the 'freedom of choice' for hundreds of thousands of apps for iPhone, or by the possibility of having more than a thousand 'friends' on Facebook, then maybe we have insisted too little on the need to desire and imagine something better. Yet alternatives to Google already exist; think of self-managed servers like Autistici/Inventati, Riseup, or Lorea. Of course, they are not *free as in beer,* but they are *free as in freedom.* Treading the never-ending paths of freedom may cost a lot, but at least you have a choice, and it allows you to undertake what you desire.

So far we have described what Donna Haraway calls the 'informatics of domination'.[15] The method that has been built (cartographic, interdisciplinary) is necessarily partial and sometimes lax, but at the same time it has allowed for problems with the technocratic delegation to emerge, long before it became obvious. Jamaican slaves used the saying, 'pull a straight lick with a crooked stick'. We like to imagine escape routes, then try to sell them; we imagine and build appropriate tools to achieve our desires. We should make them available to an audience that is made up of people, instead of publishing them through the depraved megaphone of an intrusive corporation's wall. It is as McLuhan already claimed: 'the medium is the message'.

Many of us are in the same situation; we are not cooperating since we don't want to participate in the crowdsourcing of the masses of social media. Social networking services have the compulsive urge to touch up your profile in such a way that it will stand out from the others. However, these 'touch ups' are not real differences; they are only slight variations within predefined categories (single? married? friend?). This has resulted in the formation of groups who are friends because they say that they like the same thing. In other words, it has resulted in a homophile self-imposition. Diversity appears in the approval of tastes and behaviors. Even so, as Lucius T. Outlaw enlightens us in *On Race and Philosophy,* human biodiversity, as races and ethnicities, is a valuable difference.[16] We carry on in step and apply this difference, following Braidotti and Haraway, to the entire human-tech machinic systems.[17] The more differences there are, the more valuable the system will be. If genetic variability is a value, so should be the variability of the code. The value of difference is not a principle quantity. More does not mean better, and more objects or friends does not mean greater freedom of choice.

We note that in analyses of networks (including social networks), terminology is usually heavily militarized. However, if we return to the 'material' in a more narrow sense, it should be noted that computers themselves are constructed with semi-conductor minerals, which are extracted from areas that are in constant conflict over those minerals (e.g. Congo), for that very reason. Globalization of goods is mainly the globalization of exploitation. We should not look away from the fact that our cool and ergonomic tools are produced by masses of Asian workers, especially Chinese, who are forced to declare in their contracts that they will not commit suicide at the factories they work at. Thanks, guys! The global market digests all differences. Meanwhile, when we are

---

15. Donna Haraway, 'A Cyborg Manifesto: Science, Technology, and Socialist-Feminism in the Late Twentieth Century', in Donna Haraway, *Simians, Cyborgs and Women: The Reinvention of Nature,* New York: Routledge, 1991, pp.149-181.
16. Lucius T. Outlaw Jr., *On Race and Philosophy,* New York: Routledge, 1996.
17. Haraway, 'A Cyborg Manifesto'; Rosi Braidotti, *Metamorphoses: Towards a Materialist Theory of Becoming,* Cambridge: Polity Press 2002.

purchasing the latest technological nonsense, we can perhaps gloat over how some skimpy tree was planted to offset emissions of CO_2. Green capitalism, however, remains as mad as any productivist ideology. No one is pure, and we are all involved. However, despite being immersed in this technological world, we should try to keep a distance from it and defamiliarize ourselves in order to write some kind of ethnography of social media. This should not focus on how social media work (there are enough how-to's and manuals on that already), but on the reasons why we are in this situation, and how we can influence it by injecting diversity, chaos, and germs of autonomy. We are compromised and involved, but this does not mean we have to accept everything uncritically. If we start from the collective findings, we can derive individual conclusions in a process of estrangement that proceeds from the inside out (rather than from the unfamiliar to the familiar, as happens in classical ethnographic observations). We are the savages, and we need a decidedly subjective look. We do not need the supposed objectivity of an outside observer.

Fortunately, the myth of scientific objectivity survives only in the inferior and vulgate. It has been more than a century since the hard sciences have taken the path of relativism, and it is time now that the 'human sciences' should follow them. We need radical relativism in order to observe our habits and behavior from the outside and to understand what we are doing. We have to make our actions concrete, and we have to be able to communicate them effectively in a public space, a space that must be preserved, renegotiated, and built relentlessly. In order to stop officiating at the rite of the mass of dominant technologies, we need to build new and conscious social rituals.

This is the whole problem then: the foundation of power and its transformation into domination. How do you create a device capable of not succumbing to the power of the sacred? There is a reversal of the sacred: the profane, the iconoclastic moment of carnival. Once you have built your little Olympus, you must renew it by following the correct rhythm. The autopoiesis processes we foster are the embodiment of this sense of continuous renewal.

Do you have any ideas? We have a few, so let us know!
Ippolita.net
info@ippolita.net
September, 2013
Per una corretta autopoiesi (For a proper autopoiesis)

Download *The Dark Side of Google* for free from http://networkcultures.org/publications.

References

Agamben, Giorgio. 'What Is the Contemporary', in *What is an Apparatus? and Other Essays*, Stanford: Stanford University Press, 2009, pp. 39-56.

boyd, danah. 'Facebook and Radical Transparency: A Rant', 14 May 2011, http://www.zephoria.org/thoughts/archives/2010/05/14/facebook-and-radical-transparency-a-rant.html.

Braidotti, Rosi. *Metamorphoses: Towards a Materialist Theory of Becoming*, Cambridge: Polity Press 2002.

Gerbaudo, Paolo. *Tweets and the Streets*, London: Pluto Press, 2012.
Haraway, Donna. 'A Cyborg Manifesto: Science, Technology, and Socialist-Feminism in the Late Twentieth Century', in Donna Haraway, *Simians, Cyborgs and Women: The Reinvention of Nature*, New York: Routledge, 1991, pp. 149-181.
Hodkinson, Tom. 'With Friends Like These', *The Guardian*, 14 and 16 February 2008, http://www.theguardian.com/technology/2008/jan/14/facebook.
Ippolita. *The Dark Side of Google*, Amsterdam: Institute of Network Cultures, 2013 (2007).
____, *Nell'acquario di Facebook*, Milano: Ledizioni, 2012.
____, *Open Non è Free: Comunità Digitali tra Etica Hacker e Mercato Global,* Milano: Elèuthera, 2005.
Lampedusa, Giuseppe Tomasi di. *Il Gattopardo*, trans. Archibald Colquihoun, New York: Alfred A. Knopf, Everyman's Library, 1998.
Maturana, Humberto R. and Francisco J. Varela. *Autopoiesis and Cognition: The Realization of the Living,* Boston Studies in the Philosophy of Science, Vol. 42, Dordrecht: D. Reidel Publishing Company, 1980.
Morozov, Evgeny. *To Save Everything, Click Here,* New York: Public Affairs, 2013.
Outlaw Jr., Lucius T. *On Race and Philosophy*, New York: Routledge, 1996.
Slade, Giles. *The Big Disconnect: The Story of Technology and Loneliness*, New York: Prometheus Book, 2012.
Vaidhyanathan, Siva. *The Googlization of Everything (And Why We Should Worry),* Berkeley: University of California Press, 2011.

Dominating Search: Google Before the Law

Angela Daly

Dominating Search: Google Before the Law

¬

Angela Daly

For many, particularly in the Anglophone world and Western Europe, it may be obvious that Google has a monopoly over online search and advertising and that this is an undesirable state of affairs, due to Google's ability to mediate information flows online. The baffling question may be why governments and regulators are doing little to nothing about this situation, given the increasingly pivotal importance of the internet and free flowing communications in our lives. However, the law concerning monopolies, namely antitrust or competition law, works in what may be seen as a less intuitive way by the general public.[1] Monopolies themselves are not illegal. Conduct that is unlawful, i.e. abuses of that market power, is defined by a complex set of rules and revolves principally around economic harm suffered due to anticompetitive behavior. However the effect of information monopolies over search, such as Google's, is more than just economic, yet competition law does not address this. Furthermore, Google's collection and analysis of user data and its portfolio of related services make it difficult for others to compete. Such a situation may also explain why Google's established search rivals, Bing and Yahoo, have not managed to provide services that are as effective or popular as Google's own. Users, however, are not entirely powerless. Google's business model rests, at least partially, on them – especially the data collected about them. If they stop using Google, then Google is nothing.

The Case Against Google
Google has been challenged on both sides of the northern Atlantic through competition investigations into the operation of its online search and advertising business. Complaints of anticompetitive behavior came from Google's 'vertical' search engine competitors. Vertical search engines focus on a specific part of online content, e.g. price-comparison sites, and sites offering legal and medical information. In addition to its 'generic' search engine, Google also runs its own vertical services such as Google Maps, Google Flight Search, and the mobile application Google Shopper. Google's vertical competitors alleged that Google was using its dominant position in online generic search and advertising to give it an unfair advantage in these other markets, specifically by giving its vertical services higher and more prominent places in its

---

1. 'Antitrust' is the U.S. term, whereas 'competition' is used in most other jurisdictions, including the United Kingdom and European Union, to refer to the same area of law. In this essay, I will use 'competition' except when referring specifically to the American system in which case 'antitrust' will be used.

generic search results, while lowering the 'Quality Score' of competitors' sponsored links. This practice would make users more likely to click on Google's services rather than its competitors' vertical search services.

Google's Dominance
Google is certainly the most prominent of the search engines in Europe and the U.S.; it is the market leader in the overall European market for online search, based on either proportion of searches that are conducted through Google (for no cost to users) or its proportional share of advertising revenue (which is where Google gets its funds).[2] The company's market share in Europe is around 90 percent,[3] which would be classified as 'near monopoly' according to the Commission's past practice. Google's online search and advertising is also the market leader in the U.S., but with a lesser market share of around 80 percent, though this is still enough to be considered a dominant position.[4]

However, Google does have competition from other general search engines offered by Bing and Yahoo, as well as subject-specific vertical search engines. Google itself likes to claim when on the defensive from allegations that it operates an abusive monopoly, that its competitors are only a click away. While the search engine market in the U.S. and Europe was competitive in the 1990s and into the early 2000s, it is now massively more consolidated and concentrated around Google.

Google emerged as the market leader because of its early innovations in providing better search service than its rivals. The company did this first by developing a more sophisticated search algorithm that relied on reputation (measured by links from other pages to that page) and text matching to provide the most relevant results, and second by building on its growing experience with search to deliver even more relevant advertising through paid results.[5] Google's operation also involved the accumulation of data about user searches in order to improve the accuracy of its search function: the more data collected, the more accurate its searches became. As a result, the collection, analysis, and sale of user data form a barrier to entry for any potential competitors and entrench Google's position as the leading search engine. In other words, Google's possession and contextualization of user data put it far ahead of any potential rivals starting a new search engine. This advantage makes it more difficult to compete with Google, since a company would need similar knowledge in order to do so. A further barrier to entry for potential competitors is the large investment in hardware, software, and connection capacity required by the creation and maintenance of a search.[6] In ad-

---

2. There are different methods of calculating shares of the search engine market in Europe, which are subject to various criticisms, but Google seems to come out in all of them as possessing a dominant position in this market.
3. StatCounter, 'Global Stats Top 5 Search Engines in Europe from Feb 2013 to Jan 2014', http://gs.statcounter.com/#search_engine-eu-monthly-201302-201401.
4. StatCounter 'Global Stats Top 5 Search Engines in the United States from Feb 2013 to Jan 2014', http://gs.statcounter.com/#search_engine-US-monthly-201302-201401.
5. Kristine L. Devine, 'Preserving Competition in Multi-Sided Innovative Markets: How Do You Solve A Problem Like Google?', *North Carolina Journal of Law and Technology* 10 (2009): 7.
6. Elizabeth Van Couvering, 'New Media? The Political Economy of Internet Search Engines', paper presented to the Communication Technology Policy section of the International Association of Media & Communications Researchers (IAMCR), Porto Alegre, 25-30 July 2004, http://www.academia.edu/1047079/New_media_The_political_economy_of_Internet_search_engines.

dition, Google has built up a portfolio of related products and services from which it also harvests user data for its search business.[7]

The Competition Investigations
The European Commission opened its investigation into Google in November 2010 for an alleged abuse of its dominant position contrary to Art 102 TFEU.[8] This case is the largest and most significant competition investigation into Google to date. At the time of writing the Commission and Google appear to have reached a settlement in the wake of various proposals from Google that were rejected by the Commission. In the U.S., the Federal Trade Commission (FTC) launched an antitrust investigation into Google's activities, including search and advertising, which resulted in a settlement with Google in early 2013.

The European Commission investigation was launched in 2010 after complaints were received from Google's competitors – price comparison site Foundem, ejustice.fr (a French legal search engine) and German shopping site Ciao (owned by Microsoft) – that Google was treating them unfavorably in its search results (both 'organic' or unpaid results, and the 'sponsored' or paid results), and was discriminating in favor of its own services. More specifically, there were allegations that Google had both lowered the rank of the unpaid search results of services, particularly vertical search engines that compete with Google, and had accorded preferential placement to the results of its own versions of these services.[9] Furthermore, Google is alleged to have lowered the 'Quality Score' for the sponsored links of these competing vertical search engines (the Quality Score influences the likelihood that an ad will be displayed by Google and the ranking of that ad in the search results, and is a factor determining the price paid by advertisers to Google). In 2012, the Commission issued a communication inviting Google to offer its commitment to remedy the Commission's concerns about anticompetitive behavior, including what the Commission perceived as the potential preferential treatment that Google Search gave its own vertical search services compared to the vertical search competitors.

The saga between Google and the Commission has been lengthy and drawn out. The Commission has twice rejected offers from Google to change its behavior before accepting the current proposal in early 2014. It has always been in Google's interests to reach a settlement with the Commission since otherwise the Commission would proceed with a full-blown investigation, quite probably resulting in the imposition of remedies as well as a large fine (up to 10 percent of global turnover).

Google's first proposal to the Commission in early 2013 to remedy its behavior seemed to include an offer to label its own services in search results in order to distinguish

---

7. Although this is not without controversy. Changes to Google's privacy policy in 2012 which allowed it to share users' data across all of its products and services, was considered by national data protection authorities to breach data protection laws in the Netherlands, Spain and France. For more information, see Ezra Steinhardt, 'Google Fined by the CNIL for Privacy Breaches as European Regulators Continue Investigation', Inside Privacy, 13 January 2014, http://www.insideprivacy.com/google-fined-by-the-cnil-for-privacy-breaches-as-european-regulators-continue-investigation/.
8. European Commission press release, 'Antitrust: Commission Probes Allegations of Antitrust Violations by Google', 30 November 2010.
9. This was also one of the complaints against Google forming the FTC investigation.

them from competitors' results and to provide links to rival services. The Commission rejected these proposals in July 2013. Indeed, Foundem called Google's initial offer to the Commission 'half-hearted' because it did not address the deeper problem of how Google determined the 'relevance' of links to search queries, especially when its competitors' services were involved.[10]

The second, supposedly confidential, proposal from Google came later in 2013 (whose content was leaked on an American consumer rights group).[11] This version seemed to involve Google offering to label its own services when one or other of them was displayed in the results page in case a user did a generic search for particular terms. The label should be 'accessible to users via a clearly visible icon', should show that this result has been added by Google in order to ensure that users would not confuse it with generic search results and should indicate to users where they can find alternatives provided by Google's competitors. The result from Google's own service should be displayed in a separate area to Google's generic search results and Google also offered to display links to three rival services in 'a manner to make users clearly aware of these alternatives'. These rivals' services would be selected from a pool of eligible vertical search competitors according to a complicated process set out in the document. Google included screenshots of how these results would be displayed, which included links to competitors being displayed under its own specialized search results in a separately boxed part of the screen and taking up roughly half of the space on the page that Google's specialized service results occupied.

In response to Google's offer, FairSearch (a lobby group comprising many of Google's search rivals) commissioned a survey with the aim of finding the likely impact of these proposals on actual internet users, in particular testing the extent to which users were likely to click on any of the three rival links and whether they understood and recognized the different parts of Google's proposed search results page i.e. the labeling and descriptions.[12] The survey found that 'only a modest number' of users would click on one of the rival links and that users were confused about the difference between Google's vertical search results and the other results.[13] The conclusion was that if Google presented links to its rivals in a relatively neutral fashion i.e. in a comparable way in terms of appearance and placement on the page, then this would result in higher click through rates for the competitors' links. However, the Second Commitments offered by Google did not achieve this and so were not 'likely to command materially increased consumer attention or restore competition for [Google's] rivals'.[14]

The head of a consumer advocacy group, BEUC, also condemned the second commitments proposal as 'not just inadequate to solve consumer detriment, but [...] in fact self-serving' since they continued to 'marginalize concerns' and 'bizarrely' suggested

---

10. Kelly Fiveash, 'Google's Euro Antitrust Offer: Fine! We'll Link to Our Search Rivals', The Register, 25 April 2013, http://www.theregister.co.uk/2013/04/25/ec_gives_google_rivals_one_month_to_market_test_search_tweaks/.
11. See, http://www.consumerwatchdog.org/resources/googlesettlment102113.pdf.
12. David J. Franklyn and David A. Hyman 'Review of the Likely Effects of Google's Proposed Commitments Dated October 21, 2013', 9 December 2013, http://www.fairsearch.org/wp-content/uploads/2013/12/FairSearch-Hyman_Franklyn-Study.pdf.
13. Franklyn and Hyman 'Review of the Likely Effects', p. 2.
14. Franklyn and Hyman 'Review of the Likely Effects', p. 13.

a new revenue stream for Google, since certain competitors would have to bid in a separate auction to be included as one of the rival links displayed.[15]

In the end, the European Commission again rejected Google's offer. The third and final offer made by Google at the time of writing, which the Commission appears to have accepted at least tentatively, comprises Google informing users via a label that Google's own specialized services are promoted, separating them from the other search results in order to make clear the difference between them and 'normal' results and displaying 'prominent' links to three rival specialized search services from a pool of 'eligible competitors', and showing clearly to users in a 'comparable' way to how Google displays its own services.[16] On the occasions where Google does not charge for inclusion in its specialized search results, it will also not charge its rivals for inclusion as rival links and here will select them using its 'normal' web search algorithm. But for those services for which Google does charge for inclusion, the three rivals will be chosen via an auction from a pool of eligible competitors.

The Commission includes screenshots of how Google's services will change as a result of the commitments. When results from Google's specialized Shopping service are displayed in the results page, they are done so at the top of the page in a box headed 'Google Shopping results' and directly adjacent to the right of this box is one of the same size labeled 'Alternatives', with a shaded background, displaying results from some of Google's vertical search rivals. Google Shopping is a service for which Google charges for inclusion, and so the rivals whose results will be displayed will be selected via the auction mechanism.

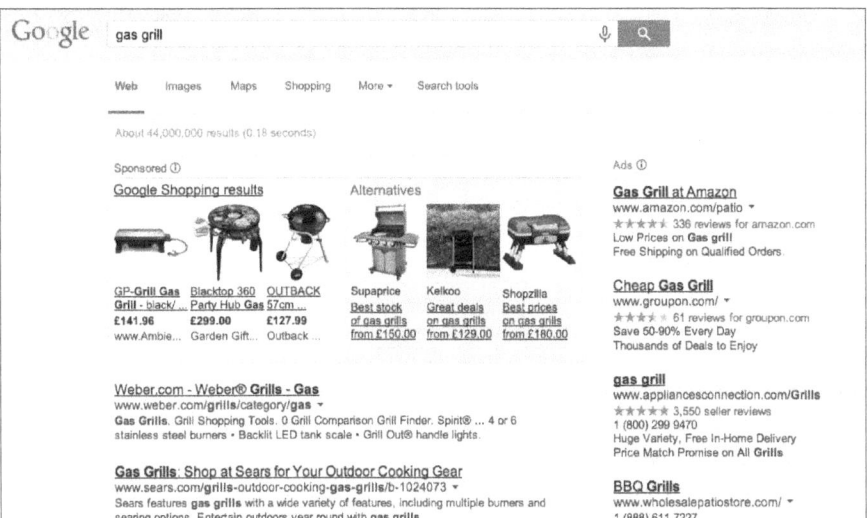

Fig. 1. Google's specialized Shopping service. Source: European Commission.

---

15. John M. Simpson, 'Consumer Groups on Both Sides of the Atlantic Oppose Google Antitrust Settlement', Consumer Watchdog, 26 November 2013, http://www.consumerwatchdog.org/newsrelease/consumer-groups-both-sides-atlantic-oppose-google-antitrust-settlement.
16. European Commission, 'Antitrust: Commission Obtains from Google Comparable Display of Specialised Search Rivals – Frequently Asked Questions', MEMO/14/87, 5 February 2014.

This would go further towards the 'parity of appearance and placement' that the Fairsearch-commission consumer research found increased consumers' likelihood of clicking on Google's rivals' results, although the research also found that the result to the furthest left on the screen was the more likely to be clicked on than those to the right.[17] If this research goes some way to reflecting accurately how European internet users in general behave, then this formulation of the results page should see an increase in clicks on rivals' results but Google's specialized service results will still have the more attractive position.

The other screenshot from the Commission includes results from Google's Local Search service, for which Google does not charge a payment for inclusion and so the rivals whose results will be displayed will be selected using Google's general search algorithm.

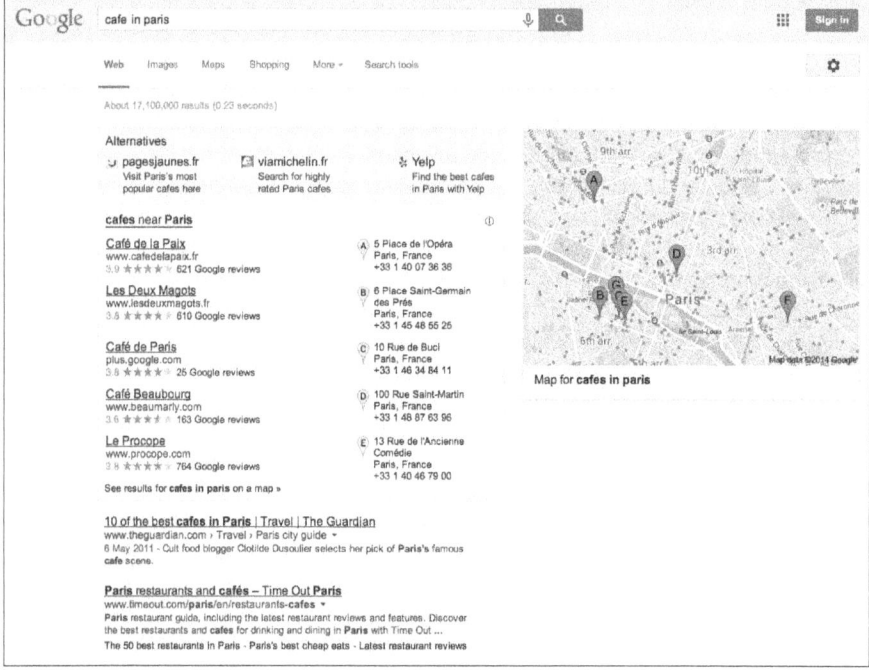

Fig. 2. Google's Local Search service. Source: European Commission.

Here, the layout is somewhat different, with the rivals' results placed at the top of the page but in a much smaller shaded area than Google's own specialized search results, which are also less clearly labeled. While the rivals' results might be thought to be in a better position, at the top of the page, their reduced size may well make them less attractive for users' clicks. This scenario does not seem to be addressed directly in the FairSearch commission and so it is unclear as to how users would react to this in practice.

---

17. Franklyn and Hyman, 'Review of the Likely Effects', pp. 10-11.

The procedure now is that the Commission will contact those who made the complaints about Google's conduct, state the Commission's views and ask for their feedback. While the Commission will consider these comments before it takes a final decision on Google's proposal, it seems unlikely that they will change the Commission's mind. Unlike Google's first two proposals, it seems that this third one will not be subject to a rigorous 'market test', during which interested third parties can offer their opinions and research, such as the FairSearch survey evidence mentioned above. This is significant since it seems that the results of the market test of Google's previous proposals contributed to the Commission's decisions not to accept them.

If this agreement does become legally binding, then Google will not have to pay a fine running into billions of euros and will escape an official finding of wrongdoing. Its previous conduct will also not officially be termed anticompetitive, which can have value as a precedent in future investigations. Perhaps an even greater victory for Google will be that it does not have to reveal to the public any more information about how its secretive algorithm works, although it may have to pass on some information about it to the independent monitoring trustee who will assist the Commission in making sure Google implements its commitments properly.

Google's competitors thus far have expressed their unhappiness with the proposed settlement. The Initiative for a Competitive Online Marketplace (ICOMP), an umbrella group of competitors, said that without another market test of the proposals, the Commission's head of competition Joaquin Almunia 'risks having the wool pulled over his eyes by Google'.[18] However Almunia himself has emphasized that his mission is to protect competition for the benefit of European consumers, not competitors, and that this proposal strikes the right balance between allowing Google to improve its services and giving users a 'real choice between different options'.[19]

Federal Trade Commission (FTC)
In the U.S., the Federal Trade Commission (FTC) also conducted an antitrust investigation into Google and came to a very different conclusion to that of the European Commission; it found that Google had adopted design changes for its search results page (it displayed its own vertical search results more prominently and had the effect of pushing the organic search links further down the page) primarily to improve the quality of its search product and the overall user experience.[20] Although Google's vertical search competitors may have lost sales as a result of this improvement, in the FTC's eyes this was just a normal part of a fierce, competitive process, and the outcome for users was that there was more directly relevant information for their search queries. So the FTC found that Google had not acted anti-competitively, and the company was not forced to label its results or otherwise change the operation or format of its search results page.

---

18. ICOMP Response to Commission's Announcement on the Google Antitrust Case, 5 February 2014, http://www.i-comp.org/blog/2014/icomp-response-commissions-announcement-google-antitrust-case/.
19. Joaquin Almunia, 'Statement on the Google investigation' European Commission SPEECH/14/93, 5 February 2014.
20. 'Statement of the Federal Trade Commission Regarding Google's Search Practices, In the Matter of Google Inc.', FTC File Number 111-0163, 3 January 2013.

Indeed, the FTC may also have found it legally difficult to insist on such changes. Certain constitutional rights in the U.S. are also enjoyed by 'legal persons' such as corporations as well as 'natural persons' (i.e. real individual people), including the right to freedom of expression under the First Amendment, as can be seen in the highly controversial Supreme Court decision in *Citizens United*.[21] Search engines including Google may be considered to be 'speakers' for the purposes of First Amendment protection, given they make 'editorial judgements' about information akin to a newspaper, with the implication that the government is not able to regulate what is presented by Google in its search results nor the way in which it is presented.[22] If the FTC had tried to impose regulations in this way, then Google may claim that it would be unconstitutional and thus illegal for them to do so.

The Users' Perspective
In any event, aside from how users might see and act on information in Google's search results pages, the perspective of users vis-à-vis a private, unaccountable, dominant online gatekeeper has not really been addressed at all so far in the competition investigations' narrow focus.

The problem that users may have with search engines is one of access to information: a search engine is a portal through which users experience the web. If a user does a search, and information thought of as 'relevant' does not appear in the results page, *and* if the search engine has had an active role in ensuring that information does not appear, then this can be characterized as censorship of sorts. Furthermore, even if certain information said to be 'relevant' or 'very relevant' is not entirely blocked from the results pages, but does not appear on the first page or even on the first five pages, then it may effectively be unavailable to users who generally will not go beyond these first few pages of results.[23] In a competitive market, according to neoclassical economic theory, when a search engine does not provide a user with the results she is seeking, that user will switch to a competitor that does provide these results. However, if the market for search engines is dominated by one entity or a small group of entities, then the user may not be able to obtain the results she wants even by switching to a competitor.[24] Her searches will be restricted either according to the economic interests or the ideological bearing of the dominant player(s). Indeed, Google has been accused of bias in how it presents its search results,[25] and there has been some evidence that it has taken steps to censor search

---

21. *Citizens United v Federal Election Commission* 558 US 310 (2010).
22. Eugene Volokh and Donald M. Falk, 'First Amendment Protection for Search Engine Search Results', Google White Paper, 20 April 2012, http://www.volokh.com/wp-content/uploads/2012/05/SearchEngineFirstAmendment.pdf.
23. Amanda Spink, Bernard J. Jansen, Dietmar Wolfram, and Tefko Saracevic, 'From E-Sex To E-Commerce: Web Search Changes', *IEEE Computer*, 35.3 (2002): 107.
24. Indeed, there are allegations that Microsoft's Bing, one of Google's competitors has been actively engaged in censoring results for certain terms that are controversial in China such as the Dalai Lama for Chinese language users doing searches from the US: http://www.theguardian.com/technology/2014/feb/11/bing-censors-chinese-language-search-results.
25. Benjamin Edelman, 'Hard-Coding Bias in Google Algorithmic Search Results', 15 November 2010, http://www.benedelman.org/hardcoding/.

terms.²⁶ However, one result of the competition investigations into Google is that very little has been revealed about its secretive website-ranking algorithm, so users are still in the dark about exactly how Google conducts its searches.

A further problem that users face regards the company's collection and use of data about them. Indeed, invasions of privacy and lack of compliance with data protection standards have been recognized in the American context as exacerbated by concentrated search markets, since consumers are left without meaningful choices given few or no competitors.²⁷

Competition Law: Could Do Better?
The result of the two investigations has been that in Europe, Google seems to have abused its dominant position regarding how it displays search results (although there is no official finding of wrongdoing), while in the U.S. Google's same conduct was found to be within the bounds of the law and, as mentioned above, possibly protected by First Amendment rights.

Indeed, it is actually unclear whether Google was acting anticompetitively and abusing its dominant position in the E.U. Aside from Google's incentives to come to an agreement with the Commission, the Commission may have been motivated to settle with Google for the reason that if it conducted a full investigation, it may not have come to the conclusion that there was anticompetitive conduct, and even if it did, Google could have appealed that decision to the European courts, which might well not have agreed with the Commission. This is because Google's conduct in favoring its own subsidiary services over those of its rivals does not fit squarely into recognized categories of anticompetitive abuses of dominance. It is not a straightforward case of 'refusal to deal' or 'refusal to supply' since Google is not refusing to deal or supply: it is 'dealing' with its competitors, but not on the terms they want. It is not blocking them entirely from its search results, whether paid or unpaid, it is just not placing them as highly and prominently as they wish to be placed. Furthermore, while certain types of discriminatory conduct by dominant entities have been found to constitute abuses of dominance, there seems to be no general duty not to discriminate against competitors on neighboring markets, and again it is unclear that Google's conduct is analogous to the cases where such abusive discrimination has been found to exist.²⁸ Furthermore, it is unclear whether Google's conduct fulfills the conditions for an abuse of dominance in the form of bundling and tying: Google certainly does 'bundle' its services i.e. its generic search engine and its vertical search engines, such that the former displays the latter in its results for a particular search term, but some conditions for finding this conduct abusive seem not to be met. Finally, the *effects* of Google's conduct are not definitively excluding competition:

---

26. Ernesto Van Der Sar, 'Google Starts Censoring BitTorrent, RapidShare and More', TorrentFreak, 26 January 2011, http://torrentfreak.com/google-starts-censoring-bittorrent-rapidshare-and-more-110126/.
27. Al Franken, 'How Privacy Has Become an Antitrust Issue', American Bar Association Antitrust Section Spring Meeting, Washington DC, 30 March 2012, http://www.americanbar.org/calendar/2012/03/antitrust_law_2012springmeeting.html.
28. Pablo Ibanez Colomo, 'Exclusionary Discrimination Under Article 102 TFEU', *Common Market Law Review*, 51 (2014) Issue 1: 141-163.

indeed, many of these competitors are still very much alive and kicking more than three years after they started to complain about Google's behavior.[29]

The Commission is empowered to take actions that can radically change the way businesses operate if it makes an official finding of abusive conduct, such as obliging certain kinds of business practices vis-à-vis competitors and customers, or even breaking up an entity into smaller constituent parts in extreme circumstances. In contrast, the terms of the agreement with Google are somewhat weak by comparison. Google will have to make some changes to the layout and content of its results page, but it will not seemingly have to be a lot more transparent about its inner machinations, nor will a general obligation of non-discrimination be imposed on Google, which were possible remedies during the investigation.[30] More transparency in particular around how Google's search algorithm works and an obligation of non-discrimination could have had positive consequences for more user-centric concerns: if the Commission had taken measures to force Google to reveal more details about its algorithm, then this would have been important for users as well as Google's competitors since they would have a lot more understanding of the hitherto secret way in which Google operates.

In comparison, the U.S. FTC did not force Google to make any changes to its search results page, since it did not find that Google had acted anticompetitively or abused its dominant position. Instead, the FTC found Google's design changes had improved its search function for consumers. This follows a line of U.S. case law including *Kodak*[31] and *IBM*,[32] which suggest that new and innovative products from the dominant entity that disadvantage competitors do not necessarily constitute abuses of the dominant position. Since this conduct was not viewed as anticompetitive, there could be no possibility of remedies for anticompetitive behavior having a positive 'spillover' effect for user-centric concerns.

These outcomes from both sides of the Atlantic may seem rather disappointing given the problems, identified above, that a dominant search engine such as Google poses for users. However, competition law is not designed to deal with all of these problems, even when they seem to flow from a concentrated market, and even when it would seem that more competition may solve or at least lessen the problem.

First, contemporary competition law's basis in neoclassical economics – due to the influence of the Chicago School of Economics in the U.S. since the 1970s and the subsequent move in the E.U. towards the 'more economic approach' in competition law and policy – has produced a legal regime that is concerned with the idea of competition as efficiency, with the maximization of 'consumer welfare' as its objective. The maximization of consumer welfare seems to trump the promotion of competition in

---

29. Pablo Ibanez Colomo, 'Exclusionary Effects in Google: Are They Relevant at All for the Outcome of the Case?', Chillin' Competition, 30 December 2013, http://chillingcompetition.com/2013/12/30/exclusionary-effects-in-google-are-they-relevant-at-all-for-the-outcome-of-the-case/.
30. Martin Cave and Howard Peter Williams, 'Google and European Competition Law', TPRC The 39th Research Conference on Communication, Information and Internet Policy, Arlington VA, 23-25 September 2011, http://papers.ssrn.com/sol3/papers.cfm?abstract_id=1992974.
31. Berkley Photo v Eastman Kodak, 444 US 1093 (1980).
32. California Computer Products v International Business Machines, 613 F.2d 727 (1979).

a market, resulting in a consequentialist approach to certain situations of (near) monopoly along with finding aggressive conduct towards competitors acceptable so long as the prices consumers pay are low or zero, as this is believed to be in their best interests. Indeed, as mentioned above, the European Commission's head of competition emphasized that he was operating within this precise approach when he described his mission as protecting competition for the benefit of consumers, not competitors. For some time in both E.U. and U.S. law, it has been established that the 'mere' accumulation of market power even up to the situation of monopoly is not in itself illegal. This can be contrasted with the past, when competition law was open to other public policy considerations that come about from the accumulation of private power, such as the effect it might have on the democratic process, a concern both of the German ordoliberals and U.S. antitrust law before the Second World War.

Second, and related to its current neoclassical incarnation, is the difficulty that competition law's economic approach has with quantifying other valuable societal goals, including vis-à-vis consumer welfare, which has resulted in them being left out of the analysis altogether.[33] Stucke, for instance, believes that competition policy can go beyond promoting economic efficiency, dispersing economic and political power, and promoting individual freedom.[34] He argues for a 'blended approach' to competition goals, yet does not explain very adequately what this would mean across the board of competition investigations and issues. His point seems simply to be a different interpretation of economic policy objectives in the scope of competition law, such as protecting small and medium businesses. In any event, it is true that competition law, as a regime that operates using mainly quantitative data, is not so well-equipped to take into account more qualitative factors. Measuring the extent to which, for instance, Google's users experience non-economic harm would seem to be a more qualitative than quantitative exercise, and generally one that would not be measured in financial terms. For non-economic objectives, it may be more expedient to use law and policy aside from competition law to achieve them, since using competition law to do so can be costly and ineffective.[35] Competition law has a particular ideology and aim that may not be conceptually flexible enough to bend to these situations.

In any event, this conception of competition law, based on principles of neoclassical economics seeing competition as efficiency with the objective of maximizing consumer welfare, may no longer reflect practice. Indeed, Buch-Hansen and Wigger have argued that at least in the E.U., competition regulation has undergone a 'neoliberal transformation' that has been primarily in the interests of transnational globalized capital rather than other social groups, challenging the view that it is consumers who are the main beneficiaries of competition.[36] Furthermore, in the U.S., one empirical study suggests that antitrust policy did not actually improve consumer welfare in practice.[37]

---

33. Christopher Townley, 'Which Goals Count in Article 101 TFEU?: Public Policy and its Discontents', *European Competition Law Review* 9 (2011).
34. Maurice Stucke, 'Reconsidering Antitrust's Goals', *Boston College Law Review* 53 (2012): 590.
35. Christopher Townley, *Article 81 EC and Public Policy*, Oxford: Hart Publishing, 2009.
36. Hubert Buch-Hansen and Angela Wigger, *The Politics of European Competition Regulation: A Critical Political Economy Perspective*, Abingdon and New York: Routledge, 2011.
37. Robert W. Crandall and Clifford Winston, 'Does Antitrust Policy Improve Consumer Welfare? Assessing the Evidence', *Journal of Economic Perspectives* 17.4 (2003): 3.

However, this is somewhat hard to square with the Commission's action against Google, since surely its investigation seems definitely not to be in the interests of the transnational globalized capital that Google constitutes. In addition, the Commission's willingness to intervene and even push for changes to Google's business practices when it is debatable that Google is behaving in an anticompetitive way would also not seem to accord with an approach minimalizing intervention in markets that neoliberalism promotes. Indeed, it seems that the Commission may have gone beyond what is 'necessary' or the bare minimum to address competition concerns. While neoliberal thought has been a dominant political current in the U.S. and U.K. at least since the 1980s, and has made inroads into the rest of the European Union, it would seem that the Commission's conduct here cannot wholly be attributed to it, and may possibly be due to factors such as European protectionism when faced with an American corporation (yet some of Google's competitors which have been making the complaints are also American) or being seen as a relevant institution to the general public and act in the face of what they perceive as a monopoly. Nevertheless, it is clear that the Commission has not been overly 'invasive' of Google's business practices, and particularly those which hold the most concern for users.

Can Other Areas of Law Help?

Although competition law seems inadequate for properly addressing the issues created by Google's dominant position for users, there are other areas of law that may go some way to alleviate these problems. First merger control, another 'head' of competition law that blocks transactions resulting in anticompetitive outcomes, could have been used more effectively to prevent Google from accumulating power through certain takeovers of other companies. Some of these mergers resulted in Google buying companies whose additional services were integrated with its existing business, becoming the object of the Commission's investigation of Google for abusing its dominant position. However the practice of the American and European merger authorities, especially when it comes to vertical or conglomerate mergers, has not been particularly circumspect. The U.S. merger authorities have been specifically criticized for being too lenient with this kind of merger as well as the resulting concentrations in technology and communications markets.[38] The European Commission's non-horizontal merger guidelines from 2008 have also been termed 'hospitable' to non-horizontal concentrations.[39] Buch-Hansen and Wigger singled out European merger control in particular as having taken the neoliberal turn in the interests of transnational capital rather than European consumers. So it is difficult to have much faith that it will address Google's dominance as a leading ambassador of globalized technological capitalism.

Some of the privacy and data protection concerns around Google's activities in Europe could at least be addressed using the European data protection regime, which is in the process of being updated from its 1995 version to reflect current technological reality. Regarding user data in the data protection regulation, there has been an attempt to include an obligation by companies to obtain the affirmative consent of individual users before profiling them. However there has been a great amount of resistance from online industry groups towards including such a term, with Google named as one of

---

38. Franken, 'How Privacy Has Become an Antitrust Issue'.
39. Cave and Williams, 'Google and European Competition Law'.

the companies lobbying against it.[40] Although in the U.S. there is growing regulatory activism around privacy and data protection, the approach taken is largely self-regulatory, with privacy activists actually appealing to the antitrust regime to intervene when dominant entities infringe on privacy. If the antitrust regime does not uphold their privacy in practice, then the limited privacy regime already in place is unlikely to help. Aside from the FTC's cognizance of the limits of its legal authority in this area, Pasquale has also identified the conceptual limits of competition law (at least in the U.S.) to govern 'dominant' search engines, such as the fact that economics-based, consumer welfare-oriented competition analysis cannot deal properly with *inter alia* privacy concerns.[41]

With regards to information access and privacy more generally and the role search engines play, the human/constitutional rights legal regimes could be called on to aid users. However, the protection of free expression (sometimes encompassing access to information as well) in Europe and the U.S. contained in the European Convention on Human Rights (ECHR) and the First Amendment to the Constitution, respectively, are usually enforceable as rights against the government and public bodies, though not against private entities such as corporations. Indeed, as mentioned earlier, in the U.S. corporations such as Google actually enjoy the protection of the First Amendment themselves. Human/constitutional rights mainly operate to prohibit government interference with citizens' rights but are largely impotent against infringements by companies or other non-public organizations. Moreover, American protection for the right to privacy (under the Fourth Amendment to the Constitution) is weaker and would seem to apply to less circumstances than the European position in the ECHR.

The Council of Europe has turned its attention to search engines, and in April 2012 its Committee of Ministers adopted a Recommendation to Member States concerning the protection and promotion of respect for human rights regarding search engines.[42] The non-binding recommendation recognizes the potential challenges of search engines to the right of freedom of expression (Art 10 of the ECHR) and the right to a private life (Art 8), which may come from the design of algorithms, de-indexing, and/or partial treatment or biased results, concentration in the market, a lack of transparency about how results are selected and ranked, the ability of search engines to gather and index content that may not have been intended for mass communication, general data processing and retention, and the generation of new kinds of personal data such as individual search histories and behavioral profiles. The recommendation, of course, is not legally binding, and it merely constitutes suggestions for the Member States to follow, if they see fit. Thus far it does not seem that the recommendation has actually been followed by Member States, and adequate protection of privacy and facilitation of free expression remain a problem for privately-owned and operated platforms like Google.

Prior or *ex ante* regulation of search engines is another possibility, especially if the legal regimes above do not adequately address user concerns. Various commentators have

---

40. EDRi, 'US Privacy Groups Believe US Officials Lobby to Weaken EU Privacy', 13 February 2013, http://www.edri.org/edrigram/number11.3/us-privacy-groups-eu-law-lobby.
41. Frank A. Pasquale, 'Privacy, Antitrust and Power', *George Mason Law Review* 20.4 (2013).
42. Council of Europe, 'Recommendation CM/Rec (2012) 3 of the Committee of Ministers to member States on the protection of human rights with regard to search engines', 4 April 2012, https://wcd.coe.int/ViewDoc.jsp?id=1929429&Site=CM.

recommended *ex ante* regulation as well as, or else appeal to these other legal regimes. In Europe, the Council of Europe's Committee of Ministers advocated a co-regulatory approach to search engines. Member States should cooperate with the private sector and civil society to develop strategies to protect fundamental rights and freedoms pertaining to search engine operation, particularly regarding transparency over how the search engines provide information, the criteria according to which search results are organized, how content not intended for mass communication (although in the public space) should be ranked and indexed, transparency as to the collection of personal data, empowerment of users to access and modify their personal data held by search engine providers, the minimization of the collection and processing of personal data, and the assurance that search engine services are accessible to people with disabilities. Member States should also consider offering users a choice of search engines, particularly to search outputs based on criteria of public value. However, as mentioned above, Member States so far have not acted on this recommendation, and as it stands the recommendation is also non-binding.

In the U.S. context, specifically given the limits of competition law to deal with privacy concerns, Pasquale argues that search engines should instead be thought of as an 'essential cultural and political facility' and regulated accordingly, using tools beyond competition law,[43] alongside other measures he has previously advocated for that relate to the increased regulation of search engines (such as protection for users' privacy and greater transparency over how search results are ordered).[44]

In order to deal with issues related to the use and exploitation of user data, Fuchs has taken a radical position and argued that as a solution, Google should not be dissolved, alternatives are not needed, and its services are not 'a danger to humanity'.[45] Instead he advocates that Google be 'expropriated and transformed into a public, non-profit, non-commercial organization that serves the common good'. He outlines what this public search engine could look like, including a non-profit organization such as a university running its services, and support by public funding. Interestingly, Vaidhyanathan has previously identified Google as remedying what he terms 'public failures' i.e. the opposite of a 'market failure', when the state cannot satisfy public needs and deliver services effectively. Google has 'stepped into voids better filled by the public sector'.[46] Aside from the fact that this is highly unlikely to happen in practice given the enormous 'intervention' in the market that such 'expropriation' of Google would entail, Fuchs also notes that this may only be possible by 'establishing a commons-based internet in a commons-based society'; this has particular resonance in the wake of the revelations of vast public/state surveillance of the internet. It would seem that internet users will only be safe in cyberspace when there is no concentration of power in one entity, whether public or private, and relations are governed on a peer-to-peer basis.

---

43. Frank A. Pasquale, 'Dominant Search Engines: An Essential Cultural & Political Facility', in Berin Szoka and Adam Marcus (eds) *The Next Digital Decade, Essays on the Future of the Internet*, Washington DC: TechFreedom, 2010, pp. 401-417.
44. Frank A. Pasquale, 'Beyond Innovation and Competition: The Need for Qualified Transparency in Internet Intermediaries', *Northwestern University Law Review* 104.1 (2010).
45. Christian Fuchs, 'Google Capitalism', *tripleC* 10.1 (2012): 47-48.
46. Siva Vaidhyanathan, *The Googlization of Everything (And Why We Should Worry)*, Berkeley: University of California Press, 2011.

Furthermore, regulation similar to that advocated for Internet Service Providers (ISPs) in the net neutrality debate has been suggested for search engines, including Google. Interestingly, Google itself was an early advocate of net neutrality regulation for ISPs, before 'modifying' its position on the issue in 2010. An equivalent obligation of Google's might encompass non-discrimination rules for its search results, as well as requiring Google not to 'block' content that would otherwise be considered a 'relevant' result for a search. However, without knowing more about how Google's search algorithm works and how 'neutral' or not it already is in determining results, it would be difficult to design such an obligation of neutrality then see that it is effectively put into place. With ISPs it is easier to determine whether they are acting in a non-neutral fashion due to their technical makeup.

Nevertheless, despite these varied suggestions for law and regulation to deal with Google's dominance, given the imperfect solutions offered (at most) by competition law, there has been no attempt to implement any of them.

This inaction may be explained by the regulatory climate in the U.S. and Europe. The regulation of communications in both jurisdictions operates according to a mostly 'market-based' approach, which, as mentioned above, has reflected the ascendancy of neoliberalism and its corresponding doctrine of 'light touch' regulation of private entities. Alongside this development, there has been the attempted capture by corporate interests of public regulatory bodies. A glaring example is the aforementioned corporate lobbying of European institutions during the legislative process for a new data protection regulation. This has resulted in governments of liberal democracies being loathe in practice to extend any further regulation of private entities, especially for seemingly 'non-economic' purposes, in accordance with the mantra that the market will provide. The legislative and regulatory solutions outlined above would entail significant intervention and 'interference' with the market for online search and advertising. Given the general environment, it is not surprising that these solutions for Google's dominance may be thought of as idealistic or going too far.

Even if the will did exist to regulate in users' interests, another issue remains: the time it takes for law and regulation to be discussed, enacted, then implemented, which is at odds with the high speed of new technological markets that govern online search and advertising.

Extra-Legal Solutions
Since the law and regulation, for various reasons listed above, seem inadequate, extra-legal solutions may be the most appropriate for search. One suggestion has been for a publicly funded search engine that would compete with Google and its ilk. This solution is advocated for by Pasquale as a real alternative to those already in operation, as a means to avoid problems with monitoring and accountability that private search engines pose. As described above, Fuchs advocated for government intervention to turn Google into a public search engine, while also admitting that a non-exploitative search engine for the benefit of humanity may only be possible through the general establishment of a commons-based internet in a commons-based society.

Nevertheless, users themselves are not entirely powerless towards search engines and do not need to wait for top-down direction. Even in scenarios where users create information for corporate expropriation, there is a weakness inasmuch as the corporations cannot force users to utilize the services and thus contribute their data. Consent is dependent on users' own views and motivations. Since the users and the data they produce become the 'product' of the company, then 'the corporation is in many ways at the mercy of users [... and] the community of users is more empowered in the face of the corporation'.[47] This suggests that if users, on whom Google's whole business model rests (at least partially anyway), realized their potential by going on 'strike' and shutting down their accounts, or refused to use Google's service and thus create data for Google, then they could avoid and successfully resist these exploitative practices.

A final option for users would be to support and use decentralized peer-to-peer search engines such as YaCy, avoiding centralized servers along with the problems they entail.[48] However, the success of such peer-to-peer search engines is dependent upon the amount of people using it 'actively' by contributing to the website index. Next to that, these search engines cannot constantly update the quality of search by accessing data to improve their results as Google does, so their results are likely to be less 'accurate' or 'relevant'.

References
Almunia, Joaquin. 'Statement on the Google investigation' European Commission SPEECH/14/93, 5 February 2014.
Berkley Photo v Eastman Kodak, 444 US 1093 (1980).
Buch-Hansen, Hubert and Angela Wigger. *The Politics of European Competition Regulation: A Critical Political Economy Perspective*, Abingdon and New York: Routledge, 2011.
California Computer Products v International Business Machines, 613 F.2d 727 (1979).
Cave, Martin and Howard Peter Williams. 'Google and European Competition Law', TPRC The 39th Research Conference on Communication, Information and Internet Policy, Arlington VA, 23-25 September 2011, http://papers.ssrn.com/sol3/papers.cfm?abstract_id=1992974.
Citizens United v Federal Election Commission, 558 US 310 (2010).
Council of Europe, 'Recommendation CM/Rec(2012)3 of the Committee of Ministers to Member States on the Protection of Human Rights with Regard to Search Engines', 4 April 2012, https://wcd.coe.int/ViewDoc.jsp?id=1929429&Site=CM.
Crandall, Robert W. and Clifford Winston. 'Does Antitrust Policy Improve Consumer Welfare? Assessing the Evidence', *Journal of Economic Perspectives* 17 (.4) (2003): 3-26.
Devine, Kristine, L. 'Preserving Competition in Multi-Sided Innovative Markets: How Do You Solve A Problem Like Google?', *North Carolina Journal of Law and Technology* 10 (2009).
Edelman, Ben. 'Hard-Coding Bias in Google Algorithmic Search Results', 15 November 2010, http://www.benedelman.org/hardcoding/.
EDRi, 'US Privacy Groups Believe US Officials Lobby to Weaken EU Privacy', 13 February 2013, http://www.edri.org/edrigram/number11.3/us-privacy-groups-eu-law-lobby.
European Commission, 'Antitrust: Commission Obtains from Google Comparable Display of Specialised Search Rivals – Frequently Asked Questions', MEMO/14/87, 5 February 2014.
European Commission press release. 'Antitrust: Commission Probes Allegations of Antitrust Violations

---

47. Mayo Fuster Morrell, 'The Unethics of Sharing: Wikiwashing', *International Review of Information Ethics* 15: 10.
48. Tyler Handley, 'P2P Search As An Alternative to Google: Recapturing Network Value Through Decentralized Search', *Journal of Peer Production: The Critical Power of Free Software* 3, http://peerproduction.net/issues/issue-3-free-software-epistemics/peer-reviewed-papers/p2p-search-as-an-alternative-to-google-recapturing-network-value-through-decentralized-search/.

by Google', 30 November 2010.

Federal Trade Commission, 'Statement Regarding Google's Search Practices, In the matter of Google Inc.', FTC File Number 111-0163, 3 January 2013.

Fiveash, Kelly. 'Google's Euro Antitrust Offer: Fine! We'll Link to Our Search Rivals', The Register, 25 April 2013, http://www.theregister.co.uk/2013/04/25/ec_gives_google_rivals_one_month_to_market_test_search_tweaks/.

Franken, Al (Senator). 'How Privacy Has Become an Antitrust Issue', American Bar Association Antitrust Section Spring Meeting, Washington DC, 30 March 2012, http://www.americanbar.org/calendar/2012/03/antitrust_law_2012springmeeting.html.

Franklyn, David J. and David A. Hyman. 'Review of the Likely Effects of Google's Proposed Commitments Dated October 21, 2013', 9 December 2013, http://www.fairsearch.org/wp-content/uploads/2013/12/FairSearch-Hyman_Franklyn-Study.pdf.

Fuchs, Christian. 'Google Capitalism', *tripleC* 10 (.1) (2012): 42-48.

Fuster Morrell, Mayo. 'The Unethics of Sharing: Wikiwashing', *International Review of Information Ethics* 15: 9-16.

Handley, Tyler. 'P2P Search As An Alternative to Google: Recapturing Network Value Through Decentralized Search', *Journal of Peer Production* 3 'The Critical Power of Free Software' (2013), http://peerproduction.net/issues/issue-3-free-software-epistemics/peer-reviewed-papers/p2p-search-as-an-alternative-to-google-recapturing-network-value-through-decentralized-search/.

Ibanez Colomo, Pablo. 'Exclusionary Discrimination Under Article 102 TFEU', *Common Market Law Review*, 51(.1) (2014): 141-163.

_____. 'Exclusionary Effects in Google: Are They Relevant at All for the Outcome of the Case?', Chillin' Competition, 30 December 2013, http://chillingcompetition.com/2013/12/30/exclusionary-effects-in-google-are-they-relevant-at-all-for-the-outcome-of-the-case/.

ICOMP Response to Commission's Announcement on the Google Antitrust Case. 5 February 2014, http://www.i-comp.org/blog/2014/icomp-response-commissions-announcement-google-antitrust-case/.

Pasquale, Frank A. 'Beyond Innovation and Competition: The Need for Qualified Transparency in Internet Intermediaries', *Northwestern University Law Review* 104.1 (2010): 105-173.

_____. 'Dominant Search Engines: An Essential Cultural & Political Facility', in Berin Szoka and Adam Marcus (eds) *The Next Digital Decade, Essays on the Future of the Internet*, Washington DC: TechFreedom, 2010, pp 401-417.

_____. 'Privacy, Antitrust and Power', *George Mason Law Review* 20.4 (2013): 1009-1024.

Rushe, Dominic. 'Bing Censoring Chinese Language Search Results for Users in the US', *The Guardian*, 12 February 2014, http://www.theguardian.com/technology/2014/feb/11/bing-censors-chinese-language-search-results.

Simpson, John M. 'Consumer Groups on Both Sides of the Atlantic Oppose Google Antitrust Settlement', Consumer Watchdog, 26 November 2013, http://www.consumerwatchdog.org/newsrelease/consumer-groups-both-sides-atlantic-oppose-google-antitrust-settlement.

Spink, Amanda, Bernard J. Jansen, Dietmar Wolfram, and Tefko Saracevic, 'From E-Sex to E-Commerce: Web Search Changes', *IEEE Computer,* 35.3 (2002): 107-109.

StatCounter, 'Global Stats Top 5 Search Engines in Europe from Feb 2013 to Jan 2014', http://gs.statcounter.com/#search_engine-eu-monthly-201302-201401.

StatCounter 'Global Stats Top 5 Search Engines in the United States from Feb 2013 to Jan 2014', http://gs.statcounter.com/#search_engine-US-monthly-201302-201401.

Steinhardt, Ezra. 'Google Fined by the CNIL for Privacy Breaches as European Regulators Continue Investigation', Inside Privacy, 13 January 2014, http://www.insideprivacy.com/google-fined-by-the-cnil-for-privacy-breaches-as-european-regulators-continue-investigation/.

Stucke, Maurice. 'Reconsidering Antitrust's Goals' *Boston College Law Review* 53 (2012): 551-629.

Townley, Christopher. *Article 81 EC and Public Policy,* Oxford: Hart Publishing, 2009.

_____. 'Which Goals Count in Article 101 TFEU?: public policy and its discontents', *European Competition Law Review* 9 (2011): 441-448.

Vaidhyanathan, Siva. *The Googlization of Everything (And Why We Should Worry),* Berkeley: University of California Press, 2011.

Van Couvering, Elizabeth. 'New Media? The Political Economy of Internet Search Engines', presented to the Communication Technology Policy section of the International Association of Media & Communications Researchers (IAMCR), Porto Alegre, 25-30 July 2004, http://www.academia.edu/1047079/New_media_The_political_economy_of_Internet_search_engines.

Van Der Sar, Ernesto. 'Google Starts Censoring BitTorrent, RapidShare and More', TorrentFreak, 26 January 2011, http://torrentfreak.com/google-starts-censoring-bittorrent-rapidshare-and-more-110126/.

Volokh, Eugene and Falk, Donald, M. 'First Amendment Protection for Search Engine Search Results', Google White Paper, 20 April 2012, http://www.volokh.com/wp-content/uploads/2012/05/SearchEngineFirstAmendment.pdf.

A 'History' of Search Engines: Mapping Technologies of Memory, Learning, and Discovery

Richard Graham

A 'History' of Search Engines: Mapping Technologies of Memory, Learning, and Discovery

Richard Graham

Can we draw a timeline onto which search engines fit? This is at once an ordinary and odd question. We constantly contextualize technology, linking new to old and contrasting similar to dissimilar; we do this implicitly through our usage, and it helps us to feel that we understand certain phenomena. For instance, most of us are implicitly aware of the history of the watch. Without consciously researching its history, a watch wearer might place their digital wristwatch in a family tree that stretches back to sundials, waterclocks, hourglasses, candle clocks, pendulum clocks, pocket watches, and quartz watches. In this example a timeline of development is easy to draw. The mechanical processes might be wildly different, but the ancestors of the modern watch all carry out a very similar purpose. The levels of material detail have changed over time, which means that a timekeeping device designed for the modern Olympics does a very different job from a sundial, but they are all manifestations of the same pursuit. This kind of timeline might be described as a lineage of intentions, whether timepieces use sand, water, or quartz crystals.

There are many different ways that we historically contextualize technologies. A second method might be called a lineage of machinery. From this perspective, instead of placing a modern digital watch in a family tree containing other timepieces, we might relate it to other digital devices. So we might implicitly link digital watches to other digital technologies regardless of their functions. This is a useful approach when thinking about how certain technologies were invented, and it also speaks to social and historical networks that constitute our historical past. Implied in the terms 'Stone Age' and 'Bronze Age' is that we form timelines and maps of history based on physical materials and machinery rather than more abstract intentions and goals. There are many other ways in which we place phenomena and technology into a historical lineage, many of which we draw on and build in our minds implicitly and that can deepen our understanding of contemporary technologies and behaviors.

Faced with the question of what lineage Google fits into, many people might recall Ask Jeeves, AltaVista, or relate the site to other methods of navigating the web. However, the broader question regarding the lineage of web search engines, and the contexts into which the collective technology fits, is much more problematic. Rather than attempting to answer this question by providing a comprehensive timeline onto which search engines neatly find a place, this essay suggests that the *process* of thinking about timelines, lineages, and networks of relationships is much more useful than the construction of one single family tree of which web search engines are the most modern descendent. I will introduce a number of examples that relate to the ways in which we conceptualize search engines. Rather than tie them all together in an overly neat way, I will attempt to provide more questions than answers.

Considering the prevalence of the internet, World Wide Web, and search engines in our lives, we do not seem to have developed the right language for talking about them. This feeling is particularly acute when I talk to family and friends about my day-to-day activities studying search engines and when the words we use become more of a barrier than an aid. 'Is the internet a medium? Is the web a platform? Are search engines tools? Or just websites? Media? Directories?' Most of the time, these questions are avoided or ignored as irrelevant to the average user. It is unnecessary for users to understand the difference between the internet and the web in order to send an e-mail. Users do not need to know how search engines work to find out the year Barack Obama was born, or the date he became president. When our tools work, specific language or specialized knowledge may seem unimportant. When our expectations, intentions, and results are in line with one another, a deeper understanding of a technology and the vocabulary with which to discuss it recedes into the background.

However, when concerns are expressed about search engines and their effects on users, these implicit expectations become more prominent. Cries of privacy violation, worries that search engines change the value of knowledge or attention spans, fears that they provide dominant homogenous perspectives which ignore cultural differences, or, on the other hand, that they create filter bubbles, parroting search results back to users so tailored to their search behavior that it prevents them from experiencing new perspectives with which to question their own values – these and many other concerns are raised when our experience of search engines becomes misaligned with our expectations. Where these expectations are drawn from is a complex issue. One element of our expectations is the historical precedent set by technologies, ideas, and institutions, which users implicitly form as a family tree or lineage in which search engines are the latest incarnation. However, I argue that when users conceptualize a phenomenon, knowledge of previous technologies and institutions that had a direct effect on present technology is not the most prominent factor in that process. More important is our implicit process of mapping instances that we feel are similar or complementary, regardless of whether other technologies or institutions had any direct effect or relationship with the existence and identity of the phenomenon at hand. In this way it is our own individual, fluid, ad-hoc contexts that determine both how technologies are used and also our perspectives concerning how they should work.

Given that search engines do not fit into an established type of technology – they are not simply a website, medium, tool, platform, network, or service – our comparisons with historical instances, with where search engines fit within wider historical development, are important in understanding what we as users implicitly feel search engines are and what their capabilities should be. Yet in reality these historical developments are not linear, nor do we tend to think about them that way. Instead our knowledge of related phenomena constitutes a constellation of associations. This kind of rhizomatic thinking leads to multiple, often contradictory, overlapping histories that form a major part of our conception of what search engines are. For this reason I want to argue that a deeper understanding of search engines and their history can be gained by moving away from neat family trees and towards a nonlinear way of conceptualizing associations. The way we conceptualize the relationship between search engines and other technologies and behaviors is much more like building constellations of the night sky. We look at the stars and map their associations with one another based on narratives that are meaningful to us rather than accurate descriptions of how these heavenly bodies actually cohere. Consciously outlining the different ways in which we contextualize search engines can help us understand our implicit makeshift definitions, which in turn mould our behavior.

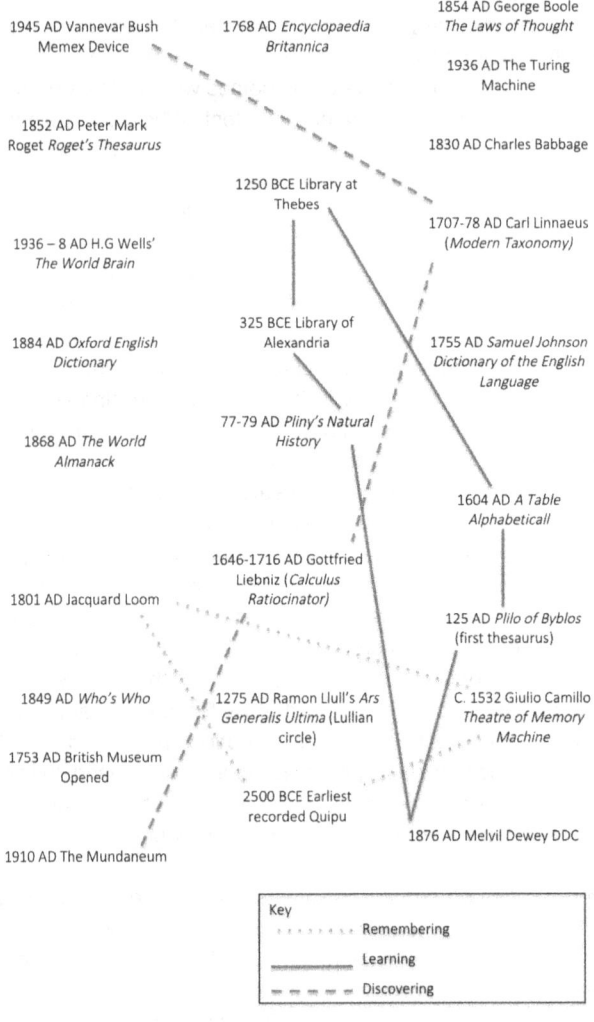

Fig. 1. An ad-hoc constellation of associations for technologies relating to remembering, learning and discovering (by the author).

Figure 1 shows a number of ideas, institutions, and technologies that relate to search engines. I could add more points of reference in the same way that star charts add more stars based on better telescopes and more thorough research. This way of presenting information decontextualizes it and in turn makes us focus our contemporary perceptions of what search engines are. We can add different categories by which the examples are grouped, build on existing categories, or remove examples entirely. This open-ended process provides us with more meaningful questions than a static timeline that simplifies the history of tools and thought. The questions opened up by making ad-hoc connections can be developed by choosing a point on our constellation of associations and discussing how search engines relate to other media in different ways.

I will outline three ways in which search engines are used, which I describe as remembering, learning, and discovering. While these are by no means exhaustive, these three ways have a range of historical ancestors and therefore provide us with a variety of overlapping constellations of association. While there are a multitude of behaviors associated with search engines, these three are important for relating to our conception of *knowledge*. Displaying them as constellations means these categories are flexible, and that new ones might be added. In doing so we widen the discourse around search engines.

Remembering concerns the use of search to recall information such as dates or names that we already have a clear contextual grasp of. Learning is searching for detailed information about areas we are partially knowledgeable about. Discovering is the use of search to provide ourselves with the unexpected. I will outline these three modes in relation to some examples from the makeshift constellation of associations I mentioned earlier, with the aim of providing a rhizomatic set of connections to other technologies and also hopefully to shift some of the conceptions regarding the newness and exceptional nature of web search engines.

Remembering, (or More Accurately, Forgetting)

> Knowledge is of two kinds. We know a subject ourselves, or we know where we can find information upon it.[1]

My use of the term *remembering* constitutes the use of search engines for jogging one's memory for things we would otherwise say we knew – sentiments crystallized by phrases such as 'Who was that guy in that film? You know, *that* guy!' and, 'It's on their second album, whatever it's called'. We often rely on these kinds of mental placeholders, however empty, because we know that correct searches will remind us of certain facts. As psychologist Stephen Kosslyn puts it: 'Once I look up something on the internet, I don't need to retain all the details for future use – I know where to find that information again and can quickly and easily do so. More generally, the internet functions as if it were my memory.'[2] Many have criticized this kind of behavior as one of the ways in which modern technology is making our levels of knowledge and understanding less

---

1. James Boswell, *The Life of Samuel Johnson Volume II*, New York: Penguin, 1986 (1791), p. 257.
2. Stephen M. Kosslyn, 'Social Prosthetic Systems' in John Brockman (ed.) *Is the Internet Changing the Way You Think?*, New York: Edge Foundation, 2011, p. 182.

substantial. Nicholas Carr in his 2008 article for *The Atlantic,* 'Is Google Making Us Stupid?', uses a metaphor that can usefully stand in for the frequently voiced opinion that the internet has fundamentally changed the way we think:

> What the Net seems to be doing is chipping away my capacity for concentration and contemplation. My mind now expects to take in information the way the Net distributes it: in a swiftly moving stream of particles. Once I was a scuba diver in the sea of words. Now I zip along the surface like a guy on a Jet Ski.[3]

Carr's metaphor reflects an entire mentality about the internet: the feeling of a profound sense of distance between the time before search engines, hyperlinking, and the web, and our wholly futuristic contemporary situation. It is as if we have passed one of, if not *the*, major technological watersheds. Carr goes on to describe how the internet, 'an immeasurably powerful computing system, is subsuming most of our other intellectual technologies. It's becoming our map and our clock, our printing press and our typewriter, our calculator and our telephone, and our radio and TV.'[4]

Carr's list of examples reinforces a version of technological change as teleological, monolithic, and always moving from less to more complex. The idea that new technology takes us places we have never been to, and also replaces ones we are familiar with, underpins the belief that there is no going back to the good old time of simplicity and authenticity. To return to Kosslyn's description of new post-internet behaviors and provide a more positive counterbalance to Carr's provocative arguments, Kosslyn reinforces the concept that, 'constant connectivity has posed various tradeoffs; nothing is without a price. But in this case – on balance – it's a small price. I'm a better thinker now than I was before I integrated the internet into my mental and emotional processing.'[5]

Even positive defences of the internet generally suffer from this kind of before and after television makeover-show metaphor. This type of thinking reinforces the attitude that media and technology affect us as if brought to us on the conveyer-belt of history, every new arrival overshadowing the rest. In the introduction I mentioned that family and friends skirt around terminology concerning what the internet is, and tend to avoid specific or technical language to avoid sounding uninformed. A similar attitude develops from many of the arguments by professional commentators, theorists, and thinkers, the majority of whom, I would hazard a guess to say, *do* have complete competency over terms and definitions. Many of these thinkers however, conflate the internet, web, search, and other aspects of new technologies for a number of reasons, perhaps for the benefit of their readers or to make their particular claims seem more fundamental or universal. However, in doing so they reinforce the idea that the issues or benefits all stem from one monolithic change in connectedness. When technology commentators talk about the internet and its ease of searching and finding, increased interconnectedness and speed compared to traditional media, they are, very often, talking primarily about the impact of search engines. If we can be more specific about

---

3. Nicholas Carr, 'Is Google Making Us Stupid', *The Atlantic,* July/August 2008, http://www.theatlantic.com/magazine/archive/2008/07/is-google-making-us-stupid/306868/.
4. Carr, 'Is Google Making Us Stupid'.
5. Kosslyn, 'Social Prosthetic Systems', p. 183.

the actual technologies that might be changing our behaviors, we have a better chance of finding points of comparison with other existing technologies, rather than talking about the internet age as if it were a journey into totally uncharted land.

While it is fashionable today to talk about Google as a mental prosthesis, technologies that extend our minds and memories are not new. There are a number of technologies and media that change the way we think and remember, some familiar and often still used, others less well known. I use the word media in a wide sense borrowed from Marshall McLuhan, whereby 'media are the intersecting points or interfaces between technologies, on the one hand, and bodies, on the other'.[6] When Samuel Johnson, in the above epigraph, referred to the knowledge of where to look, he was foremost referring to libraries. The rest of the quotation in fact states that, 'when we enquire into any subject, the first thing we have to do is to know what books have treated of it'.[7] While these kinds of structured resources will be addressed in the following section on learning, the behavior I want to address here is much more basic than the knowledge required to be familiar with a library. Rather, this lineage is based around tools for memory.

To elaborate on the question of memory, I will now introduce a very old and culturally specific technology, the Quipu.

Fig. 2. An Inca quipu, from the Larco Museum in Lima (source: Wikipedia).

---

6. Paraphrased by Friedrich Kittler in *Optical Media*, Malden, Mass.: Polity, 2010, p. 29, in reference to Marshall McLuhan, *Understanding Media: The Extensions of Man*, New York: McGraw-Hill, 1964.
7. Boswell, *The Life of Samuel Johnson*, p. 257.

In ancient Andean South America, a particular technology called a Quipu was used in a number of different regions. This device, often described as talking knots,

> consisted of a thick cord from which a number of strings were suspended in the manner of a fringe. These strings were of different colors, according to the nature of the object each represented: for example, yellow stood for gold, red for the army, white for peace. The colors, being limited in number, had different meanings depending upon the general purpose and scope of the Quipu.[8]

The Quipu could act as a memory device for complex narratives, as a record of a storehouse, rules, and decision-making, and could provide a map of an area, along with many other possible uses that historians still do not fully understand. Manipulating the strings provided sets of information that upon untying would act as a mnemonic device. Similar to the practice of tying a knot in a handkerchief to remind the user of something, except incomparably more complex, the Quipu relied on existing memories and contextual understanding from the user, the designated Quipucamayu ('keeper of the Quipus').[9] As the same sets of strings could be used for a multitude of different needs, a user must not only know the context but also the original intentions, dispositions, and other embedded behaviors that might have been encoded in its original tying. The Quipu then was not simply an exterior memory store or memory device; instead it was used as a remembering device. In it was encoded just the right level of forgetting. This level of forgetting was however not structured in terms of shallow and deep, since it did not provide a structure for more detailed memories to fall into place. Instead Quipus provided the basis for a more holistic process whereby memory was embedded in actions. The continued and repetitive use of the Quipu by many generations and in multiple regions allowed for change and adaptation but also solidified links between different types of knowledge and behavior. Quipus were dynamic, they altered the way in which their users thought and remembered and the way that individuals and societies built up their identities.

I am not trying to compare Quipus directly to Google. A direct comparison would flatten out the media-specific particularities of each technology. The historical and contextual differences are huge, so playing a spot-the-difference exercise is obviously not going to be helpful. However, if we draw on this massive gulf between contexts, pushing it to its limit, accepting all of its messiness, we can learn more about each technology on its own terms. If we tried to connect the use of Quipus to the use of search engines via a family tree or linear technological evolution, we would fail; they cannot even be described as the most distant cousins. Juxtaposing one to the other, however, can widen our thinking and draw it away from the overly specific considerations of search engines solely within our own context.

The Quipu is an ancient technology. Many archaeologists, in particular Ruth Shady, have argued that the earliest discovered examples are around 4500 years old.[10] Anthropologist Gary Urton has shown through written archival evidence that there are

---

8. Louis Baudin, *A Socialist Empire: The Incas of Peru*, New Jersey: D. Van Nostrand Company, 1961, p. 125.
9. Baudin, *A Socialist Empire*, p. 128.
10. Charles C. Mann, 'Unraveling Khipu's Secrets', *Science* 309 (12 August 2005): 1008.

descriptions of the khipus contained in documents written at the time of the Spanish conquest (beginning in 1532) [which] reveal that the Inkas used khipus to record quantitative data (e.g., censuses and tribute records) as well as songs, genealogies, and other narrative forms containing historical information.[11]

Due to the number of Quipus found between these two eras, we can argue that Quipus were no passing phenomenon. They embedded themselves in a culture and fundamentally changed the nature of knowledge and memory in that culture for thousands of years. The exact way in which they were applied, however, is uncertain, due to their use in non-literate societies, which means no written account exists. Without a written record of their use, our historical knowledge of Quipus has become almost mystical, truly embedded within its own media. For these reasons many scholars and researchers have questioned the typical descriptions of Quipus. Urton is a foremost critic of the conventional descriptions of what kinds of uses Quipus may have been put to. Urton argues against the 'idea that the khipus represented an idiosyncratic, private (i.e., individual memory-based) system of notation such that an accurate interpretation of any particular khipu could be given only by the individual who made it'.[12] Urton draws on historical evidence that the Incan empire had high levels of bureaucracy and that many Quipus were used for transmitting laws and matters of the state. Quipus' use was less like an individual memory trick and more like a range of dialects and informally borrowed ad-hoc dialogue.

It is unsurprising that certain common practices evolved as the Quipu was deployed for such a long time. What is intriguing, however, is the malleable nature of these common codes or repeated practices. The work of Quipucamayu (the Quipu user) was both intimately personal and also shared with others, remaining ambiguous due to the open-ended possibilities of combinations of strings and ties. This flexibility allowed at all times the possibility that each Quipu message was transmitting or helping different users remember more or less information. This ambiguity doubles the difficulty of ascertaining the device's precise usage from a 21st century perspective. Not only can scholars not fully understand Quipus because of a lack of translated rules, etiquette, and application, but also it is entirely possible that Quipucamayus had so many different ways in which the personal and communicative use of Quipus crossed over that we might assume there was no universal understanding of Quipus during their time. The nature of remembering and forgetting using a Quipu necessarily undermines a complete understanding of how the technology worked. Quipus were used in a variety of different and fluid ways, and it was this plasticity of behaviors that changed the relationship between thought and knowledge for its users.

On this note we return to search engines and the contemporary ways in which they are discussed. Although we cannot know the precise details of how the ancient Quipu technology was used, we know that even talking about the possible ways it might have been deployed allows us to interrogate the interplay between remembering and thinking. Could Quipus exist simply on a personal basis, did they need to be con-

---

11. Gary Urton, 'From Knots to Narratives: Reconstructing the Art of Historical Record Keeping in the Andes from Spanish Transcriptions of Inka Khipus', *Ethnohistory,* 45.3 (Summer, 1998): 409-410.
12. Urton, 'From Knots to Narratives', p. 411.

nected within an inter-medial field that took into account wider discourses? Is it inevitable that a personal memory, when structured through shared media, transmutes into semi-shared codes? Asking these questions puts my own use of search engines as a memory tool in a new light. When earlier I referred to different ways in which people use search engines to remember the names of actors or album titles, I drew a picture of how search changes the remembering and forgetting of individuals. From our experience we might develop personal codes. I frequently search the same query for names I commonly forget and have learned which searches always return the name I'm looking for and which don't. Remembering which search terms to use becomes a very personal code. I have a more direct link to certain pieces of information because I attempted to recall them before. However, search is unavoidably social. My search patterns are my own, but only because of the unspoken search behaviors of strangers. Often counterintuitive to an individual's attempted use of search engines as memory devices is that we must negotiate the combined personal mnemonic patterns of others. In my initial constellation (see Figure 1) of associated technologies, I grouped Quipus under the heading of *memory*. However, as this example shows, the collaborative contexts from which Quipus and other memory media are inextricable complicate the idealistic notion that technologies can be used simply to *remember*. Already this first example problematizes the extent to which we can establish proper boundaries between remembering, learning, and discovering.

The media archaeologist Jussi Parikka, paraphrasing the German media theorist Friedich Kittler, describes the situation by arguing that:

> Media determine our situation and are already inside our heads, inside our capacities of understanding and writing, our theoretical concepts, memories and such, yet these perspectives of a media-archaeological kind elaborate the wider intermedial fields in which the human body is trained as part of the modernization process.[13]

The link between Quipus and search engines is not direct and by no means concrete, however in the light of Parikka's comments, both technologies, by the very nature of their make-up, shape their users in comparable ways. Parikka's intermedial fields relate to the unconscious modes that develop between users of the same technologies, structuring their individual use and development of certain capacities, both in isolated and social contexts. With the Quipus we can see that the constellation of *remembering* undermines itself.

Learning, (or Searching for Details)

> At any point in history, institutions attempt to legitimate the current version of knowledge and truth by controlling the manner in which texts are ordered with respect to each other.[14]

---

13. Jussi Parikka, *What Is Media Archeology*, Cambridge: Polity Press, 2013, p. 27.
14. Gary Radford, 'Positivism, Foucault, and the Fantasia of the Library: Conceptions of Knowledge and the Modern Library Experience', *The Library Quarterly* (1992), p. 418.

A second way in which we might relate search engines to other technologies is through the behaviors that constitute *learning*. By this I mean technologies that require prerequisite knowledge that can be enhanced or deepened through their use. In many ways this description corresponds to the above distinction of technologies for memory.

A point of comparison often made between search engines and other technologies is that of the future of the printed book in an increasingly digital age. Again, this kind of comparison creates a monolithic perception of the traditional kinds of knowledge transfer and ways of expressing ideas before the internet. Much of the dialogue surrounding the place of the printed book draws from wider-ranging issues concerning the importance of scholarship, traditional boundaries, and the hierarchies between experts and amateurs. What many people mean, however, when they speak of *the future of the book* in such a general way refers back to what historian Peter Burke describes as an 'intellectual tripod composed of curricula, libraries and encyclopaedias'.[15] Burke describes how, in the 15th century, due to the uniform way knowledge was structured and taught (through the linear and sequential systems of the trivium and quadrivium), each of these components reinforced one another. 'The order of books would reproduce the order of the university curriculum',[16] and this order, unlike our modern alphabetical arrangements, structured encyclopedias. This arrangement forced a strict relationship between different types of knowledge. Grounding in grammar, logic, and rhetoric was required before students could progress onto arithmetic, geometry, astronomy, and the study of music. The fact that each area reinforced the dominant way of organizing knowledge naturalized many associations and hierarchies built into the system. It was also hard for this system to be questioned due to the fact that areas of thought would be hard to discover without sufficient context provided by the dominant university courses.

We could argue that, although much has changed since the 15th century, different institutions of knowledge still reinforce one another. The ideas that some basic disciplines must be learned to progress to certain areas, that libraries are stocked in accordance to dominant paradigms of learning, and that encyclopedias contain a condensed version of libraries, still exist. What we can say is that encyclopedias, now mostly alphabetical, give multiple points of access, making learning and understanding more flexible and individualistic. Universities allow more freedom and specialization for students and do not try to mirror the complete contents and structure of libraries and encyclopedias inside the minds of students. Libraries are now arranged in a number of different ways, and the variations show how no single order of books is ideal or objective. I will now briefly focus on libraries and their methods of arrangement. Similar to search engines, the development of a practical technology also led to very philosophical changes in attitude.

Many library traditions altered gradually over time. However, one abrupt change was due to the innovations of Melvil Dewey when he created the Dewey Decimal Classification (DDC) system in 1876. The system provided libraries with a more fluid way in which

---

15. Peter Burke, *A Social History of Knowledge: From Gutenberg to Diderot*, Malden, Mass.: Polity Press, 2000, p. 87.
16. Burke, *A Social History of Knowledge*, p. 92.

books could interact, while at the same time reinforcing older hierarchies and divisions. When demarcating constellation relationships on our map of associations (Figure 1), it might be beneficial to juxtapose the process and mindsets involved in using search engines to the changing relationship users had to books within libraries in the late 19th century. Before the DDC, library catalogs were usually arranged in the 'alphabetico-classed style' that would denote a book's subject and location.[17] Books were usually categorized under one broad category with no sub-categorizing. The remainder of the call number would refer to a specific place in the library. For instance *On the Origin of Species* might have been marked J429, where J indicated biology, 4 the fourth tier in the alcove, 2 the second self, and 9 the ninth book. When a physical library moved or grew beyond its physical limits, the collection often required renumbering.[18] Books were frequently ordered on the shelves by the date of acquisition, since if one tried to implement either alphabetical or sub-categorization of subjects, a significant part of the collection would need to be reclassed with every acquisition.

19th century libraries were significantly smaller than today, as were their number of users, and these users were typically tied to an academic institution either as teachers or students. A typical library user would discover a book via a university syllabus, encyclopedia, or academic writing, thus reinforcing what Burke describes as the 'intellectual tripod'.[19] They would then rely on their own knowledge or librarians' to ascertain the main subject and consult a written index, the only source of information regarding the book's location. There are several problems with this system. First, libraries did not allow browsing to the same extent that they do today; the major categories were too wide to allow for semi-serendipitous research behaviors. Disciplinary knowledge was needed for both cataloging and retrieval, and this forced the process of acquiring new knowledge into traditional patterns, restricting new ways of thinking. Secondly, the written indexes were time-consuming to use and maintain; if a mistake was made in cataloging a book, it would effectively be lost completely. Furthermore, the catalog was handwritten, which not only led to mistakes but meant that there was usually only one or two catalogs per library. Due to their precious nature close supervision and guidance from a librarian was required, leading to less independent research. Finally, the specificity of pre-DDC systems, which focused on where a book could be found within a specific library space, meant that libraries were not easily comparable, hindering the use of multiple libraries.

All of these problems stem from the one major difference between the DDC and the library systems it set to overcome: before the DDC library classmarks related to the physical library space, while DDC classmarks refer to the books. This is an important distinction to make. The DDC marks a reversal of the hierarchy between books and libraries. The DDC shifts emphasis from a physical library space, which is made up of a number of ordered books, to a number of ordered books which together make up a library. The books were classified in relation to one another, and although Dewey's categories were based on existing structures, this change provided a renewed flexibility and opened up new possibilities for how ideas could be accessed and related.

---

17. John Comaromi, 'Knowledge Organized is Knowledge Kept: The Dewey Decimal Classification, 1873-1976', *The Quarterly Journal of the Library of Congress* 33 (1976): 3.
18. Comaromi, 'Knowledge Organized is Knowledge Kept', p. 311.
19. Burke, *A Social History of Knowledge*, p. 87.

This change in library classification was a shift in technologies of learning, whereby the alterations in how information was navigated affected established contexts, which in turn helped provide new contexts.

The fact still remains that the books in a particular library need to be stored in a certain relationship to one another, and it is these relationships the user must understand in order to enter into its discourse. Perhaps distinct from the use of search engines as automated memory devices is the use of search engines for learning, or increasing the detail of a particular piece of knowledge the user is already familiar with. Search engine technologies provide access points, and much like a misshelved book in a library, an unindexed page on the web is removed from its context in a way that almost completely prohibits its use. Just as the links between webpages are in some ways more important than their content, the relationship of physical books within a library space provides a parallel way of thinking about context. Although the changes made to libraries in the 19th century do not link to search engines through any traditional linear progression, their juxtaposition might help us realize how technologies designed for practical purposes have changed traditional arrangements of knowledge throughout history, not just in a post-internet world. Associating the institutional structures of use that persisted through Burke's intellectual tripod to search technologies reminds us that search and retrieval are not new, and neither is the information explosion that scholars often lay claim to and have been for hundreds of years. The struggle to organize a seeming over-abundance of knowledge is much older than the digital world it is so often associated with. The balance technologies are required to strike between knowledge prerequisites for learning and open-ended discovery has been part of a much larger technological history than our modern search engine dilemmas.

Discovery (or Study Without End or Reason)

> Man would no longer need documentation if he were assimilated into an omniscient being – as with God himself. […] Everything in the universe, and everything of man, would be registered at a distance as it was produced. In this way a moving image of the world will be established, a true mirror of his memory. […] In this way, everyone from his armchair will be able to contemplate creation, as a whole or in certain of its parts.[20]

So far we have covered two areas that constitute part of the identity of web search engines – remembering and learning – and shown to some extent how similar aspects within these behaviors can be found in other unrelated media. We have seen that when placed in a new context, questions on what is important about search engines can be better formulated. As we have seen, the previous two categories blend into one another. This provides a space for new categories to be tested, and for the map connecting search engines with other phenomena to be reorganized, opening up space for new perspectives that can be further questioned. It is in this context that I will now discuss the distinction referred to in figure 1 as discovery. One of the primary aspects of web search engines that is often seen as new and unrelated to past media is their ability to

---

20. Paul Otlet, *Monde: Essaie d'Universalisme*, trans. Anthony Judge, Brussels: Editions du Mundaneum, 1935, p. 391.

provide access to unexpected areas of knowledge of which the user has little previous experience. Of course this kind of open-ended behavior is linked to the previous distinctions, since the question of prerequisite knowledge required for new discovery rears its head once more. This situation allows us to ask the question, to what extent, then, does a search engine enable unconstrained movement through unexplored information in a way that makes sense? In this case, although previous technologies have been implemented to an extent, it is perhaps more productive to compare the intentions of particular technologies. As Eric Kluitenberg argues:

> More often than not, the expectations contained in such imaginaries far exceed what actual media machines are actually capable of doing. However, the actual media machines are themselves inflicted with impossible desires that are ascribed to, or are projected onto them, by their designers as well as their perception by the public. The transition between imaginary and actual media machines, in terms of their signification can be almost seamless.[21]

The transition between the imaginary and actual occurs often when discussing search engine technologies. This is particularly the case when thinking about original intentions and future possibilities and very often happens when things go wrong. To address this transmission between real and imaginary technologies, I will now briefly outline Paul Otlet's Mundaneum, an institution that aimed to collect and make accessible all human knowledge. The Mundaneum was actually built, and aiming for the impossible was integral to its identity.

Paul Otlet (1868-1944) was a Belgian polymath who spent a large portion of his life working with Henri La Fontaine on various exploits that they hoped would promote world peace. One of Otlet's many ideas for connecting a world becoming more fragmented and hostile throughout his life, was called the Mundaneum. The Mundaneum, which was built and functioned in an unfinished state for a time (hence the ambiguity between actual and imaginary), was planned to house all the world's knowledge. Otlet described it in 1914:

> These collections are conceived as parts of one universal body of documentation, as an encyclopaedic survey of human knowledge, as an enormous intellectual warehouse of books, documents, catalogues and scientific objects. Established according to standardized methods, they are formed by assembling cooperatively everything that the participating associations may gather or classify.[22]

Not simply designed as a storehouse of information, the Mundaneum housed a number of staff who were employed to answer questions from anyone willing to pay a small fee. Knowledge would be open to many more people than the traditional model previously allowed. The time in which these inventions came about is no coincidence. Otlet wanted universal knowledge to break down nationalistic and class

---

21. Eric Kluitenberg, 'On the Archeology of Imaginary Media', in Erkki Huhtamo and Jussi Parikka (eds) *Media Archeology. Approaches, Applications, Implications*, Berkley: University of California Press, p. 48.
22. Paul Otlet, '1914 Advertising Pamphlet Qtd', in W. Boyd Rayward, 'Visions of Xanadu: Paul Otlet and Hypertext', *JASIS* 45 (1994): 240.

barriers, giving anyone the opportunity to participate in his project and become world citizens of peace in the pursuit of knowledge. He saw the Mundaneum as a centrepiece of the world city he was designing with La Fontaine. Unlike other ideas for drawing together information in a dynamic and futuristic manner, for instance H. G. Wells' idea for a World Brain or Vannevar Bush's Memex, Otlet's negotiation between the imaginary end goal of his project and the early stages of organization were key to his project. The Mundaneum had to be built in order to matter at all. Otlet's designs for a universal collection of knowledge went a step beyond familiarity with an existing system or a new structure that could be imposed on existing materials. The Mundaneum aimed to break not only national and institutional barriers but also the barriers of authorship, tradition, and the physical constraints of publishing. Otlet 'wanted to penetrate the boundaries of the books themselves, to unearth the substances and conclusions inside'.[23]

Akin to search engines, the staff at the Mundaneum would answer queries with quotations, photographs, and film footage extracted from their original work but with sufficient references to place it in context. The Mundaneum was constructed by analyzing books and other materials, selecting the most important conclusions, and translating that information onto index cards to be used as facts for any number of different contexts. At its height the Mundaneum contained over '12 million individual index cards and documents'[24] and employed full time operators who could answer questions, provide information, and work for anyone on an individual inquiry basis. During the Nazi invasion of Belgium in 1940, the Mundaneum was stripped and replaced with an exhibition of Third Reich art. Its legacy lives on, and in the late 90s many of its remains were found and have been reconstructed as a modern museum in the city of Mons.

The aims of the Mundaneum provide us with a renewed perspective for modern search engine technologies. In many ways the projects are connected. Google's mission statement 'to organize the world's information' describes Otlet's project just as well as it does Google's.[25] The beneficial element of drawing these two projects into juxtaposition is simply to argue that search engines are not internet dependent and were attempted before our contemporary connected age. The aspect I find intriguing about the Mundaneum is that, even though it seems old fashioned with its employment of index cards and physical boxes of notes, and even though its aims seem unfeasible, it still sounds inspirationally futuristic, even today. The teams of workers designed to pick out the most important parts of documents, the human contact and control when filing a request, seem at face value more sophisticated than our current situation of secret algorithms and black-boxed methods. Or are we also pleased that the world's information is out of the hands of individuals? Is the reduction of human bias or error in exchange for the computational errors of machines a cause for celebration? If we for a moment ignore the practicalities of the project and treat the Mundaneum as an institution we might aim for, does it reveal certain hopes and concerns we have for our current situation regarding search engines?

---

23. Alex Wright, *Glut: Mastering Information through the Ages,* New York: Cornell University Press, 2007, p. 187.
24. Wright, *Glut: Mastering Information through the Ages*', p. 188.
25. Google mission statement, www.google.com/about/.

Hopefully examples like the Quipu, Dewey Decimal Classification, and Paul Otlet's Mundaneum, however contextually estranged, can open up new questions and areas for debate when thinking about the ways in which we use and rely on search engines. Drawing on my metaphor of mapping constellations onto historically unrelated media, I wish to provide a wider area of analysis and more ways to question our current technologies. Through the use of examples the particular constellation categories set up at the start of this essay – remembering, learning, and discovering – have become less distinct. I believe this shows how the process of drawing up multiple non-linear narratives about a technology is perhaps more productive in our attempts to understand its effects than a traditional lineage. Rather than allowing our analysis to be shackled to unrealistically direct historical timelines, we need to decontextualize our technologies in order to see familiar ones in a new light. If search engines themselves do not respect traditional boundaries, then when we study them, why should we either?

References

Baudin, Louis. *A Socialist Empire: The Incas of Peru*, New Jersey: D. Van Nostrand Company, 1961.

Boswell, James. *The Life of Samuel Johnson Volume II*, New York: Penguin, 1986 (1791).

Burke, Peter. *A Social History of Knowledge: From Gutenberg to Diderot*, Malden, Mass.: Polity Press, 2000.

Carr, Nicholas. 'Is Google Making Us Stupid?' *The Atlantic*, July/August 2008, http://www.theatlantic.com/magazine/archive/2008/07/is-google-making-us-stupid/306868/.

Comaromi, John. 'Knowledge Organized is Knowledge Kept: The Dewey Decimal Classification, 1873-1976', *The Quarterly Journal of the Library of Congress* 33 (1976): 17-31.

Google Mission Statement. www.google.com/about/.

Kittler, Friedrich. *Optical Media*, Malden, Mass.: Polity, 2010.

Kluitenberg, Eric. 'On the Archeology of Imaginary Media', in Erkki Huhtamo and Jussi Parikka (eds) *Media Archeology. Approaches, Applications, Implications*, Berkley: University of California Press, 2011.

Kosslyn, Stephen M. 'Social Prosthetic Systems', in John Brockman (ed.) *Is the Internet Changing the Way You Think?* New York: Edge Foundation, 2011.

Mann, Charles C. 'Unraveling Khipu's Secrets', *Science* 309 (12 August 2005): 1008-9.

McLuhan, Marshall. *Understanding Media: The Extensions of Man*, New York: McGraw-Hill, 1964.

Otlet, Paul. *Monde: Essaie d'Universalisme*, Trans. Anthony Judge, Brussels: Editions du Mundaneum, 1935.

Parikka, Jussi. *What Is Media Archeology*, Cambridge: Polity Press, 2013.

Radford, Gary. 'Positivism, Foucault, and the Fantasia of the Library: Conceptions of Knowledge and the Modern Library Experience', *The Library Quarterly* (1992): 408-424.

Rayward, W. Boyd. 'Visions of Xanadu: Paul Otlet and Hypertext', *JASIS* 45 (1994): 235-250.

Urton, Gary 'From Knots to Narratives: Reconstructing the Art of Historical Record Keeping in the Andes from Spanish Transcriptions of Inka Khipus', *Ethnohistory* 45.3 (Summer, 1998): 409-438.

Wright, Alex. *Glut: Mastering Information through the Ages*, New York: Cornell University Press, 2007.

Before Google: A Pre-History of Search Engines in Analogue Times

Anton Tantner

Before Google:
A Pre-History of Search Engines in Analogue Times[1]

¬

Anton Tantner

Googling – that is, searching the internet using the Google search engine, which was developed in 1997[2] – is by now taken so much for granted that resources for searching and finding used before Google seem outdated, whether they are library catalogs on index cards, printed bibliographies, or address and telephone books – as though they belonged to a past age, an age that may be described as the 'analogue age' in the future.

On various occasions over the last few years, research has tried to consider past information technologies as precursors of the digital age. Technologies facilitating the location of information within early modern books, card catalogs, servants, and even popular German television series such as Robert Lembke's *Was bin ich?* or Eduard Zimmermann's *Aktenzeichen XY*, have been described as part of the prehistory of computers.[3] In my habilitation treatise on *intelligence* or *registry offices*, I attempted to describe these institutions as pre-modern search engines. These offices were increasingly established in major European cities from the 17th century onwards; they brokered information, but also all too often served as watchdogs.[4] In an overview article and in a collection edited with Thomas Brandstetter and Thomas Hübel in

---

1. Translated by Brita Pohl, www.bricolangue.at.
2. On the history of Google cf. among others the following journalistic accounts: David Vise and Mark Malseed, *The Google Story,* New York: Delacorte Press, 2005; Lars Reppesgaard, *Das Google-Imperium,* Hamburg: Murmann, 2008.
3. Thomas N. Corns, 'The Early Modern Search Engine: Indices, Title Pages, Marginalia and Contents', in Neil Rhodes and Jonathan Sawday (eds) *The Renaissance Computer. Knowledge Technology in the First Age of Print,* London-New York: Routledge, 2000, pp. 95-105; Markus Krajewski, *Paper Machines. About Cards & Catalogs, 1548-1929,* trans. Peter Krapp. Cambridge, MA: MIT Press, 2011; Markus Krajewski, *Der Diener. Mediengeschichte einer Figur zwischen König und Klient,* Frankfurt am Main: S. Fischer, 2010; David Gugerli, *Suchmaschinen. Die Welt als Datenbank,* Frankfurt am Main: Suhrkamp edition unseld 19, 2009. For an overview of many of the issues touched upon in this article, see Peter Burke, *A Social History of Knowledge: from Gutenberg to Diderot,* Cambridge: Polity Press, 2000.
4. Anton Tantner, *Adressbüros im Europa der Frühen Neuzeit,* Habilitation treatise, submitted at the Faculty of Historical and Cultural Studies at the University of Vienna, Wien: Universität Wien, 2011, http://phaidra.univie.ac.at/o:128115.

2012, I tried to shed more light on these past resources of searching and finding, the history of which has yet to be written.[5]

Of course, one has to be aware of the problems of such an historical approach. The term 'pre-history' might imply a kind of teleological view of history, with the assumption that the glorious advent of Google was the solution to all the problems that could not be solved in the past. This is by no means the intention of this article. What I do intend to study is how search worked in the past and what problems arose from it, assuming that some of the problems are comparable to those we are confronted with today, be it privacy issues, poor observance of the secrecy of registered data, or government use of these services.

Today's technological solutions may be new, but the problems they address are older. Thus, the extensive data collection campaigns of the Middle Ages and during the early modern period resulted, for example, in the making of the Domesday Book of medieval England, the so-called *Relaciones topográficas* composed during the reign of the Spanish king Philip II, the *enquêtes* by French minister Colbert, and the 'Political Remarks of the Imperial War Council' during the Hapsburg monarchy in 1770-1772, all which may be compared to the 'crawlers' sent out by current search engines to 'harvest' information. Their intention was to make people's property and their social and physical conditions visible and legible for state authorities, and they were often met with skepticism and resistance.[6] Even the surveillance of global internet communication by the NSA, which was made public in the summer of 2013, did not surprise historians of the early modern postal services. What nowadays are back doors allowing secret services to control the big internet companies' data traffic have famous precursors in the 'Black Cabinets' and 'Post Lodges' of European governments, which monitored correspondence via the mail services from the early modern period.[7]

In the following three sections, I will examine how knowledge was indexed and ordered in the past, the ambivalence with which human information brokers were regarded by those using their services, and finally which institutions were created in order to exchange information in the analogue age. This historical overview should not only provide new insights about the past, but should also be useful to those who study today's search engines.

---

5. Anton Tantner, 'Suchen und finden vor Google. Eine Skizze', in *Mitteilungen der Vereinigung österreichischer Bibliothekarinnen & Bibliothekare* 64 (2011): 42-69; Thomas Brandstetter, Thomas Hübel, and Anton Tantner (eds) *Vor Google. Eine Mediengeschichte der Suchmaschine im analogen Zeitalter,* Bielefeld: Transcript, 2012; the present article is based on these two last publications.
6. Peter Burke, *The Historical Anthropology of Early Modern Italy. Essays on Perception and Communication,* Cambridge: Cambridge University Press, 1987, pp. 28-31; Peter Burke, *A Social History of Knowledge,* pp. 129-132; for a monograph on Colbert's intelligence system, see Jacob Soll, *The Information Master: Jean-Baptiste Colbert's Secret State Intelligence System,* Ann Arbor: University of Michigan Press, 2009; Michael Hochedlinger and Anton Tantner (eds) '... Der größte Teil der Untertanen lebt elend und mühselig'. Die Berichte des Hofkriegsrates zur sozialen und wirtschaftlichen Lage der Habsburgermonarchie 1770-1771, Innsbruck-Wien-Bozen: Studienverlag, 2005 (Mitteilungen des Österreichischen Staatsarchivs Sonderband 8).
7. Thomas Winkelbauer, 'Postwesen und Staatsbildung in der Habsburgermonarchie im 17. und 18. Jahrhundert', in *Wiener Geschichtsblätter* 68 (2013): 69-86, at 82-85 with further literature.

Disposition and Indexation of Knowledge
How were books and bodies of knowledge arranged in order to facilitate searching for them? We need to distinguish systematic disposition on the one hand, in which books are registered and possibly arranged according to a specific system or classification – a method used often in public libraries – and, on the other hand, alphabetical organization, in which books are registered according to the name of the author or, in a subject catalog, according to keywords assigned by the librarian.

Systematic Organization: Dewey's Decimal Classification
For centuries, the systematic organization of books was pursued as an ideal. Already during the 17th century, numbers were used for classification systems; the system that is most famous today, the so-called *Dewey Decimal Classification,* was created by U.S. librarian Melvil Dewey in 1876, and later adapted and extended by Paul Otlet and Henry LaFontaine in Europe. The 'Decimal Classification' groups human knowledge into ten main classes, which are assigned the figures 0 to 9; the figure 9, for example, is reserved for the discipline of 'History'. The main classes are further subdivided, and the longer the number, the more detailed the description of the subject; for example, the history of Austria is assigned the figure '943.6'. It is no surprise, then, that this classification is strongly informed by the particular world view of its creators; thus, in the original version, all world religions outside Christianity were assigned the category '290 religions other than Christianity'.[8]

Decimal Classification is mainly used in science, technology, and medical science, and serves as an organizing pattern for systematic library catalogs, the shelving of books, and the compilation of bibliographies.[9]

Alphabetical Organization
According to Peter Burke, alphabetical order was first introduced in the 'Suidas', a Byzantine encyclopedia from the 11th century, and sporadically used over the following centuries, for example in cataloging the library of the abbey of Saint-Victor in Paris at the beginning of the 16th century. Only in the 17th century was the alphabetical organization of books established in library catalogs and bodies of knowledge such as encyclopedias, even though it was still considered so unusual that authors had to laboriously justify its use.[10]

After the acceptance of alphabetical library catalogs, distinct rules were created for them. These rules sometimes became extremely elaborate, as in the case of the 'Prussian Instructions', which were laid down during the compilation of the German General

---

8. Felix Stalder and Christine Mayer, 'The Second Index. Search Engines, Personalization and Surveillance', in Konrad Becker, Felix Stalder (eds) *Deep Search. The Politics of Search Beyond Google,* Innsbruck: Studienverlag, 2009, p. 98.
9. Harald Jele, *Wissenschaftliches Arbeiten in Bibliotheken. Einführung für StudentInnen,* München-Wien: Oldenbourg, 1999, pp. 41-49, 102-109; David Weinberger, *Everything is Miscellaneous: The Power of the New Digital Disorder,* New York: Henry Holt and Company, 2008, pp. 64-84.
10. Peter Burke, *A Social History of Knowledge,* pp. 109-10, 184-87; Neil Rhodes and Jonathan Sawday, 'Paperworlds: Imagining the Renaissance Computer' in Neil Rhodes and Jonathan Sawday (eds) *The Renaissance Computer. Knowledge Technology in the First Age of Print,* London-New York: Routledge, 2000, pp. 8-9; for a survey of the history of alphabetical sorting: Marc W. Küster, *Geordnetes Weltbild. Die Tradition des alphabetischen Sortierens von der Keilschrift bis zur EDV. Eine Kulturgeschichte,* Tübingen: Niemeyer, 2006.

Catalog in 1899. In Austria, the Prussian Instructions were adopted at the beginning of the 1930s in several research libraries, concurrent with the introduction of card indices. Its adoption also had political implications, as some German nationalist librarians welcomed the cataloging rules in force in Germany as an anticipation of the *'Anschluss'* of Austria to Germany.[11] Many libraries continued to use the Prussian Instructions up to the introduction of online catalogs. At that moment, they were replaced by another system of rules, the system of alphabetical cataloging that is usually identified by its German acronym 'RAK'.[12]

'Search Engines' in Books: Registers, Indices, Marginalia, Verse Numbers
For the location of contents in a book, too, adequate resources needed to be invented. Important tools that help a person gain an overview of a particular book are the table of contents on the one hand, and the register on the other hand, if the book contains one. The history of such book registers, however, remains to be written; according to historian Helmut Zedelmaier, they may be regarded as 'search engines of the early modern knowledge apparatus'.[13]

Scholars also unlocked the Bible's content using an entire apparatus of resources: so-called concordances; polyglots, Bible editions in several languages; canon tables, which indicate parallel passages in the Gospels; harmonies, which joined the four Gospels into one text; and synopses. Even a search aid that is self-evident to the present-day reader still had to be invented. It was the publisher Robert Estienne who, at least according to legend, divided the Bible into chapters while on horseback in the 16th century and thus introduced the numbering of verses that is still common in this fundamental text of occidental fiction.[14]

Especially in early modern times, such resources as title pages, marginalia, or chapter summaries were inserted into books; they anticipated present-day developments, and publishers succeeded in making texts more user-friendly by allowing non-serial access. This user-friendliness was, however, often paid for by a more restrictions to individual interpretation.[15]

From Bibliometric Citation Indices to Google's PageRank
One way of arranging and rating books that was invented in the 20th century is so-called bibliometric, or citation indices. By means of this method, a prioritized order of texts, articles, or books is established, depending on how often they are cited in important journals; such rankings may also be established using the footnotes of a scientific

---

11. Hans Petschar, 'Einige Bemerkungen, die sorgfältige Verfertigung eines Bibliothekskatalogs für das allgemeine Lesepublikum betreffend', in Hans Petschar, Ernst Strouhal, and Heimo Zobernig (eds) *Der Zettelkatalog. Ein historisches System geistiger Ordnung,* Wien-New York: Springer, 1999, pp. 35-36 and 42, FN 65.
12. Rupert Hacker, *Bibliothekarisches Grundwissen,* 4th edition, München: Saur, 2000, pp. 181-195.
13. Helmut Zedelmaier, 'Facilatis inveniendi. Zur Pragmatik alphabetischer Buchregister', in Theo Stammen and Wolfgang E.J. Weber (eds) *Wissenssicherung, Wissensordnung und Wissensverarbeitung. Das europäische Modell der Enzyklopädien,* Berlin: Akademie, 2004 (Colloquia Augustana 18), pp. 193 (citation) and 201.
14. Daniel Weidner, '"Wende sie um und um, denn alles ist in ihr." Über das Suchen in heiligen Texten', in Thomas Brandstetter et al. (eds) *Vor Google,* pp. 41-72.
15. Thomas N. Corns, 'The Early Modern Search Engine', p 103.

text. A rather useful analogy for these metrics is linking on the internet. Search engines rank the websites found in a query according to the number of links to them. First efforts in this direction already started in the 1920s; since the 1950s, the work of Eugene Garfield gained influence after founding current citation indices, starting with the *Science Citation Index (SCI)* dating from 1963. Such indices, today available in the form of databases, calculate the influence or 'impact' of articles. The higher the 'impact factor', i.e. the more an article is cited in journals judged to be scientifically excellent, the more important that article is considered to be and the higher it is ranked.[16] There also is a similar citation index for the field of humanities, the *Arts & Humanities Citation Index*. Currently attempts are being made to establish such an index for Europe, the *European Reference Index for the Humanities (ERIH)*.[17]

Citation analysis is crucial not only in the field of academic research, but also for its important role in our current daily search life, as the ranking processes of search engines work according to this principle. The better a page is linked, the further up on the page it will appear in search results. Linking is one of the factors used to determine the ranking of a website. In the case of Google, this principle is called 'PageRank' – its name also being a pun, as 'Page' is the name of one of Google's founders, Larry Page.[18]

Encyclopedias as Repositories of Knowledge
Another form of knowledge storage and indexing that may be regarded as characteristic of early modern times is the major encyclopedia projects, of which I will cite only three exemplary ones. The most famous of these encyclopedias is without a doubt the *Encyclopédie ou Dictionnaire raisonné des sciences, des arts et des métiers*, founded by Diderot and D'Alembert in the 18th century as one of the great projects of Enlightenment. The *Encyclopédie* appeared from 1751 to 1780 and comprises 35 volumes.[19] Even earlier, Zedler's *Universal-Lexicon* was published in German mostly during the first half of the 18th century (64 volumes, four supplement volumes).[20] Lastly, the *Encyclopédie Anarchiste*, initiated by the anarchist educator Sébastien Faure, appeared in French in four volumes from 1925 to 1934, running to more than 2,800 pages. The manner of financing such a giant enterprise was rarely employed elsewhere; some of the *Encyclopédie Anarchiste*'s funding came from the famous Spanish anarchist Buenaventura Durutti, who had seized the money from bank robberies.[21]

---

16. Bernhard Rieder, 'Zentralität und Sichtbarkeit. Mathematik als Hierarchisierungsinstrument am Beispiel der frühen Bibliometrie', in Thomas Brandstetter et al. (eds) *Vor Google*, p. 223-252.
17. For further information on the ERIH, see http://www.esf.org/hosting-experts/scientific-review-groups/humanities/erih-european-reference-index-for-the-humanities.html.
18. See e.g. Reppesgaard, *Das Google-Imperium*, p 77.
19. Cf. e.g. Robert Darnton, *The Business of Enlightenment: A Publishing History of the Encyclopédie, 1775-1800*, Cambridge, MA: Harvard University Press, 1987 (1979). For the digitized 'encyclopédie', see: http://portail.atilf.fr/encyclopedie/.
20. Digitized version: http://www.zedler-lexikon.de. For general information on encyclopedias, see Martin Gierl, 'Enzyklopädie', in Friedrich Jaeger (ed.), *Enzyklopädie der Neuzeit*. Stuttgart: Metzler, 2005 et sequ., vol. 3, 2006, pp. 344-356.
21. Hans Magnus Enzensberger, *Der kurze Sommer der Anarchie. Buenaventura Durrutis Leben und Tod*, 10th edition, Frankfurt am Main: Suhrkamp st 395, 1994, pp. 57, 64. Digitized version: http://www.encyclopedie-anarchiste.org/.

Human Information Brokering Institutions

Werner Faulstich identifies those media that work without necessarily using technology as 'primary media' or 'human media', such as the theater.[22] In an analogy, it may be possible to refer to institutions such as contact brokers, agents, or go-betweens, as well as domestics and loan lackeys, servants, and concierges, as 'human search engines'.

Contact Brokers, Servant Agents, Go-Betweens
The term *Beziehungsmakler* (contact broker) refers to the concept of a broker, a term that today is mostly used in connection with stock exchange brokers. According to a definition provided by Christoph Windler,

> brokers' arrange contacts with individuals who themselves control needed resources or can on their part establish further contacts [...]. They supervise critical connections between a local system and a broader whole [...]. Their position crucially depends on the importance of the contacts brokered by them for the involved parties and the inexistence of alternative channels of communication.[23]

Some examples are the so-called *Gesindezubringer* (servant agents), often elderly women; those looking for servants for their household were able to approach them. Servant agents possessed specialized knowledge about who was looking for work and were extremely unpopular with the early modern authorities, because they were accused of poaching servants once they had placed them, in order to collect the brokering fee as many times as possible.[24]

A similar function was fulfilled by the so-called *Unterkäufer* (go-betweens) in the late Middle Ages and the early modern period, but they were related to the sale of goods. When a foreign tradesman entered a city, he was able to turn to such a go-between, who would help him find resellers against a commission.[25]

Servants and Loan Lackeys
Servants, too, may be regarded as search engines. Here, we may differentiate between those who worked in one household for a longer period of time, and loan lackeys or porters appearing in bigger towns and cities, whose services usually were enlisted by travelers for a specified period of time.

Regarding the first group, Markus Krajewski has pointed to a literary treatment of this issue by P.G. Wodehouse, who published a series of miniatures about the Butler

---

22. Werner Faulstich, 'Medium', in Werner Faulstich (ed.) *Grundwissen Medien,* München: Fink, 2004, pp. 13, 23-25.
23. Christian Windler, 'Gemeinde und königliche Gerichte in Spanien im ausgehenden Ancien Régime', in *Zeitschrift für Historische Forschung* 24 (1997): 56; for general information on go-betweens, see Valentin Groebner, 'Mobile Werte, informelle Ökonomie. Zur 'Kultur' der Armut in der spätmittelalterlichen Stadt', in Otto Gerhard Oexle (ed.) *Armut im Mittelalter,* Ostfildern: Thorbecke, 2004, pp. 175-180.
24. Statistisches Departement im k.k. Handelsministerium (ed.) *Die Arbeitsvermittlung in Österreich,* Wien: n.p., 1898, p. 26.
25. Eberhard Schmieder, 'Unterkäufer im Mittelalter. Ein Beitrag zur Wirtschafts- und Handelsgeschichte vornehmlich Süddeutschlands', in *Vierteljahrsschrift für Sozial- und Wirtschaftsgeschichte* 30 (1937): 229-260.

Jeeves in 1923, a manservant who may be regarded as a positive information center. Jeeves functions as an interface between the master of the house and the rest of the staff, and in the course of his work, he gains deep insights into the financial and other affairs of the noble family. It was consistent, then, that one of the search engines competing with Google in the 1990s was called AskJeeves.com; this name also alluded to the ambivalence of these institutions. On the one hand, a human search engine is a helping hand, on the other however, she or he is a bearer of secrets, consistently suspect of being an informer, a spy, and of betraying these secrets to other powers. This suspicious attitude was an especially pronounced phenomenon around 1800, when in those noble or bourgeois families who were able to afford servants, there prevailed a paranoia that servants might spy on them.[26] Even today, this anxiety sometimes surfaces, as it did in a short story by Woody Allen in which Allen's nanny plans to write a scandal-mongering novel about him.[27]

The second group, loan lackeys, made their knowledge available only temporarily, and their services were mainly enlisted by travelers, as examples from Vienna and Prague show. The travel writer Johann Kaspar Riesbeck reported that within three days of his arrival in Vienna, he had found rooms for rent with the help of such a loan lackey.[28] A travel guide of Prague dated 1817 contains the following advice:

> When [the stranger] wants to be instructed about the places he wishes to visit, he should turn to the attendant at the tavern, in general called a loan lackey, who will accompany the guest to his desired destination. The loan lackey will also make all provisions so the stranger will be supplied with all the articles he asks for.[29]

Concierges
Another type of 'human search engine' in larger towns and cities were concierges; in a travel report by Friedrich Nicolai from Vienna in the 1780s, he says: 'Who therefore has to look for someone in a big house, only has to ask for the concierge, who will know all the tenants, who often are not acquainted with each other.'[30] Also when looking for an apartment, concierges could play an important role, as they kept in touch with each other and therefore knew about empty apartments, which made them a 'central con-

---

26. Markus Krajewski, 'Ask Jeeves. Servants as Search Engines', trans. Charles Marcrum, *Grey Room* 38 (Winter 2010): 6-19.
27. Woody Allen, 'Nanny Dearest', in Woody Allen, *Mere Anarchy*, New York: Random House, 2007, pp. 55-64.
28. Johann Kaspar Riesbeck, *Briefe eines Reisenden Franzosen über Deutschland an seinen Bruder zu Paris.*, vol. 1 s.l.: n.p., 1784, pp. 191-194.
29. *Prager Wegweiser zum Unterricht und Bequemlichkeit der Fremden und Kenntniß der Einheimischen (...)*, Prague: Betterl v. Wildenbrunn, 1817, p 19: 'Wenn derselbe [der Fremde, AT] von den Oertern, die er besuchen will, unterrichtet zu werden wünscht, so verwendet er sich an den Aufwärter des Gasthauses, insgemein Lehnlaquai genannt, welcher den Gast nach dem Bestimmungsorte begleitet. Dieser Lehnlaquai trifft auch Veranstaltung, damit der einkehrende Fremde mit allen Artikeln, die er verlangt, versehen würde.'
30. Friedrich Nicolai, *Beschreibung einer Reise durch Deutschland und die Schweiz, im Jahre 1781*, Berlin-Stettin: n.p., 1783. Reprint: Hildesheim: Olms, 1994 (Collected Works 16, Edited by Bernhard Fabian and Marie-Luise Spieckermann), p. 142 et sequ.: 'Wer also in einem grossen Haus jemand zu suchen hat, muß nur nach dem Hausmeister fragen, welcher alle Miethsleute kennet, die sich oft untereinander nicht kennen.'

tact point for accommodation seekers not connected to the house'.[31] Their services, however, are not as innocent as they seem at first glance, as the writings of Josef Richter, another chronicler of Vienna, show. In 1785, he called the concierges a proper 'plague of the houses'. 'Most unbearable and rude are the concierges, who are at the same time friends, advisors, and spies for the house inspectors and administrators, even though they be imperial and royal.'[32]

The profession of a concierge emerged in Vienna when large tenant houses were built, and the owner of the house often no longer lived in the house himself. The institution of the concierge was created as a link between him and the tenants. The concierge would collect the rent, and his duties included '[knowing] everything about any events in the house and if need be, to report to the owner. He knew all tenants in person, often he knew all personal and professional affairs of a family before they had even moved in.' The Viennese concierges also cooperated with the police in a reciprocal relationship. The police were informed about suspect tenants, and the concierge got advance information about prospective tenants.[33]

Institutions of Information Brokerage

Archives, libraries, and museums, as well as schools and universities, are the classic sites of occidental knowledge and information communication. Especially the catalogs of libraries with their different systems of registering and allowing access to books stored in them have informed our understanding of searching and finding for centuries. Manuscript catalogs in book form, which for a long time had been the ideal, were only replaced by index cards in the course of the 19th century, before online electronic catalogs were established at the end of the 20th century.[34]

By contrast, those sites and institutions that served to broker everyday information have attracted less interest. A selection of these will be presented in this article.

Inns and Coffee Houses

The activities of inns and coffee houses extended far beyond serving drinks and offering food. Historians of these public houses report auctioneers offering their wares, dentists practicing their profession, and travelers looking for information about foreign places. The English diarist Samuel Pepys wrote in his diary that he went to the inn solely to satisfy his desire to hear the news.[35] Inns served as information and contact exchanges. Contracts were concluded, news passed on, disputes were held,

---

31. Konstanze Mittendorfer, *Biedermeier oder: Das Glück im Haus. Bauen und Wohnung in Wien und Berlin 1800-1850,* Wien: Verlag für Gesellschaftskritik, 1991, p. 146.
32. [Joseph Richter], *Wienerische Musterkarte ein Beytrag zur Schilderung Wiens. 6 Stück,* Wien: n.p., 1785, pp. 7, 9: 'Am unerträglichsten und gröbsten sind die Hausmeister, die zugleich Freunde, Rathgeber und Spione der Hausinspektoren und Administratoren sind, falls sie auch k.k. wären.'
33. Peter Payer, *Hausmeister in Wien. Aufstieg und Niedergang einer Respektsperson,* Wien, 1996 (Wiener Geschichtsblätter Beihefte 1996, Nr. 4), p. 7: 'über alle Vorkommnisse im Haus Bescheid zu wissen und dem Hausherrn im Bedarfsfall Meldung zu erstatten. Ihm waren alle Parteien persönlich bekannt, oft wußte er über eine Familie schon bevor sie einzog sämtliche privaten und beruflichen Verhältnisse'.
34. For a concise overview on the history of libraries and their catalogs, see: Uwe Jochum, *Kleine Bibliotheksgeschichte,* Stuttgart: Reclam U-B 8915, 1993.
35. Beat Kümin, 'Drinking and Public Space in Early Modern German Lands', in *Contemporary Drug Problems,* 32 (2005): 16-20.

and protests were organized; inns were (and are) at the same time meeting points, transit points for goods, banks, employment agencies, and gathering spaces. State functions, too, were held there. In some villages that didn't have a courthouse, court sessions were held in the presence of the public at the inn. The inn also sometimes served as a place for publicizing laws. The inn was also used as lodgings for traveling diplomats, and finally, it held the media function of a point of exchange for news. No wonder, then, that clerical powers tried again and again to stigmatize the inn as a place of sin.[36]

The coffee house's distinction was as a site of political debates. As early as the mid-18th century, to be more exact in 1743, one observer, Theodor Johann Quistorp asserted that 'a coffee house was as it were a political stock exchange, where the bravest and most spirited heads from all cities converged'.[37]

Intelligence Offices: the Example of the Paris Bureau d'Adresse, 1630-1643

Emerging in the 17th century and lasting until the early 19th century, so-called intelligence offices were another specific type of information exchange in addition to inns and coffee houses. These institutions brokered employment, apartments, wares, and money against a fee, and occasionally published advertisers.[38]

The earliest and at the same time most famous of these intelligence offices was the *Bureau d'adresse* established by Théophraste Renaudot in Paris circa 1630. Renaudot – who is known as the founder of one of the first French newspapers, the *Gazette (de France)* – was convinced that, beyond detention of the poor in workhouses – the *grand enfermement* as described by Foucault – it was also necessary to provide suitable institutions for the placement of workers. After having secured the support of Cardinal Richelieu, Renaudot was able to open his *Bureau d'adresse* at the Maison du Grand-Coq on the Quai du Marché Neuf in the Rue de la Calandre.

The activities of this *bureau* were numerous and diverse. First, it provided information for people who were looking for it. Those who looked for street addresses or a traveling companion, who needed to learn the names or residences of famous

---

36. Susanne Rau and Gerd Schwerhoff, 'Frühneuzeitliche Gasthaus-Geschichte(n) zwischen stigmatisierenden Fremdzuschreibungen und fragmentierten Geltungserzählungen', in Gert Melville and Hans Vorländer (eds) *Geltungsgeschichten. Über die Stabilisierung und Legitimierung institutioneller Ordnungen,* Köln-Weimar-Wien: Böhlau, 2002, pp. 181, 186, 190, 199; Martin Scheutz, '"hab ichs auch im würthshauß da und dort gehört [...]" Gaststätten als multifunktionale öffentliche Orte im 18. Jahrhundert', in Martin Scheutz, Wolfgang Schmale, and Dana Štefanová (eds), *Orte des Wissens,* (Jahrbuch der österreichischen Gesellschaft zur Erforschung des 18. Jahrhunderts 18/19), Bochum: n.p., 2004, pp. 169-203.
37. Quoted from: Hans Erich Bödeker, 'Das Kaffeehaus als Institution aufklärerischer Geselligkeit', in Étienne François (ed.) *Sociabilité et société bourgeoise en France, en Allemagne, et en Suisse, 1750-1850. Geselligkeit, Vereinswesen und bürgerliche Gesellschaft in Frankreich, Deutschland und der Schweiz, 1750-1850,* Paris: Editions Recherche sur les Civilisations, 1986, p. 72: 'daß ein Cafféhaus gleichsam eine politische Börse sey, wo die wackersten und witzigsten Köpfe aus allen Ständen zusammenkommen'.
38. For an overview on address bureaus: Astrid Blome, 'Offices of Intelligence and Expanding Social Spaces', in Brendan Dooley (ed.) *The Dissemination of News and the Emergence of Contemporaneity in Early Modern Europe,* Farnham: Ashgate, 2010, pp. 207-222; Anton Tantner: *Adressbüros.*

individuals such as theologians, physicians, or attorneys, were able to turn to the *bureau* and hope for an answer. The *bureau* also served as a sales agency. Whoever had something to sell was able to have his or her wares entered into a register against a fee of three *sous*; whoever looked for certain goods, was able to take a look into the register, also for a fee. On sale were not only mobile goods such as antiques, books, or machinery, but also animals – once, even a dromedary was offered – as well as real estate including country estates and houses. The *bureau* was also used as an employment agency. Open positions were entered into a separate register, and teachers, servants, and journeymen looking for work were able to direct their requests to the *bureau*. The *bureau* occasionally published its own journal, the *Feuille du Bureau d'Adresse,* in which excerpts of register entries were published. In addition to this, the *bureau* supported medical care – Renaudot was a physician by education – which was mainly directed at the poor. After a first consultation, the sick were referred to physicians, surgeons, or apothecaries who treated them pro bono. The *bureau* also worked as a pawnshop. When someone needed short-term funds, they were able to deposit property at the office and mortgage it. Finally, the office assumed the role of a scientific academy. From 1633, lectures were held in the rooms of the bureau every Monday at two pm – the *conférences du Bureau d'adresse,* which covered a number of different subjects, such as medicine, physical phenomena, or economics. On 3 February 1642, a question was discussed that famously has been of tremendous interest to humanity since time immemorial: 'What was made first, the egg or the chicken?'[39]

Because of the extensive activities of the *bureau*, it repeatedly ran afoul of individuals whose business it interfered with. Thus, the journeymen's associations, which traditionally served as employment agencies, were by no means happy about the competitor that the *bureau* constituted for them in this area. Above all, however, it was the medical faculty that took action against the *bureau*, especially when Renaudot wanted to further extend his medical counseling activities. Nevertheless, Renaudot's adversaries only succeeded when his protector, Cardinal Richelieu, died. In 1643, Renaudot's *Bureau d'adresse* had to abandon most of its activities.[40]

The Universal Register Office, London 1750
One successor of the Bureau d'Adresse was the Universal Register Office founded by the Fielding brothers in 1750. According to its self-description the office's declared aim was 'to bring the World [...] together into one place'.[41] This sounds quite similar to

---

39. 'Qui a esté le premier fait de L'Oeuf ou de la Poule?', in Eusèbe Renaudot (ed.) *Cinquiesme et dernier tome du Recueil général des questions traittées ès conférences du Bureau d'addresse (...)*, Paris: Besogne, 1655, pp. 91-94.
40. On Renaudot and his *Bureau d'adresse* see: Howard M. Solomon, *Public Welfare, Science and Propaganda in Seventeenth Century France: The Innovations of Théophraste Renaudot*. Princeton: Princeton University Press, 1972; Justin Stagl, *Eine Geschichte der Neugier*, pp. 175-187; Gilles Feyel, *L'Annonce et la nouvelle. La presse d'information en France sous l'ancien régime (1630-1788)*, Oxford: Oxford University Press, 2000, pp. 11-308; Gérard Jubert (ed.) *Père des journalistes et médecin des pauvres. Théophraste Renaudot (1586 – 1653)*, Paris: Champion, 2005.
41. Henry Fielding, 'A Plan of the Universal Register-Office', in Bertrand A. Goldgar (ed.) *The Covent-Garden Journal and A Plan of the Universal Register-Office*, Oxford: Clarendon Press, 1988, pp. 3-10; on this institution see also Miles Ogborn, *Spaces of Modernity. London's Geographies 1680-1780*, New York/London: Guilford Press, 1998, pp. 201-230, 295-302.

the well-known self-description of Google: 'Google's mission is to organize the world's information and make it universally accessible and useful.'[42] The self-description of the Universal Register Office continues: 'In large and populous cities [...] every human Talent is dispersed somewhere or other among the Members; and consequently every Person who stands in Need of that Talent, might supply his Want, if he knew where to find it; but to know this is the Difficulty, and this Difficulty still encreases with the Largeness of the Society.' The Fielding brothers' Universal Register Office promised to afford remedy: It would bring together buyers and sellers, teachers and pupils, tradesmen and their partners, finally masters and apprentices or servants.[43]

Like its Parisian predecessor the Universal Register Office served as a sales agency, a labor office, a pawnshop and also a travel agency. Anyone wishing to have their names entered onto, or to consult the Universal Register Office's registries could do so for a fee between three pence and one shilling. One of the main tasks of this institution was labor exchange; the Fielding brothers understood this service also as a means of fighting crime: According to them depraved servants were responsible for most crimes; potential masters were informed, that no servant would be registered who seemed suspicious or who was living in a disreputable place. Dismissed servants would not be registered any longer if the former masters informed the office. By doing so the Universal Register Office would be a 'public eye' concerning servants.[44] In addition the methods adopted by the Fielding brothers were also directed at crime prevention by protecting newcomers from the countryside from fraud. To that end, Henry Fielding set up an information office exclusively concerned with uncovering crimes: All facts on fraud and crimes, all criminals, every robbery committed, any object lost were to be gathered at one place, and the names and descriptions of offenders recorded in a register;[45] so the Universal Register Office was also designed as a government utopia contributing to a surveillance society.

The Anfrage- und Auskunftscomptoir, Vienna, 1819
An institution similar to the information offices developed at the beginning of the 19th century, namely the offices of inquiry and information (*Anfrage- und Auskunftscomptoire*). So far, such institutions are known for Vienna, Wrocław/Breslau and Munich. Joseph Jüttner and Baron Karl von Steinau founded the *Anfrage- und Auskunftscomptoir* in Vienna in 1819, and they offered its services by arguing, amongst others reasons, that loan servants were unreliable. An 1822 travel guide has the following to say:

> For a modest fee of 20 kr[euzer]. to 1 fl. [guilder], the managers [of this establishment] offer information on resident citizens and foreigners, doctors of medicine and of the law, about civil servants, scholars, artists etc., on local affairs and the facilities of public institutes; on the authorities and state officers; on all kinds of company trading; on loans on mortgages and commodities; on available products of nature and artifice for buyers and sellers; on opportunities for travel; on employers and domestics looking for employment; on purchases and leases of houses,

---

42. See, http://www.google.com/corporate/.
43. Fielding, 'A Plan', pp. 3-6.
44. Ogborn, *Spaces*, p. 217.
45. Ogborn, *Spaces*, pp. 219-221.

realties etc., on apartments, warehouses, stables, factories etc., in short, on all civil and social dealings and affairs, of which knowledge is permitted.[46]

A satire aimed at this information office was published in *Eipeldauer* magazine in 1820:

> About the *Auskunftscomptoir*, which fortunately was established in Vienna a short while ago, I happen to know a few anecdotes. For one day, a Hungarian hay farmer went there and said: "Gentlemen, I would like to know, if my young wife, while I am in Vienna and sell my hay, is faithful to me in my Hungarian land! So please, be so kind, and look it up." Another came and wanted to know whether his rich cousin in Günz was going to die this year, and make him his heir. Oh my lord and cousin, if only the gentlemen at the *Comptoir* could find all such things, they would undoubtedly be even busier. I for my part, would have looked up whether the public will be satisfied with me for long, and whether the *Eipeldauer* will continue to increase its readership.[47]

– Here, the *Comptoir* was alleged to be able to supply information about the future; as is often the case, a new medium triggered utopias of omniscience.

Press Clipping Services
Press clipping services constitute an additional specialized institution of information exchange.[48] The initial problem these institutions promised to redress was quite clear and was expressed for example by one of Dostoyevsky's characters at the beginning of the 1870s. There was a mass of newspapers appearing daily that reported on a number of interesting events, but finding them after some time was nearly impossible.[49] Press clipping services were finally created not for retrospective use, but for searching for a subject at the current moment in time. The first such office to become famous was founded under the name *Argus de la Presse* in Paris in 1879. According to

---

46. Johann Pezzl, *Neueste Beschreibung von Wien*, 6th edition, Wien: Armbruster, n.d. (1822), p. 166: 'Die Unternehmer [dieser Anstalt] geben, gegen das mäßige Honorar von 20. kr. bis zu 1 fl. Auskunft über hier sich aufhaltende In- und Ausländer, über Doctoren der Medicin und der Rechte, über Beamte, Gelehrte, Künstler tc., über das Locale und die Einrichtung öffentlicher Institute; über Behörden und Staatsbeamte; über alle Arten von Compagnie-Geschäften; über Darlehen auf Hypotheken und Waaren; über vorhandene Natur- und Kunstproducte für Käufer und Verkäufer; über Reisegelegenheiten; über Dienstgeber und Dienstsucher; über Käufe und Pachtungen von Häusern, Realitäten tc., über Wohnungen, Magazine, Stallungen, Fabriken tc., kurz, über alle bürgerliche und gesellschaftliche Geschäfte und Verhältnisse, welche zu wissen erlaubt ist.'
47. [Adolph Bäuerle], *Briefe des jüngsten Eipeldauers an seinen Herrn Vettern in Kakran*, 5th issue, Wien: n.p. 1820, p. 230 et sequ.: 'Von dem in Wien seit einiger Zeit, mit sehr vielem Glück bestehenden Auskunfts-Comptoir weiß ich auch ein Paar Anekdoten. Da ist nämlich die Tag ein ungarischer Heubauer hinkommen und hat g'sagt: "Meine Herren, möchte ich gern wissen, ob mein junges Weibel, während ich in Wien bin und mein Heu verkauf, mir in Ungerland treu ist! Gehen's seyn's so gut und schlagens einmal nach." Wieder ein anderer ist kommen, der gern hat wissen wollen, ob sein reicher Vetter in Günz heuer noch stirbt, und ihn, zum Erben einsetzt. O mein Herr Vetter, wann die Herren in dem Comptoir lauter solche Sachen auffinden könnten, sie müßten noch mehr zu thun bekommen. Ich z.B. ließ mir aufschlagen, ob das Publikum mit mir recht lang zufrieden seyn, und ob der Eipeldauer immer mehr und mehr Leser bekommen wird'.
48. Anke te Heesen, *Der Zeitungsausschnitt. Ein Papierobjekt der Moderne*, Frankfurt am Main: Fischer, 2006.
49. Fyodor Dostoyevsky, *Demons*, trans. Richard Pevear and Larissa Volkhonsky, New York: Vintage Classics, 1995 (1872), p. 128f.

its founding legend, its inventor, Comte François-Gaston-Auguste de Chambure, often watched artists while they were looking through the newspapers at newsstands for articles about their work. De Chambure proceeded to cut reviews from a few newspapers and to forward them to the respective artists, and this evolved into a real enterprise. From Paris, press clipping services spread to other cities. For example, an employee of the *Argus de la Presse*, the writer and journalist Max Karfunkel, established this service for Berlin.[50] From a description of the early days of these services, it appears that the job of reading the newspapers was mostly done by women:

> Finally, 60 young women sat in Romeike's New York house, bowed over 1,090 newspapers and 5,000 magazines. Whenever they raise their eyes from the columns, they are caught by the list of names and subjects they have to consider; but this list contains only those which are most difficult to remember, all others they need to know by heart; 7,000 names and subjects in all. All girls have to make use of their lynx' eyes for all clients. Twice a day, a bell sounds, an overseer appears and reads off new customers and subjects. These girls don't cut out, they only mark with a pencil. The cutting is done by a group of boys. Then there is another group of girls who sort the clippings into pigeonholes.[51]

Conclusion

Obviously, this historical overview is far from complete; one could for example add the finding aids used for people search, such as address books including Nicolas de Blegny's *Livre Commode* dating from 1691/1692, state calendars, or the Red Cross Tracing Service dedicated to the search for missing people after the world wars.[52] What this survey has clearly shown, however, is that although the tools for searching can be very useful, they are not innocent. Loan lackeys and concierges provided their clients with helpful information but sometimes revealed their desires to police officers. Intelligence offices facilitated the exchange of goods but were suspected of making public what should stay secret within the families.[53]

---

50. Anke te Heesen, *Der Zeitungsausschnitt*, pp. 78-80.
51. P.A., 'Herr der tausend Scheren. Der Letzte der Romeikes, Zeitungsausschnitt', in *Sammlung Feldhaus*, Akten 7253, I. Depositum 40 Feldhaus, Blatt 1-3; my thanks to Anke te Heesen for giving me access to photocopies; the source given by te Heesen, p. 82 et sequ. – *Daheim* 36 (1899/1900), no 28, p. 22 et sequ. – is unfortunately erroneous.
52. Abraham Pradel, (= Nicolas de Blegny), *Les Adresses de la Ville de Paris avec le Tresor des Almanachs. Livre Commode En tous lieux, en tous temps, & en toutes conditions*, Paris: n.p., 1691; Reprint of the 2nd edition 1692: Abraham du Pradel (= Nicolas de Blegny), *Le livre commode des adresses de Paris pour 1692*, Édouard Fournier (ed.) Vol. 1-2, Paris: Paul Daffis, 1878. Digitized version: http://gallica2.bnf.fr/ark:/12148/bpt6k27823x and http://gallica2.bnf.fr/ark:/12148/bpt6k278248; Volker Bauer, 'Herrschaftsordnung, Datenordnung, Suchoptionen. Recherchemöglichkeiten in Staatskalendern und Staatshandbüchern des 18. Jahrhunderts', in Thomas Brandstetter et al. (eds) *Vor Google*, pp. 85-108; for a bibliography on the Red Cross Tracing Service compiled by three students in my seminar 'Digitale Medien in der Geschichtswissenschaft. Suchmaschinen im analogen Zeitalter' during the winter term of 2008/09, see: http://www.univie.ac.at/igl.geschichte/tantner/wiki /index.php?title=Suchdienst_des_Roten_Kreuz.
53. This was the case for the poet François Colletet's short-lived Bureau d'adresse: Quatorzième Journal et Suite des Avis et des Affaires de Paris. [29.10.1676], in: *Le Journal de Colletet, premier Petit journal parisien (1676)*. Supplement to: *Le Moniteur du Bibliophile. Gazette littéraire, anecdotique et curieuse*, 1.1878, p. 201.

Concerning this ambivalence, internet historian Mercedes Bunz uses the term 'frenemy' to describe the oscillation of applications such as Google between friendly usefulness and hostile control of users' desires:

> Because of their dangerously detailed knowledge, net companies possess a new form of power – it is not for nothing that Google is described as a 'frenemy'. These internet companies are dangerous like enemies because of their knowledge – and knowledge is power, today more than ever – but they appear to be friends. They make life easier. They are no rulers in a Hegelian sense. Theirs is a different form of power, and this power is dangerous – but it is not automatically subjugating, bad or evil.[54]

It appears that this Janus-faced quality can already be demonstrated of the search aids of the 'analogue age', which explains why they were sometimes met with some skepticism. Concierges, servants, information offices, and the like are situated in the contested field between private utilization and the authorities' claims, which are renegotiated with the appearance of each new search aid.

References

Allen, Woody. 'Nanny Dearest', in Woody Allen, *Mere Anarchy*, New York: Random House, 2007, pp. 55-64.

Bauer, Volker (ed.). *Repertorium territorialer Amtskalender und Amtshandbücher im Alten Reich. Adreß-, Hof-, Staatskalender und Staatshandbücher des 18. Jahrhunderts*, Vol. 1-4, Frankfurt am Main: Klostermann, 1997-2005.

____. 'Herrschaftsordnung, Datenordnung, Suchoptionen. Recherchemöglichkeiten in Staatskalendern und Staatshandbüchern des 18. Jahrhunderts', in Thomas Brandstetter et al. (eds) *Vor Google. Eine Mediengeschichte der Suchmaschine im analogen Zeitalter*, Bielefeld: Transcript, 2012, pp. 85-108.

[Bäuerle, Adolph]. *Briefe des jüngsten Eipeldauers an seinen Herrn Vettern in Kakran*, 5th issue, Wien: n.p. 1820.

Blome, Astrid. 'Offices of Intelligence and Expanding Social Spaces', in Brendan Dooley (ed.) *The Dissemination of News and the Emergence of Contemporaneity in Early Modern Europe*, Farnham: Ashgate, 2010.

Bödeker, Hans Erich. 'Das Kaffeehaus als Institution aufklärerischer Geselligkeit', in Étienne François (ed.) *Sociabilité et société bourgeoise en France, en Allemagne, et en Suisse, 1750-1850. Geselligkeit, Vereinswesen und bürgerliche Gesellschaft in Frankreich, Deutschland und der Schweiz, 1750-1850*, Paris: Editions Recherche sur les Civilisations, 1986, pp. 65-80.

Brandstetter, Thomas, Thomas Hübel, and Anton Tantner (eds). *Vor Google. Eine Mediengeschichte der Suchmaschine im analogen Zeitalter*, Bielefeld: Transcript, 2012.

Bunz, Mercedes. 'Sozial 2.0: Herr, Knecht, Feind, Freund. Soziale Netzwerke und die Ökonomie der Freundschaft', in *De:Bug. Elektronische Lebensaspekte*, 120 (11 March 2008), http://de-bug.de/mag/5422.html; short version reprinted in: *analyse & kritik* 541 (21 August 2009): 14.

Burke, Peter. *The Historical Anthropology of Early Modern Italy: Essays on Perception and Communication*, Cambridge: Cambridge University Press, 1987.

____. *A Social History of Knowledge: From Gutenberg to Diderot*, Cambridge: Polity Press, 2000.

Cooper, Alix. 'Fragen ohne Antworten. Die Suche nach lokalen Informationen in der frühen Aufklärung', in Thomas Brandstetter et al. (eds) *Vor Google. Eine Mediengeschichte der Suchmaschine im analogen Zeitalter*, Bielefeld: Transcript, 2012, pp. 73-83.

Corns, Thomas N. 'The Early Modern Search Engine: Indices, Title Pages, Marginalia and Contents',

---

54. Mercedes Bunz, 'Sozial 2.0: Herr, Knecht, Feind, Freund. Soziale Netzwerke und die Ökonomie der Freundschaft', in *De:Bug. Elektronische Lebensaspekte* 120 (11 March 2008), http://de-bug.de/mag/5422.html, short version reprinted in: *analyse & kritik*, 541 (21 August 2009): 14.

in Neil Rhodes and Jonathan Sawday (eds) *The Renaissance Computer. Knowledge Technology in the First Age of Print*, London-New York: Routledge, 2000, pp. 95-105.

Darnton, Robert. *The Business of Enlightenment: A Publishing History of the Encyclopédie, 1775-1800*, Cambridge, MA: Harvard University Press, 1987 (1979).

Dostoyevsky, Fyodor. *Demons*, trans. Richard Pevear and Larissa Volkhonsky, New York: Vintage Classics, 1995 (1872).

Enzensberger, Hans Magnus. *Der kurze Sommer der Anarchie. Buenaventura Durrutis Leben und Tod*, 10th edition, Frankfurt am Main: Suhrkamp st 395, 1994.

Faulstich, Werner. 'Medium', in Werner Faulstich (ed.) *Grundwissen Medien*, 5th edition, München: Fink, 2004, pp. 13-102.

Feyel, Gilles. *L'Annonce et la nouvelle. La presse d'information en France sous l'ancien régime (1630-1788)*, Oxford: Oxford University Press, 2000.

Fielding, Henry. 'A Plan of the Universal Register-Office', in Bertrand A. Goldgar (ed.) *The Covent-Garden Journal and A Plan of the Universal Register-Office*, Oxford: Clarendon Press, 1988, pp. 3-10.

Gierl, Martin. 'Enzyklopädie', in Friedrich Jaeger (ed.) *Enzyklopädie der Neuzeit*, Stuttgart et al.: Metzler, 2005 et sequ., vol. 3, 2006, col. 344-356.

Giesecke, Michael. *Der Buchdruck in der frühen Neuzeit. Eine historische Fallstudie über die Durchsetzung neuer Informations- und Kommunikationstechnologien*, 4th edition, Frankfurt am Main: Suhrkamp, 2006.

Groebner, Valentin. 'Mobile Werte, informelle Ökonomie. Zur 'Kultur' der Armut in der spätmittelalterlichen Stadt', in Otto Gerhard Oexle (ed.) *Armut im Mittelalter*, Ostfildern: Thorbecke, 2004, pp. 165-187.

Gugerli, David. *Suchmaschinen. Die Welt als Datenbank*, Frankfurt am Main: Suhrkamp eu 19, 2009.

Hacker, Rupert. *Bibliothekarisches Grundwissen*, 4th edition, München: Saur, 2000.

Heesen, Anke te. *Der Zeitungsausschnitt. Ein Papierobjekt der Moderne*, Frankfurt am Main: Fischer, 2006.

Hochedlinger, Michael and Tantner, Anton (eds). *'... Der größte Teil der Untertanen lebt elend und mühselig'. Die Berichte des Hofkriegsrates zur sozialen und wirtschaftlichen Lage der Habsburgermonarchie 1770-1771*, Innsbruck-Wien-Bozen: Studienverlag, 2005 (Mitteilungen des Österreichischen Staatsarchivs Sonderband 8).

Horn, Eva. *Der geheime Krieg. Verrat, Spionage und moderne Fiktion*, Frankfurt am Main: Fischer, 2007.

Jele, Harald. *Wissenschaftliches Arbeiten in Bibliotheken. Einführung für StudentInnen*, München-Wien: Oldenbourg, 1999.

Jochum, Uwe. *Kleine Bibliotheksgeschichte*, Stuttgart: Reclam U-B 8915, 1993.

Jubert, Gérard (ed.). *Père des journalistes et médecin des pauvres. Théophraste Renaudot (1586 – 1653)*, Paris: Champion, 2005.

Krajewski, Markus. *Paper Machines. About Cards & Catalogs, 1548-1929*, trans. Peter Krapp, Cambridge, MA: MIT Press, 2011.

____. *Der Diener. Mediengeschichte einer Figur zwischen König und Klient*, Frankfurt am Main: S. Fischer, 2010.

____. 'Ask Jeeves. Servants as Search Engines', translated by Charles Marcrum, II, in *Grey Room* 38 (Winter 2010): 6-19.

Kümin, Beat. 'Drinking and Public Space in Early Modern German Lands', in *Contemporary Drug Problems* 32 (2005): 9-27.

Küster, Marc W. *Geordnetes Weltbild. Die Tradition des alphabetischen Sortierens von der Keilschrift bis zur EDV. Eine Kulturgeschichte*, Tübingen: Niemeyer, 2006.

Mattl-Wurm, Sylvia and Pfoser, Alfred (eds). *Die Vermessung Wiens. Lehmanns Adressbücher 1859–1942*, Wien: Metroverlag, 2011.

Mittendorfer, Konstanze. *Biedermeier oder: Das Glück im Haus. Bauen und Wohnung in Wien und Berlin 1800-1850*, Wien: Verlag für Gesellschaftskritik, 1991.

Nicolai, Friedrich. *Beschreibung einer Reise durch Deutschland und die Schweiz, im Jahre 1781*, Berlin-Stettin: n.p., 1783. Reprint: Hildesheim: Olms, 1994 (Collected Works 16, Edited by Bernhard Fabian and Marie-Luise Spieckermann).

Ogborn, Miles. *Spaces of Modernity. London's Geographies 1680-1780*, New York/London: Guilford Press, 1998.

P.A., 'Herr der tausend Scheren. Der Letzte der Romeikes, Zeitungsausschnitt', in *Sammlung Feldhaus*, Akten 7253, I. Depositum 40 Feldhaus, sheet 1-3.

Payer, Peter. *Hausmeister in Wien. Aufstieg und Niedergang einer Respektsperson*, Wien. 1996 (Wiener Geschichtsblätter Beihefte 1996, Nr. 4).

Petersen, Thomas et al. 'Der Fragebogen Karls des Großen. Ein Dokument aus der Vorgeschichte der Umfrageforschung', in *Kölner Zeitschrift für Soziologie und Sozialpsychologie* 56 (2004): 736-745.
Petschar, Hans. 'Einige Bemerkungen, die sorgfältige Verfertigung eines Bibliothekskatalogs für das allgemeine Lesepublikum betreffend', in Hans Petschar, Ernst Strouhal and Heimo Zobernig (eds) *Der Zettelkatalog. Ein historisches System geistiger Ordnung,* Wien-New York: Springer, 1999, pp. 17-42.
Pezzl, Johann. *Neueste Beschreibung von Wien,* 6th edition, Wien: Armbruster, n.d. (1822).
Pradel, Abraham (=Blegny, Nicolas de). *Les Adresses de la Ville de Paris avec le Tresor des Almanachs. Livre Commode En tous lieux, en tous temps, & en toutes conditions,* Paris: n.p., 1691; reprint of the 2nd edition 1692: Abraham du Pradel (= Nicolas de Blegny), *Le livre commode des adresses de Paris pour 1692,* Édouard Fournier (ed.) Vol. 1-2, Paris: Paul Daffis, 1878.
Prager Wegweiser zum Unterricht und Bequemlichkeit der Fremden und Kenntniß der Einheimischen (...). Prague: Betterl v. Wildenbrunn, 1817.
Rau, Susanne and Schwerhoff, Gerd. 'Frühneuzeitliche Gasthaus-Geschichte(n) zwischen stigmatisierenden Fremdzuschreibungen und fragmentierten Geltungserzählungen', in Gert Melville and Hans Vorländer (eds) *Geltungsgeschichten. Über die Stabilisierung und Legitimierung institutioneller Ordnungen,* Köln-Weimar-Wien: Böhlau, 2002, pp. 181-201.
Reinöhl, Fritz. 'Die österreichischen Informationsbüros des Vormärz, ihre Akten und Protokolle', in *Archivalische Zeitschrift* 38 (1929): 261-288.
Renaudot, Eusèbe (ed.). *Cinquiesme et dernier tome du Recueil général des questions traittées és conférences du Bureau d'addresse (...),* Paris: Besogne, 1655.
Reppesgaard, Lars. *Das Google-Imperium,* Hamburg: Murmann, 2008.
Rhodes, Neil and Jonathan Sawday. 'Paperworlds: Imagining the Renaissance Computer' in Neil Rhodes and Jonathan Sawday (eds), *The Renaissance Computer. Knowledge Technology in the First Age of Print,* London-New York: Routledge, 2000, pp. 1-17.
[Richter, Joseph]. *Wienerische Musterkarte ein Beytrag zur Schilderung Wiens. 6 Stück,* Wien: n.p., 1785.
Rieder, Bernhard. 'Zentralität und Sichtbarkeit. Mathematik als Hierarchisierungsinstrument am Beispiel der frühen Bibliometrie', in Thomas Brandstetter et al. (eds) *Vor Google. Eine Mediengeschichte der Suchmaschine im analogen Zeitalter,* Bielefeld: Transcript, 2012, pp. 223-252.
Riesbeck, Johann Kaspar. *Briefe eines Reisenden Franzosen über Deutschland an seinen Bruder zu Paris,* 2 volumes, 2nd edition, s.l.: n.p., 1784.
Scheutz, Martin. '"hab ichs auch im würthshauß da und dort gehört [...]" Gaststätten als multifunktionale öffentliche Orte im 18. Jahrhundert', in Martin Scheutz, Wolfgang Schmale and Dana Štefanová (eds) *Orte des Wissens,* (Jahrbuch der österreichischen Gesellschaft zur Erforschung des 18. Jahrhunderts 18/19), Bochum: n.p., 2004, pp. 169-203.
Schmieder, Eberhard. 'Unterkäufer im Mittelalter. Ein Beitrag zur Wirtschafts- und Handelsgeschichte vornehmlich Süddeutschlands', in *Vierteljahrsschrift für Sozial- und Wirtschaftsgeschichte* 30 (1937): 229-260.
Soll, Jacob. *The Information Master: Jean-Baptiste Colbert's Secret State Intelligence System,* Ann Arbor: University of Michigan Press, 2009.
Solomon, Howard M. *Public Welfare, Science and Propaganda in Seventeenth Century France: The Innovations of Théophraste Renaudot,* Princeton: Princeton University Press, 1972.
Stagl, Justin. *A History of Curiosity: The Theory of Travel, 1550-1800* (Studies in Anthropology and History), London-New York: Routledge, 1995.
Stalder, Felix and Mayer, Christine. 'The Second Index. Search Engines, Personalization and Surveillance', in Konrad Becker, Felix Stalder (eds) *Deep Search. The Politics of Search Beyond Google,* Innsbruck: Studienverlag, 2009, distributed by Transaction Publishers, New Jersey, pp. 98-115.
Statistisches Departement im k.k. Handelsministerium (ed.), *Die Arbeitsvermittlung in Österreich,* Wien: n.p., 1898.
Tantner, Anton. *Adressbüros im Europa der Frühen Neuzeit,* Habilitation treatise, submitted at the Faculty of Historical and Cultural Studies at the University of Vienna, Wien: Universität Wien, 2011, http://phaidra.univie.ac.at/o:128115.
_____. 'Suchen und finden vor Google. Eine Skizze', in *Mitteilungen der Vereinigung österreichischer Bibliothekarinnen & Bibliothekare,* 64 (2011): 42-69.
Vise, David and Malseed, Mark. *The Google Story,* New York: Delacorte Press, 2005.
Weidner, Daniel. '"Wende sie um und um, denn alles ist in ihr." Über das Suchen in heiligen Texten', in Thomas Brandstetter et al. (eds) *Vor Google. Eine Mediengeschichte der Suchmaschine im analogen Zeitalter,* Bielefeld: Transcript, 2012, pp. 41-72.
Weinberger, David. *Everything is Miscellaneous: The Power of the New Digital Disorder,* New York:

Henry Holt and Company, 2008.
Windler, Christian. 'Gemeinde und königliche Gerichte in Spanien im ausgehenden Ancien Régime', in *Zeitschrift für Historische Forschung* 24 (1997): 53-87.
Winkelbauer, Thomas. 'Postwesen und Staatsbildung in der Habsburgermonarchie im 17. und 18. Jahrhundert', in *Wiener Geschichtsblätter* 68 (2013): 69-86.
Zedelmaier, Helmut. 'Facilitas inveniendi. Zur Pragmatik alphabetischer Buchregister', in Theo Stammen and Wolfgang E.J. Weber (eds) *Wissenssicherung, Wissensordnung und Wissensverarbeitung. Das europäische Modell der Enzyklopädien,* Berlin: Akademie, 2004 (Colloquia Augustana 18), pp. 191-203.
Zwahr, Helmut. 'Das deutsche Stadtadreßbuch als orts- und sozialgeschichtliche Quelle', in *Jahrbuch für Regionalgeschichte* 3 (1968): 204-229.

Search Control in China

Min Jiang and Vicențiu Dînga

Search Control in China

Min Jiang and Vicențiu Dîngă

Min Jiang is an Associate Professor of Communication at UNC Charlotte and an affiliate researcher at the Center for Global Communication Studies, University of Pennsylvania. Min Jiang was a speaker at the second edition of the Society of the Query conference in Amsterdam, 7-8 November 2013. She participated in the session called 'Search Across the Border', where she talked about borders on web search in China, expanding on her previous research on search results in China.

Vicențiu Dîngă: Firstly, I'd like to talk about your work involving the comparative study of Baidu and Google's search results in China. Could you tell me more about this research?
Min Jiang: The impetus for this research came from my own varied experiences with search engines in China, the U.S. and elsewhere. How is search experienced differently became a question that I wanted to explore. Search engines are interesting media to me. They are an important interface between the user and available knowledge and information. More interestingly, they are also popularly regarded as neutral and almost god-like while search's political and commercial nature is often downplayed. I explored this aspect in the Chinese context. In an article published in *New Media & Society* I compare Baidu's and Google's search results in China, focusing on a few aspects: search filtering, ranking, overlap, and bias.[1]

First, we know that filtering has always been an issue with the Chinese internet, and search filtering is a part of it. Google, upon entering China in 2006, consented to filtering. But in January 2010, Google announced that it would stop censoring its search results in mainland China because of security threats. Subsequently Google moved its servers to Hong Kong because the region is a free speech zone in China. Many suspected the censorship burden shifted from Google to the 'Great Firewall', a filtering infrastructure erected at the Chinese borders so that international information coming through can be filtered ('The Great Firewall of China' is the colloquial term for the 'Golden Shield Project'), but nobody knew how effective the Great Firewall was. Part of my data shows that there were quite complex filtering patterns in China. Top 10 search results from both Google China and Baidu were collected inside mainland China in late 2010 using 316 popular event keywords. The table below indicates that after Google

---

1. Min Jiang, 'The Business and Politics of Search Engines: A Comparative Study of Baidu's and Google's Search Results of Internet Events in China', *New Media & Society*, 22 April 2012, http://nms.sagepub.com/content/early/2013/04/18/1461444813481196.full.

left mainland China, the filtering burden indeed shifted to the Chinese state. While inaccessibility of Baidu's search results was caused mainly by broken links, for Google, it was largely because of filtering by the Great Firewall. Baidu also performs this task of filtering as Chinese laws mandate content filtering by commercial operators within its borders. So, Baidu filters too, but its filtering patterns are much subtler and more nuanced than that performed by the Great Firewall.

	Baidu	Google
Total number of links	3160	3160
Links inaccessible from China	171	400
Bad links	125	91
Links inaccessible due to search engine filtering	22 (partial filtering or blockpage by Baidu)	10 (by Google SafeSearch auto-block)
Links inaccessible from China but accessible from the U.S. (blocked by GFW)	24	299 (among them, 180 'connection reset')
Links inaccessible due to GFW blocking	24	299

Table 1. Distribution of Baidu and Google's Link Accessibility (2011).

Second, in terms of search results overlapping and ranking, I found Google and Baidu are actually quite different. Based on the search results of 316 popular Chinese events, the overlap, or the appearances of the same URL in top 10 search results from both search engines, is quite low. Maybe this is not so shocking to those of us who study search engines, but for the general public, an overlap of search results between Google and Baidu of less than 7% might come as a big surprise. This tells us that based on the search engine you use, your search results and the knowledge you obtain as a result can vary in significant ways. When it comes to news and current events, search engines can be quite important in shaping what we know.

With regard to search bias, I focused on self-bias, or the extent to which a search engine links search results to its own content. This is because, as we know, Google and Baidu are no longer only search engines; they offer many other related information products and services. For instance, Baidu owns Q&A websites and real time messaging services. It has incentives to direct searchers to its own content, with effective regulation or strong competition absent. At the time of my study in late 2010, it turned out that Baidu rarely links to Chinese Wikipedia or other competitors in China, but often to Baidu Baike, its own Wikipedia-like service. On the other hand, Google back then was more likely to link to Chinese Wikipedia. It seems at times that Chinese Wikipedia is Google's default choice even though Chinese domestic competitor Hudong Baike was more popular with many more entries and users at the time. The latter case is not about Google's favored treatment of its own service, but its preferences certainly shaped users' information experiences and outcomes. In a follow-up study with a component examining Google's linking patterns to Wikipedia-type services, I found Google has since shifted its strategy.[2] Based on the longitudinal data I collected in 2011 and 2012, Google no longer seems to privilege Chinese Wikipedia and instead has given Baidu Baike and Hudong Baike an almost equal chance in mainland China.

Search bias is a real concern. Even Chinese official media CCTV has exposed Baidu for punishing advertisers who refused to pay for their search rankings. I think this issue will persist as long as search engines remain a critical information access point in our societies. More and more people will start to realize this is a huge problem. While China's political and market situation may be somewhat unique, search bias and unfair business practices can occur in every information society and market.

VD: How do these search engines behave throughout China?
MJ: Although search results can vary for a variety of reasons, regional differences are notable. Search results in Hong Kong, Taiwan, and Macau, for instance, differ in important ways from those retrieved from mainland China. This is not only because of politics, but also because of linguistic and cultural differences among other things. As an example, Hong Kong, previously a British colony, was returned to mainland China in 1997 but the two regions remain distinct under the 'one country, two systems' principle (where Hong Kong practices a capitalist economic and political system and mainland uses a socialist one). In Hong Kong, local laws continue to protect free speech – that's why Google moved its servers there and to this day is able to remain in 'China'. The legal systems in these regions differ in marked ways from mainland China's. Linguistically, Hong Kong natives continue to speak Cantonese and Taiwan natives Taiwanese. Traditional Chinese characters are more commonly used in Hong Kong, Macau and Taiwan rather than simplified Chinese characters, the latter used more dominantly in mainland China. In all its complexity, the notion of China may include Hong Kong, Macau, and often Taiwan (although mainland and Taiwan still have unresolved territorial and political disputes). These historical legacies continue to shape how search is used and regulated today. In the Chinese case, search tends to conform to these linguistic, cultural and legal boundaries rather than transcending them. Search is re-territorialized rather than de-territorialized. My colleague Han-Teng Liao from Oxford's Internet Research Institute has a paper that discusses the different patterns of search results that one gets in Chinese-speaking regions including mainland China, Hong Kong and Taiwan.[3]

VD: In your presentation for the Society of the Query conference you stated that 'the popular depiction of the search engine as a borderless, global medium is an illusion'. Can you expand on that?
MJ: Yes. I believe there is a huge gap between what we think search can offer versus how we use it in reality. We have this dream, almost a fantasy, that search engines are

---

2. Min Jiang, 'Search Concentration, Bias, and Parochialism: A Comparative Study of Baidu, Jike, and Google's Search Results from China', presented at the 41st Research Conference on Communication, Information and Internet Policy (TPRC), 27-29 September 2013, George Mason University School of Law, Arlington, VA, USA.
3. Han-Teng Liao, '"Wikipedias" (or its Copycat) Dominate "Chinese" Search Engine Result Pages (SERPs)', 6 May 2013, http://people.oii.ox.ac.uk/hanteng/2013/05/06/wikipedias-or-its-copycat-dominate-chinese-search-engine-result-pages-serps/.

a borderless and global medium. In reality, I think our experiences are very much conditioned by our location, by who we are, how we search, and what we know. In many ways, search is more local or parochial, if you will, rather than cosmopolitan or global. Search engines are popularly mentioned in the same breath as the internet as part of a *global village*, a McLuhanian dream built on an information system radiating throughout the world, producing positive outcomes. As with any new technology, however, as time went by, more and more governments also started to figure out how to use law and other means to set the boundaries for search and in extreme cases to filter any undesirable content. Structurally, we have a global digital infrastructure that is more or less connected, but in terms of content and information flows, I think it's quite a local or national experience for many, especially in countries such as China. At the inception of the internet and search engines, those who were able to use them were more educated and cosmopolitan to begin with. Today, in China alone, there are almost 600 million internet users and 450 million searchers. For many, their search experiences are not at all as borderless as projected.

Borders are frames. People think about them often in terms of physical borders and territory. On the internet, there are no physical borders; borders are invisible. In the realm of search, various search engines employ complex criteria to collect, sort, rank, and present results to us, adopting certain factors and excluding others, operating largely in secrecy and expanding their collection of user data to ever more spheres. Eli Pariser describes such criteria or algorithms as 'filters' and the resulting state of individualized information as 'filter bubbles'.[4]

Geo-linguistic borders, the kinds of existing differences in location and language, for instance those between Chinese mainland, Hong Kong, and Taiwan as noted previously, certainly form the basis for distinct sources and domains of information and knowledge from which search engines may crawl. They are reflected in search results. Politics, regional or national, could also play an important role, especially in places where freedom of political speech is not guaranteed. Another aspect of 'borders' has to do with technology itself in the form of geo-location. If you are located in Amsterdam, your search results are more likely to receive localized results based on your IP address. This aspect has become more and more prevalent over time, as search engines do not offer universal results to a query anymore. The degree and scope of personalization, however, remains largely a mystery. It has been revealed that Google uses over 70 different 'signals' to personalize results. Broadly, Google defines a person in three aspects: your geographical location, search history and your relationships or social networks. These are frames or 'borders' imposed on the user. A last aspect I want to emphasize is economic incentives for localized delivery of information. A lot of our search behavior is 'local' – whether you want to get a haircut or buy a product at a nearby grocery store. Localized advertising is pushing for localization in search results. While localization makes sense in some cases, it can turn out badly in others where the need to transcend parochialism is more important. In general, a variety of factors aside from personal idiosyncrasies – linguistic/cultural, political, technological and economic – have come to shape our search results to be more local or parochial.

---

4. Eli Pariser, *The Filter Bubble: What the Internet Is Hiding from You*, New York: Penguin, 2011.

VD: You mentioned that possible alternatives could be offered to reimagine what search engines could become. What possible alternatives do you have in mind?
MJ: When it comes to news, to current events, it is quite inadequate for the user to only receive results that are based on location. China is a very extreme example. In some cases, you do not get any alternative perspectives at all on critical events. During the Arab Spring, search results were filtered in such a way that the only news you got in China were from state sanctioned sources. It tended to focus on the government's efforts of rescuing the Chinese from the troubled regions and China's investments in those areas. Search results made little to no mention of the protests or demonstrations for fear of domestic repercussions. When these did get mentioned, they were presented as chaotic and threatening. Stability trumps everything. That is all you get. Given the current political arrangement in China, change will be hard to come by. Search reflects rather than challenges the political make-up of the regime.

But people elsewhere may have more options. Imagine, if Google can personalize your search results, then why doesn't Google give you the option to personalize your own results? For instance, why can't I design my own filters if I choose to be more internationally minded? Search engines could give users more freedom in the design of their own search results and the kinds of information they want to receive. Google, for instance, has been experimenting with personalized Google News since 2011 where 'borders' could be rendered less relevant by users themselves. Certainly, by choosing one's own filters, one has to live with a set of self-imposed 'filter bubbles'. But this may allow for a greater degree of self-determination rather than an opaque set of algorithmic rules over which we have no control. There have been suggestions that users should minimize or completely abandon the use of search engines because using them would subject users to a set of opaque algorithms (not unlike a robotic monster) that feeds on, lives off, and profits from our incessant use. This is a difficult dilemma. Will people stop using search engines entirely? Probably not. But could there be more algorithmic scrutiny, user control and privacy protection? Much more likely. In fact, there are alternative search engines out there (e.g. DuckDuckGo and Blekko) that offer users more privacy protection and options.

There is also a lot of room for independent evaluation of search and search quality. Many of us use one search engine on a regular basis, be it Google in much of the world or Baidu in China. As the amount of information explodes, the job of delivering better information becomes harder, not easier. The notable differences between search results delivered to the same person from different search engines naturally beg such questions as 'which is better?' and 'based on what standards?' The problem, however, is that perfectly ranked search results for any given query do not exist. Algorithms are a kind of simulacra in the Baudrillardian sense. Yet, we can still compare search engines and reveal their preferences or prejudices, and in some cases even abuses of their surveillance and monopolist power.

VD: What about the Chinese state search engines, how do they perform?
MJ: In China, there are three state-run search engines. One of them is well known as the first national Chinese search engine. It's called Jike, which in Chinese means 'instant' or 'immediate'. Some call it 'geek'. Its parent company is *People's Daily Online*, which is publicly listed on Shanghai Stock Exchange. Another one is Panguso; it's a search engine backed by Xinhua News Agency (a state news agency)

and China Mobile (also a state-owned enterprise publicly listed on both the New York Stock Exchange and the Hong Kong Stock Exchange). The third one is a search engine associated with CCTV, China's official television station, now with an online presence through CNTV. Recently, Jike got into financial troubles and has merged with Panguso.

So diverse parties of interest are at play here and the reasoning behind state-sponsored search engines is quite complex and convoluted. I explored the phenomenon of 'national search engines' in a paper that will appear in *Policy & Internet*. First, security was a major concern. All three state-backed search engines were put into play immediately after Google left mainland China as a response to Secretary Hilary Clinton's 'Internet freedom' speech. It was clear from publicly available Chinese Communist Party's documents that China's top leaders consider 'internet sovereignty' and control over information within Chinese borders a top priority. They attached great importance to the 'management' of the internet in China and understood the centrality of search engines in an information society.

Second, such an acute sense of security was heightened by two subsequent pivotal events – the Arab Spring and the Snowden revelations, both of which have prompted a global trend of re-nationalization of the internet. Repercussions of the Arab Spring are still unraveling but the quick toppling of several dictatorships sent a palpable jolt to Chinese leaders in Beijing who were obsessed with 'stability'. National search engines were part and parcel of increased government control asserted over the Chinese internet. In the post-Snowden world, there were several important signs of re-nationalization of the internet, including Russia's development of its own national search engine *Sputnik*, and discussions of a 'national internet' in both Germany and Brazil. To what extent 'national internets' will materialize in Germany and Brazil is not clear but in China, there is already a *de facto* 'national internet'.

Third, financial considerations also played an important role in China's state search engine experiment, where the Party wishes to profit from China's surging information and search markets. Since China started to implement economic reforms in the late 1970s, state media have become more independent financially, although not quite free from the state's ideological management. Chinese mainstream media, a euphemism for state-owned media, absolutely dominate China's traditional media from books and magazines to radio and TV, however not so much in online media. State propaganda has been trying to figure out how to engage users and do propaganda work online. *People's Daily*, the party's mouthpiece, has developed a successful website *People's Daily Online* whose online traffic is among the top 20 in China (based on Alexa data). It seems that, with national search engine Jike, *People's Daily Online* hopes to expand its sphere of influence and become more profitable financially. However, I think authorities may have underestimated the effort it takes to develop a commercially viable search engine. Jike failed technologically, strategically and managerially. Jike's failure, however, has not put an end to state search engine experiments in China. After Jike's merger with Panguso, the future of state search engines remains highly uncertain but is undoubtedly subject to both politics and competition.

VD: You mentioned the Great Firewall of China, and I remember reading somewhere that it is suspected that regimes such as Cuba, Zimbabwe, or Belarus have

obtained surveillance technology from China. So it seems that China actually exports this kind of approach.

MJ: That's right. When we talk about Chinese search engines or the Chinese internet in general, we tend to neglect or underestimate China's reach overseas. Apart from domestic growth driven by nearly 600 million Chinese internet users, China's rise technologically, politically, economically, and military is also manifested overseas. In fact, Chinese technology companies, state-owned or commercially operated, seek to grow abroad through international trade as many others do. This includes a unique category of surveillance and filtering technologies that the state or state-related companies have developed and wanted to export. While China has previously imported surveillance technologies from such Western companies as Cisco, Microsoft, and Nokia, it has been developing its own surveillance technologies that might end up in other countries as you mentioned. Chinese companies such as Huawei (a telecommunication company and the largest producer of telecommunications equipment in the world) have been quite successful in exporting tech products. Lately, news reports surfaced that Huawei plans to sell technologies to Iran to help 'clean' its internet. While many of Huawei's low-cost, functional tech products can aid growth and development in some of the world's poorest areas in Africa, South America, and Asia, it is also competing against other Western companies in selling filtering technologies to authoritarian regimes.

VD: What do we know about the way that users deal with these censorship regimes? Is there research being done on how they try to counteract this?

MJ: This issue has attracted the attention of a lot of Western countries and reporters. Sure, some Chinese users are aware that their search results are being filtered. Users who are knowledgeable and tech-savvy are able to use proxy servers and VPNs to route around censorship. But we do not know how many people are aware of this issue or how many actually care about their search results enough to seek alternative search engines and processes. I believe the majority of users either don't know or don't care. Maybe their information needs are met by the filtered results. Maybe they will not bother paying extra money or doing extra work just to get 'better' search results. I am not too optimistic about it. People who have a lot of business or academic connections with the outside world are more likely to employ alternative strategies. In fact, most foreign businesses in China have been using proxies or VPNs for a long time. For them, it's a standard operation. Also, individuals who rely on a daily dosage of alterative information from valuable external sources such as *The New York Times*, the Chinese version of *Wall Street Journal*, BBC Chinese or Twitter are likely to use circumvention tools on a more regular basis.

VD: We talked about Google and Baidu, the biggest players in China. I recently read that Bing was reportedly censoring results from searches conducted in simplified Chinese[5], so the ones used in mainland China, but not the ones in traditional Chinese characters used in Hong Kong, Taiwan, or Macau.

MJ: I believe that confirms what we talked about earlier. Bing's censoring of its search results in mainland China is to comply with (mainland) Chinese laws. It does not censor results in traditional Chinese perhaps because most of the people who use traditional

---

5. Pete Cashmore, 'Bing Accused of Censoring Simplified Chinese Language Searches', Mashable.com, 21 November 2009, http://mashable.com/2009/11/21/bing-chinese-queries/.

Chinese are from Hong Kong, Taiwan, or Macau, regions with different speech regulations. But it would be interesting to learn, for instance, if mainland searchers using traditional Chinese for their queries might get uncensored results. In many ways, censorship is a language game.

VD: One more thing: what is your opinion on the importance of search engines? Can Google and other search engines substitute knowledge somehow? Or are they more like a tool that shapes and distributes knowledge through their rankings and mechanisms? And if these search engine mechanisms can be controlled by political authorities and interest groups, how does that affect knowledge?
MJ: Many people equate search engines with knowledge, and probably most search engines want people to think that way. A lot of us use search engines to access information and search engines do matter. Wikipedia is so popular precisely because search engines like Google have made it a default 'knowledge site.' By doing so, search engines like Google define to some extent what constitutes useful information or knowledge. Every search engine wants to crawl and index as much online content as possible, but it's impossible to index everything. In 2008 Google announced it had indexed one trillion unique URLs. Lately the number has gone up to 60 trillion. But even that is a small fraction of what's available out there and it is not clear that all that gets indexed can be considered useful knowledge.

It is misleading, I think, to equate search engines with knowledge. To me, knowledge means a set of facts, truths and beliefs learned throughout time. Knowledge can be gained through experience and human interactions. People have always learned through curiosity, trial and error, intuition, rational thinking, and we learn a lot from others. Since learning is situated in various social and institutional contexts, knowledge can be considered the result of a highly social and culture-specific process. Lately, we have been able to locate information much faster through a process facilitated by search engines, but it is dangerous to think knowledge is a mere result of filtering and algorithms.

The equation of search with knowledge, I suspect, may have something to do with our fear in dealing with information overload and our huge investments in information technologies. By equating search with knowledge, we take comfort in the fantasy that the world's information and knowledge is at our fingertips. The linear progression 'data-information-knowledge-wisdom', to me, represents our wishful thinking rather than a real process of acquiring knowledge that is always messier, harder and more serendipitous. This is not to deny the usefulness of search, but to point out knowledge is much more than search filtering and algorithms.

Search engines, political authorities, business interests and powerful interest groups can certainly impact the process and mechanisms of search. In the end, whatever results Google, Baidu, or any search engine presents to the user depends very much on what the search engine can crawl and index, what it desires or is allowed to present. It's a highly problematic process. Unfortunately, we don't have a very good understanding of its specifics. In certain regimes, the information sought by users is sometimes hidden and forbidden. Steep barriers still exit, preventing people from participating fully in global conversations and knowledge productions. Much needs to be done to open dialogues and increase access to information and knowledge without losing sight of the need to preserve user privacy and integrity.

References

Cashmore, Pete. 'Bing Accused of Censoring Simplified Chinese Language Searches', Mashable.com, 21 November 2009, http://mashable.com/2009/11/21/bing-chinese-queries/.

Jiang, Min. 'The Business and Politics of Search Engines: A Comparative Study of Baidu's and Google's Search Results of Internet Events in China', *New Media & Society*, 22 April 2012, http://nms.sagepub.com/content/early/2013/04/18/1461444813481196.full.

Jiang, Min. 'Search Concentration, Bias, and Parochialism: A Comparative Study of Baidu, Jike, and Google's Search Results from China', Presented at the 41st Research Conference on Communication, Information and Internet Policy (TPRC), 27-29 September 2013, George Mason University School of Law, Arlington, VA, U.S.

Liao, Han-Teng. '"Wikipedias" (or its Copycat) Dominate "Chinese" Search Engine Result Pages (SERPs)', 6 May 2013, http://people.oii.ox.ac.uk/hanteng/2013/05/06/wikipedias-or-its-copycat-dominate-chinese-search-engine-result-pages-serps/.

Pariser, Eli. *The Filter Bubble: What the Internet Is Hiding from You*, New York: Penguin, 2011.

'I Am not a Web Search Result! I Am a Free Word': The Categorization and Commodification of 'Switzerland' by Google

Anna Jobin and Olivier Glassey

'I Am not a Web Search Result! I Am a Free Word': The Categorization and Commodification of 'Switzerland' by Google

Anna Jobin and Olivier Glassey

Imagine a world in which all your questions meet calculated answers defined and achieved by an opaque process. A place where your various interrogations are tracked and stored so that the knowledge the system possesses about you is continuously refined. Your behavior, centers of interest, habits, and languages are endlessly monitored, collected, and transmitted to a secret, remote command center.

That command center, which provides a massive map of the known world, gathers information about all the inhabitants of this place. The scope and the ramifications of the actual use of that massive intelligence remain unknown to you, but you are told that everything is geared towards collective benefits. Indeed, the system supports its users and spares no effort to organize and offer seamless access to varied information about any topic you seek to explore. Moreover, it has been designed in a way which helps you to stay focused by filtering out pieces of information that it has decided are of limited use for your future projects. The system 'cares' so much about your precise understanding of the world that it will even try to anticipate your questions. In order to smother unfiltered social interactions and increase its own efficiency, the system will also strongly suggest a transparent digital classification of individual identities.

While most people thrive within the system, a few lonely inhabitants are resisting. Nostalgic for their former world, these individuals try not to share their personal information, although the system episodically tries to trick them into doing so. A typical hardcore resister keeps raising critical questions about the opaque management of the command center and is tirelessly trying to find out which intelligence agencies might actually benefit from the collected data. He takes a symbolic stance and refuses the digital identity that he has been assigned.

Overall, the reach of the system seems all-encompassing, except for those who are limited by it and are subtly, and sometimes forcefully, brought back within its realms, as it is in the system's interest to keep people within boundaries.

No, this is not necessarily the description of the 'Googlization of everything',[1] despite its resemblance, but a condensed summary of the universe of the late sixties cult TV series *The Prisoner*. The hero of the show, a former spy, tries to make sense of a new world where he has been abducted, a tidy seaside holiday village apparently controlled by a secret organization, the goal of which is to extract the information of intelligence agents.

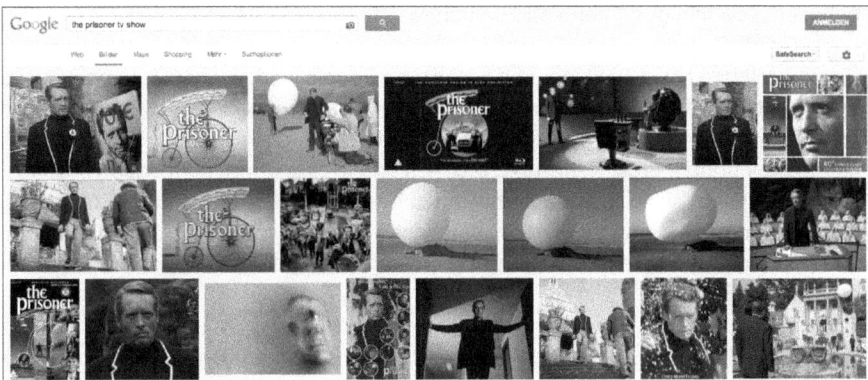

Fig. 1. Googling *The Prisoner*.

Like many successful science fiction stories, this work has become, over time, a generic metaphor used to deconstruct different forms of confinement.[2] While the universe of the TV series is quite remote from any actual stakes raised by information technologies, we nevertheless consider the depicted organization of the village (the 'system') a stimulating entry point to a critical discussion about our current relationship with search engines.

We will therefore examine in more detail the forms of confinement enabled by Google, their organization, and their performativity with regard to accessing content through this service. We begin not from a small village but from a word, in order to understand how it is processed by passing through the 'mills' of Google.

Why Words Matter for Google

Google's search algorithms determine the relevance of websites for particular search terms. More specifically, they determine which search results (links, pictures, videos, etc.) seem to be most relevant for particular search terms for a particular user.[3] And while other attributes such as technical specificities of a website or geographical location are taken into account, Google depends heavily on words because they are the

---

1. Siva Vaidhyanathan, *The Googlization of Everything (And Why We Should Worry)*, Berkeley: University of California Press, 2011.
2. Pierre Sérisier, *Le prisonnier: sommes-nous tous des numéros?* Paris: PUF, 2013.
3. Cf. e.g. James Grimmelmann, 'The Google Dilemma', *New York Law School Law Review* 53.939 (2009), http://works.bepress.com/james_grimmelmann/19. Or Martin Feuz, Matthew Fuller, and Felix Stalder, 'Personal Web Searching in the Age of Semantic Capitalism: Diagnosing the Mechanisms of Personalisation', *First Monday* 16.2 (July, 2011), http://firstmonday.org/htbin/cgiwrap/bin/ojs/index.php/fm/article/view/3344/2766.

base of any query.[4] The query terms trigger search results, which are links to webpages that have been evaluated according to keywords as well as to the words in the anchor text of the pages pointing at them. In order to display the most relevant search results for a user, Google evaluates the relevancy of potential search results for this user's initial query terms. Since most query terms consist of only two to three words,[5] Google depends on understanding the meaning of these words as accurately as possible; its algorithms are iterative and 'learn' whether or not the association between a certain query term and search results is adequate.

The importance of written language to the way Google works cannot be understated. Even content which is *a priori* not text – e.g. images and videos – will be indexed, ranked, and searched for in terms of the words that are associated with it: title, file name, description, tags, meta-text, etc. Nothing in this world, supposedly, escapes the possibility of being represented with words. The underlying paradigm of the way Google works is a 'semantic determinism': the vision of a world where everything that exists can and will be expressed through the symbolic form of words… and then be indexed by Google.

But Google does not only depend on words for the constitution of its index. Words are also a *commodity* the company earns money with, because Google has commodified words by offering advertisers the opportunity to bid on certain search terms with which they want their ads associated.[6] Indeed, the entire company, Google Inc., owes almost its entire revenue – tens of billions of dollars each year – to advertising.[7] It is on Google's platform AdWords that advertisers are presented with a price-list for search terms they could potentially associate their ad with.

The very same search terms that trigger previously indexed web search results (websites, links, pictures, videos, etc.) *also* trigger ads that are displayed at the same time. These ads have been esteemed 'relevant' with regard to the search terms by advertisers who have bid on these words, as well as by Google, which evaluates relevance within the *Quality Score* attributed algorithmically to each ad.[8] The process of commodification of words is thus not only the transformation of words into monetary value; it is also the (re-)production of representations by linking words and meaning. And, words have the highest value for Google when their meaning can unambiguously be determined and commodified.

---

4. Admittedly with the exception of image search based on an existing image, a lesser known and comparatively little used feature.
5. Dirk Lewandowski, 'New Perspectives on Web Search Engine Research', in Dirk Lewandowski (ed.) *Web Search Engine Research*, Bingley: Emerald Group Publishing, 2012, p. 4.
6. Cf. Micky Lee, *Free Information? The Case Against Google*, Champaign: Common Ground Publishing, 2010. And Theo Röhle. *Der Google-Komplex: Über Macht Im Zeitalter Des Internets*, Bielefeld: Transcript, 2010.
7. Christian Fuchs, 'A Contribution to the Critique of the Political Economy of Google', *Fast Capitalism* 8.1 (October, 2011), http://www.uta.edu/huma/agger/fastcapitalism/8_1/fuchs8_1.html.
8. Check and Understand Quality Score – AdWords Help, Google, https://support.google.com/adwords/answer/2454010?hl=en.

What is 'Switzerland'?

We have decided to explore how 'meaning' is attributed to a word by undertaking a case study of the (in-)visibility of the categorization of one particular word by Google. As will become obvious below, the linguistic particularities of Switzerland provide an ideal context for our exploration.

Our case study starts with the following question: What is *Switzerland*? Isolated, the word Switzerland is free from meaning, because it is only the usage, contexts, and intentions that will assign meaning to the word.[9] For Switzerland, Wikipedia's disambiguation page already lists about a dozen possibilities to begin with. Then, consider how a particular meaning of Switzerland may or may not be equivalently expressed by e.g. *Schweiz* (in German) or *Suisse* (in French). Finally, think of all the different meanings Switzerland can have for individual people.

If one types 'Switzerland' into Google's search query field, there is no disambiguation – only web search results and ads. (Plus search options, which actually add to the lack of transparency rather than act as a remedy for it, as we will see later.) Of course, results will be shaped according to profiling, (personalization, localization, language settings, etc.), and in 2011, Eli Pariser has brought mainstream attention to what he named the filter bubble: the focus on *the Google search results we are not getting* due to personalized filtering.[10] Our case study, however, shows that the phenomenon goes beyond a personal filter bubble impacting individuals. The Google search results we are *not* getting are a symptom of a complex dispositive based on linking words and their meaning: a symptom of a semantically determined lifeworld imposed on us, without transparency, on various levels.

'Switzerland' in Switzerland

What happens if you search for the word 'Switzerland' in Switzerland? Well, it depends. Switzerland is a polyglot country. There are four official languages (German, French, Italian, and Romansh) and English is widely used as well.

The default language option for Google's Swiss search portal, google.ch, is set to German. But if your browser settings allow cookies,[11] google.ch can – and according to your general settings will – be used in any other of those five languages. It goes without saying that our case study is based on the most general options, allowing for as little personalization as possible with available settings (e.g. no browser or search history), which does not exclude the possibility that people use platforms in a specified language. Let's first search for 'Switzerland' on Google Switzerland, the English version of google.ch, because there are many plausible scenarios where someone's language settings are set to English.

---

9. Lev S. Vygotskij, *Denken und Sprechen: psychologische Untersuchungen*, trans. Joachim Lompscher and Georg Rückriem, Weinheim; Basel: Beltz, 2002.
10. Eli Pariser, *The Filter Bubble: What the Internet Is Hiding from You,* London: Penguin Books Ltd., 2011.
11. In September 2013, Google announced that the company intends not to rely on cookies anymore in the near future (cf. Claire Cain Miller. 'Google Is Exploring an Alternative to Cookies for Ad Tracking', The New York Times Bits blog, 19 September 2013, http://bits.blogs.nytimes.com/2013/09/19/google-is-exploring-an-alternative-to-cookies-for-ad-tracking/).

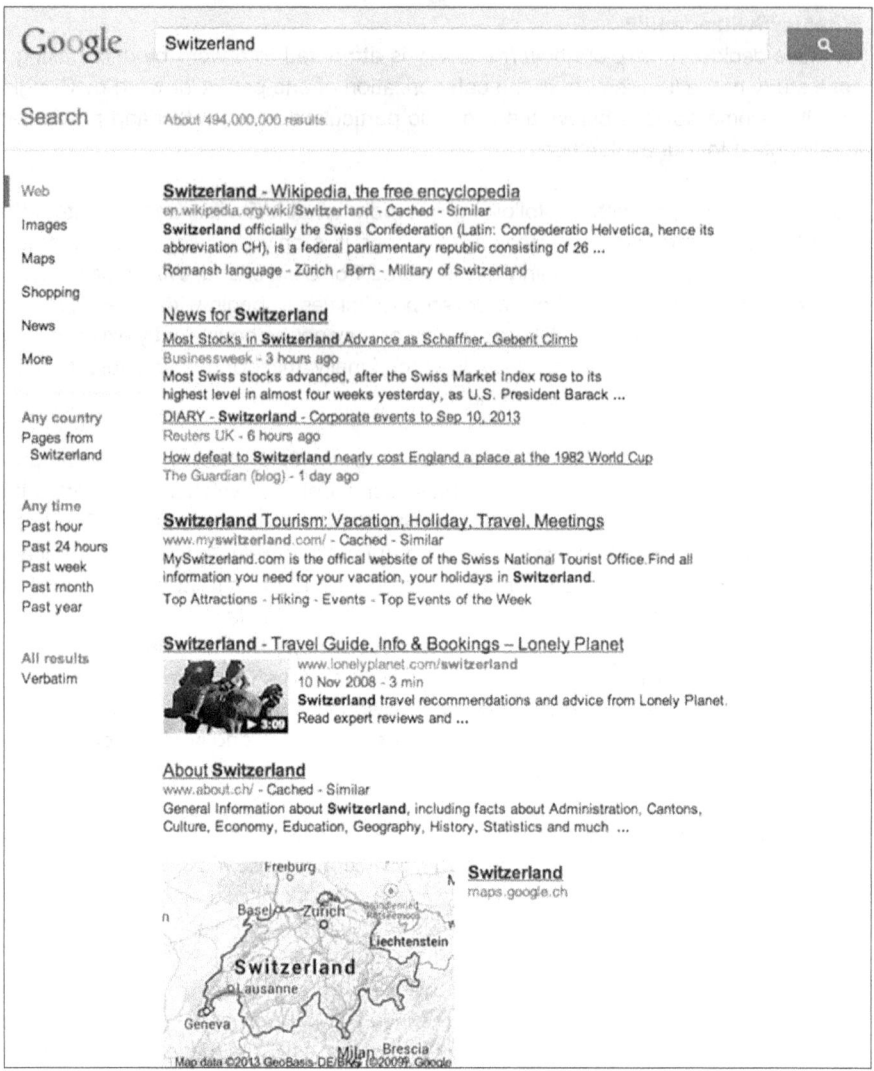

Fig. 2. Search results for 'Switzerland' on Google Switzerland (i.e. google.ch in English).

Further, let's see what happens when the language settings were set to German, French, Italian, or Romansh, and search again for 'Switzerland' on google.ch. The results on the search engine results page (SERP) are not identical, although Wikipedia, tourism promotion portal MySwitzerland.ch, and about.ch turn up on each SERP, albeit in slightly different ways.[12]

According to Google's web search results, the word Switzerland is most closely related to tourism (MySwitzerland, Lonely Planet), a geographical entity (map), and a

---

12. Pictures are available in an online appendix, see networkcultures.org/publications.

Wikipedia entry. The google.ch in French and German puts links to MySwitzerland on top, whereas in other languages Wikipedia is first. The SERP of Google Switzerland features 'News for Switzerland', a different set of results than the general 'web results' (including all results from any country, any time, as the settings to the left indicate). 'News for Switzerland' shows up solely on Google Switzerland. This is already a first indicator that the word 'Switzerland' is interpreted in a different manner by Google according to the language of the interface.

The particular result of 'News' brings us to the next question: what if, in fact, we are searching for specific kinds of results? I might actually be looking only for news, images, or videos. Suddenly, the very same word triggers very different results, depending on the language settings for google.ch.

Video search results on Google Switzerland consist mainly of travel and tourism videos (dating from 2008-2013), plus three videos about recent events (Oprah's visit in Zurich and a football match). The search for the very same word on Google Schweiz shows striking differences: the results consist mainly of videos in German about a Swiss TV singing show, plus one about a sports event and travel information.

You might say that different language settings lead to different search results because the search results are based on the language settings. Indeed, this is how Google works; it assumes that our language settings are a manifestation of the search results we seek. Why would anyone use Google Schweiz if they did not privilege German language results?

There are at least two problems with this reasoning:

1. It is not true!
The assumption that language settings always state individual language preference is simply wrong. In Switzerland, a small polyglot country with four co-existing official languages, plus English being the lingua franca on the internet, there are many reasons why someone might be using Google in a certain language without wanting results to be filtered according to this specific language setting. An important illustration of this wrongful assumption is Google's default of German for most Swiss IP addresses.[13] As a result, people from the French or Italian speaking part of Switzerland have to use Google Schweiz (in German) if they are browsing as privately as possible and not allowing cookies. Or someone may, for example, own a personal computer with English language settings, yet their workplace computer is set to German. Why would this person be looking for inherently different information when googling Switzerland depending on which computer she is using? Neither geographical location nor language settings can unambiguously predict a user's actual language preference.

2. It is patronizing and misleading!
Have you noticed the settings to the left of the SERPs? Whatever language setting is enabled, the search settings state that the results come from the 'web', without limi-

---

13. Even distinct regional defaults would provide no solution because many Swiss IP addresses are generated dynamically and thus indicate the internet provider's, not the location of a user.

tation. Furthermore, it is mentioned that it is possible on Google Schweiz to limit the results from German websites – nowhere does it say that the results have already been filtered based on language. Users are made to believe that the language setting applies only to the interface, not the results.

But does this really matter? Someone who wants to find videos related to Switzerland other than the TV show 'Voice of Switzerland' will keep looking, won't they? This presupposes that people already know what search results they want, which is far from being the default case and is especially not true when we search for news – by definition recent items of information we might not yet know. Checking out Google search results for news, the difference between the English google.ch and the German google.ch is striking. Again, to the left of the results Google suggests that these results have not yet been filtered based on language nor on country of origin.[14]

'Switzerland' in Switzerland in Swiss Languages
Up to this point, we have been searching for a single word: 'Switzerland'. Already, search results for the word's English expression have been seen to depend on the platform (or language setting) on which the term is entered, despite all of them coming under the umbrella of the local Google portal, google.ch. In what way do things change if we search on each platform in the respective language?

For 'Schweiz', 'Suisse', and 'Svizzera', Wikipedia and MySwitzerland.ch are constant results, as well as a map of Switzerland. In addition, each SERP integrates News as a second search result, but similarities in the results end here. Where the official political portal admin.ch appears both on Google Suisse and Google Svizzera, it is absent from Google Schweiz.

The SERP of 'Svizzera' on Google Svizzera highlights images as well, which differs from Google Schweiz and Google Suisse. And whereas news sources on Google Schweiz and Google Suisse are actually Swiss, Google Svizzera displays news only from Italian (!) media. Yet another very different world is the one of Google Svizra: most of the results are websites of national media stations.

Maybe we should not be surprised to get different results. Ethan Zuckerman writes:

> When we look for information through most search engines, the language we use to build a query limits the results we get. Search Google in the United States for "apple" and you won't get the same results as you would get by searching for the Spanish equivalent, "*manzana*," on Google.mx. This makes sense, of course – many of the people searching in the United States would prefer English-language results. But this limitation can constrain what information is available.[15]

Indeed, this 'constraint' on the availability of information is very real. It is even more important in our case, considering that our examples all come from one single platform

---

14. See the screenshots on networkcultures.org/publications for a side-by-side comparison.
15. Ethan Zuckerman, *Rewire: Digital Cosmopolitans in the Age of Connection*, New York: W. W. Norton & Company, 2013, pp. 164-165.

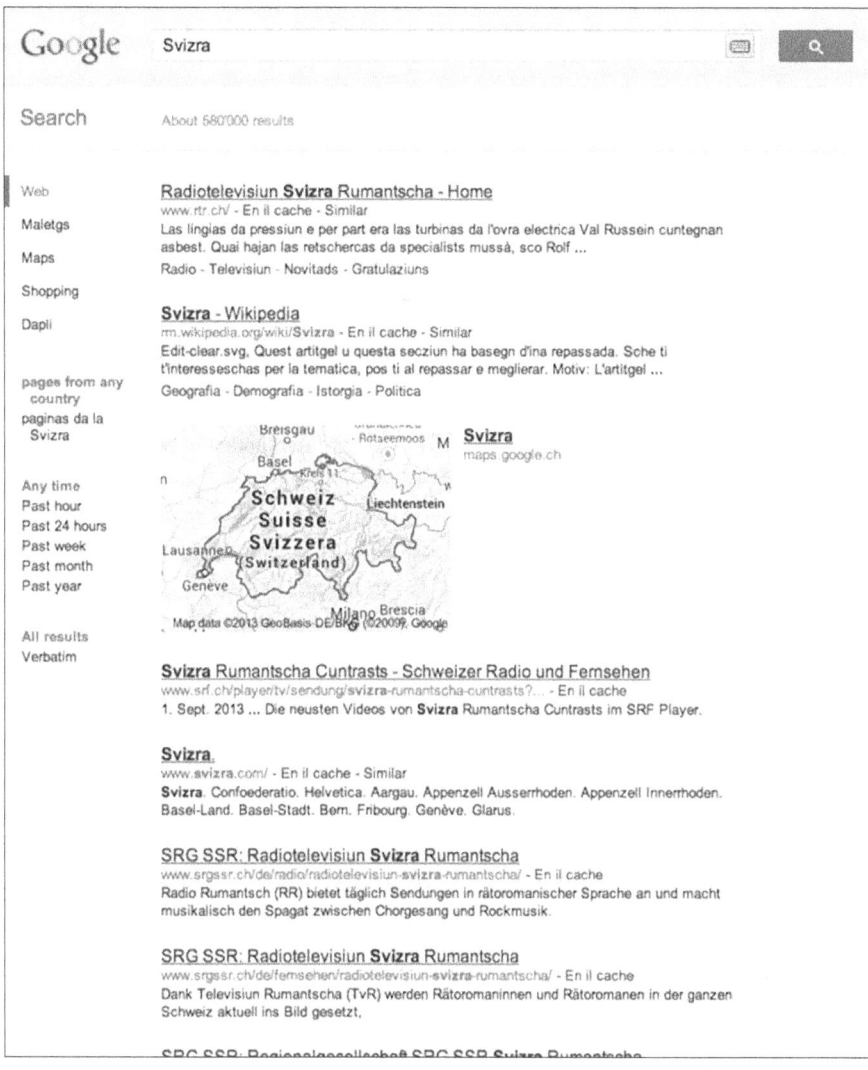

Fig. 3. Searching for 'Svizra' on Google Svizra (i.e. google.ch in Romansh).

(google.ch), i.e. from the same country. Is it still appropriate to declare what 'makes sense' based on majorities? The Swiss law defines four official languages without privileging one over the others – is it acceptable that citizens of the *same* country get different information depending on the language they use?

What Is in Switzerland Stays in Switzerland

'So what?' you might say. If we are looking for different pieces of information than we are presented with, all we have to do is search again, search differently... But in practice, our next search will most probably not be independent of our first query, even without taking into account filter bubble issues. If our keywords do not trigger the results we expect, we will adjust our search by modifying or adding a keyword. We might not even have to type; Google's 'Related Searches' are just a click away.

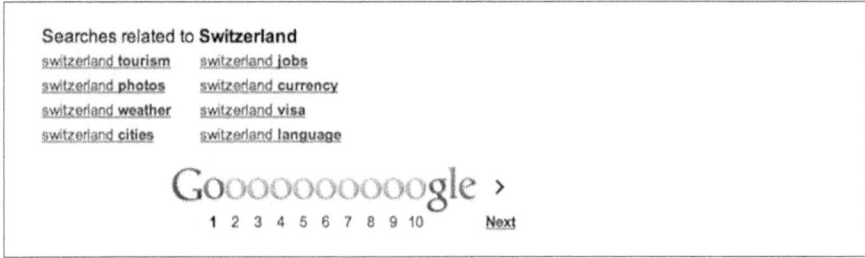

Fig. 4. Related searches to 'Switzerland' on Google Switzerland.

Have you ever misspelled a word in the search query field? Google's algorithms will immediately ask 'Did you mean...?' and suggest the corrected word. Even without misspelling, Google's autocompletion will suggests words and expressions to us *before we finish typing*. Thus, these algorithms mediate semantically between what we *mean* and which *words* we will use to describe it. All of them are so-called 'linguistic prosthesis', potentially impacting the written expression of our thoughts.[16]

```
swi,swisslos
swi,swiss pass
swi,swiss news
swit,http://en.wikipedia.org/wiki/Switzerland
swit,switzerland
swit,switch
swit,switzerland weather
swit,http://switch.ch
swit,http://switcher.ch
swit,switzerland train
swit,switcher
swit,switzernet
swit,switch plus
swit,switzerland mobility
swit,switched at birth
swit,switzerland news
swit,switzerland map
swit,switzerland weather forecast
swit,switzerland holidays
swit,switzerland hiking
swit,switzerland tourism
swit,switzerland public holidays
swit,switzerland public holidays 2013
switz,switzerland
switz,http://en.wikipedia.org/wiki/Switzerland
```

Fig. 5. An excerpt of autocompletion retrievals why typing 'Switzerland' (to the right of the comma are Google's autosuggestions for the expression on the left).

Just as Rover, the big white balloon, prevents the Prisoner from leaving the village, algorithms may prevent a user's potential search queries from escaping the lexicon with which they are familiar by suggesting words whose meanings make sense for Google. The algorithms create and impose their own invisible hermeneutics by interpreting words, reframing queries, and shaping entire semantic fields according to their own rules-based associations of words and their meaning.

Behind the Scenes: How Words Are Grouped and Sold
Remember how a Google search triggers not only search results but also ads? On Google AdWords, advertisers can consult Google's ranking of keywords, including

---

16. Anna Jobin and Frederic Kaplan, 'Are Google's Linguistic Prosthesis Biased Towards Commercially More Interesting Expressions? A Preliminary Study on the Linguistic Effects of Autocompletion Algorithms', *Digital Humanities 2013 Conference Abstracts*, Lincoln, NE: Center for Digital Research in the Humanities, 2013, pp. 245-248.

their popularity and estimated price (cost per click, or CPC) on the Keyword Planner (formerly known as Keyword Tool), and are able to buy keywords; i.e. bid on those with which they would like to associate their ad.[17]

It might not be a surprise that the way the Keyword Planner deals with words is limiting and far from transparent. The Keyword Planner is not transparent for the same reasons that the search above has shown: because the Keyword Planner presents groups and lists of words without explaining how the lists were established. The Planner is limiting because words and expressions find themselves categorized in certain groups of meanings, thereby dismissing other interpretations.

Google suggests certain things as pertinent Ad group ideas related to the keyword 'Schweiz' for all languages and all locations. The Ad group ideas are sorted 'by relevance'; it is not entirely clear how this relevance has been established however. As for the categorizing, it appears rather arbitrary. Why would 'Wohnungen Schweiz' ('Appartments Switzerland') be in 'Schweiz Sehenswürdigkeiten' ('Switzerland Sights') rather than in 'Schweiz Immobilien' ('Switzerland Realties')? How can 'der Schweiz' ('the Switzerland', using a wrong article) be a category? What is the difference between the categories 'Jobs Schweiz' (Jobs Switzerland) and 'Stellenangebote' ('Job Offers')? Why is 'Schweizer' ('Swiss') a category on its own, including keywords such as 'Schweizer Wetter' ('Swiss Weather'), which would make more sense within 'Wetter Schweiz' ('Weather Switzerland')? These examples are evidence of a tremendous lack of semantic understanding, which does not prevent the platform from patronizing users by suggesting these (non-)categories as valuable information to be taken into account.

Another striking aspect are the different ad prices: the suggested price for 'Schweiz' is 0.66 CHF, the one for 'Switzerland' 0.41 CHF, for 'Suisse' 0.35 CHF, for 'Svizzera' 0.2 CHF, and no suggested price for 'Svizra'.

It may not be surprising that the prices, Ad group and keyword ideas for 'Schweiz', 'Suisse', 'Svizzera', 'Svizera', and 'Swizerland' are not congruent. After all, Google probably bases its suggestions on people's search queries and the potential search results, and people who search in a certain language might be more likely to look for a specific topic than people searching in another language. When many people searching for 'Svizzera' are looking for work-related results, Google's algorithms will deem everything around 'lavoro/lavorare in Svizzera' ('work in Switzerland') to be most relevant for the query 'Svizzera'. If most people searching for 'Schweiz' do so with regard to tourism or housing, this will be reflected in what Google associates with 'Schweiz'. This seems logical, but the problem lies in the fact that we find ourselves very quickly confined within a world of meaning based on our language preference, constantly confronted with supposedly relevant meanings established through algorithmic procedures. No disambiguation, no freedom, and no accountability, only conformity.

---

17. According to Micky Lee, *Free Information?*, both the providing of a ranking and the commodification of keywords are part of the three main values Google sells to the advertisers, the third being the Google Search user's attention.

The 'Word Selling' Business Becomes a Trade of 'Meaning'

The Prisoner illustrates with astonishing accuracy our relationship with Google by raising crucial questions: What processes are shaping our representation of the world? Who is in charge? Why is it impossible to get away? What does it mean to be free? *The Prisoner* finds himself trapped in a pleasant yet mysterious village where everyone refers to him as 'Number Six'. He opposes that designation, proclaiming 'I am not a number. I am a free man.'

It is in the same spirit that we criticize Google for erasing the distinction between *words* and *meaning*. A complex structure of integrated processes offers its own fragmented and oriented interpretation of the world through query results proposed as relevant, accurate, and meaningful. While answers to users' queries are rephrased or reframed by obscure rules and words proposed as packages, a major shift occurs: the words selling business become a trade of meanings. From Saussure to Wittgenstein, Berger, Luckmann, and beyond, countless scholars have pointed out how power structures are reflected by, built into, and maintained through language. The fundamental question is, then, what kind of power is embedded in Google's deconstruction and contextual reconfigurations of words such as 'Switzerland'?

A first answer could be found if we look at *The Prisoner*'s village. What is most disturbing is not the display of power and control over information that we can actually see, but those that are concealed, out of reach. We still have limited technical and theoretical tools with which to understand how information is processed within Google.[18] Moreover – not unlike Lewis Mumford's concept of mega-machines – we know that we are an active part of a huge, epistemic infrastructure that includes rulers and managers, yet the different roles and the responsibilities are blurred. The lack of transparency and accountability of Google, by pretending to simply mirror the collective actions of its users, sets an asymmetric power relationship. This discourse constructed and maintained through practices operates like a mega-machine:

> The perception of the system as providing the limits to action (and possibility) rather than an actual (locatable) ruler, helps authority defuse most of the resistance from democratic technics. This is not to argue there are not individuals or groups with power in society but, that such power is partly masked by the technological system's "needs".[19]

A second level of power is economic, and this is explicitly at play when considering the strategic moves of major web companies. Various information retrieval systems – search engines in their many forms – find themselves at the core of a long-lasting struggle for influence, still largely dominated by Google, over the booming capitalist

---

18. Which is why we agree with Lev Manovich (*Software Takes Command: Extending the Language of New Media,* New York and London: Bloomsbury, 2013) and Barocas et al. (Solon Barocas, Sophie Hood, and Malte Ziewitz, 'Governing Algorithms: A Provocation Piece', *SSRN Scholarly Paper*, Rochester, NY: Social Science Research Network (2013), http://ssrn.com/abstract=2245322 or http://dx.doi.org/10.2139/ssrn.2245322) that the study of software and, more fundamentally, algorithms deserves our utmost attention.
19. Christopher May, 'The Information Society as Mega-Machine', *Information, Communication & Society* 3 (2000): 251.

economy of word commodification. While it is impossible to assess how this domain will evolve, such confrontations by search engines overwhelmingly operated by business-oriented private companies challenge the very idea of common good.

Finally, at a more fundamental level, endeavours to control and market questions, answers, words, and meaning could also be perceived as a major shift in the way we think as a society. In his book *The Order of Things*, Michel Foucault defines the concept of *episteme* as 'the strategic apparatus which permits of separating out from among all the statements which are possible those that will be acceptable within, I won't say a scientific theory, but a field of scientificity, and which it is possible to say are true or false'.[20] While Foucault refers to change in modern society and the rise of science as the leading way to conceptualize the world, we might ask ourselves to what extent do hundreds of billions of monthly queries, with their processed answers, participate in the framing of our collective way of recognizing what is 'possible' and what is 'acceptable'. The issue here is not about a kind of censorship or about voluntary control of content but concerns a much more subtle and distributed influence in which the ontological status of information depends on its transformation and translation in the multiple processes we have described above. In other words, will the *googleability* of a piece of information become a condition of its social existence?

At this general level, the critical issue in terms of power and accountability is the search engines' non-visibility. If we accept this situation as such we would be following the path of the vast majority of *The Prisoner*'s village inhabitants: thankful and happy to live in a cozy, tidy, and artificial place they call their world. However, opening the 'black box' of meaning (re-)production through search engines could be an unsettling experience as we discover how much we have already delegated to algorithms and their owners, and how we are all entangled through our practices. Hopefully, transparency also would lay the ground for a much needed public debate about how to conceptualize systems where the (re-)production of meaning is not subordinated to economic interests. At this point it's important to remember how the search engine operates between us and our words.

NB: All data from Google (i.e. screenshots of SERPs, autocompletion, Keyword Planner data) were retrieved on 11 September 2013, between 11.30am and 2pm, from Lausanne, Switzerland.

References
Barocas, Solon, Sophie Hood, and Malte Ziewitz. 'Governing Algorithms: A Provocation Piece', *SSRN Scholarly Paper*, Rochester, NY: Social Science Research Network (2013), http://ssrn.com/abstract=2245322 or http://dx.doi.org/10.2139/ssrn.2245322.

Cain Miller, Claire. 'Google Is Exploring an Alternative to Cookies for Ad Tracking', The New York Times Bits blog, 19 September 2013, http://bits.blogs.nytimes.com/2013/09/19/google-is-exploring-an-alternative-to-cookies-for-ad-tracking/.

Feuz, Martin, Matthew Fuller, and Felix Stalder. 'Personal Web Searching in the Age of Semantic Capitalism: Diagnosing the Mechanisms of Personalisation', *First Monday* 16.2 (2 July 2011),

---

20. Michel Foucault, quoted by Yves Viltar, 'L'étrange carrière du concept foucaldien d'épistémè en science politique', *Raisons Politiques* 23 (2006): 3.

http://firstmonday.org/htbin/cgiwrap/bin/ojs/index.php/fm/article/view/3344/2766.

Fuchs, Christian. 'A Contribution to the Critique of the Political Economy of Google', *Fast Capitalism* 8.1 (October 2011), http://www.uta.edu/huma/agger/fastcapitalism/8_1/fuchs8_1.html.

Google.com. Check and Understand Quality Score - AdWords Help, https://support.google.com/adwords/answer/2454010?hl=en.

Grimmelmann, James. 'The Google Dilemma', *New York Law School Law Review* 53.939 (2009), http://works.bepress.com/james_grimmelmann/19.

Jobin, Anna and Frederic Kaplan. 'Are Google's Linguistic Prosthesis Biased Towards Commercially More Interesting Expressions? A Preliminary Study on the Linguistic Effects of Autocompletion Algorithms', *Digital Humanities 2013 Conference Abstracts*, Lincoln, NE: Center for Digital Research in the Humanities, 2013, p. 245-248.

Lee, Micky. *Free Information? The Case Against Google,* Champaign: Common Ground Publishing, 2010.

Lewandowski, Dirk (ed.). *Web Search Engine Research,* Bingley: Emerald Group Publishing Ltd., 2012.

Manovich, Lev. *Software Takes Command: Extending the Language of New Media,* New York; London: Bloomsbury, 2013.

May, Christopher. 'The Information Society as Mega-Machine', *Information, Communication & Society* 3.2 (2000): 241-265.

Pariser, Eli. *The Filter Bubble. What the Internet Is Hiding from You,* London: Penguin Books Ltd., 2011.

Röhle, Theo. *Der Google-Komplex: Über Macht Im Zeitalter Des Internets,* Kultur- Und Medientheorie, Bielefeld: Transcript, 2010.

Sérisier, Pierre. *Le prisonnier: sommes-nous tous des numéros?* Paris: PUF, 2013.

Vaidhyanathan, Siva. *The Googlization of Everything (And Why We Should Worry)*, Berkeley: University of California Press, 2011.

Viltar, Yves. 'L'étrange carrière du concept foucaldien d'épistémè en science politique', *Raisons Politiques* 23.3 (2006): 193-202.

Vygotskij, Lev S. *Denken und Sprechen: psychologische Untersuchungen,* trans. Joachim Lompscher and Georg Rückriem, Weinheim; Basel: Beltz, 2002.

Zuckerman, Ethan. *Rewire: Digital Cosmopolitans in the Age of Connection*, New York: W.W. Norton & Company, 2013.

Keywords, Trademarks, and Search Engine Liability

Amanda Scardamaglia

Keywords, Trademarks, and Search Engine Liability

¬

Amanda Scardamaglia

In 2012 the Language Council of Sweden added the word 'ungoogleable' to its annual list of Swedish words that are not in the Swedish dictionary but have become part of the common vernacular. The word, which in Swedish translates to 'ogooglebar', was defined as something that cannot be found on any search engine. Google objected and demanded the definition be amended to refer specifically to its search engine, incorporating a disclaimer stating that Google is a trademark of Google Inc. The Swedish Language Council resisted, and, after observing that language development and the protection of trademarks are anomalous, it declared the word would not be included on its final list.[1]

The irony of Google taking issue with the use of its trademark in this way is surely not lost on those familiar with the spate of lawsuits around the world brought against the search engine in recent times for its perceived lack of respect for trademarks and trademark law. It is certainly not lost on the trademark owners who have instituted these proceedings, although their condescension is not exclusively reserved for Google of course, with trademark owners equally concerned about any use of their trademarks by internet intermediaries and their advertisers.

So how did we get here?

The proliferation of information available on the internet and the growth of internet-related businesses has resulted in an exponential rise in the power of the search engine – as both repositories of information and advertising platforms with enormous reach. This shift in the business landscape has led to a swell in litigious claims and a growing jurisprudence on search engine liability, much of which relates to questions of trademark infringement arising from the use of third party trademarks as keywords in the online advertising services offered by web search engines.

The following discussion will explore the judicial response to such claims in Europe, the United States, and Australia, but with a particular focus on Google, since allegations of search engine liability concerning trademark infringement have almost exclusively

---

1. See Language Council of Sweden, 'Google Does Not Own the Language', 26 March 2013, http://www.sprakradet.se/15922 (in Swedish).

been leveled against Google, as the market leader.[2] It will also consider the application of consumer protection legislation as an alternative means of regulating the use of third party trademarks as keywords in online search and advertising. The purpose of this study is to test whether search engine liability, in the jurisdictions subject to review, is a reality, a possibility, or largely illusory. In order to undertake this analysis, it is necessary to first touch on the operation of internet search engines and their advertising services, including the use of keyword advertising.

Understanding Keyword Advertising
Keyword advertising enables search providers and their advertisers to deliver relevant, tailored, consumer-specific ads to internet users. It also allows search engine operators to generate substantial revenue from the sale of keyword advertising. For example, in 2012 the global internet advertising market was worth U.S. $100.2 billion, representing a year-on-year growth of 17 percent, and a 20 percent share of the total global advertising market.[3] Given its profitability, some search engines operate on a pay for placement basis only, where search results are primarily based on paid placements and not relevance.[4] The distinction between relevance-based search results, or natural search results, and sponsored ads is best explained in the present context, by reference to the Google search engine.[5]

When a user enters a term in the Google search engine, users are given two main search results: natural (or organic) search results and sponsored links. Organic search results provide links to web pages that are ranked in order of relevance to the search terms entered, as determined by a complex algorithm developed by Google. Although the precise nature and workings of the algorithm remain unknown, its use means that organic search result rankings cannot be purchased.

Sponsored links on the other hand, are a form of advertising, created by advertisers who pay the relevant search provider each time a user clicks on it. With respect to the Google search engine, sponsored links are displayed separately from organic search results and can appear in a box marked 'Ad' or 'Ad/s related to...' usually above the organic search results. Significantly, the order and ranking of sponsored links and

---

2. As the market leader, Google generates more than U.S. $50 billion in revenue annually, the majority of which is generated from its advertising. See Google Inc, 'Form 10-K: Annual Report', 29 January 2013, http://edgar.secdatabase.com/1404/119312513028362/filing-main.htm. According to NetMarketShare, as of January 2014, Google's global desktop search engine market share was 71.36 percent. Its closest competitors were Baidu (16.35 percent) and Bing (5.83 percent). In the past, this figure was above 90 percent, but has been pegged back significantly by the growth of the Chinese language search engine Baidu. See NetMarketShare, 'Desktop Search Engine Market Share', January2014, http://www.netmarketshare.com/search-engine-market-share.aspx?qprid=4&qpcustomd=0.
3. In 2017 this figure is expected to grow to U.S. $185 billion. See Pricewaterhouse Coopers, 'Global Entertainment and Media Outlook: 2013-2017: Internet Advertising', http://www.pwc.com/gx/en/global-entertainment-media-outlook/segment-insights/internet-advertising.jhtml.
4. See for example GoTo.com v Walt Disney Co, 202 F 3d 1199 (9th Cir, 2000), where GoTo.com ran a pay for placement search engine which produced search results using an algorithm weighted in favour of paid advertisers.
5. For more on the operation of the Google search engine see Google Inc v Australian Competition and Consumer Commission [2013] HCA 1 at [18]-[33] per French CJ, Crennan and Kiefel JJ. Also see Interflora Inc v Marks and Spencer Plc [2013] EWHC 1291 (Ch) at [87]-[111] per Arnold J.

whether they will appear at all in response to a user query is determined by Google's AdWords program and not the Google web search algorithm.

The AdWords program allows advertisers to create, change, and monitor the performance of sponsored links. These sponsored links consist of three parts. The first part is the headline, which incorporates a link to a webpage. The second part is the address of the webpage. The third part of the link is the advertising text, which usually consists of a brief summary of the subject of the sponsored link and sometimes the advertiser's business.

A third and more recent addition to Google's search results page is the Knowledge Graph box. According to Google, '[t]he Knowledge Graph enables you to search for things, people or places that Google knows about – landmarks, celebrities, cities, sports teams, buildings, geographical features, movies, celestial objects, works of art and more – and instantly get information that's relevant to your query.'[6] The relevant information Google refers to appears on the right hand side of the search results page, linking to public sources including Wikipedia. The information shown in this section is derived from a collection of information about real-world things and their connections to other things, where Knowledge Graph gathers information about a topic from several sources, before refining the information based on the most popular questions people ask about that subject.

For an example of Google's search layout see Figure 1 which shows the results page generated in Australia in response to a desktop search query using the LACOSTE trademark as a keyword, including both organic search results and sponsored links, as well as Google Knowledge Graph.

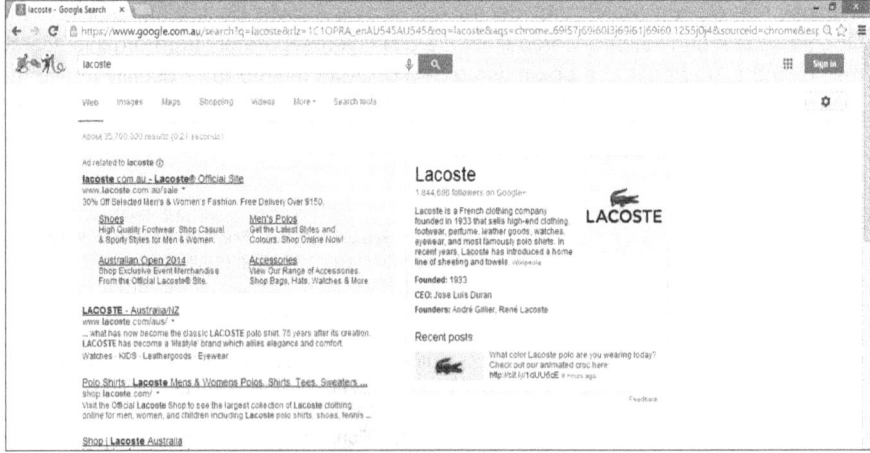

Fig. 1: Google Search Engine Response to Keyword Search for LACOSTE.

---

6. 'Introducing the Knowledge Graph: Things not Strings', Google Official Blog, 16 May 2012, http://googleblog.blogspot.com.au/2012/05/introducing-knowledge-graph-things-not.html

Returning to sponsored links, advertisers using AdWords are able to specify each part of the three-part sponsored link. The advertiser can also specify keywords that will trigger the appearance of the sponsored link when that keyword is entered as a search term in the Google search engine. Furthermore, advertisers are able to take advantage of keyword insertion, a special feature of AdWords, where the search phrase entered by a user is then used as the clickable headline for the sponsored link.

There was a period when Google did not allow advertisers to link their ads to the trademarks of others, but in 2004 its advertising policy was amended in the United States and Canada to allow advertisers to purchase their competitors' trademarks as keywords.[7] This policy was subsequently applied to the United Kingdom and Ireland in 2008 and the rest of Europe in 2010.[8] In early 2013 the policy was rolled out further in countries including China, Hong Kong, and Australia, with Google announcing it '…will no longer prevent advertisers from selecting a third party's trademark as a keyword in ads targeting these regions'.[9]

As to its competitors, Microsoft's Yahoo! and Bing search engines also provide keyword advertising services, as does Baidu. With respect to Microsoft, initially its keyword policy differed somewhat from Google's, but in 2011, the company announced it was amending its Intellectual Property Policy so as to no longer review complaints in relation to the use of trademarks as keywords in the United States and Canada, in order to align its practices with the current industry standard, namely Google.[10] Microsoft will however, still investigate a complaint about trademark use in the text of a search ad,[11] as will Google, if it is inconsistent with its AdWords Trademark Policy.[12] Furthermore, in Australia, Brazil, France, Hong Kong, Indonesia, Italy, New Zealand, Ireland, Singapore, and the United Kingdom, Microsoft will investigate a complaint about trademark infringement with respect to keyword use.[13]

These changes in search engine policy and the consequential practice of advertisers purchasing competitors' trademarks as keywords have created a number of challenges for judges in having to adapt and apply laws and legal doctrines to technologies

---

7. Google Advertising Policies Help, 'AdWords Trademark Policy', https://support.google.com/adwordspolicy/answer/6118?rd=1.
8. Matthew Saltmarsh, 'Google Will Sell Brand Names as Keywords in Europe', The New York Times, 4 August 2010, http://www.nytimes.com/2010/08/05/technology/05google.html?_r=0.
9. Google Advertising Policies Help, 'Updates to AdWords Trademark Policy', https://support.google.com/adwordspolicy/answer/177578.
10. Eric Goldman, 'Microsoft Adopts Google-Style Trademark Policy for Keyword Advertising', Technology & Marketing Law Blog, 15 February 2011, http://blog.ericgoldman.org/archives/2011/02/microsoft_adopt.htm.
11. Bing Ads, 'Intellectual Property Guidelines', http://advertise.bingads.microsoft.com/en-us/editorial-intellectual-property-guidelines#1.
12. Google Advertising Policies Help, 'AdWords Trademark Policy'. That is, where a third party trademark is being used and the exceptions do not apply. Thus, advertisers can use a trademarked term in an ad if they are authorized to do so, or if they are using the term descriptively. Furthermore, advertisers can use a trademark in ad text if the advertiser complies with Google's policy on resellers and informational sites, which can be found at http://support.google.com/adwordspolicy/answer/6118?hl=en.
13. Bing Ads, 'Intellectual Property Guidelines'.

and trademark uses unimagined at the time of enactment.[14] As previously noted, most of the litigation in this space concerns the potential liability of Google for trademark infringement flowing from its sale of trademarks as keywords to third parties, although some trademark owners have also pursued the advertisers directly.

Trademarks as Keywords and Trademark Infringement
In most jurisdictions, trademark infringement is premised on the assessment of consumer confusion, which flows from the alleged infringing use of a mark where that use is consistent with the function of a trademark in the course of trade. For example, in the United States, trademark infringement is defined as '[...] any reproduction, counterfeit, copy, or colorable imitation of a registered mark in connection with the sale, offering for sale, distribution, or advertising of any goods or services on or in connection with which such use is likely to cause confusion, or to cause mistake, or to deceive [...]'.[15] In order to succeed in a claim for infringement therefore, one must show (1) that the defendant has used (2) an identical or similar mark (3) in commerce (4) and that the defendant's use is likely to confuse consumers.[16]

Confusion is also a central tenant in the conceptualization of trademark infringement under Article 5(1)(a) of the First Council Directive to Approximate the Laws of the Member States Relating to Trade Marks.[17] According to case law, a claim for infringement under Article 5(1)(a) can only succeed if the following conditions are satisfied: (1) there must be use of a sign by a third party within the relevant territory; (2) the use must be in the course of trade; (3) it must be without the consent of the proprietor of the trademark owner; (4) it must be of a sign that is identical to the trademark; (5) it must be in relation to goods or services which are identical to those for which the trademark is registered; (6) and it must affect or be liable to affect the functions of the trademark.[18]

In Australia, the grounds for relief under the Trade Marks Act 1995 (Australia) are somewhat similar. Here, infringement occurs when a person uses as a trademark a sign that is substantially identical to or deceptively similar to a registered trademark in relation to the same class of goods (or services) for which the trademark is registered.[19] As in the United States and Europe, there is a threshold requirement that the alleged infringer

---

14. As acknowledged by Circuit Judge Hartz in his opening statement of 1-800 Contacts Inc v Lens. com Inc, No 11-4114, 11-4204, 11-4022 (10th Cir, 2013) at 2.
15. §32 of the Lanham Act, 15 USC §1114(1) (2005). Also see §1125(a) which provides a cause of action for the infringement of unregistered trademarks.
16. As to the recognized categories of confusion see Australian Gold Inc v Hatfield, 436 F 3d 1228 (10th Cir, 2006).
17. *First Council Directive 89/104/EEC of 21 December 1988 to Approximate the Law of the Member States Relating to Trade Marks,* Article 5, which has subsequently been replaced by a codified version under the European Parliament and Council Directive 2008/95/EC of 22 October 2008 to Approximate the Law of the Member States Relating to Trade Marks. The Directive further provides that a trademark owner can prevent the use of a sign on goods and services that are similar to those covered by the trademark where there exists a likelihood of confusion on the part of the public.
18. As set out by Arnold J in Interflora Inc v Marks and Spencer Plc [2013] EWHC 1291 at [177].
19. Trade Marks Act 1995 (Australia) s 120(1). Trademark infringement can also occur where a sign is being used in relation to goods which are the same description as the goods (or services) for which the trademark is registered or in relation to closely related services (or goods). See section 120(2) of the *Trade Marks Act 1995* (Australia).

must use the registered trademark as a trademark, so as to distinguish the goods and services to which it is attached. Further, trademark infringement is based on the use of a mark that is either substantially identical to or deceptively similar to a registered trademark, so as to confuse or deceive consumers.[20]

When it comes to the use of trademarks as keywords, cases of infringement usually hinge on whether the use of a trademarked term in search results constitutes use as a trademark, consistent with the legal definition of use. Another precarious issue pertains to consumer confusion. Both of these issues have come to surface in the suite of infringement lawsuits brought against Google over the last decade, where trademark use and confusion have been pivotal in determining whether the search engine could or should be liable for direct or contributory trademark infringement.

Now while some of the first reported cases involving internet intermediaries looked to have broadened the class of people who could face legal liability for trademark infringement,[21] in the subsequent cases involving Google, the potential for liability has seemingly contracted, as most of the lawsuits instituted against the search engine have been largely resolved in its favor. Perhaps the most publicized trademark infringement action involving Google is the famed European Court of Justice (ECJ) case of Google France SARL v Louis Vuitton Malletier SA.[22]

Culminating over several years and bringing together three separate lawsuits, this case was considered a victory for Google and search engine operators in general. Here, Louis Vuitton brought proceedings against Google France, alleging it had allowed advertisers to purchase Louis Vuitton trademarks as keywords via Google's AdWords program and link to websites selling imitation Louis Vuitton goods and to competing websites, in breach of Article 5 of the First Council Directive. The claim ultimately failed, with the ECJ deciding that search engine operators do not infringe trademarks by selling keywords that correspond to third party trademarks. This is because although search engines are carrying out commercial activity in the course of trade, these activities do not constitute use, as required for the purposes of trademark infringement:

> The fact of creating the technical conditions necessary for the use of a sign and being paid for that service does not mean that the party offering the service itself uses the sign. To the extent to which it has permitted its client to make such a use of the sign, its role must, as necessary, be examined from the angle of rules of law other than Article 5 [...].[23]

After determining that the use requirement could not be established, the ECJ terminated its inquiry at the first step of the above mentioned framework for infringement,

---

20. Trade Marks Act 1995 (Australia) s 10.
21. See especially Playboy Enterprises Inc v Netscape Communications Corp, 354 F 3d 1020 (9th Cir, 2004) which held that search engines could face liability for allowing advertisers to use trademarks as keywords where such use was not authorized by the trademark owner – for either direct or contributory infringement.
22. Google France SARL v Louis Vuitton Malletier SA [2010] C-236/08, C-237/08 and C-238/08.
23. Google France SARL v Louis Vuitton Malletier SA [2010] C-236/08, C-237/08 and C-238/08 at [57].

without examining some of the other more pertinent questions relating to infringement, such as whether AdWords undermines the function of the trademark, including the economic function, which is central to the rationalization of trademark law.[24] Nevertheless, this decision has become a reference point for the milieu of claims brought against Google around the world, where the company has similarly escaped liability.

This success has prompted some commentators to assert that Google has won the trademark and keyword advertising battle,[25] paving the way for the company and its competitors to continue selling trademarks as keywords, unfettered and without legal consequence. There is some truth to this claim, although a closer examination of the legal basis for such decisions and the circumstances surrounding the search engine's success would suggest that such an assertion is somewhat of an exaggeration. There are several reasons for this.

First, a number of lawsuits brought against Google have been dismissed before the issues could be tested in court. For example, Soaring Helmet, manufacturers of the VEGA motorcycle helmet, voluntarily dismissed Google from its trademark lawsuit against Bill Me Inc and others.[26] More recently, Google was successful in defending a claim of trademark infringement, among a laundry list of other claims.[27] As far as the trademark infringement claim was concerned, the matter was dismissed after the Court held the plaintiff's trademark, Home Decor Center, was too generic to warrant protection.

Furthermore one cannot say definitively that Google has been victorious against aggrieved trademark owners, given that several lawsuits have been settled out of court, including the long-running dispute between Google and software company Rosetta Stone.[28] Indeed it is worth noting that while Google was successful in the first instance;[29] on appeal the Fourth Circuit reversed the District Court on several key points, including claims of direct trademark infringement, contributory infringement, and dilution, before both parties settled on confidential terms.[30]

As a result, several substantive issues related to trademark infringement in the search engine context are yet to be considered by the courts, let alone resolved. In Australia for example, the issue of search engine liability for trademark infringement has not even come before the courts, although perhaps this is because the likelihood of success is seen as too remote, especially with respect to the interpretation of the trade-

---

24. William M. Landes and Richard A Posner, 'Trademark Law: An Economic Perspective', *Journal of Law and Economics* 30 (1987): 266-268 and William Landes and Richard Posner, *The Economic Structure of Intellectual Property*, Cambridge, MA: Harvard University Press, 2003.
25. Eric Goldman, 'More Confirmation that Google Has Won the AdWords Trademark Battles Worldwide', *Forbes*, 22 March 2013, http://www.forbes.com/sites/ericgoldman/2013/03/22/more-confirmation-that-google-has-won-the-adwords-trademark-battles-worldwide/.
26. Soaring Helmet Corporation v Bill Me Inc, 2:2009cv00789 (WD Wash, 2009). Similarly see Ezzo v Google, 2:09-CV-00159 (MD Fla, 2010) and Jurin v Google Inc, WL 5011007 (ED Cal, 2012).
27. Home Decor Center Inc v Google Inc, CV 2:12-cv-05706-GW-SH (CD Cal, 2013).
28. Reuters, 'Rosetta Stone and Google Settle Trademark Lawsuits', 31 October 2012, http://www.reuters.com/article/2012/10/31/us-usa-court-rosettastone-google-idUSBRE89U1GE20121031.
29. Rosetta Stone Ltd v Google Inc, 1:09-cv-00736-GBL-TCB (ED Va, 2010).
30. Rosetta Stone Ltd v Google Inc, WL 1155143 (4th Cir, 2012).

mark use doctrine.[31] And even when the courts have been given an opportunity to make a clear statement on the application of trademark law in the context of search engines, against the most dominant search engine in the world no less, they have not done so. The most obvious case in point is the Google France decision, when the Court dismissed the claim for trademark infringement on the basis that the use as a trademark requirement had not been established. Critically however, the court did not make any assessment as to the other elements of trademark infringement, including likelihood of confusion, much to the dismay of some:

> [...] the ECJ left open the door for future misbehaviour. For example, suppose that, as a bonus for its most loyal clients, Google modified its natural search results so that on occasion the link to a trademark proprietor's website diverts users to an advertiser's page. This behaviour would surely cause significant confusion, yet it would be difficult to attribute to the underlying advertiser, as opposed to Google itself. Under the Court's analysis, however, Google would still be immune from trademark infringement liability.[32]

Another point worth observing is that while the ECJ concluded that Google's conduct does not constitute use sufficient enough to found a cause of action for trademark infringement, this is not entirely consistent with some of the American case law on this issue, which in itself is conflicting.[33] As such, there is a real possibility for future test cases to shed further light or clarification on the concept of trademark use, consumer confusion, and, particularly, whether keyword use is likely to affect the function of the trademark. The latter issues are especially crucial, since there is conflicting evidence as to whether consumers are actually confused or understand the nature and operation of sponsored links.[34] Another area that has not been sufficiently flushed out is the case of contributory trademark liability, as opposed to primary liability, an issue that was in dispute in the aforementioned Rosetta Stone case but was settled out of court.

Whether such test cases will materialize in the near future is unclear but is probably unlikely, with trademark owners seemingly resigned to the fact that as Google has continued to successfully stave off trademark infringement lawsuits, the legality of its AdWords program is becoming more entrenched and legitimated. Consequently, trademark owners have shifted their focus to the advertisers responsible for purchasing third party

---

31. For further discussion see Althaf Marsoof, 'Online Service Providers and Third Party Trademark Infringement in Australia', *International Journal of Law and Information Technology* (2013): 1-32. Also available from http://ijlit.oxfordjournals.org/content/early/2013/07/18/ijlit.eat010.full.pdf. The lack of case law in Australia may also be attributed to the fact that unlike other jurisdictions, the Trade Marks Act 1995 (Australia) does not make any provision for contributory or indirect liability.
32. 'Trademark Law – Infringement Liability: European Court of Justice Holds that Search Engines do not Infringe Trademarks', *Harvard Law Review* 124 (2010): 648, 654-655.
33. See for example Rescuecom Corp v Google Inc, 562 F 3d 123 (2d Cir, 2009) and compare with the earlier case of 1-800 Contacts Inc v WhenU.com Inc, 414 F 3d 400 (2d Cir, 2005).
34. For example in Rosetta Stone Ltd v Google Inc, 2012 WL 1155143 (4th Cir, 2012), the District Court cited an internal Google study finding that even sophisticated consumers were sometimes unaware that sponsored links were advertisements. Compare this to the findings set out in David J. Franklyn and David A. Hyman, 'Trademarks as Search Engine Keywords: Much Ado About Something?', *Harvard Journal of Law and Technology* 26.2 (2013): 1-65.

trademarks as keywords, with better success.[35] The possibility of holding advertisers as opposed to intermediaries liable was actually foreshadowed in Google France, although the ECJ deferred a decision about the advertiser's liability to the referring Court.

We have seen the flow on effect of this in the recent Interflora Inc v Marks and Spencer Plc decision. In this case Arnold J held that in purchasing 'Interflora' (and similar variations) as keywords, Marks and Spencer, was liable for trademark infringement because it did not enable reasonably well-informed and reasonably attentive internet users, or enabled them only with difficulty, to ascertain whether the service referred to in the advertisements originated from the proprietor of the trademarks or an undertaking economically connected with it, or else originated from a third party.[36] The Federal Court of Australia also recently found an advertiser liable for trademark infringement in similar circumstances.[37]

Given these decisions, it would not be surprising to see trademark owners pursue the advertisers responsible for the purchase of keywords exclusively, rather than the search engines responsible for facilitating that purchase.[38] This does not mean however, that search engines such as Google have or will escape all liability for their role in the sale of trademarks as keywords. To say that would be to ignore the potential scope and application of laws that govern against misleading and deceptive conduct in advertising – laws which in all likelihood, are better suited to regulating new and emerging market activities such as keyword advertising than trademark law is or ever could be.

Misleading and Deceptive Conduct and False Advertising
Some litigants have sought to test the legitimacy of Google's AdWords facility under the laws regulating misleading and deceptive conduct and false advertising, as an alternative to the often argued claim of trademark infringement. One of the most notable examples came to a head in Australia, when the Australian Competition and Consumer Commission (ACCC) instituted proceedings against Google and the Trading Post for breaching section 52 of the Trade Practices Act 1974 (Cth), now section 18 of the Australian Consumer Law (ACL),[39] which prohibits traders from engaging in conduct that is misleading and deceptive or is likely to mislead or deceive.

This section and its predecessor have been interpreted broadly, so that they can serve their function as '[…] a norm of commercial conduct which applies in dealings with the public at large, with individuals and between traders'.[40] As such, section 18 has

---

35. Although see 1-800 Contacts Inc v Lens.com Inc, No 11-4114, 11-4204, 11-4022 (10th Cir, 2013) and Allied Interstate LLC v Kimmel & Silverman PC, WL 4245987 (SDNY, 2013) as examples of trademark infringement lawsuits instituted by trademark proprietors against advertisers who have used third party trademarks as keywords, but which were unsuccessful, for want of sufficient evidence of confusion.
36. Interflora Inc v Marks and Spencer Plc [2013] EWHC 1291 at [318].
37. REA Group Ltd v Real Estate 1 Ltd [2013] FCA 559.
38. They should do so with caution however as the Interflora decision may be confined to its facts, where confusion only arose given the unique nature of the Interflora business. Accordingly, it is possible the case will not serve as a precedent such that all advertisers will be liable for trademark infringement in the future. Rather, in most instances, such as the aforementioned 1-800 Contacts and Allied Interstate decisions, evidence of confusion will not be usually sufficient.
39. This is a schedule of the *Competition and Consumer Act 2010* (Cth).
40. Robert French, 'A Lawyer's Guide to Misleading or Deceptive Conduct', *Australian Law Journal* 63 (1989): 250, 268.

been applied to sanction the use of misleading brand names, get-up, or packaging of products,[41] misleading business and company names,[42] as well as domain names.[43] It also prohibits misleading statements and representations made in advertising including online advertising, and in this way, is analogous to the false advertising prohibitions found in other jurisdictions.[44]

The ACCC's case against Google related to its broader claim relating to various sponsored links.[45] The essence of this broad claim was that each of the disputed sponsored links were misleading or deceptive, or likely to mislead or deceive, because they included a headline that linked to the advertisers' webpage rather than to a webpage of the advertisers' competitor whose trading or product name featured in the headline. For example, the first named respondent, the Trading Post, a classified advertising business, was alleged to have purchased 'Just 4x4s Magazine' among others as keywords (with Just 4x4s Magazine being a competitor of the Trading Post in providing classified advertising for four wheel drives). Thus, when a user entered the search terms 'Just 4x4s Magazine' into the Google search engine, they would be returned the following search result:

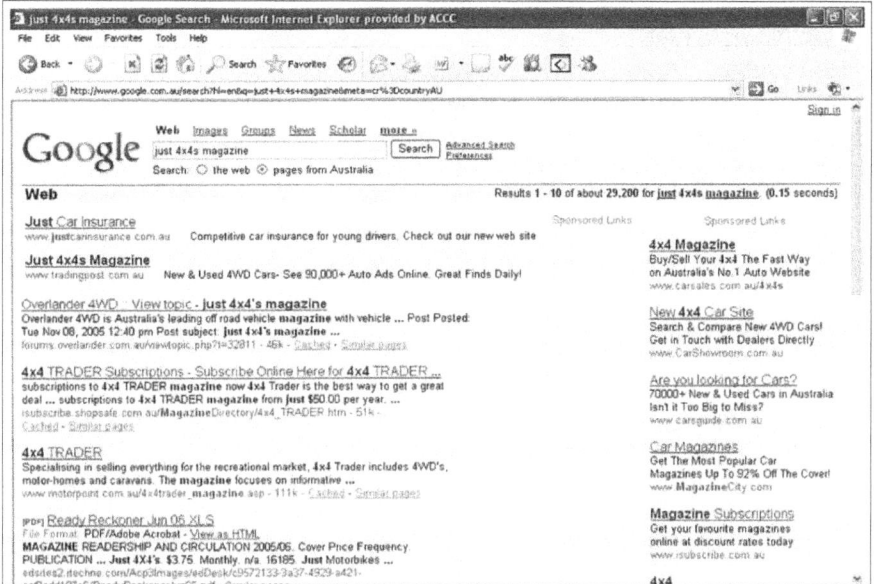

Fig. 2. Google Search Engine Response to Keyword Search for JUST 4X4S MAGAZINE.

---

41. For imitation of product shape and get-up see for example Parkdale Custom Built Furniture Pty Ltd v Puxu Pty Ltd [1982] HCA 44 and Interlego AG & Lego Australia Pty Ltd v Croner Trading Pty Ltd [1992] FCA 624. For the imitation of a product name and get-up see Apand Pty Limited v the Kettle Chip Company Pty Limited [1994] FCA 1370.
42. Re Taco Company of Australia Inc [1982] FCA 136.
43. Architects (Australia) Pty Ltd v Whitty Consultants Pty Ltd [2002] QSC 139.
44. In the United States see §43 of the Lanham Act, 15 USC §1125 (2005). Also see Directive 2006/114/EC of 12 December 2006 on Misleading and Comparative Advertising.
45. For a detailed analysis of this case see Amanda Scardamaglia, 'Misleading and Deceptive Conduct and the Internet: Lessons and Loopholes in Google Inc v Australian Competition and Consumer Commission', *European Intellectual Property Review* 35 (11) (2013): 707-713.

The dispute, so far as it relates to Google, centered on its publishing the misleading and deceptive sponsored links, including the advertisement mentioned above. Specifically, the ACCC alleged that by publishing or displaying the sponsored links in question, Google was liable for misleading and deceptive conduct, as the *maker* of those advertisements. The ACCC further claimed that Google had engaged in misleading and deceptive conduct by failing to distinguish sufficiently between its organic search results and its sponsored links.

Although the proceedings against the Trading Post were settled, the case against Google was subject to protracted litigation. The matter was heard at first instance before Justice Nicholas in the Federal Court. He found that although four out of the 11 sponsored links subject to dispute were misleading and deceptive such that the advertisers were liable, Google had not made those representations.[46] Rather they had merely communicated those representations as the publisher – and as the publisher, Google was not liable. As to the claim that Google had failed to sufficiently distinguish between its organic search results and its sponsored links, the primary judge found that ordinary and reasonable members of the public who have access to a computer connected to the internet would have understood sponsored links were advertisements that were different from Google's organic search results such that Google was not liable.

The ACCC appealed, challenging the finding that Google had not made any false and misleading representations. The finding that Google had not differentiated between its organic search results and sponsored links was not subject to appeal. Here, the Full Court unanimously reversed the decision of the primary judge, finding that Google had engaged in misleading and deceptive conduct. Keane CJ, Jacobson and Lander JJ distinguished Google's role as publisher from publishers of traditional advertising, including newspapers and television stations, finding that it had acted as more than a mere conduit and was the maker of the advertisements:

> The circumstance that the sponsored link is displayed as Google's response to a user's insertion of a search term into Google's search engine prevents any analogy between this case and the case of the bill-board owner or the owner of a telephone network or the publisher of a newspaper or a telecaster who simply displays an advertisement of another. In those cases the medium is not concerned with the content of the advertiser's message: in the four instances in question here Google created the message which it presents. Google's search engine calls up and displays the response to the user's enquiry. It is Google's technology which creates that which is displayed. Google did not merely repeat or pass on a statement by the advertiser: what is displayed in response to the user's search query is not the equivalent of Google saying here is a statement by an advertiser which is passed on for what it is worth.[47]

---

46. Australian Competition and Consumer Commission v Trading Post [2011] FCA 1086.
47. Australian Competition and Consumer Commission v Google Inc [2012] FCAFC 49 at [95] per Keane CJ, Jacobson and Lander JJ.

Perhaps unsurprisingly, Google appealed, and the matter went before the High Court of Australia, where in a much publicized and anticipated decision,[48] the bench unanimously allowed the appeal. Significant to this finding was the fact that the evidence against Google '[...] never rose so high as to prove that Google personnel, as distinct from the advertisers, had chosen the relevant keywords, or otherwise created, endorsed, or adopted the sponsored links'.[49] As such, Google was not liable as the maker of misleading and deceptive advertising content.

Some consider the High Court's decision a lost opportunity, since the statutory language of section 18 of the ACL and its precursor are '[...] sufficiently open-ended to catch the situation at hand'.[50] Even so, one should not dismiss the possibility of search engine liability on this front entirely, since the High Court did not consider a number of complex issues that are critical to the application of consumer protection laws to online service providers, including Google.

For example, while the High Court found that Google was not the maker of the misleading and deceptive advertising content, it did not assess whether Google had engaged in misleading and deceptive conduct by aiding, abetting, counseling, or procuring misleading conduct, on the part of the advertisers. Obviously this was beyond the scope of the claim alleged by the ACCC, and so it was not necessary for members of the Court to make any determination on this issue. Even so, it may still be open for persons aggrieved by Google's conduct, including consumers and trademark owners, to take legal action against Google on this ground.

It is further possible that Google may yet be found liable for the publication of misleading organic search results in breach of section 18 of the ACL, especially since although the ACCC alleged there was a class of consumers who did not understand the distinction between organic search results and sponsored links, they did not produce any survey evidence to support this proposition.[51] Thus, the production of such consumer evidence in the future may prove to be significant. This issue might be enlivened sooner rather than later if Google moves towards the introduction of banner ads as speculated,[52] while the addition of Google's Knowledge Graph adds another layer to the vexed issue of confusion.

Another issue that was not adequately clarified was the application of the publisher's defense, which provides immunity to publishers when they publish advertisements that are false or misleading but has no reason to suspect they would be in

---

48. See Megan Richardson, 'Before the High Court: Why Policy Matters: Google Inc v Australian Competition and Consumer Commission', *Sydney Law Review* 34 (2012): 587-598.
49. Google Inc v Australian Competition and Consumer Commission [2013] HCA 1 at 71 per French CJ, Crennan and Kiefel JJ.
50. Megan Richardson, 'Before the High Court', 588.
51. On this point, the Trkulja v Google Inc LLC & Anor (No 5) [2012] VSC 533 case is relevant. Here, the Supreme Court of Victoria found Google liable as the publisher of defamatory material as published in its organic search results. It is entirely plausible that such a claim could have been made out under the ACL as well.
52. Charles Arthur, 'Google Breaks 2005 Promise to Never Show Banner Ads on Search Results', *The Guardian*, 25 October 2013, http://www.theguardian.com/technology/2013/oct/24/google-breaks-promise-banner-ads-search-results.

breach of the law.[53] Because Google was not found to have engaged in misleading and deceptive conduct, the High Court did not think it necessary to consider the relevance of this defense. The majority of French CJ, Crennan, and Kiefel JJ did however observe that:

> [...] an intermediary publisher who has endorsed or adopted a published representation of an advertiser without appreciating the capacity of that representation to mislead or deceive may have resort to the statutory defence. In those circumstances, recognising that its business carried a risk of unwitting contravention, an intermediary publisher may need to show that it had some appropriate system in place to succeed in the defence that it did not know and had no reason to suspect that the publication of that representation would amount to a contravention.[54]

Whether Google's policies and practices would have been considered an appropriate system by which it could rely on the publisher's defense was not discussed. Given this, there may still be some life to this limb of liability, in terms of regulating the conduct of internet search engines and, even more broadly, their advertisers in the future. Indeed, in the current landscape, such provisions seem the most likely legal avenue to fill this regulatory hole.

There are a number of reasons why this might be true. First, this alternative may prove more palatable for the courts, since it does not require them to apply trademark doctrine in a way which might depart from traditional principles of trademark law in order to guard against confusion.[55] Second, consumer protection legislation, particularly in Australia, is also flexible enough for the courts to interpret broadly, so as to accommodate new and emerging commercial practices such as internet advertising.

Where to From Here?
Claims of search engine liability require carefully balancing a number of interests – the interests of trademark owners, consumers, and competition more generally. In exercising this juggling act, the courts have recognized that internet advertising is simply a modern form of comparative advertising that is ultimately good for consumers and good for competition because it promotes choice, placing priority on these interests above all else. This much was acknowledged by Arnold's J in the aforementioned Interflora decision, where it was observed that '[...] keyword advertising is not inherently or inevitably objectionable from a trade mark perspective. On the contrary, the case law [...] in this field recognises that, as a general rule, keyword advertising promotes competition [...]'.[56]

---

53. Section 85(3) of the Trade Practices Act 1974 (Cth), now 251 of the ACL.
54. Google Inc v Australian Competition and Consumer Commission [2013] HCA 1 at 75 per French CJ, Crennan and Kiefel JJ.
55. Such as the contextual approach to trademark infringement as suggested in Dinwoodie and Janis, 'Confusion Over Use: Contextualism in Trademark Law', *Iowa Law Review* 92 (2007): 1597-1667.
56. Interflora Inc v Marks and Spencer Plc [2013] EWHC 1291 at [288].

As such, the courts have resisted applying a cheapest cost avoider[57] interpretation to questions of search engine liability and have instead recognized Google's advertising service as a legitimate undertaking. Perhaps this is because the alternative would '[...] jeopardize the internet's potential as an information resource and a catalyst for competition [...]'.[58] It may also have an undesirable chilling effect in restricting the dissemination of truthful comparative advertising and unnecessarily sanctioning legitimate behavior by internet intermediaries.[59] Thus, as Eric Goldman puts it:

> To increase the odds of efficient and successful searches, searchers should be able to pick the search terms they want and search providers should be able to use those search terms to deliver the most helpful content to searchers. Thus trademark law must step aside when searchers receive content they may want.[60]

As the preceding discussion has demonstrated, the case law in this area indicates that the courts have for the most part accepted this proposition, and have been prepared to quarantine the use of trademarks and keywords from the realms of trademark infringement by search engine operators, although the advertisers have not been afforded the same protection. Thus, while there is still some scope to test the ambit of such claims further, it appears that search engine liability, at least for the moment and at least from the perspective of trademark law, is an unlikely proposition. Any potential liability for trademark infringement therefore would more likely rest against the advertisers. And as to the laws relating to misleading and deceptive conduct or false advertising – well, in the absence of any statutory intervention, they seem the most viable and appropriate mechanism to regulate the conduct of both search engines and advertisers in this context in the future.

References

1-800 Contacts Inc v WhenU.com Inc, 414 F 3d 400 (2d Cir, 2005).
1-800 Contacts Inc v Lens.com Inc, No. 11-4114, 11-4204, 11-4022 (10th Cir, 2013).
Allied Interstate LLC v Kimmel & Silverman PC, WL 4245987 (SDNY, 2013).
Arthur, Charles. 'Google Breaks 2005 Promise to Never Show Banner Ads on Search Results', *The Guardian*, 25 October 2013, http://www.theguardian.com/technology/2013/oct/24/google-breaks-promise-banner-ads-search-results.
Australian Competition and Consumer Commission v Google Inc [2012] FCAFC 49.
Australian Competition and Consumer Commission v Trading Post [2011] FCA 1086.
Australian Gold Inc v Hatfield, 436 F 3d 1228 (10th Cir, 2006).
Bing Ads, 'Intellectual Property Guidelines', http://advertise.bingads.microsoft.com/en-us/editorial-

---

57. That is, accept that liability should fall on the 'cheapest cost avoider', being the party that could have avoided the harm most cheaply. On this, see Guido Calabresi, 'Some Thoughts on Risk Distribution and the Law of Tort', *Yale Law Journal* 70 (1961): 499-533 and Guido Calabresi and Jon T. Hirchshoff, 'Towards a Test for Strict Liability in Torts', *Yale Law Journal* 81 (1972): 1055-1085. For a discussion of the application of this principle in the search engine context, see generally Megan Richardson, 'Before the High Court', 587-598.
58. Eric Goldman, 'Deregulating Relevancy in Internet Trademark Law', 509.
59. Also see Stacey L. Dogan and Mark A. Lemley, 'Trademark and Consumer Search Costs on the Internet', *Houston Law Review* 41 (2004): 782. Also available from http://www.houstonlawreview.org/archive/downloads/41-3_pdf/dogan.pdf.
60. Eric Goldman, 'Deregulating Relevancy in Internet Trademark Law', 510.

intellectual-property-guidelines#1.
Bundesgerichtshof, I ZR 140/10 of 19 October 2011, *Vorschaubilder II*.
Calabresi, Guido and Jon T. Hirchshoff. 'Towards a Test for Strict Liability in Torts', *Yale Law Journal* 81 (1972): 1055-1085.
Calabresi, Guido. 'Some Thoughts on Risk Distribution and the Law of Tort', *Yale Law Journal* 70 (1961): 499-533.
Competition and Consumer Act 2010 (Cth).
Dinwoodie, Graeme B. and Mark D. Janis. 'Confusion Over Use: Contextualism in Trademark Law', *Iowa Law Review* 92 (2007): 1597-1667. Also available from http://www.repository.law.indiana.edu/cgi/viewcontent.cgi?article=1361&context=facpub.
Dogan, Stacey L. and Mark A. Lemley. 'Trademark and Consumer Search Costs on the Internet', *Houston Law Review* 41 (2004): 777-838. Also available from http://www.houstonlawreview.org/archive/downloads/41-3_pdf/dogan.pdf.
European Parliament and Council Directive 2006/114/EC of 12 December 2006 on Misleading and Comparative Advertising.
European Parliament and Council Directive 2008/95/EC of 22 October 2008 to Approximate the Law of the Member States Relating to Trade Marks.
Ezzo v Google, 2:09-CV-00159 (MD Fla, 2010).
First Council Directive 89/104/EEC of 21 December 1988 to Approximate the Law of the Member States Relating to Trade Marks.
Franklyn, David J. and David A. Hyman. 'Trademarks as Search Engine Keywords: Much Ado About Something?', *Harvard Journal of Law and Technology* 26.2 (2013): 1-65.
French, Robert. 'A Lawyer's Guide to Misleading or Deceptive Conduct', *Australian Law Journal* 63 (1989): 250-260.
Goldman, Eric. 'Deregulating Relevancy in Internet Trademark Law', *Emory Law Journal* 54 (2005): 507-596.
_____. 'Microsoft Adopts Google-Style Trademark Policy for Keyword Advertising', Technology & Marketing Law Blog, 15 February 2011, http://blog.ericgoldman.org/archives/2011/02/microsoft_adopt.htm.
_____. 'More Confirmation that Google Has Won the AdWords Trademark Battles Worldwide', *Forbes*, 22 March 2013, http://www.forbes.com/sites/ericgoldman/2013/03/22/more-confirmation-that-google-has-won-the-adwords-trademark-battles-worldwide/.
_____. 'With Rosetta Stone Settlement, Google Gets Closer to Legitimizing Billions of AdWords Revenue,' *Forbes*, 1 November 2012, http://www.forbes.com/sites/ericgoldman/2012/11/01/with-rosetta-stone-settlement-google-gets-closer-to-legitimizing-billions-of-adwords-revenue/print/.
Google Advertising Policies Help, 'Updates to AdWords Trademark Policy', https://support.google.com/adwordspolicy/answer/177578.
Google France SARL v Louis Vuitton Malletier SA [2010] C-236/08, C-237/08 and C-238/08.
Google Inc v Australian Competition and Consumer Commission [2013] HCA 1.
Google Inc, 'Form 10-K: Annual Report', 29 January 2013', http://edgar.secdatabase.com/1404/119312513028362/filing-main.htm.
GoTo.com v Walt Disney Co, 202 F 3d 1199 (9th Cir, 2000).
Home Decor Center Inc v Google Inc, CV 2:12-cv-05706-GW-SH (CD Cal, 2013).
Interflora Inc v Marks and Spencer Plc [2013] EWHC 1291 (Ch).
'Introducing the Knowledge Graph: Things not Strings', Google Official Blog, 16 May 2012, http://googleblog.blogspot.com.au/2012/05/introducing-knowledge-graph-things-not.html.
Jurin v Google Inc, WL 5011007 (ED Cal, 2012).
Landes, William M. and Richard A. Posner. 'Trademark Law: An Economic Perspective,' *Journal of Law and Economics* 30 (1987): 266-268.
_____. *The Economic Structure of Intellectual Property*, Cambridge, MA: Harvard University Press, 2003.
Language Council of Sweden, 'Google Does Not Own the Language,' 26 March 2013, http://www.sprakradet.se/15922 (in Swedish).
Lanham Act 15 USC §1051 et seq. (2005).
Marsoof, Althaf. 'Online Service Providers and Third Party Trademark Infringement in Australia',

International Journal of Law and Information Technology 2013: 1-32. Also available from http://ijlit.oxfordjournals.org/content/early/2013/07/18/ijlit.eat010.full.pdf.

Moffat, Viva R. 'Regulating Search', *Harvard Journal of Law and Technology* 22 (2009): 475-513.

NetMarketShare, 'Desktop Search Engine Market Share', January 2014, http://www.netmarketshare.com/search-engine-market-share.aspx?qprid=4&qpcustomd=0.

Playboy Enterprises Inc v Netscape Communications Corp, 354 F 3d 1020 (9th Cir, 2004).

Pricewaterhouse Coopers, 'Global Entertainment and Media Outlook: 2013 – 2017: Internet Advertising', http://www.pwc.com/gx/en/global-entertainment-media-outlook/segment-insights/internet-advertising.jhtml.

REA Group Ltd v Real Estate 1 Ltd [2013] FCA 559.

Rescuecom Corp v Google Inc, 562 F 3d 123 (2d Cir, 2009).

Reuters, 'Rosetta Stone and Google Settle Trademark Lawsuits', 31 October 2012, http://www.reuters.com/article/2012/10/31/us-usa-court-rosettastone-google-idUSBRE89U1GE20121031.

Richardson, Megan. 'Before the High Court: Why Policy Matters: Google Inc v Australian Competition and Consumer Commission', *Sydney Law Review* 34 (2012): 587-598.

Rosetta Stone Ltd v Google Inc, 1:09-cv-00736-GBL-TCB (ED Va, 2010).

Rosetta Stone Ltd v Google Inc, WL 1155143 (4th Cir, 2012).

Saltmarsh, Matthew. 'Google Will Sell Brand Names as Keywords in Europe' *The New York Times*, 4 August 2010, http://www.nytimes.com/2010/08/05/technology/05google.html?_r=0.

Scardamaglia, Amanda. 'Misleading and Deceptive Conduct and the Internet: Lessons and Loopholes in Google Inc v Australian Competition and Consumer Commission', *European Intellectual Property Review* 35 (11) (2013): 707-713.

Soaring Helmet Corporation v Bill Me Inc, 2:2009cv00789 (WD Wash, 2009).

'Trademark Law – Infringement Liability: European Court of Justice Holds that Search Engines do not Infringe Trademarks', *Harvard Law Review* 124 (2010): 648-655.

Trade Marks Act 1995 (Australia).

Trkulja v Google Inc LLC & Anor (No 5) [2012] VSC 533.

Towards an Anthropology of Location-Based Recommendation and Search

Martin Reiche and Ulrich Gehmann

Towards an Anthropology of Location-Based Recommendation and Search

Martin Reiche and Ulrich Gehmann

With the increase and advance of software for mobile devices, the paradigm of *relevance* for the user has experienced a major shift. Functionality that was earlier heavily bound to software on stand-alone machines such as mainframes is now available for citizens with sufficient spare change wherever they are located in the world. Cell phones have advanced to smart phones and so increased in complexity, computational power, and practicability. However, an even more important change has taken place: computers are no longer bound to a specific place, but rather can be easily carried in a person's pocket and are therefore as mobile as their owner. This new mobile freedom and independence is of course also applicable to the software on the phone,[1] which by now enables the user to use the phone in almost any way that a software developer envisions and that hardware allows.

Thus, software itself has become mobile, and this new mobility leads inarguably to a paradigm shift: through the hardware of the mobile device, software becomes aware of its own mobility and can leverage the new kinds of information it acquires: location, acceleration, proximity to other devices,[2] and access to local infrastructure through Wi-Fi. These new parameters address the user's notion of space, place, and relevance drastically, as these terms now have to be defined not only through the eyes of the user, but also through the 'eyes' of the software. The software can no longer be seen as independent from the user but is intertwined with some of his properties in physical space. This paradigm shift will be the focus of this article.

Relevance
We all have a deep understanding of what is relevant for us in our life. Although understanding what is relevant might be very subjective, the idea that some things are more relevant than others is part of our cultural heritage. When it comes to breaking down a definition of relevance though, we can argue with the *conditio humana*: the basic notion of the human being, i.e. what makes us human after all. If we accept that relevance is what serves this basic notion of the *conditio humana*, then relevance is subjective. If relevance is subjective from the very start of its definition, we have to question whether a definition of relevance that has its roots in computer science and mathematics –

---

1. Of course not completely independent of location, as smart phones still need access to power supply regularly and wireless connectivity for many of its main functions to work.
2. E.g. through GPS, accelerometers, and near-field communication sensors.

domains that are precise and, as an effect, computable – is an adequate definition of relevance for a human being.

At this point, there are two aspects of general importance pertaining to discussions of the *conditio humana*. Even if it is true that the human condition embodies a subjective concept, there are conditions that serve as a framework within which these subjectivities remain embedded. First of all, it was a specific sociocultural and economic context that gave rise to an unprecedented use of technology, and, in its wake, our dependence on technological devices to such a degree that our very conceptions of the self (and hence of the human condition) became strongly influenced by it. First of all, our daily life worlds became technologized to such a degree that living without technology turns out to be almost impossible. To provide an example, at the onset of a third wave of modernization shortly after World War II, Schelsky notes our increasing dependence on 'automatization' (as he terms it), with respective social consequences.[3]

This dependence was the case long before the arrival of the internet. The technological condition became an intrinsic part of the human condition; this effect shouldn't be forgotten when discussing its continuous accelerations manifested in the paradigm shift toward mobile devices mentioned in the beginning. We have been technologically determined for a long while (as Schelsky wrote in 1957), and in such an overall environment, which has been characterized as a *technogene* space,[4] we encounter not only new paradigms but also ontologies. Seen against the background of a continuous generation of non-places[5] associated with that technogene space, that paradigm shift – or more precisely, the ontology it announces – perfectly fits with a scenario of generating a literal utopia (that is, a non-place).

Second, when considering possible determinants of the present human condition, we should look back at the long history of discussions occurring under the aegis of technology-driven modernity. Any discussion about a new ontological status (expressed in the paradigm shift) must consider all the past shocks related to the *conditio humana*, from 19th century metropolization onwards to the present state.[6] We must consider these shocks in order to take a broader perspective of the phenomena discussed as they deserve, and for them to be understood at all.

Location-Based Recommendation and Search
Location-based recommendation is a concept from mathematics and computer science that has made a great impact on our experience of the web, especially in the last decade. Almost every online shop offers some sort of recommendation to its users: either they recommend products based on what they learn about the user's previous interests or based on what other users have bought independently of each other.

---

3. Helmut Schelsky, 'About the Social Consequences of Automatization', *Auf der Suche nach Wirklichkeit* [On the Search for Reality], Munich: Goldmann, 1979, pp. 118-147.
4. Günther Oetzel, 'On Technotopian Spaces', in Ulrich Gehmann (ed.) *Virtuelle und ideale Welten* [Virtual and Ideal Worlds], Karlsruhe: KIT Publishing, 2012, pp. 65-83 (73-76 on the *technogene* space in particular).
5. Marc Augé, *Non-Places: Introduction to an Anthropology of Supermodernity*, London/New York: Verso, 1995.
6. See for instance Helmuth Plessner, *Conditio Humana*, Frankfurt: Suhrkamp, 2003.

Sometimes recommendations appear completely random to outsiders. Location-based recommendation can formally be seen as a mathematical function that puts an entity in space in relation to other entities in (the same or another) space by utilizing a common space called *feature space*.[7] Thus, in order to compute relations, the entities are processed and reduced to *features* that resemble the entity. It must be clear that this reduction is intentionally done by the designer of the recommender system and that the designer's beliefs about *what makes an entity to be the entity it is* might be highly subjective. Taking into account that every next step of the recommendation is first and foremost based on this reductive step, it is obvious that the designer's subjective beliefs about the world are subsequently affecting every user of the system.

Like the *conditio humana*, the problem of reduction has a long modern history as well, one aligned with the dominance of technogene spaces addressed earlier. A space generated by technology has to be reductive *eo ipso* since the essence of the technical approach to reality is to functionalize things. The question 'what makes an entity to be the entity it is' has to be interpreted in these terms, too, because we are discussing functionalities. And functionality *is* reductive, otherwise it wouldn't work. Based on these fundamental relations that cannot be overcome, a functionalized entity is a reduced entity, and the feature space that is made of functionalized entities is reductive, too, by necessity.

With regards to *relevance*, an additional aspect comes into play. For functionalized features, only functions are relevant at the proverbial end of the day, whether technical functions enabling performance and the use of apps (a point to come), economic functions sustaining the technical ones, or last but not least, social 'functions' as the result of all of this, since social functions are one of the main *applications* of the former. So, the relevant world becomes the world of the functional, that is, the world of functions.

By reducing the world to features, location-based recommendation algorithms calculate the relevance of every entity in relation to another entity. This other entity does not have to be of the same kind as the entity that will be recommended; it might just be the location of the user, that is a recommendation could respond to the relation of the user's current location to a set of night clubs (based on proximity) as well as a night club's relation to other night clubs (based on e.g. music genre and proximity). Note that this notion of location-based recommendation already includes the concept of location-based search. While search delivers information to its user based on a query and thus can be seen as a reactive way to present information ('search results'), recommendation provides results without requiring the user to execute a concrete query. The effects of search and recommendation for the user, though, remain the same, which is why in the course of this article we will use these two terms synonymously. In the case of location-based recommendation algorithms, we will from now on assume that the user's proximity to the recommended entities plays an important role in the calculation process of the recommendation.

---

7. A feature space is an abstract space whose dimensions are properties of the entities. How the dimensions are chosen and what the dimensions resemble is highly dependent on the entities themselves. A text document for example could have the number of occurrences of words as dimensions, while a car could have the dimensions make, model, color, gearing, etc.

Besides the problem that already emerges from processes of reduction, a problem occurs in the calculation of the results. At this stage all entities are already reduced to a set of features, and the calculation involves the computation of distance between these feature sets. While there is extensive literature on metrics that can be used in order to compute these distances,[8] modern recommender systems usually try to learn users' habits and interests, then apply this knowledge to the recommendation process by using *weighted metrics*. These weighted metrics deploy different factors of influence for each feature in the calculation process in order to resemble the information the system has already learned about the user.[9]

Finally, the results of the recommendation might consist of entities nearby, entities that match the user's interests to a high degree, as well as entities that increase the chance of serendipity as they are drawn from a number of other entities, and the system is not sure whether they are of interest to the user or not.[10] These results all have in common that their relevance to the user has been mathematically calculated, and that this calculation has followed a model of the world that has been created by people who might have different beliefs about the world than the user. This means that all recommender systems not only resemble the user's spatial properties or interests but also the designer's very own notion of relevance on all the levels of calculation.

The World as a Set of Apps and the New Spatiality

Taking into account the perspective of a smart phone user, we should think over a few more problems arising from the conception of relevance that are deeply intertwined with the idea of the *app*. The basic idea of an app is to encapsulate one functionality into a single piece of software and to distribute this software worldwide. This concept concentrates the efforts of a single piece of software into the optimization of its functionality, eventually reaching the point where the piece of software becomes the de facto standard for the solution to a specific problem.[11] This single task's degree of perfection is one of the key benefits of the app and a big reason for its success story.[12]

However, providing one functionality per software piece also produces a variety of problems. First of all, basic functionalities such as textual communication are duplicated over a multitude of apps; the average smart phone today has at least one app for standard text, one for Facebook messages, and one for Twitter, not to mention the number of apps for taking pictures or writing notes. All these apps have their

---

8. Eleza Deza and Michelle Marie Deza, *Encyclopedia of Distances*, Heidelberg: Springer, 2009, p. 3f.
9. For example if the user is in close physical proximity to some of the best techno night clubs in town but the system has learned that the user anticipates other genres, it might reflect this information when computing the recommendations, maybe resulting in some very close techno night clubs nearby as well as other clubs further away that better resemble the user's interests. That way, spatial as well as learned information have been taken into account in the computational process of the recommender system.
10. And by this, the system is able to learn more about the user as it can extract information about the behavior towards these unforeseen results.
11. As is Facebook for the wider social network of many of its users.
12. At this time, we see a multitude of app stores from many different companies and service providers, such as Apple, Google, Amazon, Intel, and much more.

rightful purpose as they offer a certain approach towards one functionality and therefore might serve a user better than an app with the same functionality but a different approach. This in itself is not yet a problem, but it starts to become a problem (for example for communication) when the existing systems cannot communicate with each other, or users cannot communicate across these platforms. You can refer to this problem as the *lock-in effect*.[13] Ultimately it forces users to work with a variety of apps that all provide the same functionality, thus effectively undermining the whole idea of the app.

The information that can be used to make a recommendation must be gathered by the apps themselves, which means that every app can only supply recommendations on the basis of its own investigations about the user, and this significantly affects the quality of the recommendation. If the recommendation calculation itself can only be done on the basis of the information gathered by the single app, then important information might be missing when recommending entities. Even more, self-learning recommender systems will learn only a small subset of the variety of the user's interests (as they can only learn interests that have to do with the functionality of the app itself) and therefore will optimize their algorithms in a direction that no longer fully resembles the user's interests, so that the relevance of the recommended entities decreases.

At the same time, the relevance of the recommended entities of each app increases in the mathematical model of the app (which simply results in the app optimizing its recommendations based on a model and the learned characteristics and interests of the user). What then happens is that each app develops its own optimized model of the world and offers this view to the user, and the world gets functionally segmented based on the optimizations of each app on the phone. Instead of showing the user the relevant world, smart phone apps show the user a world that is optimized based on her location and interests for each specific functionality, each represented by a different app. The user becomes the inhabitant of a functionally segmented environment, meaning that the relevant world around the user cannot be modeled based on the concept of the app.[14]

If you turn from the single app and allow data acquired from functions of different apps to merge into one single user profile, as with a Google or Amazon account, then the recommendation quality may increase again as the functional segmentation might not take place in such a drastic way. However, new problems arise regarding a major concern with all recommender systems: in order to work the way they are supposed to, recommender systems create profiles from an extensive collection of data acquired from users' behavioral patterns, leading to very understandable privacy concerns. In essence, to get rid of the problems of functional segmentation, user profiles must be created that are shared among several (not necessarily all) apps, giving away this potentially valuable data to the third party that is maintaining the profile. In order to avoid the functional segmentation, we have to give our data away.

---

13. S.J. Liebowitz and Stephen E. Margolis, 'Path Dependence, Lock-in and History', *Journal of Law, Economics, and Organization* 11 (1995): 205-226.
14. Ulrich Gehmann and Martin Reiche, 'Virtual Urbanity', Hybrid City II Conference, Athens, 2013.

New Spatial Relevance
One can still argue that the models of the world that are generated by smart phones and apps are not intrinsically affecting the world of the user, but as we have shown in earlier publications,[15] there is reasonable suspicion that this functional segmentation, as well as the system designer's beliefs about the world, influence the users' notion of relevance and also the users' behavior. In addition, there is an economic reason why the apps work in such a way: the recommendation creates a *personalized experience* that might greatly differ from your experience without the app (unwanted people can be blocked, conflicting thoughts can get filtered out, etc.[16]) and that thus gives you a more enjoyable user experience, resulting in an increase in the usage of specific apps and lowering the inhibition threshold to pay for extra services or advanced versions of the software itself.

Optimization of different functionalities through apps thus creates a new spatial relevance. The idea that the sum of the apps on a mobile device describes your world (at least the one reachable through the device) to a certain extent simply stems from the experience that these apps are being developed for almost all functionalities in life that can be converted into an app (be it sport, gaming, dating, communication, or work). It therefore is important to address the problems of relevance in this anthropological context.

Conclusion
Mobile devices show us a world that is highly optimized for every function that is transferable to the concept of an app. We have outlined how apps are able to optimize their functionality through recommendation by learning about the user's interests and characteristics, and we have shown how this leads to a paradigm shift in the notion of (spatial) relevance. *Relevant for the user* becomes an algorithmic mixture of the subjective world view of the system designer, the user's interests that have been learned by the app, as well as the lack of information that results from the encapsulation of functionality in each app. This new notion of relevance simultaneously becomes a new viewpoint of the world due to the duty of the mobile device to become our personal assistant and our gateway to parts of the world that are not immediately accessible to us. At the same time, the personalized experience that the mobile device is offering us is compelling, which makes it easy for us to sell away our very own notion of relevance for the notion(s) of relevance created by the apps on the devices – and these foremost address a notion of relevance based on the pragmatic idea of increased user interaction resulting in more sales.

---

15. Martin Reiche and Ulrich Gehmann, 'How Virtual Spaces Re-Render the Perception of Reality Through Playful Augmentation', in Proceedings of ACM International Conference on Cyberworlds, Darmstadt, 2012.
16. Jacob Weisberg, 'Bubble Trouble, Is Web Personalization Turning Us Into Solipsistic Twits?', Slate, 10 June 2011, http://www.slate.com/articles/news_and_politics/the_big_idea/2011/06/bubble_trouble.html.

References

Augé, Marc. *Non-Places: Introduction to an Anthropology of Supermodernity*, London/New York: Verso, 1995.

Deza, Eleza and Michelle Marie Deza. *Encyclopedia of Distances*, Heidelberg: Springer, 2009.

Gehmann, Ulrich and Martin Reiche. 'Virtual Urbanity', Hybrid City II Conference, Athens, 2013, in press.

Oetzel, Günther. 'On Technotopian Spaces', in: Ulrich Gehmann (ed) *Virtuelle und ideale Welten* [Virtual and Ideal Worlds], Karlsruhe: KIT Publishing, 2012.

Liebowitz, S.J. and Stephen E. Margolis. 'Path Dependence, Lock-in and History', *Journal of Law, Economics, and Organization* 11 (1995): 205-226.

Reiche, Martin and Ulrich Gehmann. 'How Virtual Spaces Re-Render the Perception of Reality Through Playful Augmentation', in Proceedings of ACM International Conference on Cyberworlds, Darmstadt, 2012.

Schelsky, Helmut. 'About the Social Consequences of Automatization', *Auf der Suche nach Wirklichkeit* [On the Search for Reality], 1979, Munich, Goldmann.

Weisberg, Jacob. 'Bubble Trouble, Is Web Personalization Turning Us Into Solipsistic Twits?' Slate, 10 June 2011, http://www.slate.com/articles/news_and_politics/the_big_idea/2011/06/bubble_trouble.html.

Historicizing Google Search: A Discussion of the Challenges Related to Archiving Search Results

Jacob Ørmen

Historicizing Google Search: A Discussion of the Challenges Related to Archiving Search Results

Jacob Ørmen

Who would not want to know which results you would have gotten if you had entered the keyword 'terrorism' into Google's search bar just before September 11? And what if you could compare it to a search conducted on exactly 11 September 2001 or two weeks after? Or what about tracing the search rankings of websites associated with the query 'USA' through the last ten years?

Subjects like these and related types of questions trouble imaginative researchers (probably historians the most), and often the depressing answer presents itself: yeah, you actually could... if someone had just thought of archiving it then. The main issue with historical sources is that someone had to have the idea to produce them in the first place. Luckily such sources have been produced and made available to us in many formats, from newspaper articles, film, and video recordings to official documents and personal correspondence. In recent years we have been able to supplement these types of sources with digital data from social network sites such as Twitter that extend the variety and depth of communication, which we are then able to analyze retrospectively. Now, I argue, we also need to pay attention to those areas of communication that are not as easily stored as newspaper articles or tweets, but nonetheless are relevant sources to future understandings of how events like September 11 or discourses around a particular topic such as 'USA' have unfolded. One such area would be Google Search.

Google Search is a particularly interesting case because of its total dominance over the search engine market. Google Search is a central entry point to the web for the majority of people in large parts of the Western world – approximately 65 percent in the U.S. and probably more than 95 percent in Europe.[1] It is an important gateway for people to find information about various topics, events, disasters, etc. and for that reason it is relevant to investigate the type of information that is being presented to individuals in the form of ranked search results. To document the development of search is also important for the general preservation of culture. As Sanz and Stancik put it, Google

---

1. Ken Hillis, Michael Petit, and Kylie Jarrett, *Google and the Culture of Search,* New York, NY and Oxon, UK: Routledge, 2013.

Search offers us a 'unique empirical window into the study of culture'.[2] Furthermore, if we want to understand search engines such as Google as a specific 'meta-genre'[3] on the internet, it is important that we attend to how these search engines arrange, or mediate, information on the web in the form of ranked search results.

Search results are however not easy to archive since the exact rankings of websites are re-evaluated by proprietary and inaccessible algorithms (including Google's Page-Rank) for each query and thereby subject to change constantly. They are not documents in the same fashion as newspaper articles, tweets, or Facebook posts published online by someone and that appear more or less in a similar way for anyone accessing them. Knowing how a specific website fared or which websites were associated with a particular keyword at any point in time is impossible to assess if the information has not been archived properly. Since the quality of the sources relies heavily on the precise ways they have been archived, these are important issues for scholars in the digital humanities and related fields. Here, I cannot provide a clear answer to the challenges related to archiving search results (since I do not believe there are clear answers here), but I raise some of the most pertinent challenges and suggest some ways forward. Hopefully, this analysis can shed some new light on how search results can be used as historical sources in future research.

'All Those Moments Will Be Lost in Time, Like Tears in Rain'
The problem of irretrievable information is anything but new – in fact, the majority of communication has always been (and still is) lost for eternity. Just think of all oral communication that is not being recorded. It is, as the android Roy Batty so poetically utters in *Blade Runner*, as if 'all those moments will be lost in time, like tears in rain'. This also entails that we of course cannot archive everything (not even all the material on the web), and therefore we must choose carefully what type of information we want to archive and how we want to store it. I believe that search results can serve as important primary sources in the future, and we therefore should worry about which search results merit archiving and how to archive them. Before we can go as far, we need to understand the intricacies of conducting this kind of archiving.

Search engine results exist as a particular type of document online. Since search engines provide an index of retrievable documents on the web, they are on the one hand general access points to a wealth of information (somewhat like a traditional library index). Yet, search engines, by way of various algorithms, also adjust the specific search results to the person making the search (more like the librarian in human form). In that sense the particular search results are a co-creation of the person searching (by the keyword decisions and earlier search history as well as numerous other factors) and Google (by providing an index to search). The results are, so to speak, both 'found' through the index and 'made' by the interaction – referring to discussions of different

---

2. Esteve Sanz and Juraj Stancik, 'Your Search – "Ontological Security" – Matched 111,000 Documents: An Empirical Substantiation of the Cultural Dimension of Online Search', *New Media & Society* (29 April 2013): 0-19.
3. Klaus Bruhn Jensen, 'Meta-Media and Meta-Communication: Revisiting the Concept of Genre in the Digital Media Environment', *MedieKultur. Journal of Media and Communication Research* 51 (2011): 8-21.

types of data raised by Jensen and others.[4] They simply don't exist prior to the particular act of searching. Therefore search results are likely to appear differently not only in time and across space as the index and algorithms change, but also between different individuals ('searchers') making the queries. Results do not simply exist 'out there' waiting to be found, scraped, and analyzed as are offline documents, online articles, or tweets, but have to be created in the act of searching. This ontological peculiarity poses a number of unique methodological challenges for researchers studying search results.

The practical question of how to archive Google Search has only become more complicated in recent years. The official API to search through the entire index of Google Search was discontinued by Google as of November 2010 and replaced by a Custom Search API that offers very limited search options.[5] It appears to be possible to circumvent the limitations set up by Google through a manual customization of the present API, but it remains unclear whether this is in line with Google's Terms of Service (ToS). Furthermore, the present Custom Search API will be discontinued soon (according to rumors on Stack Overflow).[6] Last but not least, it looks like the search results produced by the search APIs (both the present one and the discontinued) produce quite different search results from manual searches. A different option would be to construct a web scraper and query Google through this device. However, Google has previously explicitly banned this option in the ToS, and it is generally seen as a 'dirty research method'.[7] Using APIs or server-side access has its clear advantages, but the risk is always that access to or functionalities of services might change suddenly, thereby severely harming the research project. Therefore it is always a risky solution, and even more so for studies taking place over a longer period of time. This is obviously not a unique phenomenon related to studying Google Search, but a common problem that one encounters when retrieving data from online services in general (scholars of Twitter for instance are well aware of the limits the Twitter API sets on research projects).

So it seems that the only really viable option is to collect the results through manual search requests on google.com (and the affiliated sub-domains). An inelegant yet quite feasible method with which to do this is to use research tools that can make automated screen dumps of search results at regular intervals.[8] This approach has the benefit of containing all the visual information from the browser window, which might work well in research projects that are interested in the constellation of search results (e.g. the size of each result in the query list, the placement of links, images, videos, and other

---

4. Klaus Bruhn Jensen, 'New Media, Old Methods – Internet Methodologies and the Online/Offline Divide', in Mia Consalvo and Charles Ess (eds) *The Handbook of Internet Studies*, Oxford, UK: Wiley-Blackwell, 2010, p. 43.
5. See, https://developers.google.com/custom-search/.
6. See, 'Google Web Search API Deprecated – What Now?', Stackoverflow, http://stackoverflow.com/questions/4082966/google-web-search-api-deprecated-what-now, or 'What Free Web Search APIs Are Available?', Stackoverflow, http://stackoverflow.com/questions/6084096/what-free-web-search-apis-are-available.
7. As Richard Rogers described how people view this kind of research in the plenary session 'The Network Tradition in Communication Research and Scholarship', at the International Communication Association (ICA) Conference, London, June 17-22, 2013.
8. One such tool is Siteshoter (only for PC), which can take screen dumps of various websites at specified intervals. The program runs in the background and seems to be quite reliable over longer periods of time (e.g. one week). Thank you to Aske Kammer for making me aware of this tool.

contextual data). This method has its obvious drawbacks if the goal is to conduct statistical analysis, since the information is 'flattened' in one image instead of being nicely ordered in a structured database. Manual recoding is of course possible, but will be quite tedious work even with smaller samples of screen dumps. Therefore, screen dumping functions best in more qualitative studies that integrate the visual elements into the analysis. I will discuss the more general issue of why qualitative methods in search engine studies might be more feasible than quantitative later on.

The second important question to consider is how much material is relevant to archive. That of course depends on the purpose for which the material is collected, and there really is no overall answer here. Instead I will present two different archetypical models of archiving that I believe offer alternative ways of approaching search results as documents:

1. *The longitudinal model*: A basic approach would be to archive search results for specific queries on a regular pre-planned basis (e.g. once per week for several years in a row). The point here would be to document certain keywords that retain salience in the popular mind (in other words: that get queried a lot over a longer period of time). Examples of keywords such as this could be 'terrorism', 'United States', and 'E.U.'. Here the goal would be too look for associations between the keywords and websites, pictures, videos, discourses, or anything else one could find as relevant units of analysis. This approach, first of all, makes it possible to engage with how search results of specific terms appear in various stages (in time)[9] and in various locations (in space) – what Marres and Weltevrede have called the *liveliness* of issues.[10] This approach also entails that we can attend to the contexts of the particular search action and take into account the contextual details of the individual doing the searching (see below). In this way we could conduct what Laura Granka has called 'studies at the micro-level'[11] as a supplement to general search trends at the macro-level. However, by creating an archive of specific queries at regular intervals throughout time, researchers could compare the different search result constellations across queries and across time. This way it becomes easier to historicize Google search.

2. *The short burst model*: Another approach would be to collect more material in shorter, yet more intensive, waves of documentation. This could be a relevant method if one suspects that a certain event could cause great disruption in the search rankings. Here the goal is to zoom in on the minute changes happening in the course of the event and then analyze these changes in light of the event (e.g. by relating it to the various sub-events happening or contrasting it to news media coverage, social media activity, etc.) The (hypothetical) documentation of September 11 would be an

---

9. A perfect example of this is Eric Borra and René König's longitudinal study of which websites were associated most prominently with the search term '9/11' in Google Search across a six year period. See a summary of their conference presentation here: Catalina Iorga, 'Erik Borra and René König Show Google Search Perspectives on 9/11', Institute of Network Cultures, 11 November 2013, http://networkcultures.org/wpmu/query/2013/11/11/erik-borra-and-rene-konig-google-search-perspectives-on-911/.
10. Noortje Marres and Esther Weltevrede, 'Scraping the Social? Issues in Real-Time Social Research', *Journal of Cultural Economy* 6.3 (2012): 313-335.
11. Laura A. Granka, 'The Politics of Search: A Decade Retrospective', *The Information Society* 26.5 (September 27, 2010): 364.374.

example of this. By archiving search results before, during, and after certain influential events have occurred (e.g. major pre-planned spectacles such as elections, or sudden disruptive incidents such as natural disasters), we are able to investigate the fluctuations in search results during big events. In this sense the documentation of search results can be used in natural experiment studies, where the event is treated as the exogenous shock. These types of experiments have been used beforehand in the context of Google Search, but there the focus has been on the relationship between click behavior and online advertisement campaigns for certain keywords.[12] However, since we don't have access to Google's algorithms, it is impossible to isolate variables and thereby very difficult to establish a causal link between exogenous events and search result rankings. Nonetheless, this model can provide an interesting insight into the shifting constellations of search results during important events.

Of course it is possible to combine these models into a hybrid (see for example the Danish web archive[13]), and the models outlined above should be seen more as archetypical approaches to the archiving of search results than precise recipes.

Perhaps the greatest challenge spanning both models is that fluctuations in search rankings are very difficult to explain, since the number of factors informing the search rankings and the individual weight of each factor is impossible for us mortal researchers (read: not employed by Google) to decipher. Dirk Lewandowski has ordered these factors into 'query dependent' (considering the position and order of search terms and relating the search terms to amount and types of relevant keywords in documents) and 'query independent' factors (notably the popularity of web sites, determined among other things by the PageRank algorithm).[14] Here I will add personalized factors, which are all those signals stemming from the individual user such as geographical location, prior search history, behavior on other sites Google is able to monitor, and whether one is logged into services (e.g. Google accounts). Thereby, any changes in the search rankings might be due to changes in the algorithms, updates in the index, as well as individual level and country-specific factors. In the following, I discuss ways to tackle this serious issue and suggest a possible path forward. To guide the discussion I introduce a small case study that was originally intended to provide empirical material for another article, but ended up being the cause for why I decided to write this article instead.

The Cat and the Mouse in the Google Sphere

On 14 October 2012 at about 12:08 MDT, some 38 kilometers above the face of the earth, Felix Baumgartner stepped out of the capsule that had carried him up there and jumped out into the stratosphere, thereby beginning his four minute long free-fall towards the ground. After about 40 seconds he reached a top speed of about 1,342 kilometers per hour (or about the height of the Empire State Building per second)

---

12. Thomas Blake, Chris Nosko, and Steven Tadelis, 'Consumer Heterogeneity and Paid Search Effectiveness: A Large Scale Field Experiment', The National Bureau of Economic Research Working Paper, 6 March 2013, http://conference.nber.org/confer/2013/EoDs13/Tadelis.pdf.
13. Danish web archive (netarkivet.dk) archives certain culturally and politically important websites on a routine basis and then archives an extensive number of websites decided on an *ad hoc* basis for specific pre-planned or suddenly occurring events. In that way they combine the models presented here.
14. Dirk Lewandowski, 'Web Searching, Search Engines and Information Retrieval', *Information Services & Use* 25 (2005): 137-147.

breaking the speed of sound before he descended to the ground and landed safely minutes afterwards. The event (named the 'Red Bull Stratos' after its main sponsor) was followed by millions through simultaneous live streams on the web (YouTube alone reported more than seven million viewers at its peak moments) and on Discovery Channel (which obtained the highest ratings for a non-primetime program ever). On Twitter most of the trending hashtags throughout the event were related to the Stratos, and on Facebook Baumgartner's fan page received about half a million new likes and a plethora of comments from ecstatic fans. Even though the global significance of the event might be questionable (cynics might be tempted to re-phrase Neil Armstrong's famous line into 'A giant leap for a man, one small step for mankind') the Stratos was truly a huge media event – though not necessarily in the terms of Dayan and Katz's now classical definition of the genre[15] – that happened across platforms. More importantly for this context it provided a clear-cut case for the study of Google Search (roughly following the short burst model) and an even better case for discussing issues of archiving the searches in real time. The latter proved to be a frustrating yet enlightening game of cat and mouse, which started with the selection of relevant search queries.

Finding the Right Key
I decided to map the Red Bull Stratos about a week before the event took place because it had already received quite a lot of attention from established news media at that point. So I figured that the Statos could be an important event to document for future research. Obviously, when one tries to document an event like this through Google Search the exact keywords used as search queries are of the greatest importance, since they determine the exact angle taken on the subject. Therefore the keywords must be chosen with care and consideration.

Before the event occurred I couldn't know for sure which queries would be most relevant in a research context, so I tested a number of different keywords in the days leading up to the jump. I eventually decided to map two different keywords: 'red bull stratos' (the official name of the jump) and 'Felix Baumgartner' (the name of the jumper). I also tried with more general keywords such as 'jump', 'stratos', 'felix', and 'baumgartner', but they proved to be too general by including clearly irrelevant search results for the purpose of mapping the event. Therefore I decided to stick with the more precise keywords, which of course meant that I excluded many searches (obviously many people looking for information about the event would use different search terms). Faced with this issue, I decided that false negatives (excluding relevant results) were the better option in this particular context than false positives (including too many irrelevant results).

---

15. Media (read: TV) events are defined as the pre-arranged 'high holidays of mass communication' that interrupts the daily routines, monopolizes media communication, and encapsulate viewers across the nation and world. Media have the power to unify and speak the language of social integration and reconciliation. (Daniel Dayan and Elihu Katz, *Media Events: The Live Broadcasting of History,* Cambridge, Mass.: Harvard University Press, 1992). Even though the Red Bull Stratos might showcase some of these characteristics, it is unclear whether the event could be said to dominate the media's attention and encapsulate viewers on the same emotional level as traditional media events (the obvious – and very problematic – comparison would be the moon landing in 1969).

By comparing the search volume on Google Trends for the two queries it is very clear that 'Felix Baumgartner' had a greater resonance as a keyword in the population of searchers.[16] It is also clear that the popularity of the search terms are greatest in the Central European countries, particularly Austria, even though the event took place in air space above Nevada, U.S. Since Felix Baumgartner is Austrian, the fact that Austria is the most popular place is not that surprising, but these numbers suggest that there would be a point in looking at various country-specific Google domains in Europe as well.[17]

So it seems that the best solution with search queries is either to zoom in on a specific keyword one suspects will retain its relevance over the course of the study (e.g. a very general keyword) or to map different keywords that together can encapsulate the different aspects of the event. This challenge is very much related to the difficulties of determining the proper hashtags to find debates about certain events on Twitter. When comparing queries for 'Red Bull Stratos' and 'Felix Baumgartner' at the same time slot, it is quite obvious that these two keywords capture very different aspects of the event. 'Red Bull Stratos' associates the event much more with official sources (including Red Bull itself), whereas a search for the astronaut yields more person-focused results (among other things, his Facebook page). Similar to how exact hashtags in Twitter research determine the type of debate you can capture, the keywords will demarcate Google Search studies. The words have to be chosen with care. Here, pilot studies (simply trying different keywords in different contexts) and data from Google Trends are a tremendous help.

Who Is the Subject and Who Is the Researcher?
The hard part about studying Google Search on a systematic basis is that Google soon realizes that it is being studied. Even though the so-called 'Hawthorne effect' (the fact that human subjects are conscious of researchers studying them and adapt their behavior accordingly) has been contested in subsequent studies,[18] it might be relevant to ask in the context of studies of Google (and similar companies): to what extend do these services adapt to us studying them? As I see it, this adaption can either be in a very indirect manner, manifesting in the way the search results are shown, or it can be very direct if the search engine intervenes in the study. An example of the latter is shown in Figure 1, where the search engine detects suspicious behavior from the IP address and blocks further requests from that particular computer for a while.

Ethan Zuckerman has described two important ways Google might indirectly interfere. In the first, when Google receives a number of queries from the same IP address, it might try deliberately to randomize search results a bit in order to mask the workings of the algorithm. Zuckerman states, 'The faster you poll the engine, the more variability

---

16. Comparison made with the free tool Google Trends. Available at: www.google.com/trends/.
17. I actually did exactly that, but because of the issues with personalization the results from the country specific Google domains were rendered more or less meaningless. The language settings simply overruled the specific domain, and I was redirected from the Austrian version of Google to the Danish or U.S. version.
18. Steven D. Levitt and John A. List, 'Was There Really a Hawthorne Effect at the Hawthorne Plant? An Analysis of the Original Illumination Experiments', *American Economic Journal: Applied Economics. American Economic Association* 3.1 (January 2011): 224-238, http://www.nber.org/papers/w15016.

you get, making it harder to profile the engine's behavior'.[19] The second is experimentation. Google is constantly conducting tests (e.g. A/B comparisons) to detect which kind of search results (and design elements) users are most likely to interact with. Because of these issues it becomes very difficult to establish why something is placed at a particular position in the rankings.

Fig. 1. Google Search error message.

The question we need to ask ourselves as researchers is: How can we study Google when Google is studying us? The only answer I can provide to this question is that we need to be aware of the settings used when searching, then accept that in the end we can never really know the causal relationship involved.

We Know Where You Are... and What Language You Speak
Two particular ranking factors that we need to be acutely aware of are the language settings and IP address. Figure 2 shows the outcome of an attempt to query 'Felix Baumgartner' on google.at (the Austrian version of Google Search) to see the event from an Austrian perspective. Even though I specifically tried to avoid particular Danish search results by doing this, Google still placed these results prominently. There was a video from the Danish-language version of Redbull's website (redbull.dk) as well as a news story from the largest Danish TV channel (nyhederne.tv2.dk). Furthermore, the language settings in the panel on the left side remained Danish. Apart from that, there was only one site in German (wikipedia.de), which seems rather suspicious, especially given the huge attention the event garnered in Austria. Since I did not change my IP address to a server in Germany and had Danish as my default language setting, it was quite likely that these factors informed the search engine's decision to provide me with these search results.

---

19. Ethan Zuckerman, 'In Soviet Russia, Google Researches You!', ...My Heart's in Accra blog, 24 March 2011, http://www.ethanzuckerman.com/blog/2011/03/24/in-soviet-russia-google-researches-you/.

Fig. 2. Search query 'Felix Baumgartner' on google.at.

To get a clearer idea of whether the language setting of the IP address influenced the constellation of search results, I conducted a mini-experiment (see Figure 3). Here I queried 'Felix Baumgartner' on Google.de (German domain) with four different settings: one with the language set to Danish with my normal IP address in Copenhagen, Denmark (Figure 3a); one with the language set to German with my home IP address in Denmark (Figure 3b); one with the language set to German and with a German IP address (Figure 3c); and one with the language set to Danish and with a German IP address (Figure 3d). The greatest changes in the organic search results seemed to come from the language settings. Notice for example how the country domains on Wikipedia follow the language settings and not the IP address. Meanwhile, the IP address informs the type of ads that are shown to the user in the top banners. So if one wants to appear as if coming from another country when searching Google, it is not enough simply to change the IP address. At a minimum it is required to change the language setting accordingly.

Fig. 3. Search on google.de with varying settings for language and IP-address.

Personalization – the Known Unknowns of Search
Apart from the choice of keywords, language settings, and location-based results, there is of course the increasingly 'black-boxed' issue of personalization. Earlier a number of studies tried to 'second-guess' Google's search algorithm(s) through the systematic mapping of search rankings across queries.[20] In recent years it has become increasingly clear that the multitude of factors that informs the exact constellation of search results for any given query[21] as well as the increasing personalization of users

---

20. See e.g. Benjamin Edelman, 'Hard-Coding Bias in Google "Algorithmic" Search Results,' 15 November 2010, http://www.benedelman.org/hardcoding/.
21. Granka, 'The Politics of Search: A Decade Retrospective'; Zuckerman, 'In Soviet Russia, Google Researches You!'.

have made this task very hard, if not impossible.[22] There simply exists no vantage point from which the researcher can analyze the search results objectively. We know that the results are personalized (partly because Google confirms this repeatedly),[23] but we don't know exactly how. This fact forces scholars to give up on these strict quantitative designs and either abandon search studies altogether (as I sense quite a few have chosen to do) or work with these limitations actively in their studies.

Richard Rogers, among others, has suggested one way to mitigate the effects of personalization. Rogers advises researchers to operate with a 'research browser', which is a browser cleaned of any history of prior usage and boots directly from scratch each time it is opened.[24] Another method commonly applied is to use some kind of IP scrambler that changes the IP address to a random or specified IP address (e.g. through VPN servers) or disguises the IP address (e.g. through TOR). Both of these are definitely viable ways to deal with personalization issues (not to mention surveillance issues) since they make it easier to distort some of the factors that inform the search engine. From a research perspective they also have one downside, as I see it: they run the risk of being too artificial and detached from real-world search situations. Most people are either logged into Google when searching (knowingly or unknowingly), or they do not change their IP address each time to avoid the prior search history to inform their present results. Accordingly, with this approach it might be possible to strip the search engine of some personalized factors and achieve more stable search results across various researchers. The results might be reliable, but not necessarily very valid.

Another way would be to discard strict notions of reliability and embrace search results more as documents intended for qualitative research than precise data points to be used in statistical studies. In this way it might be more appropriate to discuss the scientific value of these types of documents in terms of 'trustworthiness, rigor and quality'[25] and to triangulate the queries across searchers (possibly employing human subjects as participants in this process). By these standards would we be able to discuss properly the changes in search results in a more sophisticated manner? Naturally, it would still be virtually impossible to assess which changes in search results are the outcome of personalization and which changes are due to numerous other factors, such as A/B tests and randomization of search results, that are included in the algorithm. But assessing these changes would not be the goal of such a study either. By treating search results as historical documents archived at a specific time and place by researchers with more or less clear biases in their approach (here shown concretely in the personalization mechanisms), they operate on the same level as every other type

---

22. Martin Feuz, Matthew Fuller, and Felix Stalder, 'Personal Web Searching in the Age of Semantic Capitalism: Diagnosing the Mechanisms of Personalisation', *First Monday* 16.2 (1 February 2011), http://firstmonday.org/ojs/index.php/fm/article/view/3344/2766; Eli Pariser, *The Filter Bubble: How the New Personalized Web Is Changing What We Read and How We Think*, New York, NY: Penguin Books, 2012.
23. An example: search personalization is a topic on Google Support and has its own fairly detailed subpage: https://support.google.com/accounts/answer/54041?hl=en.
24. Richard Rogers, *Digital Methods*, Cambridge, Mass.: MIT Press, 2013.
25. Nahid Golafshani, 'Understanding Reliability and Validity in Qualitative Research', *The Qualitative Report* 8.4 (2003): 597-607.

of source we have access to. Sources can illuminate new aspects of a historical situation or period, but they will never be a complete representation of the subject matter. Sources (like data) can never speak for themselves.

In short, because of all the challenges related to archiving shown here, second-guessing Google is probably not the right way to proceed for research. Instead we should use the search results for a different purpose and in context with other information at hand.

So What's Next...?
As historians would know, relying on single sources is a haphazard affair that could lead to dangerous conclusions (who says that this one source is willing to or capable of telling the truth?). The same goes for search results, whether they are collected as short bursts to document specific events or over a longer period of time for longitudinal studies. Alone they are difficult to verify and thereby almost impossible to analyze in a systematic manner. But in conjunction with other sources (e.g. newspaper articles, activity on social network sites, TV coverage, etc.) they can shed some new light on aspects of societal development and important events that would otherwise remain in the dark. Google is still one of the dominant entryways to the web for many people, as shown in the staggering penetration numbers mentioned earlier, and as such can be an important looking glass into the mentality of the day. For this reason it is important to archive the search results and make them available for future studies.

Throughout the discussion of the various methodological challenges related to online archiving, I have presented some ways forward. To sum this up in a more coherent manner, what I am suggesting here is the following: whether one wants to conduct a longitudinal study or follow a short burst model, it is important to compare (or triangulate) the results from various participants, preferably positioned at different geographical places with appropriate language settings, and either from more or less anonymous networks where IP addresses are not tied to individual machines or from the participants' own computers. If browsers from personal computers are used the criteria for the sampling of human participants are an integral part of the setup. This means, among other things, that the researcher has to consider the personal characteristics of the participants, such as age, gender, place of residence, and search habits, when assessing the search results.[26] One such design could employ a 'maximum variation sampling strategy,'[27] where the researcher attempts to compile a pool of participants with characteristics as different as possible according to specified criteria. If search results vary little across this group of participants, one could establish a stronger case for the consistency of these particular results. As such, this approach to archival research resembles many traditional qualitative research designs.

---

26. Apart from contextualizing search results with content from other media, there is also the possibility of studying the participants themselves as primary objects of research. This would be a more anthropological, rather than historical, take, but nonetheless important. This method could add interesting insights into our understanding of what people see as important keywords and the reasons they provide for querying specific events.
27. Anton J. Kuzel, 'Sampling in Qualitative Inquiry', in Benjamin F. Crabtree and William L. Miller (eds) *Doing Qualitative Research*, Thousand Oaks, CA: Sage Publications, Inc, 1992, pp. 31-44.

If reliable VPN servers are available, then it is possible to conduct geographical stratification by changing the IP address and language settings instead of relying on human participants. This is indeed a more practical solution (you can do it from one computer and control all the aspects of the archiving yourself), so it is probably more feasible for most individual researchers, but from my experience it seems to be difficult to get assurance that this exercise works in practice. I still believe that a group of human searchers are preferable to this solution, since it offers more detailed and analytically fruitful discussions of how search results differ across profiles.

As a final note, the issue of personalization that I have discussed here in relation to Google seems to be spreading rapidly to new areas, e.g. news websites. Huffington Post is already using an algorithmically informed front-page that adapts to the (perceived) interests of the user.[28] This poses an obvious challenge to scholars doing content analysis and makes this conundrum unavoidable for an even greater part of online research. If we want to continue to archive and analyze online content, this is an issue we need to face. The only real solution seems to be to adapt research designs to the limitations of the material and embrace the uncertainties we must accept as researchers. I have suggested one way of doing this here. Maybe others can carry the torch a bit further.

References

Blake, Thomas, Chris Nosko, and Steven Tadelis. 'Consumer Heterogeneity and Paid Search Effectiveness: A Large Scale Field Experiment', The National Bureau of Economic Research Working Paper, 6 March 2013, http://conference.nber.org/confer/2013/EoDs13/Tadelis.pdf.

Dayan, Daniel and Elihu Katz. *Media Events: The Live Broadcasting of History,* Cambridge, Mass.: Harvard University Press, 1992.

Edelman, Benjamin. 'Hard-Coding Bias in Google "Algorithmic" Search Results,' 15 November 2010, http://www.benedelman.org/hardcoding/

Feuz, Martin, Matthew Fuller, and Felix Stalder. 'Personal Web Searching in the Age of Semantic Capitalism: Diagnosing the Mechanisms of Personalisation', *First Monday* 16.2 (1 February 2011).

Fishman, Rob. 'Stories You Might Like: Join Our Beta Program to Test HuffPost Recommendations', *The Huffington Post,* 6 January 2011, http://www.huffingtonpost.com/rob-fishman/stories-you-might-like-jo_b_800427.html.

Golafshani, Nahid. 'Understanding Reliability and Validity in Qualitative Research', *The Qualitative Report* 8.4 (2003): 597-607.

Granka, Laura A. 'The Politics of Search: A Decade Retrospective', *The Information Society* 26.5 (September 27, 2010): 364-374.

Hillis, Ken, Michael Petit, and Kylie Jarrett. *Google and the Culture of Search,* New York, NY and Oxon, UK: Routledge, 2013.

Iorga, Catalina, 'Erik Borra and René König Show Google Search Perspectives on 9/11', Institute of Network Cultures, 11 November 2013, http://networkcultures.org/wpmu/query/2013/11/11/erik-borra-and-rene-konig-google-search-perspectives-on-911/.

Jensen, Klaus Bruhn. 'Meta-Media and Meta-Communication: Revisiting the Concept of Genre in the Digital Media Environment', *MedieKultur. Journal of Media and Communication Research* 51 (2011): 8-21.

---

28. See e.g. Rob Fishman, 'Stories You Might Like: Join Our Beta Program to Test HuffPost Recommendations', *The Huffington Post,* 6 January 2011, http://www.huffingtonpost.com/rob-fishman/stories-you-might-like-jo_b_800427.html.

———. 'New Media, Old Methods – Internet Methodologies and the Online/Offline Divide', in Mia Consalvo and Charles Ess (eds) *The Handbook of Internet Studies*, Oxford, UK: Wiley-Blackwell, 2010.

Kuzel, Anton J, 'Sampling in Qualitative Inquiry', in Benjamin F. Crabtree and William L. Miller (eds) *Doing Qualitative Research*, Thousand Oaks, CA: Sage Publications, Inc, 1992, pp. 31-44.

Levitt, Steven D. and John A. List, 'Was There Really a Hawthorne Effect at the Hawthorne Plant? An Analysis of the Original Illumination Experiments', *American Economic Journal: Applied Economics. American Economic Association* 3.1 (January 2011): 224-238, http://www.nber.org/papers/w15016.

Lewandowski, Dirk. 'Web Searching, Search Engines and Information Retrieval', *Information Services & Use* 25 (2005): 137-147.

Marres, Noortje and Esther Weltevrede, 'Scraping the Social? Issues in Real-Time Social Research', *Journal of Cultural Economy* 6.3 (2012): 313-335.

Pariser, Eli. *The Filter Bubble: How the New Personalized Web Is Changing What We Read and How We Think,* New York, NY: Penguin Books, 2012.

Rogers, Richard. *Digital Methods,* Cambridge, Mass.: MIT Press, 2013.

Sanz, Esteve and Juraj Stancik. 'Your Search – "Ontological Security" – Matched 111,000 Documents: An Empirical Substantiation of the Cultural Dimension of Online Search', *New Media & Society* (29 April 2013): 0-19.

Zuckerman, Ethan. 'In Soviet Russia, Google Researches You!', …My Heart's in Accra blog, 24 March 2011, http://www.ethanzuckerman.com/blog/2011/03/24/in-soviet-russia-google-researches-you/.

Exploratory Search and Extended Cognition in Health Information Interaction

Martin Feuz

Exploratory Search and Extended Cognition in Health Information Interaction

Martin Feuz

While researching expert Tetris players, cognitive scientists David Kirsh and Paul Maglio made the following interesting observation: these players typically rely on rotating the falling objects to more easily identify their shape or moving them to the far right to determine and set up their exact position for high-drops. The researchers name these moves *epistemic action*, as their interpretation of such actions in the world is that they improve cognition. 'Certain cognitive and perceptual problems are more quickly, easily, and reliably solved by performing actions in the world than by performing computational actions in the head alone.'[1]

What does epistemic action have to do with search interaction, you may ask? Actually, a lot! Search for information, about health for example, is conducted in high volumes and affects people's decision-making processes, so we should take it seriously. Health search interactions are of an exploratory nature and different in kind from other searches. Current black-boxed search engine mechanisms may do more harm than good in these exploratory search interactions. More profoundly, supporting exploratory health search interactions effectively requires shifting models of interactivity and cognitive processes from an information processing model of mind towards understanding cognition as extending into and performing through the artifactual and social environment.

The Context: Health Search and Search Engines
According to Pew Research from June 2009, 57 percent of adults turn to the internet as a source of health information; for 60 percent, information found online influenced their decision-making process regarding treatment options.[2] By the end of 2010, Pew reports that 'searching for health information, an activity that was once the primary domain of older adults, is now the third most popular online activity for all internet users 18 and older'.[3]

Before we dive into specific ways in which search engines play a substantial role in health information search, a bit of contextualization is needed. This context will help

---

1. David Kirsh and Paul Maglio, 'On Distinguishing Epistemic from Pragmatic Action', *Cognitive science* 18 (1994): 513.
2. Susannah Fox and Sydney Jones, *The Social Life of Health Information*, Pew Research Center, 11 June 2009.
3. Kathryn Zickuhr, *Generations 2010*, Pew Research Center, 16 December 2010.

illustrate how the development of search engines and interactions with them in the context of health information search is problematic.

Search engines have played a vital role since the early days of the web. This is mainly due to the fact that the web lacks an inherent indexing and categorizing mechanism. While some organizations have tried to compile a directory using human experts, this approach quickly runs into deep problems. On the one hand this method simply can't cope with the rapid growth of the web and thus runs the risk of becoming incomplete. On the other hand the complexity and dynamics of the web lead to ontological problems with categorizing the information found. Subsequent search engine providers started to build automated indexing and ranking mechanisms. The index is the part of a search engine that search crawlers continuously update by scanning the web for new websites and new content on those indexed websites. Ranking, on the other hand, is concerned with matching a user's search query with the index and, based on a set of rules, presenting the user with a selection of search results. At the core of ranking lies the trade-off between precision and recall. Precision is concerned with the accuracy of the match between search query and retrieved search results, while recall is concerned with the number of relevant search results produced. When the precision of the match between search query and results is increased, recall is reduced and vice versa. We will see that this tension is of ongoing concern in the development and improvement of search engines.

While better suited to cope with the enormous growth of the web, early automated search engines nevertheless suffered from a number of problems. Key among the issues was that their ranking mechanism chiefly relied on a relatively crude statistical keyword matching process between search query and indexed webpages. With the growth of content on the web, this produced enormous amounts of search results (recall). More often than not, it was a strenuous effort to find useful, relevant search results.

While the front end of most search engines has not seemed to change much in recent years,[4] the back end has changed substantially. Search results for a given search query are nowadays automatically filtered by a number of variables that remain hidden from immediate user interaction. The goal of this filtering is to further increase the relevancy of search results. Among others, search results are typically filtered based on the search user's geo-location derived from her IP (Internet Protocol) address. Thus, if a user enters 'restaurant' as a search query on Google, the search engine assumes that the user is looking for a restaurant within the city she currently accesses the internet from. This geographic sensitivity may obviously be useful in some cases but largely depends on context. However, a more substantial and unidentifiable change to the ranking mechanism began some time ago when Google, among others, began personalizing users' search results, promising to deliver more relevant results to the user whose query is now contextualized by her search history and other data previously compiled into a personal profile. In order to produce this context, vast amounts of personal information need to be collected, organized, and made actionable. Within the quickly receding limitations of storage space and computing power, profiles can never

---

4. Richard Rogers, *Digital Methods*, Cambridge: MIT Press, 2013.

be too comprehensive, detailed, or up-to-date. Google for example, compiles personal profiles in three dimensions: the knowledge person (what an individual is interested in, based on search and click-stream histories), the social person (whom an individual is connected to, via email, social networks, and other communication tools), and the embodied person (where an individual is located in physical space and the states of the body).[5] Together, these three profiles promise to provide a detailed, comprehensive, up-to-date context for each search query with the potential to deliver precise results that reflect not only the information 'out-there', but also the unique interest a user has at any given moment. Personalized search does not simply aim to provide a view of existing reality, which is problematic enough.[6] Rather, personalized search promises an 'augmented reality' in which machine intelligence interprets the user's individual relationship to reality and then selects what's good for that relationship. As a result, it has become highly unlikely that two users see the same search results for a particular search query even when accessed from the same IP address.[7] Unfortunately, many search engine users do not seem to be aware of this development.[8]

To fully understand the implications of search personalization, it is necessary to take a more nuanced focus in light of different types of search interactions and today's typical search engine interface. Andrei Broder suggests differentiating between three types of search interactions, which, while crude, is a useful taxonomy for our purposes here.[9] First, navigational search queries are used when users want to find the URL for a specific website. Second, transactional search queries, such as checking flight prices, can be performed on a number of different but nevertheless specific websites. Third, informational search queries may find information on multiple websites and are useful when the search goal may not always be clear at the beginning but could emerge through the search process itself. Thus, with this type of search activity, people are typically trying to learn aspects about a topic of interest and exploring new knowledge domains. This kind of search could include anything from school or university research for an essay, to a person thinking of moving into a new professional domain or learning more about a health issue, as is the focus of this text. From such a perspective it starts to become clear that search results personalization, with its self-referential mechanisms – termed by some an echo chamber[10] or filter bubble[11] – is especially problematic for informational search queries. This is because it is precisely the user's intention to move beyond already familiar knowledge and explore novel terrain. Thus, the analysis and argument I develop will focus on this type of search interaction.

---

5. Felix Stalder and Christine Mayer, 'The Second Index. Search Engines, Personalization and Surveillance', in Konrad Becker and Felix Stalder (eds) *Deep Search: The Politics of Search Beyond Google,* Innsbruck: Studienverlag, 2009.
6. Lucas Introna and Helen Nissenbaum, 'Shaping the Web: Why the Politics of Search Engines Matters', *The Information Society* 16.3 (2000): 169-180.
7. Martin Feuz, Matthew Fuller and Felix Stalder, 'Personal Web Searching in the Age of Semantic Capitalism: Diagnosing the Mechanisms of Personalisation', *First Monday* 16.2 (2011).
8. Bing Pan, Helene Hembrooke, Thorsten Joachims, Lori Lorigo, Geri Gay, Laura Granka, 'In Google We Trust: Users' Decisions on Rank, Position, and Relevance', *Journal of Computer Mediated Communication* 12.3 (2007): 801-823.
9. Andrei Broder, 'A Taxonomy of Web Search', *ACM SIGIR Forum* 36.2 (2002): 3-10.
10. Cass Sunstein, *Echo Chambers: Bush v. Gore, Impeachment, and Beyond*, Princeton: Princeton University Press, 2001.
11. Eli Pariser, *The Filter Bubble: What the Internet is Hiding from You*, London: Penguin UK, 2011.

Exploratory Search

Recently researchers have developed and characterized the notion of informational search as 'exploratory search',[12] which is the term I will use from now on.

Exploratory search can be used to describe an information-seeking problem context that is open-ended, persistent, and multi-faceted; and to describe information-seeking processes that are opportunistic, iterative, and multi-tactical. In the first sense, exploratory search is commonly used in scientific discovery, learning, and decision-making contexts. In the second sense, exploratory tactics are used in all manner of information seeking and reflect seeker preferences and experience as much as the goal.[13]

Exploratory search interactions are characterized by a number of typical features. To start with, very often there is a complex information problem at hand and a desire to learn about it. Also, people engaging in exploratory search may be unfamiliar with the knowledge domain their search goal relates to, including a lack of understanding of dominant and peripheral actors within that domain. Furthermore, people may not have good knowledge about relevant keywords, concepts, and information sources that might be relevant to formulate search queries and evaluate search results. Lastly, it is also possible that exploratory searchers might not have a specific search goal in mind initially. The goal may only evolve and become clearer through a process of learning about a specific knowledge domain, its concepts, and actors within it. Given these characteristics, the exploratory search process typically develops over the course of multiple sessions, which may last days, weeks, or months.

The Interface and Models of Interaction

Many search engine interfaces are typically built on a 'commonly accepted' set of action grammars and handles suggested by the Human Computer Interaction (HCI) domain.[14] The action grammar applied more often than not aims to describe a context-free meta syntax and thereby suggests universal applicability and usability. In the case of universal search engines such as Google or Bing, the interface is typically made of a single search box with a search button on an otherwise almost empty page. A user enters her search query, clicks on the search button, and is then presented with the most relevant search results for that search query. Typically, the user then has a few general refinement options available to further narrow the search. What remains hidden are the numerous assumptions at work that lead to the ranking of the most relevant search results, mentioned above. This approach arguably works well for simple navigational tasks in web search. While there have been a number of useful attempts to change the dominant search interaction paradigm, sadly these ventures have died after some time. I can only speculate on the reasons why they weren't successful, but a key determining factor seems much less related to the interaction paradigm than to index comprehensiveness, explained earlier. The computation-intensive processes for

---

12. Ryen W. White and Resa A. Roth, 'Exploratory Search: Beyond the Query-Response Paradigm', *Synthesis Lectures on Information Concepts, Retrieval, and Services* 1.1 (2009): 1-98.
13. Gary Marchionini and Ryen White, 'Find What You Need, Understand What You Find', *International Journal of Human Computer Interaction* 23.3 (2007): 205-237.
14. Action grammar and handles refer to the standardized styles and design metaphors suggested by the professional Human Computer Interaction domain.

approaching comprehensiveness and accuracy require Google and other popular universal search engine providers to invest massively in hardware and human expertise. This appears to be an increasingly high entry barrier for potential competitors entering the global search engine sector. Danny Hillis, a well-known supercomputing pioneer and founder of the Long Now Foundation, has argued in *The New York Times* that 'Google has constructed the biggest computer in the world, and it's a hidden asset'.[15]

The core of the problem of why today's search engine interfaces don't support exploratory search well lies in both a specific perspective on the model of interaction as well as the model of cognitive processes assumed by search interaction designers. Today's search engine interfaces can be described as relying on a few core assumptions that resonate strongly with an information-processing model of the mind. Cognition is typically represented and described as a purely mental process consisting of 'identifying an information need, followed by the activities of query specification, examination of retrieval results, and if needed, reformulation of the query, repeating the cycle until a satisfactory result set is found'.[16] Alternate models of the search process, such as Marcia Bates' berrypicking, have made very useful contributions to a more interactive style of search by including iterative aspects of the process, including learning and shifting focus and goals.

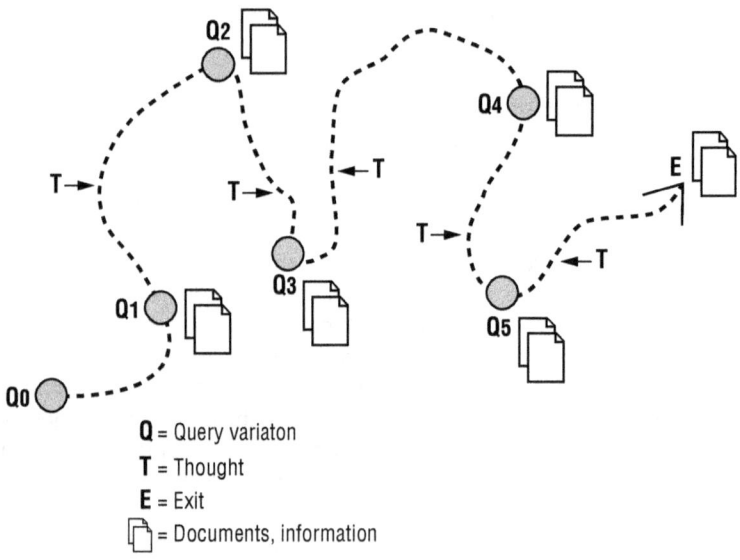

Q = Query variaton
T = Thought
E = Exit
= Documents, information

Fig. 1. Berrypicking Model (Bates).

---

15. John Markoff and Saul Hansell, 'Hiding in Plain Site, Google Seeks More Power', *The New York Times*, 14 June 2006, http://www.nytimes.com/2006/06/14/technology/14search.html?pagewanted=1&_r=1.
16. Marti A. Hearst, *Search User Interfaces*, Cambridge: Cambridge University Press, 2009.

While the model itself seems a bit formal, Bates more recently clarified her perspective by stating: 'In my view, our understanding of information seeking is not complete as long as we exclude the biological and anthropological from our study.'[17] Unfortunately, such an understanding has not yet been adopted by the information seeking research community.[18] Further arguments about why models with a more embodied understanding and style of interactivity are particularly desirable in the realms of health search interaction will be developed in the next section.

Methods and Issues of Evidence-Based Medicine
In order to appreciate why a lack of supporting exploratory types of search interaction is particularly problematic when searching for health and medical information, we need to briefly unpack the methods on which such knowledge is produced and some of the issues this generates.

For the past four decades, Evidence-Based Medicine (EBM) has slowly but increasingly become dominant as a knowledge paradigm and clinical practice approach in Western medicine. This paradigm is evident in the forms of new institutions such as the Cochrane Collaboration and the National Institute for Clinical Excellence in the U.K., new journals, recurring editorials in leading medical journals, as well as the adoption of EBM-methods, such as randomized controlled trials in mainstream medical research.[19] Greenhalgh and Donald define Evidence-Based Medicine as follows:

> The use of mathematical estimates of the risk of benefit and harm, derived from high-quality research on population samples, to inform clinical decision-making in the diagnosis, investigation or management of individual patients.[20]

This sounds all good and well; however, as research transpires through the growing body of systematic reviews, the scientific robustness of medical evidence increasingly reveals some of the problematic foundations and processes whereby medical knowledge has been and continues to be generated and distributed. Ben Goldacre, a physician and EBM researcher, has framed these issues as the 'broken information architecture of Medicine'.[21] This phrase refers to his analysis, which exposes the fact that there is a fundamental gap in the publishing of negative trial results.[22] Put differently, the structural bias towards publishing mostly positive trial results leads to an overstatement of the benefits of treatments. To understand why, it is useful to consider the recent research by John Ioannidis, a leading meta-analytic medical researcher with an interest in the quality of medical research. In his study 'Contradicted and

---

17. Marcia J. Bates, 'Toward an Integrated Model of Information Seeking and Searching', *The New Review of Information Behaviour Research* 3 (2002): 1-15.
18. Amanda Spink and Michael Zimmer, *Web Search: Multidisciplinary Perspectives*, Berlin: Springer-Verlag, 2010.
19. Stefan Timmermans and Marc Berg, *The Gold Standard: The Challenge of Evidence-Based Medicine and Standardization in Health Care,* Philadelphia: Temple University Press, 2003.
20. Trisha Greenhalgh, *How to Read a Paper: The Basics of Evidence-Based Medicine*, Oxford: Blackwell, 2010.
21. Ben Goldacre 'The Information Architecture of Medicine is Broken', 29 February 2012, http://www.youtube.com/watch?v=AK_EUKJyusg.
22. Ben Goldacre, *Bad Pharma. How Drug Companies Mislead Doctors and Harm Patients*, London: Fourth Estate Harper Collins, 2012.

Initially Stronger Effects in Highly Cited Clinical Research', he analyzed actual medical publication patterns and how initial research findings were only slowly corrected over time.[23] For this, he studied 49 of the most important published research findings that were influential in popularizing treatments, 'such as the use of hormone-replacement therapy for menopausal women, vitamin E to reduce the risk of heart disease, coronary stents to ward off heart attacks'. What he found was that '41% of these findings had been convincingly shown to be wrong or significantly exaggerated'.[24] This problem may be explained to a large extent by selective reporting of research results and publication bias. The former is the choice of data that scientists document, whereas the latter is the 'tendency of scientists and scientific journals to prefer positive data over null results'.[25] While in some cases this choice merely means an ineffective treatment for some patients, in others it has grave consequences by actually increasing morbidity.[26]

From our previous discussion on search interaction models, it is becoming evident that such issues in evidence-based medicine may not be easily identified or explored with either navigational or transactional search interaction approaches nor with the tools search engines provide to assess the relevancy of search results and their sources of authority. This is because these types of search interactions presume the search user to fully understand the knowledge domain at the outset and thus to be able to identify relevant information via the mere listing of search results. Instead, an exploratory model of search interaction would, for example, support the identification of central and peripheral actors in a knowledge domain and thus provide multifarious means of assessing contextual relevancy.

Cognitive Conceptions of Human Decision-Making
Having briefly reflected on the methods and issues underlying contemporary evidence-based medicine, I posit that a more open-ended and exploratory form of health information interaction is strongly desirable. Desirable on the one hand due to the inherent question of the kinds of lives that are deemed valuable and desirable to live,[27] and on the other hand for allowing more engaged patient participation. Decision-making, and the ways in which it can be supported, thus figures as a core element within interactivity. We can turn to shared decision-making processes[28] that aim to support exploratory interaction and decision-making. This approach will also allow us to illustrate the cognitive assumptions underlying the design of decision support provisioning, which also informs much contemporary human computer interaction design.

---

23. John P. Ioannidis, 'Contradicted and Initially Stronger Effects in Highly Cited Clinical Research', *JAMA*, 294.2 (2005): 218-228.
24. David H. Freedman, 'Lies, Damned Lies, and Medical Science', *The Atlantic*, November 2010, http://www.theatlantic.com/magazine/archive/2010/11/lies-damned-lies-and-medical-science/8269/.
25. Jonah Lehrer, 'The Truth Wears Off', *The New Yorker*, 13 December 2010, http://www.newyorker.com/reporting/2010/12/13/101213fa_fact_lehrer.
26. Craig M. Pratt and Lemuel A. Moye, 'The Cardiac Arrhythmia Suppression Trial: Background, Interim Results and Implications' *The American Journal of Cardiology*, 65.4 (1990): 20-29, http://circ.ahajournals.org/content/91/1/245.short.
27. Nikolas Rose, *Politics of Life Itself*, Woodstock: Princeton University Press, 2006.
28. Klim McPherson, John E. Wennberg, Ole B. Hovind, and Peter Clifford, 'Small-Area Variations in the Use of Common Surgical Procedures: An International Comparison of New England, England, and Norway', *The New England Journal of Medicine*, 307.21 (1982): 1310.

Shared decision-making processes often make use of different kinds of decision aids. Typically these are pamphlets that present information about treatment options for a specific illness in a structured format. For example the pamphlets incorporate if-then scenarios for when deciding on a certain treatment option and the probable health implications, including potential side effects. Where available, such information is augmented by quantitative probabilities, which aim to support the decision-making process by trading off the probabilities of different treatment options along with healing or side effects prospects.

Decision aids belong to the larger field of decision support systems and span across academic disciplines such as economics, psychology, statistics, and computer sciences. A decision support system (DSS) can be defined as a formal system designed to support the evaluation of decision alternatives and assess the likely consequences following each course of action; it thereby aids at arriving at optimal decisions.

Two aspects from the above definition of DSS require attending to: the 'formal' and the 'optimal', both of which resonate strongly with some of the earliest work on decision-making in administrative organizations by Herbert Simon, an economist and highly influential researcher in the field of decision-making processes. The 'formal' is related to the positivism-oriented style of Simon's work, focused on 'scientific authority by means of reproducibility'. 'Optimal', in the spirit of his book, is to be understood normatively, as he makes clear that his (developing) theory of administrative behavior is not a 'description of how administrators decide so much as a description of how good administrators decide'.[29] Coupled with such normative formalisms are his conceptions of rationality, which in this context he sees as means-ends chains 'concerned with the selection of preferred behavior alternatives in terms of some system of values whereby the consequences of behavior can be evaluated'.[30] He proposes the concept of bounded rationality: instead of maximizing strategies in light of pre-given sets of choices, human individual decision-makers follow satisficing strategies. Characteristic of bounded rationality for him is when decision-makers employ heuristics, or rules of thumb decisions in the 'face of the limits of human knowledge and reasoning'.[31] For example, one such heuristic that seems to be readily applied by doctors today is 'err on the safe side', by which is meant, in case of doubt recommend medical intervention. As the literature suggests, the logic behind this heuristic is mainly a way to avoid being taken to court in case a patient does fall ill.[32] To sustain his arguments for bounded rationality, Simon points to four decades of progress in psychology research to describe 'difficult problem-solving and decision-making in terms of basic symbol-manipulating processes'[33] and also what has come to be called an information processing theory of the mind.

While Simon aimed to differentiate his view on rational decision-making from those of game theoretic approaches to strategic decision-making, his concept of bounded rationality nevertheless remains within very strong theoretical boundaries concerning cog-

---

29. Herbert A. Simon, *Administrative Behavior*, New York: Free Press, 1976, p. 73.
30. Simon, *Administrative Behavior*, p. 84.
31. Simon, *Administrative Behavior*, p. 119.
32. Studdert et al., 'Defensive Medicine Among High-Risk Specialist Physicians in a Volatile Malpractice Environment', *JAMA* 293.21 (2005): 2609-2617.
33. Simon, *Administrative Behavior*, p. 120.

nitive processes. For his concept of bounded rationality, the environment within which decision-making takes place, as well as, more importantly, the cognitive capacities and mechanisms of individuals, introduce significant constraints that need to be recognized in order to fully understand and successfully design for decision-making strategies.

Secondly and more fundamentally, bounded rationality operates within the confines of a cognitive theory that follows an information processing model of cognition and mind, also known as cognitivism. This model of cognition assumes that knowledge, understanding, and sensations operate as clear mental representations upon which cognitive processes then perform mental changes. Importantly, cognitive processes are conceptualized as symbolic computations, including semantic meaning. Cognitivism, as a theoretical framework within psychology, developed as a reaction to, and yet largely an extension of behaviorism, the dominant psychological approach for much of the early 20th century. In contrast to behaviorism, which reduced all thinking to behavior that could in various ways be conditioned by stimuli, cognitivism holds that thinking influences behavior and cannot thus be behavior itself. Nevertheless, cognitivism shares behaviorism's positivist orientation by assuming that cognition can be fully explained by following the scientific method and experimentation. Furthermore, typically the brain is conceptualized as a machine-like device that is the sole and sufficient locus of human cognition.[34]

Rethinking Cognition in Exploratory Healthcare Information Interaction
Crucially, and in contrast to classic cognitive theories discussed above, from the perspective of the Extended Mind Thesis (EMT) cognition is not delimited by processes that occur within our skin and skull, but extends into and operates through the social and artifactual environment. As evidence suggests such artifactual and social ecologies play a productive and significant role in cognitive processes, as well as in human development and evolution more fundamentally. The thesis of the Extended Mind for Andy Clark and David Chalmers, who first formulated it, is that 'when parts of the environment are coupled to the brain in the right way, they become parts of the mind'.[35] At the heart of such considerations, and in relation to EMT, lies the insight that meaningful interaction with the world seems to rely profoundly on intentional interactivity facilitated by various means and channels of perception in action.

I can usefully illustrate the role of the artifactual environment in cognition for EMT in its simplest form with the example of Tetris players. Epistemic action from within the cognitive sciences field is an area relevant to exploratory health search interaction. As Kirsh and Maglio argue, epistemic actions 'are actions performed to uncover information that is hidden or hard to compute mentally' as differentiated from pragmatic actions 'performed to bring one physically closer to a goal'.[36] Kirsh and Maglio observed players of Tetris, an interactive video game for which the player must arrange objects of various shapes in order to fill in rows at the bottom of the screen. Whenever a row

---

34. Robert M. Harnish and Denise D. Cummins, *Minds, Brains, and Computers: A Historical Introduction to the Foundations of Cognitive Science*, Oxford: Blackwell Publishers, 2000.
35. Andy Clark, *Supersizing the Mind: Embodiment, Action, and Cognitive Extension*, Oxford: Oxford University Press, 2008.
36. David Kirsh and Paul Maglio, 'On Distinguishing Epistemic from Pragmatic Action', *Cognitive science* 18 (1994): 513-549.

is fully filled, it disappears and makes space available. When rows cannot be fully filled, they will build up, creating less space to maneuver the falling objects. While the objects fall from the top of the screen, the player can either rotate or move them from left to right. What Kirsh and Maglio observed was that 'certain cognitive and perceptual problems are more quickly, easily, and reliably solved by performing actions in the world than by performing computational actions in the head alone'.[37] The authors' interpretation of such actions in the world is that they improve cognition. Exemplary epistemic action, as mentioned in the beginning, occurred when users turned objects to more easily identify their shape or moved them to the far right to determine the exact position for a high drop. From their study, the authors conclude that standard information processing models of Tetris cognition are unable to explain many of the actions performed by the players and also make them seem unmotivated and superfluous. Furthermore, they find that such 'traditional accounts are limited because they regard action as having a single function: to change the world. By recognizing a second function of action – an epistemic function – we can explain many of the actions that a traditional model cannot.'[38]

Similar types of epistemic action can easily be imagined as useful interactions in the context of exploratory search – for example, the ability to explore the sources of authority a given search result entry enjoys, or its dominance as a search result on a timeline. Such epistemic actions would provide multifarious means to make sense of search results and assess their contextual relevancy, or, as Venturini puts it, to gain a second-degree objectivity.[39]

The field of behavioral economics has also recognized and come to exploit opportunistically the ways in which human cognition operates through and participates in artifactual ecologies. The field has been popularized by Richard Thaler, an economist and behavioral scientist, and Cass Sunstein, a legal scholar and behavioral economist, as a suitable means to address 'solving' contemporary social and health related issues. Interventions following this approach are based on the idea that the artifactual environment can be designed to 'nudge' people to behave in ways thought to be more beneficial for them than others. For example, healthy foods could be placed at the beginning of a long array of food displays in a school canteen rather than at the end. This tactic, it is believed by proponents of behavioral economics, will make it more likely that students will choose healthy foods than otherwise. Such an approach also goes by the term 'choice-architecture'.[40] Typically, evidence for the performance of such an approach is experimental. Indeed, as Gigerenzer, a psychologist, and Berg, an economist, argue, the evidence base is rather thin because rather than researching how people actually make decisions, it only looks at what decisions they make and then generalizes from such experimental evidence.[41] From a more political perspective,

---

37. Kirsh and Maglio, 'On Distinguishing Epistemic from Pragmatic Action': 513.
38. Kirsh and Maglio, 'On Distinguishing Epistemic from Pragmatic Action': 513.
39. Tommaso Venturini, 'What is Second-Degree Objectivity and How Could It Be Represented', http://www.medialab.sciences-po.fr/publications/Venturini-Second_Degree_Objectivity_draft1.pdf.
40. Richard H. Thaler and Cass R. Sunstein, *Nudge: Improving Decisions about Health, Wealth, and Happiness*, London: Penguin Books, 2009.
41. Tim Harford, 'Why We Do What We Do', *Financial Times*, 28 January 2011. http://www.ft.com/cms/s/2/76e593a6-28eb-11e0-aa18-00144feab49a.html#axzz1lAG3KbL5.

one critique is that 'nudge' interventions are seen as 'liberal paternalism' because they are designed and imposed top-down. Due to their nebulous presence, nudge tactics also do not invite participation, reflection, and thus do not incite learning and long-term behavioral change.

As this and other diverse research projects have come to suggest and support,[42] cognition emerges out of a much more complex entanglement of internal and external processes, involving perception, attention, memory, and the material and cultural environment.[43] Such a perspective makes clear that black-boxing parts of the assumptions that underlie the design of interactions comes at the cost of people's ability to make sense of them contextually.

The Extended Mind Thesis thus provides an interesting and potentially productive perspective for rethinking and engaging with the issues identified above, such as the ways in which search results are filtered, ranked, and presented in a black-boxed way. Rethinking interactivity in these areas with EMT in mind reopens problem- and design-spaces and raises interesting questions about the relationship of action to cognition in these specific areas, along with how we might approach the challenge to redesign interfaces that match the potential for the web's complexity.[44]

References

Bates, Marcia J. 'Toward an Integrated Model of Information Seeking and Searching', *The New Review of Information Behaviour Research* 3 (2002): 1-15.
Broder, Andrei. 'A Taxonomy of Web Search', *ACM SIGIR Forum* 36.2 (2002): 3-10.
Castiglione, Chris. 'Matthew Fuller: Search Engine Alternatives', Institute of Network Cultures, 14 November 2009, http://networkcultures.org/wpmu/query/2009/11/14/matthew-fuller-search-engine-alternatives/.
Clark, Andy. *Supersizing the Mind: Embodiment, Action, and Cognitive Extension*, Oxford: Oxford University Press, 2008.
Feuz, Martin, Matthew Fuller and Felix Stalder. 'Personal Web Searching in the Age of Semantic Capitalism: Diagnosing the Mechanisms of Personalisation', *First Monday* 16.2 (2011).
Fox, Susannah and Sydney Jones. *The Social Life of Health Information*, Pew Research Center, 2009.
Freedman, David H. 'Lies, Damned Lies, and Medical Science', *The Atlantic*, November 2010, http://www.theatlantic.com/magazine/archive/2010/11/lies-damned-lies-and-medical-science/8269/.
Goldacre, Ben. 'The Information Architecture of Medicine is Broken', 29 February 2012, http://www.youtube.com/watch?v=AK_EUKJyusg.
____. *Bad Pharma. How Drug Companies Mislead Doctors and Harm Patients*, London: Fourth Estate Harper Collins, 2012.
Greenhalgh, Trisha. *How to Read a Paper: The Basics of Evidence-Based Medicine*, Oxford: Blackwell, 2010.
Harford, Tim. 'Why We Do What We Do', *Financial Times*, 28 January 2011, http://www.ft.com/cms/

---

42. Alva Noë, *Out of our Heads*, New York: Farrar, Straus and Giroux, 2009.
43. James Hollan, Edwin Hutchins, and David Kirsh, 'Distributed Cognition: Toward a New Foundation for Human-Computer Interaction Research', *ACM Transactions on Computer-Human Interaction* 7.2 (2000): 174-196.
44. See Matthew Fuller's presentation at Society of the Query Conference 2009. Chris Castiglione, 'Matthew Fuller: Search Engine Alternatives', Institute of Network Cultures, 14 November 2009, http://networkcultures.org/wpmu/query/2009/11/14/matthew-fuller-search-engine-alternatives/.

s/2/76e593a6-28eb-11e0-aa18-00144feab49a.html#axzz1lAG3KbL5.
Harnish, Robert M. and Denise D. Cummins. *Minds, Brains, and Computers: A Historical Introduction to the Foundations of Cognitive Science*, Oxford: Blackwell Publishers, 2000.
Hearst, Marti A. *Search User Interfaces*, Cambridge: Cambridge University Press, 2009.
Hollan, James, Edwin Hutchins, and David Kirsh. 'Distributed Cognition: Toward a New Foundation for Human-Computer Interaction Research', *ACM Transactions on Computer-Human Interaction* 7.2 (2000): 174-196.
Introna, Lucas and Helen Nissenbaum. 'Shaping the Web: Why the Politics of Search Engines Matters', *The Information Society* 16.3 (2000): 169-180.
Ioannidis, John P. 'Contradicted and Initially Stronger Effects in Highly Cited Clinical Research', *JAMA*, 294.2 (2005): 218-228.
Kirsh, David and Paul Maglio. 'On Distinguishing Epistemic from Pragmatic Action', *Cognitive Science* 18 (1994): 513-549.
Lehrer, Jonah. 'The Truth Wears Off', *The New Yorker*, 13 December 2010, http://www.newyorker.com/reporting/2010/12/13/101213fa_fact_lehrer.
Marchionini, Gary and Ryen White. 'Find What You Need, Understand What You Find', *International Journal of Human Computer Interaction* 23.3 (2007): 205-237.
Markoff, John and Saul Hansell. 'Hiding in Plain Sight, Google Seeks More Power', *The New York Times*, 14 June 2006, http://www.nytimes.com/2006/06/14/technology/14search.html?pagewanted=1&_r=1.
McPherson, Klim, John E. Wennberg, Ole B. Hovind, and Peter Clifford. 'Small-Area Variations in the Use of Common Surgical Procedures: An International Comparison of New England, England, and Norway', *The New England Journal of Medicine* 307.21 (1982): 1310-4.
Noë, Alva. *Out of Our Heads*, New York: Farrar, Straus and Giroux, 2009.
Pan, Bing, Helen Hembrooke, Thorsten Joachims, Lori Lorigo, Gery Gay, Laura Granka. 'In Google We Trust: Users' Decisions on Rank, Position, and Relevance', *Journal of Computer Mediated Communication* 12.3 (2007): 801-823.
Pariser, Eli. *The Filter Bubble: What the Internet is Hiding From You*, London: Penguin UK, 2011.
Pratt, Craig M. and Lemuel A. Moye. 'The Cardiac Arrhythmia Suppression Trial: Background, Interim Results and Implications', *The American Journal of Cardiology*, 65.4 (1990): 20-29, http://circ.ahajournals.org/content/91/1/245.short.
Rogers, Richard. *Digital Methods*, Cambridge: MIT Press, 2013.
Rose, Nikolas. *Politics of Life Itself*, Woodstock: Princeton University Press, 2006.
Simon, Herbert A. *Administrative Behavior*, New York: Free Press, 1976.
Spink, Amanda and Michael Zimmer. *Web Search: Multidisciplinary Perspectives*, Berlin: Springer-Verlag, 2010.
Sunstein, Cass. *Echo Chambers: Bush v. Gore, Impeachment, and Beyond*, Princeton: Princeton University Press, 2001.
Stalder, Felix and Christine Mayer. 'The Second Index. Search Engines, Personalization and Surveillance', in K. Becker and F. Stalder (eds) *Deep Search: The Politics of Search Beyond Google*, Innsbruck: Studienverlag, 2009.
Studdert, David M., et al. 'Defensive Medicine Among High-Risk Specialist Physicians in a Volatile Malpractice Environment', *JAMA*, 293.21 (2005): 2609-2617.
Thaler, Richard H. and Cass R. Sunstein. *Nudge: Improving Decisions about Health, Wealth, and Happiness*, London: Penguin Books, 2009.
Timmermans, Stefan and Marc Berg. *The Gold Standard: The Challenge of Evidence-Based Medicine and Standardization in Health Care,* Philadelphia: Temple University Press, 2003.
Venturini, Tommaso. 'What Is Second-Degree Objectivity and How Could it Be Represented' http://www.medialab.sciences-po.fr/publications/Venturini-Second_Degree_Objectivity_draft1.pdf.
White, Ryen W. and Resa A. Roth. 'Exploratory search: Beyond the Query-Response Paradigm', *Synthesis Lectures on Information Concepts, Retrieval, and Services* 1.1 (2009): 1-98.
Zickuhr, Kathryn. *Generations 2010*, Pew Research Center, 16 December 2010.

Educating for Search: Understanding the Past and Present Search Technology to Teach for Future Resilience

Dave Crusoe

Educating for Search: Understanding the Past and Present Search Technology to Teach for Future Resilience

Dave Crusoe

Who taught you web search? What do you remember learning? My formal introduction to web search was made in the mid 1990s, when I was in high school. I was taught to think about search as a way to excavate resources that included or excluded specific characteristics. My instruction was linked to set theory and Boolean algebra, which are the visual, mathematical, and conceptual languages that enable us to illuminate objects' relationships. We might use a Venn diagram, for example, to visually separate sweet from sour fruit, or distinguish those fruit that display both sweet and sour characteristics from others. In the United States, students are typically introduced to the Venn diagram in middle school. More sophisticated Boolean algebra, such as written notation, may be part of a high school math class.[1]

Fig. 1. Venn diagram.

Central tenants of Boolean algebra and set theory were adopted and applied by computer scientists in their quest to solve problems generated by the volume and messiness of digital information. Early search pioneers – and developers since – have applied Boolean algebraic logic to help users and software identify relevant information. Early search engines, for example, required users to apply literal Boolean as a means to define their queries. Search engine Excite.com, for example, allowed searchers to apply AND, OR, AND NOT logic, and even to bracket terms parenthetically to apply term precedence.[2]

This symbiosis – a relationship between search logic, search engine function, and education – has led to a situation in which set theory and some Boolean concepts are taught alongside search engine instruction. The result is a situation in which education about search logic, including keyword structure and syntax, presents a false concep-

---

1. The Common Core references algebraic set theory in its high school appendices. See http://www.corestandards.org/assets/CCSSI_Mathematics_Appendix_A.pdf for more information.
2. Way Back Machine, 21 November 1996 archive of 'How to Use Excite Search', http://web.archive.org/web/19961219003220/http://www.excite.com/Info/advanced.html?aqt.

tual depiction about how search engines work at a time when common search engine function is far less about explicit algebraic operation and increasingly about how a user taps prior knowledge to construct, manipulate, and rephrase a series of queries.

While observing a number of U.S. middle and high school class sessions focused on teaching web search to students, I learned that educators' understanding of how search engines work were often reflective of an earlier or different era. As a result, I concluded that educators would benefit from a brief, but holistic depiction of how search engines have historically functioned and evolved since, due to a number of pressing information challenges, and a discussion of why, as a result of shifting technologies, instruction must shift from teaching logic to teaching search function and practices. The result is, I hope, an experience that engages educators in cognitive dissonance over the nature of the topical education we provide, with the hope that a stronger educational experience will emerge.

A Starting Point: Boolean in the Digital Space
To have a productive discussion about the use of Boolean logic in the digital space, it's important that we share an understanding of what Boolean algebra actually is, and how its logic functions. Boolean algebra includes many of the familiar conceptual, linguistic, and symbolic tools we use daily: ANDs, ORs, and NOTs, among others. These tools can be expressed linguistically ('AND'), notationally ($\wedge$ for AND), and programmatically ('&' in many programming languages).

There are also a number of logic operations that may be less familiar, save to programmers. Some search engines may still utilize precedence grouping, which we know as brackets (and). Bracketing allows certain set operations to happen before other set operations. Another operation, a logical disjunction, ('XOR', expressed symbolically as $\oplus$), indicates that an operation validates as true if A or B are true, but not both A and B simultaneously. Other logic structures in Boolean Algebra include equivalence, tautology, and contradiction. However, the user-facing syntax utilized by most search engines is less technically powerful than the true syntax of full Boolean algebra. For example in the searches we conduct, we may utilize:

– AND: A *conjunction* implies a necessary relationship between keywords such that subsequent words are required to appear in results listing the initial term. For example, show me all fruit that are [sweet AND sour].

– Implied AND: When an AND is implied, keywords are implicitly linked with a conjunction. For example, parsing [sweet sour] with an implied AND would be recognized as [sweet AND sour].

– Implied phrase: Another interpretation of keywords is by implied phrase. This is a transformation of the multiple keywords in a query into an explicit phrase for the purposes of search matching. For instance, were [sweet salty sour] an implied phrase, we'd receive results that literally contained the specific words 'sweet salty sour' together, in that order.

– Exact phrase: Explicit indication of a phrase for the purposes of search matching.

Yet depending on the search engine, the effect our syntax has upon results may differ based upon how developers have stated that the engine should act. For example, for many years, Google utilized an implied 'AND' between keywords that were entered without a phrase. According to online discussions, that is no longer the case.[3]

It's helpful to think about the syntax we're provided as one layer in a series of interpretations. Programmers have provided the user with Boolean functionality that they interpret in managing the communication between input (what we provide) and output (what they have to instruct the engine to do, to provide us with results). For example, let's pretend that we're searching a simple literary database for books by Jules Verne. As that query translates directly into MySQL, a popular database engine, it might look something like this:

> Select title,year,dewey-id from books where author = (Jules Verne AND language = English)

In this case, we're asking the database to tell us the title, year, and the Dewey Decimal information from a table of books, when the author of the book is Jules Verne and the language is English. Yet search engine creators have found that related or similar results might also be helpful – but not included by the literal query. As a result, the search we type is further interpreted. Imagine we're searching for a book by Jules Verne, but we misspell his name as 'Julez Vern'. Search engine programmers have crafted their algorithms not only to show us all strict matches, but also those matches that sound the same. Their algorithms automatically translate our query into something like:

> Select title,year,dewey-id from big-search-database where SOUNDEX(author) = SOUNDEX(Julez Vern)

This is, of course, a *gross oversimplification* of how a search engine might locate information, but it serves to illustrate how queries we have expressed in simple terms evolve into queries that search engine operators might use to develop and display results. Understanding this shift puts us on a good footing to explore the pressures that have forced the relationship between information seeking practices and search to evolve past the 'Boolean' phase. In this next section, we'll investigate those pressures.

Evolution: Pressures to 'Do Better'

Perhaps the most fundamental goal of any engine is to provide users quickly with high quality content that responds accurately to the information need. To accomplish this feat, major search technologies break various challenges into separate, interconnected systems. Query pages help support and guide users through the process of creating accurate queries for the engine to parse. The query engine probes an index, built by an indexing engine typically spread across tens, hundreds, or thousands of machines, to identify individual results. In turn, the indexing engine builds its results with input from a crawler, which identifies and retrieves content to feed into the index.

---

3. Anthony Stuart, 'Re: Boolean + Operator Removed? Why?' posting to Google Search Forum, 5 November 2011, http://productforums.google.com/forum/#!searchin/ websearch/%22implied$20and%22/websearch/3olWbew9xdE/xuKBfNk5wjwJ.

Along each step of the process, various algorithms are applied to rank, weigh, judge, and vet content on various quality dimensions. At each step of the way, internal and external pressures provide impetus for technological evolution. Perhaps the most important factor is economic – a business imperative. If the user isn't satisfied, then he or she will move search activity elsewhere.[4] Yet the pressures are primarily technological.

One primary pressure is the need to eliminate spam. Search engineers face the dual task of immediately surfacing query-relevant documents, while reducing or eliminating documents that have been made to *seem* relevant to indexing algorithms through search engine optimization techniques. Search Engine Optimization (SEO) is the practice of artificially enhancing the ranking or rating of a website to increase traffic. The central challenge for search engine creation is to determine not only what is legitimate, but also what is relevant and high quality. You can expect that, for any given search, a significant body of content has been excluded for its potential to be spam.

Alternatively, there are many websites or resources that present high-quality information but have not been optimized in any way. As a result, these sites are tough or even impossible to discover. Publications, particularly content published prior to digitization or accessible beyond a paywall, are an especially common example. Historical research or dialogue, including materials published by the web's precursor, Gopher, are also hidden from search engines' view. Similarly, not all discussion forums are entirely public. Microcommunities, including Howard Rheingold's Brainstorms bulletin board system, which has supported fifteen years of discussion about the future of technology, are accessible only through a membership process. This important material can be classified as part of the 'deep' web.

Either way, what's important to understand is that search engine providers work to balance the results they provide so that the results reflect a minimum of 'spammy' returns, and a maximum of high-quality results for any query. The result of their work is that certain content may or may not actually appear for any given search. Another pressure is to ensure freshness. Freshness relates to the newness of content and is based upon how quickly crawled items can be indexed and made available to searchers through search results. As technologies improve, freshness increases.[5] For instance, users expect to find the latest news articles or the latest version of a website when they visit a site. Just as with spam filtering, content is filtered for its freshness. A particular news article, for instance, may not appear on the first or second results page if much newer news articles appear. Alternatively, a particularly well-liked older article may appear above much fresher news or content.

Beyond serving spam-free, fresh results, search engine providers want to understand the intention beyond the query. Is a user conducting a navigational query (e.g., to find

---

4. Victor Hu, Maria Stone, Jan Pedersen, and Ryen W. White, 'Effects of Search Success on Search Engine Re-use', in Bettina Berendt, Arjen de Vries, Wenfei Fan, Craig Macdonald, Iadh Ounis, and Ian Ruthven (eds) *Proceedings of the 20th ACM International Conference on Information and Knowledge Management (CIKM, '11)*, New York: ACM, 2011.
5. Vanessa Fox, 'Google's New Indexing Structure "Caffeine" Now Live', Search Engine Land weblog, 8 June 2010, http://searchengineland.com/googles-new-indexing-infrastructure-caffeine-now-live-43891.

a specific website), informational query (to 'acquire some information assumed to be present on one or more web pages'), or a transactional query ('to perform some web-mediated activity')?[6] Delivering results that match the user's desires will ensure satisfied and returning customers.

In his testimony before Congress in 2011, Google CEO Eric Schmidt related that in 2010, his company undertook thousands of algorithmic tweaks and, ultimately, implemented '516 changes' to improve search quality.[7] This volume of changes virtually ensures that search results do change over time. Is this important? I believe that it is, and that it's vital we view search engines not as stable technologies, but as vibrant and frequently evolving tools. The content we retrieve has been filtered and ranked, although we may not retrieve all there is to know about a topic, and what we do retrieve will not be the same for long. These are quiet, non-obvious changes.

Yet one of the most profound advances doesn't have to do with spam filtering, speed, freshness, or even content ranking algorithms. It has to do with providers' desire to read far beyond the simple textual query that a user has entered – the search provider wants to understand and interpret what the user really wants *to know*. What the provider utilizes to produce this portrait of intent is called *signals*.

The Result: From Interpreting a Query to Interpreting Intent
Writing about the future of search, a 2002 research team proposed: 'We need a new generation of web searching tools based upon a more thorough understanding of human information behaviors. Such tools would assist users with query construction and modification, spelling, and analytical problems that limit their ability or willingness to persist in finding the information they need.'[8] Ten years later, the query (in the formal sense) remains relevant; it *is* a primary means through which a search engine divines what a searcher seeks. So what is the query? The text of the query is only a small part of what we might conceive of as the entire request. The query is a combination of who and where the searcher is, what the searcher tells the engine to retrieve, and what the searcher may have told the engine in the past.[9] These are 'signals', and increasingly search engines collect signals to interpret *user intent*.

Geospatial reference information – location – is a powerful signal, particularly for many commercial queries. For instance, a searcher interested in movie times may actually intend to search for movie times local to their current location. As I type 'movie time' into my search bar, I receive a suggestion: '"movie time" atlanta', which is my current location. Were I to wish for movie times in New York, I'd have to craft my query to be more specific.

---

6. Andrei Broder, 'A Taxonomy of Web Search', *ACM Sigir Forum* 36.2 (2002): 3-10.
7. Eric Schmidt, 'Testimony of Eric Schmidt, Executive Chairman, Google Inc. before the Senate Committee on Judiciary Subcommittee on the Antitrust, Competition Policy and Consumer Rights', retrieved from Search Engine Land weblog, 21 September 2001, http://searchengineland.com/figz/wp-content/seloads/2011/09/Eric-Schmidt-Testimony.pdf.
8. Amanda Spink, Bernard J. Jansen, Dietmar Wolfram, and Tefko Saracevic, 'From E-Sex to E-Commerce: Web Search Changes', *IEEE Computer* 35.3 (2002): 107-109.
9. Google, 'Verbatim Tool', http://support.google.com/websearch/bin/answer.py?hl=en&p=g_verb&answer=1734130.

Some search engines may also tap the history of our searches to predict the kind of information we'd like to gain through our current or future searches. Were I conducting a research project about a particular historical figure, this tailoring could be helpful – particularly if it were to help me refine my keywords (the syntax I'd enter). For example, Google

> [...] now considers over 200 factors in assessing site quality and relevance. When a user types a query into Google Search, Google's proprietary technology analyzes these signals to provide a determination as to what the user is looking for. Google uses this ever-improving technology to organize information, rank sites, and present results to users. Google's search results are ultimately a *scientific opinion* as to what information users will find most useful.[10] [emphasis added]

We can read this to mean that the language we use to express our query, whether typed, spoken, or otherwise communicated, may not be interpreted literally. Search engines take into account a variety of linguistic devices to better match our intent with quality results. Stemming, for instance, is used to match queries like 'child's' to 'children's', or 'runner' to 'run' and 'running'. So, a search for one word may yield other, very similar stems. Additionally, the engine might match for synonyms. A search for 'stationary' may also yield information about 'office supplies' and 'staples' since these are a popularly used, similar terms.[11]

The way that Boolean syntax is applied is also shifting, although the language of the syntax has not. By now, we're familiar with AND, NOT, and OR, which are the basic Boolean search operators. Search engine providers frequently modify how these operators interact with their search technology to display matching results. For example, until fall of 2011 Google search software applied AND to link keywords, and utilized a '+' to indicate essential and exact keywords.[12] In fall of 2011, the syntax evolved to reduce the utilization of implied AND and transform the '+' operator syntax to quotes, "". Furthermore, it is only possible to receive exact responses to queries via its Verbatim tool, which provides search results 'using the exact keywords you typed'.[13] Queries conducted through its standard tool may include items not specifically designated by AND or + syntax.[14]

While writing this essay, I was also surprised to find that Google's interpretation of the long-standing quotation mark syntax, "", which request exact-phrase matching,

---

10. Schmidt, 'Testimony of Eric Schmidt'.
11. Vanessa Fox, 'Is Google's Synonym Matching Increasing? How Searchers & Brands Can Be Both Helped and Hurt by Evolving Understanding Of Intent', Search Engine Land weblog, 27 August 2012, http://searchengineland.com/is-googles-synonym-matching-increasing-how-searchers-and-brands-can-be-both-helped-and-hurt-131504.
12. Barry Schwartz, 'Google Removes the + Search Command', Search Engine Land weblog, 24 October 2011, http://searchengineland.com/google-sunsets-search-operator-98189.
13. Google, 'Search for Exact Words or Phrases', http://support.google.com/websearch/bin/answer.py?hl=en&p=g_verb&answer=173430.
14. For example, at one point the help text of the Google Basic Search page was amended to read: 'A particular word might not appear on a page in your results if there is sufficient other evidence that the page is relevant.' This change was cited by respondents in help discussions in Google forums, including http://productforums.google.com/forum/#!topic/websearch/x3Pt5XB29Pc.

may also be shifting in application. These searches now return results with characters between the elements ('standardization test' yields matches for 'standardization: test') and searches with a singular, plural, or passive voice return some 'corrected' results ('world serie' returns results for 'world series'). Autocorrection is also enforced. Exact phrase searching for 'thsi American life' using Google's standard tool returns results for 'This American Life', yet searching for the same incorrect phrase using Google's Verbatim tool yields a significantly different results set. As a point of comparison, Bing's search results reflect a similar approach to exact phrase auto-correction. A Bing search for 'literar device' returns only results for 'literary device', despite that Bing's syntax guide indicates that quotes should return 'results that contain the specified phrase, exactly'.[15]

The increasing emphasis on geolocation, an increase in the use of fuzzy matching and synonyms, the rapidity with which the index is updated, and the evolving nature of how our precise syntax is interpreted points to the shifting nature of our query syntax. Our search is no longer about the keywords we enter. It is nothing less than an interpretation of the sum of all signals we send to the engine. In sum, *we must think of the query as the sum of all signals we send to the engine* and not simply the words that we type into the search box.

Search Education in a Signals World

To respond to these shifts, search education must focus on what's appropriate, of high value, and leads learners to develop an understanding responsive and resilient to technological change. Where is instructional time best spent?

First: Teach About How Search Engines Work
First and most fundamentally, it's important for searchers to possess a basic understanding of what a search engine is and how it works. It's essential to teach that a search engine may crawl large portions of what we can conceive of as the internet but that not all portions will be visible to us through the searches we conduct. Engines' parsing or ranking may be beneficial, for instance, in the filtering of spam, but it may also be detrimental. In which cases would it be detrimental, and what are some ways to overcome artificial barriers? What tools might be built into search engines that can allow a searcher to take more advantage of what the technology has to offer? By helping learners understand what a search engine is, how it works, and how and where to learn more about it, we provide them with tools to adapt more easily to the unforeseen.

Second: Teach Learners to Use Keywords, Phrases, or Sentences that are Likely to Occur in a Page
On major search engines, keywords are the primary signal a user shares with the search engine to drive the search engine's results. But what should those keywords be for any particular search? How do we know? In some engines, particularly in academic engines like EBSCO, keywords may have to match pre-defined keywords that relate to an article or specific entry fields.[16] But these keywords are decreasingly correlated

---

15. Microsoft Bing, 'Phrase', http://msdn.microsoft.com/en-us/library/ff795609.aspx.
16. EBSCO, 'Advanced Search Guided-Style Find Fields – Help Sheet', http://support.epnet.com/knowledge_base/detail.php?id=3821 and EBSCO, 'Searching with Boolean Operators – Help Sheet', http://support.ebsco.com/knowledge_base/detail.php?id=3883.

with success when using major search technologies. In the case of Google and other providers, it's more important that keywords or phrases target the language that a web page may use, or even attempt to replicate a sentence that might be found on a particular page.

What does this mean for the teaching of Boolean keywords like AND, OR, and NOT? It is decreasingly important that we educators teach young people specific keyword syntax, and much more important to teach about the overall technological function that search engines fulfill.

Third: Teach Patience and Refinement
Educators must also teach patience. Fellow educators and I have described this as *refinement thinking*.[17] It's quite common for searchers to select one of the first four options on a page, but far less frequent for one of the first four options to be 'the best' or 'the only'. Social psychologists call this 'cognitive miserism', in which 'the basic idea is that people do not like to take a lot of trouble thinking if they do not have to'.[18] Yet it's an important habit to break, particularly because the quick path is so very quick. How often have you observed the same practices? What were your responses, and how might they be improved?

One good response is to engage learners actively in a discussion about the merits and drawbacks of information from any particular source, and to challenge them to synthesize information from multiple sources. But don't treat this as a passive assignment by simply grading the number of sources a learner might cite. Instead, ask for elaboration and thinking – how do sources corroborate one another, and where do they differ? Which sources seem to be of higher quality than others, and why? What can one take from this knowledge to future research? These are all valuable questions to ask of learners.

Finally, for older learners, we must at least mention the code-switching necessary to make the transition from successfully searching sophisticated web engines to the far simpler search technologies used by libraries and research databases. Quite often, research databases function with explicit Boolean operators. Negotiating these databases is an essential skill for students of secondary and higher education institutions. Yet we must recognize and differentiate between the instruction required for success in one 'code', that of web engines, and the other, or older Boolean-based databases.

Fourth: Teach About Content Sources
No discussion would be complete without relaying the importance of recognizing high-quality sources. High-quality sources for information provide a level of vetting, and potential detail, beyond what many readily available sources might yield. A search for 'how a cat purrs', for example, yields a large number of results from sources as divergent as content aggregators (http://ask.com and http://answers.com), government websites (http://www.loc.gov, the Library of Congress), and publications (such

---

17. This term emerged through discussions with D. Abilock and others on the ALA's Information Literacy listserv.
18. Susan T. Fiske, 'Social Cognition', in Abraham Tesser (ed.) *Advanced Social Psychology*, New York: McGraw-Hill, 1995, p. 154.

as *Scientific American*) – all within the first dozen Google search results. The content and probable quality of the results is as diverse as the result sources themselves, but knowing and understanding which locations are most likely to be detailed and of high quality (such as the Library of Congress or *Scientific American*) is important.

Yet, we must ask: how do learners come to identify which sources are of the highest quality and which are of dubious quality? At school? Home? Whose responsibility is it to ensure that a young person can identify a small handful of high-quality resources? As educators, I believe it is *our* responsibility. A librarian-educator recently remarked to me that she wished subject educators would not only grade classroom assignments, but would also grade the overall quality of resources that a learner had utilized to derive the information in their report. Additionally, what if it were an assignment to improve upon resources that had already been identified? Perhaps, as educators, we could work harder to engage learners in critiquing their own sources – and at an earlier age.

Conclusions

In the past decade, search engine technology has become immeasurably more sophisticated. Paradigms that were once helpful, including the user paradigms of Boolean logic as a tool for searching, have faded in importance as more sophisticated paradigms emerge. In crafting this essay, I wanted to provide a grounding for how search engines function and the challenges that search providers face. By sharing a common understanding and respect for these challenges, I believe we can provide ourselves with a firm footing through which to engage our learners in understanding the same.

Yet there's more. I hope this has prompted thinking about how search education must be delivered at a time when the search technologies themselves have moved beyond the straightforward and logical tools that we may have once learned. Many of us educators must evolve our conceptual understanding of what it is to teach search. To teach search now, we are best teaching how search engines actually work. What do they find – 'index' – and why? What's missed in the process? With that understanding in place, it's trivial to move forward with teaching about why patience, 'refinement thinking', is an important practice. Yet that practice won't be embedded unless we educators take more care with our students – not only by teaching them how to synthesize information and about sources they can trust and reference, but by helping them to critique the sources they've already found. As a whole, these practices, well learned, will enable future researchers to thrive now and to be resilient through inevitable technological evolution.

Special thanks to Mary Roth, IBM Research, and Sara Armstrong, OnCUE, for their feedback.

References

Broder, Andrei. 'A Taxonomy of Web Search', *ACM Sigir Forum* 36.2 (2002): 3-10.
EBSCO, 'Advanced Search Guided-Style Find Fields – Help Sheet', http://support.epnet.com/knowledge_base/detail.php?id=3821.
EBSCO, 'Searching with Boolean Operators – Help Sheet', http://support.ebsco.com/knowledge_base/detail.php?id=3883.
Fiske, Susan T. 'Social Cognition', in Abraham Tesser (ed.) *Advanced Social Psychology*, New York: McGraw-Hill, 1995, pp. 145-194.
Fox, Vanessa. 'Google's New Indexing Structure "Caffeine" Now Live', Search Engine Land weblog, 8 June 2010, http://searchengineland.com/googles-new-indexing-infrastructure-caffeine-now-live-43891.
_____. 'Is Google's Synonym Matching Increasing? How Searchers and Brands Can Be Both Helped and Hurt by Evolving Understanding Of Intent', Search Engine Land weblog, 27 August 2012, http://searchengineland.com/is-googles-synonym-matching-increasing-how-searchers-and-brands-can-be-both-helped-and-hurt-131504.
Google. 'Search for Exact Words or Phrases', http://support.google.com/websearch/bin/answer.py?hl=en&p=g_verb&answer=1734130.
_____. 'Verbatim Tool', http://support.google.com/websearch/bin/answer.py?hl=en&p=g_verb&answer=1734130.
Hu, Victor, Maria Stone, Jane Pedersen, and Ryen W. White. 'Effects of Search Success on Search Engine Re-Use', in Bettina Berendt, Arjen de Vries, Wenfei Fan, Craig Macdonald, Iadh Ounis, and Ian Ruthven (eds) *Proceedings of the 20th ACM International Conference on Information and Knowledge Management (CIKM, '11)*, New York: ACM, 2011, pp. 1841-1846.
Schmidt, Eric. 'Testimony of Eric Schmidt, Executive Chairman, Google Inc. before the Senate Committee on Judiciary Subcommittee on the Antitrust, Competition Policy and Consumer Rights' 21 September 2001, http://searchengineland.com/figz/wp-content/seloads/2011/09/Eric-Schmidt-Testimony.pdf.
Schwartz, Barry. 'Google Removes the + Search Command', Search Engine Land weblog, 24 October 2011, http://searchengineland.com/google-sunsets-search-operator-98189.
Spink, Amanda, Bernard J. Jansen, Dietmar Wolfram, and Tefko Saracevic. 'From E-Sex to E-Commerce: Web Search Changes', IEEE Computer, 35.3 (2002): 107-109.
Stuart, Anthony. 'Re: Boolean + Operator Removed? Why?' posting to Google Search Forum, 5 November 2011, http://productforums.google.com/forum/#!searchin/websearch/%22implied$20and%22/websearch/3oIWbew9xdE/xuKBfNk5wjwJ.
Way Back Machine, 21 November 1996, archive of 'How to Use Excite Search', http://web.archive.org/web/19961219003220/http://www.excite.com/Info/advanced.html?aqt.

Finding Knowledge: What Is It to 'Know' When We Search?

Simon Knight

Finding Knowledge:
What Is It to 'Know' When We Search?

Simon Knight

You walk into the exam room, breathe a nervous sigh, sit down, and plug your laptop in. The URL for the questions is sent out, and you are reminded that while you may search for information and browse pages as you wish, you may not communicate with any other person. You look at the first question; it gives you a poem from an author you know little about, along with some brief historical context, and another source you have studied before. You are asked to draw comparisons between the perspectives of the sources, using your knowledge of the period. 'Right,' you think, as you open up a popular search engine, 'what do I need to know…'

Consider the preceding vignette; Andy Clark and David Chalmers propose that in such cases the external apparatus (the internet) fulfills the same functional role as the internal apparatus (the brain) and thus should be considered an extension of our mind.[1] For the purposes of this essay readers need not 'buy into' the extended mind thesis whole scale. Rather, this example is intended to illustrate a general point regarding the relationship between technology and the mind: When analyzing the functional role of technology we should consider how it shapes our activities, its implications for epistemic concepts such as 'knowledge', and the differences between pre- and post-technology practices.

Such an analysis has profound implications in education, for example. Under what circumstances do we accept that students 'know' something? How do we decide that they know something (that is, how do educators claim knowledge of their student's knowledge states) and also that such knowledge is important? Furthermore, how do we think about the future of technology and the ways that technology might change what we believe is important (for better or worse)?

Indeed, the issue of external tools is not an abstract problem. Open book exams have existed for some time, as have 'take home' exams and coursework. Moreover, in Denmark a three-year trial – now implemented – started in 2009 to permit the use of the internet in exams.[2] The inclusion of the World Wide Web in examinations (excluding sites

---

1. Andy Clark and David Chalmers, 'The Extended Mind', *Analysis* 58.1 (1998): 7-19, http://www.philosophy.ed.ac.uk/people/clark/pubs/TheExtendedMind.pdf.
2. Simon Knight, 'Danish Use of Internet in Exams – Epistemology, Pedagogy, Assessment…' Finding Knowledge blog, 23 July 2013, http://people.kmi.open.ac.uk/knight/2013/07/danish-use-of-internet-in-exams-epistemology-pedagogy-assessment/.

which could be used to communicate with other students) was a natural extension of earlier Danish examinations that had included multimedia resources ranging from CD-ROMs to videos, audio, and webpages. The aim was to give students the opportunity to work with a variety of resources and to probe analysis skills and metacognitive skills, such as checking mathematical outputs using multiple methods.

I find the Danish example particularly interesting because it is so far removed from what my own assessment experience has been – both as a teacher and student. Moreover, as I and others have argued, our assessment methods implicate particular epistemological assumptions; measuring 'knowledge' of unconnected 'facts' suggests a rather different way of thinking about knowledge than those that require testing the filtering and analysis of resources towards some critical, evaluative output. The epistemological implications of our social and technical interactions with information is the subject of this essay. I will specifically look at the role of search engines as informants offering testimonial knowledge on a query, then at the question of how the receiver of testimony should be taken into account by those giving the information, and finally at how we should deal with multiplicity of perspectives, or even gaps in our knowledge.

Of course, the simple retrieval of precise information on the internet may be a challenge for many. Readers may recognize the experience of having a friend or colleague ask a question, which you respond to by turning to a search engine and finding an answer to the request with the first query. Indeed, the website www.lmgtfy.com – 'let me google that for you' – exists for that purpose, animating a search for any given query. The Danish example, though, shows that it is still required for students in this case to remember ('know' according to some) information, while still allowing them to engage critical literacy skills to connect pieces of information from across multiple web sources.

As mentioned above, we should examine the implications of technology concerning how we think and how our activities are shaped. However, we should not assume *prima facie* that these technological changes actually represent new epistemologies, whether positive or negative, nor new ways of thinking about what it means to 'know'. Rather, we should seek to understand the nature of 'knowledge', and how informants – including non-human informants – mediate our understanding of the world around us and have always done so. This essay considers these questions, first by discussing some issues regarding research on technological changes, then by asking what role search functions fulfill and how these functions affect our own understanding of 'knowledge'.

Researching Search

The impact of the internet on how we think has caught popular attention in the many articles – often critical.[3] However, many of these articles assume that change is a bad thing – particularly any indication of neurological change – and they often report studies of very particular circumstances. Yet neurological change is unsurprising given the

---

3. See for discussion and critique of these articles Simon Knight, 'Is Google Making Me [Stupid|smarter]...How About Bing?' Finding Knowledge blog, 23 January 2013, http://people.kmi.open.ac.uk/knight/2013/01/is-google-making-me-stupid-or-smarter-how-about-bing/.

human brain's high plasticity, and it is incredibly difficult to conduct solid research that tracks abilities over time given the challenges to control across multiple cohorts of ages and educational systems.

Much of the substance of these debates boils down to what we value. We have previously valued memory and memorization of facts, in part because they are easy to assess.[4] However, presumably most people would agree that the purpose of education is not the speedy recall of facts – it is not to develop world-class pub quizzers, capable of reciting the dates of monarchy. Instead, the idea behind assessments is that if students can recall facts, then – by proxy – they have knowledge about those facts, meaning they can engage with critical skills of evaluation, etc. Fundamentally, these skills – understanding the connectedness of knowledge, of evaluation, of making credibility judgments – are what knowledge consists of, not the recall of individual 'facts' in constrained contexts. Critical skill is also what the Danish system seeks to measure; given the easy access to facts through search engines, a focus on synthesis and evaluation becomes easier. However, the question of how the tools help shape our thinking still stands. Just as books, with indexes, chapters, reference lists, and so on, present information in certain ways, so too does the internet and its tools of access, such as search engines, browsers, and social network sites.

Search Engines as Informants
An interesting aspect of the Danish example is the prohibition of communication websites in examinations. Yet the line between search engines and social networking sites is increasingly blurring. Indeed, while Google's advertising rhetoric has tended to focus on a desire to 'know what you want, before you do',[5] Bing (with Facebook), at least in North America, has developed 'Bing Social'[6] with the headline: 'For every search, there is someone who can help.'

Google's strategy is to use developments in semantic web technology to identify key facts associated with any particular query; thus, a search for Florence Nightingale brings up a standard search engine results page (SERP) with key links on it. However, in addition to that SERP, there is a box on the right hand side with some key facts about Florence Nightingale populated from her Wikipedia entry. Bing Social, in contrast, uses similar developments in social network data to infer whether someone might be a good 'informant' for any particular query – for example, whether or not that person has qualifications in the subject of historical figures. Thus Google's Knowledge Graph has been developing more as a direct informant – providing the information itself – while Bing Social (and Facebook Graph search) aim to provide you with good informants from your social network.

---

4. Amongst others, Dan Russell discusses these issues: 'Why Knowing Search Isn't the Same as Having an Education', SearchReSearch blog, 1 August 2011, http://searchresearch1.blogspot.co.uk/2011/08/why-knowing-search-isnt-same-as-having.html.
5. Tim Adams, 'Google and the Future of Search: Amit Singhal and the Knowledge Graph', *The Guardian*, 19 January 2013, http://www.theguardian.com/technology/2013/jan/19/google-search-knowledge-graph-singhal-interview.
6. Derrick Connell, 'Bing Social Updates Arrive Today: For Every Search, There is Someone Who Can Help', Bing Blogs, 17 January 2013, http://www.bing.com/blogs/site_blogs/b/search/archive/2013/01/17/bing-social-updates-arrive-today-for-every-search-there-is-someone-who-can-help.aspx.

Both of these approaches have obvious uses and advantages but also potential problems. Examples of the risks of seeking informants in one's own social network (the Bing Social and Graph Search approach) are:

- If your social network mediates your information seeking, there is likely to be a confirmation bias in the returned results. If our results are influenced by our friendship groups (particularly biased in ways we might not be aware of), this raises serious concerns about the epistemic properties of the search, which we might expect will return both all relevant results (recall), and specific results that meet the criteria we have stated (precision).
- The above concern is particularly true for those who do not (or who rarely) use the internet – both in terms of an offline searcher's access to information, and in terms of an online searcher's access to information about those offline.
- Such data is likely to be *messy* – many people may not want all facets of their life to be searchable (indeed, there's a Tumblr for that[7]); plenty of people post information to their social networks that might make them prominent in search results, but not necessarily good informants. For example they 'like' pages for signaling some attribute they don't actually have, or to get discounts from brands, or to monitor activity (e.g. watching a political opponent's activity).

Two key ideas from the work of philosopher Miranda Fricker strike me as particularly fruitful here,[8] and to my knowledge they have not yet been explored in this context:

- The risk of testimonial injustice – the risk that some types of user knowledge will be marginalized by specific agents on the basis of their (demographic or personal) characteristics. Whether such a risk is greater or lesser in a particular search (or recommender) system is an interesting question (and might be thought of as a case of prejudice exercised by individuals).
- The risk of hermeneutical injustice – the risk that some types of user knowledge will be marginalized by the system, perhaps in such a way as to make those users unaware of their own epistemic injustice. Again, whether such a risk is greater or lesser in particular search (or recommender) systems is interesting. (This risk might be thought of as a case of marginalization, as opposed to explicitly enacted prejudice.)

These problems are arguably a part of the more general problem of the filter bubble: the concern that search engines through personalization and demographic characteristics filter SERPs to provide individuals with biased information, affirming prior beliefs. It is to this issue that I now turn.

Search as an Epistemic Tool – More of What You Want

The use of search engines to find information or sources of information is a common activity in which students must frequently engage. In a 2012 paper, Thomas Simpson suggests search engines fulfill the role of 'surrogate experts', and that we should be concerned about their epistemic properties – their ability to return relevant results (precision),

---

7. See, http://actualfacebookgraphsearches.tumblr.com/.
8. See for example Miranda Fricker, *Epistemic Injustice: Power and the Ethics of Knowing*, Oxford: Oxford University Press, 2009.

not exclude relevant results (recall), return results in a timely manner, and prioritize credible sources.[9] In particular, they should be 'objective'. By this he means that if two sides to a story exist and are equally linked to across the web, then they should be interleafed and not stacked. SERPs should not present a biased perspective on credible sources.

However, Simpson and various other authors argue that personalization of search results fails this 'objectivity' criterion. His claim is that presenting information that is likely to affirm a user's prior beliefs is problematic because – unless the individual is an 'epistemic saint'[10] – the search engine fails to represent the domain being searched. Simpson suggests two solutions: first, turning off personalization or querying search engines that do not use personalization, and second, legal regulation of search engines' objectivity.

While there are certainly valid concerns regarding this issue, here I want to discuss some of the motivations for personalization and personal recommendation (such as the Bing Social example discussed above) in light of testimonial knowledge. In the context of filter bubbles we should consider:

- Searchers may well search for biased information in their queries – searching for 'Al Gore inconvenient truth' may bring up rather different results than 'Al Gore liar'.
- SERPs may present bias for two reasons:
    1. Bias will arise from personalization of results (this is broadly *testimonial injustice*).
    2. Bias will arise from an epistemically biased landscape – for example, language and gender dominance among Wikipedia articles and editors (this is broadly hermeneutical injustice and may be more challenging for search engines to address).
- Social search is likely to present many of the same problems, but many non-personalized search engines will too.

It is worth considering the role of the search engine in epistemic inquiry, and how search engines could foreground their assumptions about searchers to fulfill their roles as informants.

Testimonial Expertise

You're conducting a school research project on a local Spanish festival that happens to be a namesake of an English clothing brand. You ask your parents for some useful websites on the festival; they give you the details of a U.K. arts festival nearby, along with a link to a website with a primary school level English description of the clothing brand...

When we seek information we are interested in different things in different contexts. One of the challenges of the 'semantic web' is to understand the varied meanings that any particular word can indicate – in short, to understand context. For that reason, some researchers began talking about the 'pragmatic web', the development of technologies to support language in action perspectives in order to understand how

---

9. Thomas W. Simpson, 'Evaluating Google as an Epistemic Tool', *Metaphilosophy* 43.4 (2012): 426-445, http://people.ds.cam.ac.uk/tws21/preprints/2012_Metaphilosophy_Evaluating%20Google%20as%20an%20Epistemic%20Tool_preprint.pdf.
10. Simpson, 'Evaluating Google as an Epistemic Tool', p. 439.

queries might be *used*.[11] Of course, in education we also want to train people to care about the right things in the right context.

The example given above highlights how irritating such 'help' could be; similarly, while search engines rarely are true surrogate experts (Knowledge Graph being a counterpoint), they do strive for quality by pointing out good informants – that is, by testifying that a website is a good source in the given context. We expect informants – human and otherwise – to take into account salient factors about ourselves, although we might expect some of these to be left implicit (e.g. geolocation of information) but not others (e.g. political leanings, or perhaps facets such as literacy level).

Personalization
A search function returns English results, and when you check quantities it defaults to metric, always using a base 10 numeric system.[12] *When you search for your morning news, a set of left-wing blogs you like to read are returned, along with a new source and an article a friend of yours has recommended on a popular social networking site.*

While certainly in the latter case the search engines' complicity in confirmation bias may be an issue, the real concern is the searcher's own epistemic standpoint and his or her openness to other perspectives (which the search engine might be able to present the searcher with while still highlighting recommendations). We should pay more attention to the level of the *agent* when considering the filter bubble.

However, despite this claim, there are at least two major cases where we can imagine filter bubbles in which the searcher is not complicit:

- The 'racist classmate' case. In this example, we imagine a searcher who, without knowing, has a classmate who searches for white supremacist websites. In fact, we can imagine a more innocuous case in which the searcher's classmate is particularly fond of one local café; unknown to the searcher, their searches are thus pushed towards that café as opposed to other – equally well liked, reviewed, and known – local establishments. The concern here is not that the search engine knows one's geolocation, but that by tailoring to repeated searches – while not making this explicit in the search interface – the SERP provides a non-objective set of results (this is true even if one's own searches have developed the bias).
- The 'biased community' case. In this example, we imagine a country where the majority of searchers are more inclined towards one perspective on an issue than another. Thus, despite the presence of credible, timely, and well-linked online resources from the other perspective, searchers in that country are more likely to be directed towards the majority perspective.

In both cases the search engine mediates our access to information in ways that make understanding that information *less* transparent – they thus fail to act as objective informants.

---

11. See for example this post and references on it in Simon Knight, 'The Pragmatic Web: More than Just Semantics Contextualized', Finding Knowledge blog, 4 January 2014, http://people.kmi.open.ac.uk/knight/2013/01/the-pragmatic-web-more-than-just-semantics-contextualised/.
12. I am grateful to Rebecca Ferguson at the Open University for these examples.

We can see that to some extent personalization is exactly what we expect informants to deliver – I want information that understands my context. However, I also want to be able to interrogate the informant's understanding of my context, to ensure we are 'on the same page' as it were, and in this respect search engines often fail. I would suggest that personalization is bad not because it's non-objective, but that, when giving an 'objective' judgment of testimony, we expect informants to tell us about the substantive assumptions they make in order to come to their conclusions. We expect to have some shared understanding of the assumptions informants make about our information needs. Search engines often fail to offer this kind of disclosure, except when there is good reason for them to do so (often advertising-based, for example asking searchers to clarify their postal code for the purposes of geo-located targeted advertisements). However, where these assumptions are explicit, their impacts are often not made clear. I will now discuss another example of the socio-technical mediation of our understanding of information, before presenting a final challenge to the current status quo.

When No Answer Is Answer Enough
An interesting, related problem concerning how we think about information comes in the form of the 'testimony of silence' – when the absence of information informs you of something.[13] We can imagine this happening in a number of cases:

1. When a searcher queries a search engine, receives no answers, and takes that to imply positive knowledge (e.g., searching for information on traffic jams and finding nothing, leading the searcher to believe there are no current traffic problems).
2. When searchers seek information, receive no answer, and take that to mean poor community support or expertise (e.g. in the above example, assuming that no answer is due to a failure of technology, or in a scientific context thinking lack of an answer means there is no research on the topic searched).
3. When people search for information and receive irrelevant answers (e.g. in the 'bad informant' example above, a search is conducted to find information on a festival, but the only results returned are about another concept).
4. When people search for information but do not see the response (e.g. where search results are weighted against the answer they are looking for, as in some filter bubble cases above).

Again, in this context search engines, searchers, and the epistemic environment all play a part in the state of knowledge. To give an example of a complex case, I conducted a study in which I asked 11-year-old children in a classroom to find the answer to the question, 'How many women have won The Nobel Prize?'[14] This query is relatively simple in many respects, and in fact simply entering the query into most search

---

13. Interestingly Garfield discussed this in Eugene Garfield, *When Is a Negative Search Result Positive? Essays of an Information Scientist* vol. 1, 12 August 1970, pp. 117-118, http://www.garfield.library.upenn.edu/essays/V1p117y1962-73.pdf. According to Google Scholar (September 2013) that paper has been cited six times since then, most prominently by Marchionini discussing exploratory search – readers might be entertained to consider whether this is a positive negative result...Certainly it suggests an interesting lack of exploration of this area.
14. Simon Knight and Neil Mercer, 'The Role of Exploratory Talk in Classroom Search Engine Tasks', in *Technology, Pedagogy and Education*, forthcoming, 2014.

engines will bring up a relevant result with the correct answer. However, slightly to my surprise, some of the children visited 'answer'-style websites and took the user-submitted claims made there without checking the date of the answer given, thereby reflecting a lack of attention to the nature of change in such knowledge claims. For other questions some children decided there was no answer when they could not find one, failing to adjust their search terms or to think about how other information might be relevant to their problem. Educational contexts are further complicated by the presence of content filters that can prevent students from seeing highly relevant results.

In each of these instances, search results' presentation and user interaction have an impact. Users may be more likely to see information that confirms their prior beliefs; this bias relates to their queries, the results they click, and the information they take away from chosen results. For example, recent evidence from Microsoft Research indicates that in the health domain, searchers favor positive over negative information *as do search engines* – thus creating a filter bubble based on a 'testimony of silence' around negative results.[15] Importantly, this bias leads to the uptake of incorrect health information in many cases.[16]

Diversity Aware Search

In the preceding sections I have noted some concerns over how we look for information and why understanding the socio-technical factors involved might be interesting. There are a number of suggested solutions to these problems, but many have issues. For example:

- One solution to the filter bubble is not to personalize results. However, this is problematic because, as discussed above, we expect a degree of personalization from good informants. We expect information to be in accord with our prior understandings, our context (geographic if nothing else), etc. However, search engines such as DuckDuckGo follow exactly this approach.
- Another solution is to use friends and other social contacts as informants. Our friends understand our common knowledge and can address this and be interrogated as to their reasons more directly; of course, there are still important biases here, and my friends may not be able to inform me about a rather large range of topics. Moreover, often we don't want our social contacts to know about our information needs in the first place.
- Another solution is to show results deliberately that are beyond the area of enquiry, either topic-wise, socially, or in terms of perspective taken.

This last approach is interesting as it attempts to diversify perspectives and contexts; it has been described as 'Diversity Aware Search'.[17] As has been noted, 'diverse exposure' may be a means to burst your filter bubble, with methods ranging from clustering results, depictions of the 'balance' of articles searchers have actually viewed, and ask-

---

15. Ryen W. White, 'Beliefs and Biases in Web Search', *SIGIR'13*, Dublin, Ireland, 28 July-1 August, 2013, http://research.microsoft.com/e
16. See also Martin Feuz's article in this volume, pp. 203-215.
17. See for example, Elena Simperl et al., 'DiversiWeb 2011', In *ACM SIGIR Forum*, 45 (2011): 49-53, http://dl.acm.org/citation.cfm?id=1988861.

ing readers to engage in discourse based on considering multiple perspectives.[18] The 'liquid publications'[19] project for example developed a diversity-aware scholar search that can be used to avoid homophily in one's academic network by down-ranking papers by authors with whom the searcher has co-authored in the past.

Other solutions could be to look for diverse ways of clustering the same set of documents or present searchers with clusterings from different users;[20] this could particularly work in cases where the user is 'exploring' the information landscape and has no well-defined information need at initial stages.[21] In this case, searchers may be unaware of alternative groupings and of various ways their information need could be defined. Such approaches may foreground facets of personalization that usually remain hidden.

An additional benefit of such diversity-aware search tools is that they offer the opportunity to address 'content holes' in a searcher's knowledge.[22] Indeed, such an approach may assist in addressing some of the issues of 'silence' raised above. To give an example taken from Nadamoto et al., we might imagine a Mexican community in which swine flu in Mexico is widely discussed and known.[23] However, if that community does not also relate to the wider global risk of swine flu, it has a content hole; such gaps might be identified in community discussions across blogs through comparisons with content on related Wikipedia pages.

It is interesting to note that such an approach might also lead to unintended consequences, for example insofar as some research indicates that exposure to opposing perspectives can reinforce one's own viewpoint (and prepare one for arguing against opposition). Furthermore, technical approaches that increase diversity by reducing redundancy (repetition of information) may lead a person to question an important credibility cue, given that repetition may be highly salient in the context of seeking to corroborate sources. Therefore diversity-aware search is not a definitive solution to the problems presented above, but rather an indication of a design feature that might present interesting alternatives and lead to different interactions with search users. A big problem of search engines that are not diversity-aware is that the user will almost never learn how biased the retrieved information is. It would help if search engines would state what kind of filtering and interpretative steps they perform.

---

18. Paul Resnick et al., 'Bursting Your (Filter) Bubble: Strategies for Promoting Diverse Exposure', in *Proceedings of the 2013 Conference on Computer Supported Cooperative Work Companion*, 95-100, 2013, http://dl.acm.org/citation.cfm?id=2441981.
19. See, http://project.liquidpub.org/tools.
20. Mathias Verbeke, Bettina Berendt, and Siegfried Nijssen, 'Data Mining, Interactive Semantic Structuring, and Collaboration: A Diversity-Aware Method for Sense-Making in Search', in *Proceedings of First International Workshop on Living Web, Collocated with the 8th International Semantic Web Conference (ISWC-2009). CEUR Workshop Proceedings, Washington, DC, USA.* Vol. 515, 2009, http://www.liacs.nl/home/snijssen/publications/iswc2009.pdf.
21. Rahul Singh, Ya-Wen Hsu, and Naureen Moon, 'Multiple Perspective Interactive Search: a Paradigm for Exploratory Search and Information Retrieval on the Web', *Multimedia Tools and Applications* 62.2 (2013): 507-543.
22. Akiyo Nadamoto et al., 'Content Hole Search in Community-type Content Using Wikipedia', in *Proceedings of the 11th International Conference on Information Integration and Web-based Applications & Services*, 25-32, 2009, http://dl.acm.org/citation.cfm?id=1806353.
23. Nadamoto et al., 'Content Hole Search'.

Conclusions

You are asked to draw a comparison among the perspectives in the sources, using your knowledge of the time. 'Right', you think, as you open up a popular search engine, 'what do I need to know...'

Access to external resources prompts us to consider what it means to 'know' something and what types of knowledge are important. Asking you what a 'clepsydra' is has a different connotation in a closed book or an open (or internet-enabled) examination. That is not to say that memorizing 'facts' has no value; it is sometimes rather important, for example in the case of remembering road sign meanings. However, facts aren't disconnected from meaning, and exploring how people *use* information gives insight into their knowledge states.

On the internet, the tools at hand provide paths to information, offer particular routes, and often obfuscate alternative paths to the same or other destinations. Designing search engines is a hard challenge; many searches are 'precision' searches aimed at the recall of an individual token, but many others, such as holiday planning or weighing scientific literature, involve 'exploratory' activities and credibility judgments of sources. Thinking about how best to represent results for these multiple purposes is complex (and indeed, Google is currently soliciting feedback on how it might improve in this respect[24]). Even with technological improvements, we should raise awareness about the ways in which technology mediates our access to information, and education should reflect the importance of this awareness while also training our associated critical evaluation and credibility judgment skills.

References

Adams, Tim. 'Google and the Future of Search: Amit Singhal and the Knowledge Graph', *The Guardian*, 19 January 2013, http://www.theguardian.com/technology/2013/jan/19/google-search-knowledge-graph-singhal-interview.

Clark, Andy, and David Chalmers. 'The Extended Mind', *Analysis* 58.1 (1998): 7-19.

Connell, Derrick. 'Bing Social Updates Arrive Today: For Every Search, There is Someone Who Can Help', Bing Blogs, 17 January 2013, http://www.bing.com/blogs/site_blogs/b/search/archive/2013/01/17/bing-social-updates-arrive-today-for-every-search-there-is-someone-who-can-help.aspx.

Fricker, Miranda. *Epistemic Injustice: Power and the Ethics of Knowing*, Oxford: Oxford University Press, 2009.

Garfield, Eugene. *When Is a Negative Search Result Positive? Essays of an Information Scientist* vol. 1, 12 August 1970, http://www.garfield.library.upenn.edu/essays/V1p117y1962-73.pdf.

Knight, Simon. 'Danish Use of Internet in Exams – Epistemology, Pedagogy, Assessment...' Finding Knowledge blog, 23 July 2013, http://people.kmi.open.ac.uk/knight/2013/07/danish-use-of-internet-in-exams-epistemology-pedagogy-assessment/.

———. 'Is Google Making Me [Stupidlsmarter]...How About Bing?' Finding Knowledge blog, 23 January 2013, http://people.kmi.open.ac.uk/knight/2013/01/is-google-making-me-stupid-or-smarter-how-about-bing/.

———. 'The Pragmatic Web: More than Just Semantics Contextualized', Finding Knowledge blog, 4

---

24. Patrick Thomas, 'Give Us Your Feedback on Search Policies', Inside Search blog, 23 August 2013, http://insidesearch.blogspot.co.uk/2013/08/give-us-your-feedback-on-search-policies.html.

January 2014, http://people.kmi.open.ac.uk/knight/2013/01/the-pragmatic-web-more-than-just-semantics-contextualised/.

Knight, Simon and Neil Mercer, 'The Role of Exploratory Talk in Classroom Search Engine Tasks', in *Technology, Pedagogy and Education*, forthcoming, 2014.

Nadamoto, Akiyo, Eiji Aramaki, Takeshi Abekawa, and Yohei Murakami. 'Content Hole Search in Community-type Content Using Wikipedia', in *Proceedings of the 11th International Conference on Information Integration and Web-based Applications & Services*, 25-32, 2009, http://dl.acm.org/citation.cfm?id=1806353.

Resnick, Paul, R. Kelly Garrett, Travis Kriplean, Sean A. Munson, and Natalie Jomini Stroud. 'Bursting Your (Filter) Bubble: Strategies for Promoting Diverse Exposure', in *Proceedings of the 2013 Conference on Computer Supported Cooperative Work Companion*, 95–100, 2013, http://dl.acm.org/citation.cfm?id=2441981.

Russell, Dan. 'Why Knowing Search Isn't the Same as Having an Education', SearchReSearch blog, 1 August 2011, http://searchresearch1.blogspot.co.uk/2011/08/why-knowing-search-isnt-same-as-having.html.

Simperl, Elena, Devika P. Madalli, Denny Vrandevcić, and Enrique Alfonseca. 'DiversiWeb 2011', In *ACM SIGIR Forum*, 45 (2011): 49-53, http://dl.acm.org/citation.cfm?id=1988861.

Simpson, Thomas W. 'Evaluating Google as an Epistemic Tool', *Metaphilosophy* 43.4 (2012): 426-445.

Singh, Rahul, Ya-Wen Hsu, and Naureen Moon. 'Multiple Perspective Interactive Search: a Paradigm for Exploratory Search and Information Retrieval on the Web', *Multimedia Tools and Applications* 62.2 (2013): 507-543.

Patrick Thomas, 'Give Us Your Feedback on Search Policies', Inside Search blog, 23 August 2013, http://insidesearch.blogspot.co.uk/2013/08/give-us-your-feedback-on-search-policies.html.

Verbeke, Mathias, Bettina Berendt, and Siegfried Nijssen. 'Data Mining, Interactive Semantic Structuring, and Collaboration: A Diversity-Aware Method for Sense-Making in Search', in *Proceedings of First International Workshop on Living Web, Collocated with the 8th International Semantic Web Conference (ISWC-2009). CEUR Workshop Proceedings, Washington, DC, USA*. Vol. 515, 2009, http://www.liacs.nl/home/snijssen/publications/iswc2009.pdf.

White, Ryen W. 'Beliefs and Biases in Web Search', *SIGIR'13,* Dublin, Ireland, 28 July-1 August, 2013, http://research.microsoft.com/en-us/um/people/ryenw/papers/WhiteSIGIR2013.pdf.

Polluted and Predictive, in 133 Words

⌐

Mél Hogan and M.E. Luka

Polluted and Predictive, in 133 Words

¬

Mél Hogan and M.E. Luka

Never forget that Google collects data for a commercial purpose. It is not a public archive. Besides this, the Google search engine is getting more and more 'polluted', coming up with useless and predictable search outcomes.
– Geert Lovink[1]

For the *Society of the Query Reader*, we present here segments of a conversation done via email, inspired by interventions into Google 'suggestions', collected and compared over time. The discussion is between communications and media consultant and doctoral scholar M.E. Luka (Montréal and Halifax, Canada), and digital curation postdoc and media scholar-practitioner, Mél Hogan (Colorado University, Boulder, U.S.), collaborators on various projects including recent Korsakow[2] workshops and developing theories of archival production.[3] For both, professional and scholarly interests are deeply intertwined and more generally concerned with creativity, the arts, and digital media and the archive. Showcasing a collection of 133 words selected by Mél Hogan, and captured through a series of screen grabs in April 2010, 2011, 2012, and 2013, M.E. Luka leads a dialogue that revolves around the parameters of this 'polluted' and predictive archive, the process and display of the political poetry it generates, and the choice of (the 133) words that constitute the basis of this search.

Conceived for the web, an earlier iteration of this interview can also be found in a 'clickable' version online at melhogan.com and http://moreartculturemediaplease.com/interview-mel-hogan-and-google-query.

---

1. Geert Lovink, 'Back from Gent: Notes on Memories of the Future', Net Critique blog, 26 June 2010, http://networkcultures.org/wpmu/geert/2010/06/26/back-from-gent-notes-on-memories-of-the-future/.
2. For example, Korsakow workshops held at the Brakhage Center at the University of Colorado in Boulder, 2013. See, http://brakhagecenter.com/?tag=korsakow.
3. Mél Hogan and Mary Elizabeth Luka, 'Archiving Art Spots with Mary Elizabeth Luka', No More Potlucks, vol. 25, (January/February 2013), http://nomorepotlucks.org/site/archiving-artspots-with-mary-elizabeth-luka-mel-hogan.

2013
woman is: the future of man   that meant to insult me   a woman   the earth   the reflection of her man   a danger cat   too pretty to work   the weaker vessel   a devil   beheaded

All tables are representations of queries performed on Google (in bold) and the suggestions Google gives.

M.E. Luka: What is Google Suggest?

Mél Hogan: Though refined over the years, Google Suggest has been an experimental feature since 2004. Currently, not every user is privy to the same suggestions by Google; it's therefore needed to address the intentions of the algorithm and its discrimination based on location, language, as well as a series of other factors. According to Google's blog, terms pertaining to nationality (but not religion) are removed from suggestions, as are hate- or violence-related queries, personally identifiable information, porn and adult content, legally mandated removals, and piracy-related items. But reading through this archive, it's incredibly violent, so it would be great to see how Google defines violence and how it polices it.

Everyday words become defined through user queries, feeding into a weird, increasingly funneled and frenzied, though not entirely random, pool of associations between stereotypes, lyrics, memes, as well as sincere searches.

As you type in Google's search bar, its algorithm predicts and displays search queries based on users' search activities, including the contents of web pages indexed by Google (known as Google Suggest or Autocomplete). While this drop-down list of calculated suggestions completing user queries has spawned several memes, inspired game-like interaction, and invited scrutiny over the so-called collective archive it generates, I want our conversation to go in an exploratory direction and expose some of Google's suggestions over the course of the last four years.

ML: OK, then let's start with the words. You really picked 133 words? Why 133? What are they? Are they thematic?

MH: By way of free association and without counting how many words were going to be part of this archive, the 133 words I selected to track in Google Search over the course of the past four years are: academia, activism, arab, arabic, body, boy, boyfriend, bush, canada, capitalism, care, catholic, chance, change, christianity, communication, control, courage, cowboy, culture, daughter, death, destiny, dude, enemy, evil, faith, fascism, father, fear, female, femininity, feminism, fool, free speech, friendship, gay, gender, girl, girlfriend, god, goddess, goodness, gospel, government, grace, greed, gun, happiness, hate speech, heterosexuality, homophobia, homosexuality, hope, identity, insanity, instinct, integrity, is, islam, jew, jewish, joy, justice, labour, law, laziness, life, love, luck, lust, male, man, masculinity, mind, money, morality, mother, muslim, need, obsession, passion, peace, perception, perfection, phd, poverty, power, pride, procrastination, property, prostitution, quebec, race, racism, rage, reality, reason, religion, respect, right, sadness, sanity, satan, sex work, sex, sexiness, sexism, sexuality, shyness, sin, slavery, socialism, son, soul, spirit, terror, terrorism, thought, tom cruise, transgender, trouble, trust, want, war, woman, work, and xy.

The entire archive is available at http://melhogan.com.

For the first year, the process included selecting the words. Inspired by my trajectory in cultural studies/media studies, and my growing interests in the link between human emotion and algorithms, these words were the words I chose for this collection. At the time I had a few of these collections going, but this particular thread is the one I kept collecting over the past four years.

ML: Why these words, in particular?
MH: I think the words and the searches they suggest point to things people are searching out in private. Real questions. Real worries. It might show how fucked up we all are. What do you think? Look below at 'daughter is' – while the suggestions change a little over time, the sentiment remains the same. I find that it's the words that denote a relationship – daughter or boyfriend, for example – are the most deranged. People searching out answers about (and maybe on behalf of) others? Can Google suggestions become a way to suss out what others are experiencing? Is it where we go to feel normal, even if that normal is twisted?

ML: Hmm. I don't know. There's something about the creepily fast predictive suggestions that kind of freaks me out. But maybe, yes, it could be a way to combine with others, emotionally, about shared topics. To have a conversation without having to engage in actual, live dialogue. I found the lists really compelling. And I found myself comparing the lists from one year to the next, because you gave them to me in a way that was easy to compare.

2010	2011	2012	2013
daughter is:	daughter is:	daughter is:	daughter is:
overweight	mean	pregnant	pregnant
depressed	pregnant	depressed	calling ringtone
moving away	always cold	cutting herself	spanish
pregnant	constipated	spanish	an atheist
a bully	a bully	pregnant with dads child	sexting
mean	a loner	constipated	getting married
tired all the time	cutting herself	mean	depressed
calling ringtones	tired all the time	out of control	a brat
losing hair	overweight	disrespectful to mother	taller than me
a prostitute	calling ringtone	a brat	a tomboy

boyfriend is:	boyfriend is:	boyfriend is:	boyfriend is:
depressed	distant	distant	depressed
distant	depressed	selfish	immature
ignoring me	selfish	a virgin	a virgin
selfish	sick	boring	a douchebag
insecure	ignoring me	depressed	boring
a virgin	cheap	a jerk	ignoring me
moving away	too big	sick	moving away
a jerk	gay	controlling	selfish
too big	boring	too clingy	distant
	mad at me	insecure	gay

What's more, when I see each of the columns of phrases typed up formally in a table (rather than just as screen grabs), they seem to gain authority, and I find myself fighting emotionally with the meanings thrown at me by the lists. Does every word cause this to happen?

MH: Not every word produces a result, so in that way this social experiment is biased to words that generate results, popular enough searches. What I've noticed is that these are the kinds of words that tend to provoke and trigger strange – and very sad – results from the pooled mindset that has become Google Search. I think, in part, that's because there are genuine queries mixed in with vile equations that together form a sad but somewhat accurate definition of these words, as conceived of generally. Most of it is disgustingly violent. Some of it is more ambivalent. Some of it is just funny. I guess that's a mirror of us…?

2013			
muslim is:	mother is:	male is:	poverty is:
not a race	the name for god	x or y	state of mind
evil	spanish	xy	the worst form of violence
gonna get you	crazy	spanish	
religion of peace	dying	pregnant	the parent of revolution and crime
wrong	an alcoholic	the capital of what country	
fake	narcissistic		relative
cult	a freshman	a boy or a girl	a disease
the new black	a sociopath	better than female	a choice
the right religion	depressed	in which country	real
not a religion of peace	emotionally abusive	the capital of my capital city	found to be correlated with worse than crack
quebec is:	racism is:	transgender is:	sex work is:
racist	good	wrong	work
a nation	stupid	bullshit	part of the community
a joke	the pits	a mental disorder	
stupid	the wrong way	a sin	immoral
poor	hoodie	not real	is real work tumblr
a good place to live	taught	stupid	not sex trafficking
	funny	sexist	
	over	a choice	
	schism on a serious tip	real	
		a disorder	
	prejudice plus power		
	dead		

It's true though that if the results didn't show something this sad and vulgar, the project would probably be far less interesting; it wouldn't have drawn me in or consumed all of my time collecting and comparing and deciphering WTF is going on with us all. There are a few other projects that document the sad state of Google Search results, like 'Pure Sadness: The Top 10 Google Searches Of 2012'[4] and 'Google Proves Humanity Is Sick and Sad, Yet Absolutely Hilarious'.[5] Sad and hilarious, I think that's mostly where we are at. So, I'm certainly not the only one to collect like this. Many of my projects resemble others', but I think we all come to these urges to collect and document for different reasons. People came to the hilarity (or sadness) of this function and started to document it in different ways. For (a recent) example, I just came across this Twitter hashtag for #sadgooglesearches.[6]

ML: Hilarious. There's so much action on this front that there's a Twitter hashtag about it. When I was looking through the #sadgooglesearches posts, I noticed there were hundreds of them on 14 August 2013. And then I found a commentary on the twitter hashtag stream.[7] So now there's of-the-moment commentary on the topic, not just annual round-ups at year-end. This is what we have spent years and billions on perfecting, in order to have the speediest #sadgooglesearches? How is this helping humankind? What kind of social values are we involved in generating? Also, on a more mundane level, I'm curious to know – are Sad Google Searches the equivalent of cat videos on YouTube?
MH: I think we're back to 'sad' as the agreed upon state of the search archive...

ML: It feels like a terribly sad loss of potential to me. Is there a way to look at this that could be a little more optimistic? What about the predictive elements of this particular conundrum? Do you see Google as an oracle?[8]
MH: Ha! No. It's the opposite. Actually, I don't know, maybe it is. We're going to look back on all this one day and see how messed up we are, at this particular juncture, where what's possible technologically is far ahead of any culturally agreed upon norms. If we're following technology, and that's what's documented here, then it's an oracle that is reductively predictive and polluted. We may look back on this in a decade or two and be embarrassed by our paltry beginning efforts. But chances are most traces of these searches will be long gone... which is why art projects like this become important, right?

ML: Yes! So if you do enough iterations, the danger might be that the searches only take us down increasingly narrow or reprehensible paths. But the upside (to use a horrible corporate term) is that there will actually be traces of these searches.
MH: I'm not sure how to describe what it produces exactly, but in terms of content

---

4. 'Pure Sadness: The Top 10 Google Searches', Geekologie.com, 12 December 2012, http://geekologie.com/2012/12/pure-sadness-the-top-10-google-searches.php.
5. Jesus Diaz, 'Google Proves Humanity Is Sick and Sad Yet Absolutely Hilarious', Gizmodo.com, 2 December 2009, http://gizmodo.com/5152141/google-proves-humanity-is-sick-and-sad-yet-absolutely-hilarious.
6. See, https://twitter.com/search?q=%23sadgooglesearches&src=tren.
7. Alexis Rhiannon, 'Other Sad Google Searches: Twitter Hashtag Trending', Crushable.com, 14 August 2013, http://www.crushable.com/2013/08/14/other-stuff/sad-google-searches-twitter-hashtag-trending.
8. Thanks to Frédérick Belzile of BRUCE (http://vimeo.com/user5001083) for this insightful query.

alone, it often points to books, movies, and music, popular lyrics and quotes. For example: love, death, grace, respect, and courage, when looked at more closely:

2013
love is: patient patient love is kind all you need a battlefield blindness a battlefield lyrics war lyrics blindness lyrics my religion verb lyrics

'Love is patient' is a biblical verse.[9] 'Love is all you need' is a 2012 romantic movie[10] as well as a famous lyric from a Beatles song. 'Love is a battlefield' is a Pat Benatar hit from the 80s.[11] 'Love is blindness' is a U2 song,[12] but brought to life again by Jack White in 2013 because of the 2013 Great Gatsby film (also a remake) soundtrack.[13] So all of this is very much a commentary on popular culture.

ML: Popular culture, or the vernacular – this is the very foundation of the nation-state, according to Benedict Anderson.[14] How we construct our social selves and articulate shared values: these are critical markers. We imagine ourselves into existence. Music, poetry, journalism. Metaphor, imagination, love, loss. I don't like to think that Google Search/Suggest might one day lead us to the Republic of Google Nation. But, oh right, it already has. In fact, more than one Google Nation.[15]

2013
death is: nothing at all not the end the road to awe certain life is not bad blog but crossing the world not the greatest loss in life not dying just around the corner lyrics a star book

9. Mary Fairchild, '"Love is Patient, Love is Blind" Bible Verse', About.com Christianity, http://christianity.about.com/od/prayersverses/qt/Love-Is-Patient-Love-Is-Kind.htm.
10. See, http://www.rottentomatoes.com/m/love_is_all_you_need/.
11. See, http://www.youtube.com/watch?v=j9J9rTZJBmw.
12. Copies of the U2 music video are easily found on YouTube by searching 'U2' and the song title. For example, at the time of printing: http://www.youtube.com/watch?v=FLNFw9EYXOw.
13. See, for example, the Jack White music video on Vimeo, http://vimeo.com/69265782.
14. Benedict Anderson, *Imagined Communities*, London and New York: Verso, 2006 (1983).
15. See an iteration of Google nation here: http://www.googlenation.net/.

MH: 'Death is nothing at all' is a poem by Henry Scott Holland: 'Death is nothing at all. I have only slipped away to the next room. I am I and you are you. Whatever we were to each other, That, we still are [...]'[16] 'Death is not the end' is a Bob Dylan tune. 'Death is the road to awe' links to a Soundcloud account,[17] and 'Death is certain life is not' leads to a Yahoo! Forum where the phrase needs to be explained.[18] 'Death is not the greatest loss in life' is a quote attributable to Norman Cousins: 'Death is not the greatest loss in life. The greatest loss is what dies inside us while we live.'[19] It's also a quote by Tupac Shakur: 'Death is not the greatest loss in life. The greatest loss is what dies inside while still alive. Never surrender.'[20]

ML: Or, as long as we have a place to go to assert that we are alive, we can survive death. As Banana Yoshimoto suggests: 'When I'm dead worn out, in a reverie, I often think that when it comes time to die, I want to breathe my last in a kitchen. Whether it's cold and I'm all alone, or somebody's there and it's warm, I'll stare death fearlessly in the eye.'[21]

2013
grace is: gone lyrics gone gone dave matthews sufficient gone chords gone tab gone movie enough enough chords overrated

MH: 'Grace is gone' is a poorly rated 2007 movie,[22] and also a song by the Dave Matthews Band.[23] 'Grace is overrated' is not just a statement about grace but rather a blog about hand-drawn guided journals: http://www.graceisoverrated.com/.[24]

---

16. 'Death is Nothing at all', Poemhunter.com, 28 November 2004, http://www.poemhunter.com/poem/death-is-nothing-at-all.
17. See, https://soundcloud.com/clint-mansell/death-is-the-road-to-awe.
18. See, http://answers.yahoo.com/question/index?qid=20090913085839AAP4KkP.
19. See, http://www.goodreads.com/quotes/41499-death-is-not-the-greatest-loss-in-life-the-greatest.
20. See, http://www.goodreads.com/quotes/80268-death-is-not-the-greatest-loss-in-life-the-greatest.
21. Banana Yoshimoto, *Kitchen*, trans. Megan Backus, New York: Washington Square Press/Simon & Schuster Inc., 1993 (1988), p. 4.
22. See, http://www.imdb.com/title/tt0772168/.
23. See, http://www.youtube.com/watch?v=ssylkxyqB_w.
24. See, http://www.graceisoverrated.com/.

2013
respect is: earned earned not given earned not given quote earned quotes a must tour burning just the minimum love not earned everything

'Respect is earned' is a typical saying. 'Respect is a must tour' is a search for a hip hop band tour.[25] I started to sing along to Lauryn Hill's 'Respect is just the minimum'.[26] 'Respect is burning' is also a music compilation CD.[27] So a lot of it is about music, but arguably a lot of music is about life, so it's very fitting for the effect produced by this kind of archive.

2013
courage is: not the absence of fear lyrics change grace under pressure not the absence of fear quote my strength contagious not always a roar the strange familiar absence of fear

'Courage is not the absence of fear' and 'Courage is the absence of fear' likely points to an Ambrose Redmoon quote: 'Courage is not the absence of fear, but rather the judgment that something else is more important than fear.'[28] 'Courage is grace under pressure' is an Ernest Hemingway quote.[29] 'Courage is contagious' is also a quote[30] but reveals many other things too as top hits: WikiLeaks paraphernalia, a TED talk on courage, and a URL for a website documenting 'the amazing events of 2010, and the unraveling of the worlds governments thanks to the courage of many people and one man in particular'.

---

25. Jake Paine, 'Webbie "Savage Life 4Ever" Release Date, Trill Fam "Respect Is A Must Tour" Dates', Hip Hop DX, 27 June 2013, http://www.hiphopdx.com/index/news/id.24471/title.webbie-savage-life-4ever-release-date-trill-fam-respect-is-a-must-tour-dates.
26. See, http://www.lyrics007.com/Lauryn%20Hill%20Lyrics/Doo%20Wop%20(That%20Thing)%20Lyrics.html.
27. See, http://www.amazon.com/Respect-Is-Burning-Various-Artists/dp/B00000D9VM.
28. See, http://thinkexist.com/quotation/courage_is_not_the_absence_of_fear-but_rather_the/220774.html.
29. 'Ernest Hemingway', BrainyQuote.com, Xplore Inc, 24 December 2013, http://www.brainyquote.com/quotes/quotes/e/ernesthemi131094.html.
30. 'Billy Graham', BrainyQuote.com, Xplore Inc, 24 December 2013, http://www.brainyquote.com/quotes/quotes/b/billygraha113622.html.

2012	2013
culture is: not your friend not optional your operating system ordinary learned ordinary raymond williams dynamic destiny symbolic	**culture is:** learned not your friend defined as shared ordinary not optional integrated not supported symbolic like an iceberg

Then there are sequences that are harder to qualify: 'culture is like an iceberg', which becomes really interesting when you follow the Google suggestion all the way through to the query... what happened in 2013 to make culture be like an iceberg?

ML: The power of metaphor and simile at our fingertips through Google Search/Suggest. 'Culture is an iceberg' is a quote from a 1976 book no longer in print, *Orientations to Intercultural Communication*, by Sharon Ruhly.[31] It has persisted so strongly that a recent blog post by another intercultural communications scholar, Milton Bennett, goes to great lengths to insist that such communication is a process, not an object understandable through this metaphor.[32] Or maybe there is some kind of poetic essence that is shaken into existence by the ritualistic repetition of 'xxx is ...'. Or even better, through the plaintive addition of 'why?', as in 'Why is the measure of love loss?'[33] So ... why do you collect?

MH: In the case of this Google Suggestion project, collecting screengrabs was the only way to record a search and to document it over time. These queries shift all the time – it's probably technologically impossible to do the same search twice. I think in this case, collecting is a way to hold onto evidence of a phenomenon and also to share iterations easily online. It's also fun.

Personally, this process began during the time I was writing my dissertation in 2012, and it became a means by which to procrastinate/meditate, almost at the same time.[34] I've been collecting stuff online – users' comments are still my favorite;[35] I've collected desktop screengrabs.[36] This collection of people's desktop was selected to be in the next exhibition for the Screen Saver Gallery project, a contemporary digital art gallery

---

31. Sharon Ruhly, *Orientations to Intercultural Communication*, Chicago: Science Research Associates, 1976.
32. Milton Bennett, 'Culture is Not Like an Iceberg', IDR Institute blog, 6 May 2013, http://www.idrinstitute.org/page.asp?menu1=14&post=1&page=1.
33. Jeannette Winterson, *Written on the Body*, Toronto: Random House of Canada, 1992, p. 9.
34. See, http://spectrum.library.concordia.ca/973890/.
35. See, http://www.youtube.com/watch?v=v6O6UqLnZqI.
36. I collect, more generally, as people do, to recall and remember things. As a collector-scholar, I also collect (and sometimes it feels like hoarding) digital objects as a means of conducting research. My Desktop Archive (http://melhogan.com/website/show-me-your-desktop/) project was about seeing who would and wouldn't submit to the archive. A desktop can be (too) private to share. But it can also be tidied. Some people liked the project, but felt it exposed too much and so didn't share it. So what I don't show of that project are the conversations – usually with warnings – that I get from people who submit to the project. There's a lot of shame around the dirty desktop!

of screensavers run by Czech artists Barbora Trnková and Tomáš Javůrek.[37] And of course, the Google Suggestion searches we're talking about now.[38]

During grad school, I also took a photo of myself every day, for more than seven years, to see time pass. To see myself fall apart because of stress. So I think this urge to collect is a form of meditative hoarding, which speaks to my academic work on digital archives[39] and my production work on collections management as well.[40] It all really comes together when you account for change – to see yourself as positioned differently in relation to objects in time, and a photo of yourself can be an object.

The week of 9-17 September 2013, I collected tweets from the Boulder Floods (#boulderflood) because, re-assembled, they tell a story.[41] The happy sporty Boulder avatars, the politics of blame, the importance of animal rescue, the comparisons to New Orleans' Katrina – these all become fodder for a more scholarly intervention, but this select archive of tweets also tells a story about the event, and as well, inadvertently, about me and what I value as a collector.

Conceptually, I collect because word objects start to make more sense in relation to one another; they give each other context(s).

ML: Do you mean – dialogic? Conversational? Perhaps this is generated simply through juxtaposition? Or maybe the self-focused (sometimes self-centered, or self-ish) nature of the comments don't allow for dialogue at all. No responsibility to others, just a delight in hearing one's own voice in the ether.
MH: The Comments Collection project I did in 2010 was about collecting comments on YouTube videos, ones about the anticipated 2012 end of the world phenomena.[42] I like to select and carefully reorganize these bits of texts, usually in PowerPoint, so that it tells its own story, without additional contextual information. As in, you can just read it and get it.

ML: I remember when you did this project. Definitely, I found the level of violence in the commentary disturbing. No real space for compassion. But I also like to think about the *People this 2012 shit is hype* **piece in tandem with your 52-pickup project on the end of the world.[43] Which I think is brilliant, optimistic, funny, and** *conversational*. **I believe that's because you are at the heart of it, prompting discussion and thoughtful (and/or hilarious) responses to the question you posed about the end of the world.[44]**

---

37. See, http://screensaver.metazoa.org/about/.
38. See, http://melhogan.com/website/google-suggestions-archive-of-human-sense.
39. Mél Hogan, *Crashing the Archive: A Research-Creation Intervention into the SAW Video Mediatheque*, PhD thesis, Concordia University, 2012, http://spectrum.library.concordia.ca/973890/.
40. See, http://archinodes.com/.
41. See, http://melhogan.com/website/sept-boulderflood/.
42. See, http://www.youtube.com/watch?v=v6O6UqLnZqI.
43. See 'People this 2012 Hype is Shit!', http://www.youtube.com/watch?v=v6O6UqLnZqI.
44. Also see: http://www.salon.com/2013/10/20/new_campaign_uses_real_google_searches_to_expose_how_the_world_talks_about_women/.

MH: With the Comments Collection, assembling the story from other peoples' comments worked really well. I did about 20,[45] dealing with things from music sampling to WikiLeaks as perceived in different newspapers across the world. I like to collect other people's words because the text itself is all that matters – tone, spelling, word choice. Like many people, I often skip the article and go directly to the comments to get a quicker sense of the important issues within the piece.

With this Google Search project, it was a similar incentive. But I wanted to mark the Search over time – which is always as much a commentary on the mode of documentation (whether the screen grab or PowerPoint, copy and paste) as it is about the contents. For me, the simplicity of the tools for collection and display are really important. I rarely think of what to make of the collection. I just like to collect and make 'lists' and organize the content into a story. Collecting is the best way for me to document web phenomena and simultaneously comment on web cultures. There's something in the gesture of collecting that's in itself a means to expose meaning.

ML: How is collecting different from the massive growth in self-tracking through digital technology (e.g. on Facebook, through fitness apps, etc.)? For example, technology journalist Nora Young explores self-tracking in her new book, *The Virtual Self: How Our Digital Lives Are Altering the World Around Us*,[46] though she doesn't see it as a narcissistic practice – more as a meditation. The repetitive nature of the collection is what is important, i.e. a kind of processing or transforming ourselves while doing.
MH: I haven't read Young's work but I do believe there's a correlation. I think that the NSA debacles since the summer have more than proven that everything is tracked and stored, even if there's always the problem of information overload, including making sense of huge pools of data. The ways in which it is different from biofeedback apps is that it's much more collective and in some ways, more anonymous on the surface. Fitness apps really focus on your body, improvements, and motivation. Facebook is also profile focused and serves to link data to specific individuals within a network. Google Search and Suggestion mashes us all together!

ML: Web-based practices are often referred to as 'virtual' practices. This term – 'virtual' – is tantalizingly close to the terms 'virtuous' (be-good), and 'virtuosity' (display excellence and expertise). Are your interventions virtuous rummagings into the dominance of Google-as-web? Why are you seeking virtuosity in your practice – if you are? And/or why are you probing to see whether and how Google's Cache and Search functions are performing a kind of virtuosity in predictive 'pollutability' themselves?
MH: For my collection, I became interested in the process of documenting searches via screen grabs over a period of a few years. The results will become increasingly telling over time – especially in terms of documenting popular culture in unexpected ways:

---

45. Examples can be found at http://melhogan.com/website/comment-collection-what-is-this-pay-word-you-speak-of/ and http://melhogan.com/website/comment-collection-les-sources-de-quoi-cheri/.
46. Nora Young, *The Virtual Self: How Our Digital Lives Are Altering the World Around Us*, Toronto: McClelland & Stewart, 2012. Also see http://norayoung.ca/.

2013
friendship is: witchcraft magic dragons magic wiki witchcraft the movie magic season 4 witchcraft episode 1 magic part 1 magic episodes witchcraft tvtropes

I am wondering how these searches might change based on the ongoing queries made to Google – 5,134,000,000 searches per day in 2012.[47]

But I think this is what Geert Lovink's quote at the beginning of this conversation gets at: Google is not a public archive. But in a sense, if thought of as an archive – the possibilities for creative intervention are endless.

ML: OK, I'm all for this – generating endless creative possibilities. But let's think it through on a theoretical level as well as through the research-creation you've undertaken. Does the theory match what you are finding in your collections?
MH: Google is now highly synonymous with the web, as the main search tool and for browsing the web (rivaled in its ubiquity only by the likes of social networking tools like Facebook and Twitter, which serve decidedly different primary functions than to provide rapid web-based searches). While highly technical, Google's search function can be analyzed from a user/researcher perspective, contributing to an important dialogue about access, and more specifically about access to the web's 'past'. Google has been making its index available through cached copies – Google Cache – since 1998.

To make its collection accessible, Google uses parallel processing 'on a distributed network of thousands of low-cost computers', which means it can crawl and harvest the web rapidly and in many 'places' simultaneously.[48] More simply, Google's Googlebot 'crawls' around the web. From these crawls, the indexer sorts every word into a database, against which users' queries are compared and for which search results are generated. Based on Google's own Technological Overview, the vision and mission for the 'perfect search' is something that 'understands exactly what you mean and gives you back exactly what you want', according to Google co-founder Larry Page.[49]

However, this notion of the search is complicated by Siva Vaidhyanathan, who argues in his book, *The Googlization of Everything* that 'search' in Google is as much

---

47. See Google Annual Search Statistics at http://www.statisticbrain.com/google-searches/.
48. See the Google Guide Online, http://www.googleguide.com/.
49. See, http://www.google.com/corporate/tech.html.

about what is concealed as what is revealed.[50] Google's process is based on four elements: relevance, comprehensiveness, freshness, and speed. Combined, these are meant to allow searches to be at once comprehensive and subjective. These algorithms are updated weekly or even daily and are increasingly customized for each user, based on search history and location. Because algorithms are constantly changing, a search can hardly reproduce the same results (though this is difficult to verify and track because it rarely gets recorded). This, according to Vaidhyanathan, demonstrates that searches are not mathematical calculations based solely on correlations that objectively benefit users; they are largely the product of careful decisions by programmers working with and within large corporations. Vaidhyanathan also points out that the search privileges the recent over the classic, the local over the global, and the personal over the universal; all criteria that are largely about making consumption (online shopping) more effective, not research that relies on consistency in primary and secondary sources.[51]

ML: Aha. So Google searches are simultaneously about: shopping, random but funneled research, seeking specific kinds of solutions, and... something else entirely.
MH: Google aims to index all media and formats, and to do so continually, eventually moving into what they call 'Realtime Search'. While the function itself 'went missing' in July 2011 when Google put forth its Google +1 platform, the concept itself remains intact.[52] Google's Realtime Search (likely to re-emerge eventually) suggests that there is no difference between information created and information published – much like the Twitter application – where access is also said to be instantaneous.[53]

Interestingly, speed is the emphasis for – and increasing speed, the priority of – Google, whose query response time is 'roughly one-fourth of a second'.[54] By relying on Realtime Search, Google's archive shifts into the mode of a live or living archive, where events are not only documented moments after they occur in 'real time', but are also indexed and made available within seconds. The 'distance' between the past and the present is shortened, putting into question the proximity of primary and secondary sources within an online archival strategy. Furthermore, given Google's super servers, a site can often be accessed more rapidly through the cached version than the 'live' page itself – and this is important as it effectively thwarts the notion of an original source and any idea of a singular 'present' moment or site as point of reference. As Google indexes content on the web to provide its search tool, it simultaneously makes copies of every document in the index (the Google index is roughly 100 million gigabytes).[55]

---

50. Siva Vaidhyanathan, *The Googlization of Everything (And Why We Should Worry)*, Berkley: University of California Press, 2011.
51. Despite this trend, or direction, Vaidhyanathan points out that for the last decade, Google has provided an efficient tool for searches that facilitate access to the web for research – even if it is likely to move in the direction of catering to the user as consumer.
52. Vanessa Fox, 'Google Realtime Search Goes Missing', Search Engine Land, 3 July 2011, http://searchengineland.com/google-realtime-search-goes-missing-84130.
53. Danny Sullivan, 'What Is Real Time Search? Definitions & Players', Search Engine Land, 9 July 2009, http://searchengineland.com/what-is-real-time-search-definitions-players-22172.
54. See, http://www.google.com/corporate/tech.html.
55. See, http://www.google.de/intl/en/insidesearch/howsearchworks/crawling-indexing.html.

ML: That is mind-blowing. But, not entirely 'real', right? You talk about the significant role played by caches and caching as a key element of data management.
MH: In their on-site documentation, Google glosses over the fact that their index and archive is limited to files at 101 kilobytes of text; that is, the 'cached version of the page will consist of the first 101 kbytes', 120 kbytes for PDFs.[56] How and if this replicates the true size and complete document is not factored into the summary, an important lack in the overall framework that constitutes Google Cache's collection of the past.

In Google's cache, a cached copy is a version of a web page as it appeared when it was indexed, which is not necessarily a reflection of the present or most current page. Website owners can opt out of the index, but their site is still likely to be cached despite the 'cache' button and access to the cached version being omitted from the interface (made invisible). As John Battelle dramatizes in *The Search*, Google creates 'a world in which every click can be preserved forever'.[57] The default of multiplying remains even if the cached version is hidden or made inaccessible to the general public; files exist across servers, continually indexing the web's data. However, since the cache exists as an opt-out process (rather than as an informed opt-in), most users overlook the issue of copies as they pertain to these mass automated indexing projects. Part of what makes Google Cache so valuable is its span, despite being largely understated in its current (re)presentation. Google restricts access to the index, making only the most recent indexed version available. Access is limited to one single revision. Needless to say, Google's collection of the web's past grows continuously, exponentially in size and, in turn, in value. However, because it is a corporation working in a competitive environment, Google's indexing and its reliance on metadata standards are kept as trade secrets, which is a stark contrast to archives and library environments where this information is shared freely – and becomes more valuable for it.[58] This brings attention to the ways the online realm is not accessible or 'open' simply by virtue of being online.

ML: I think this is an important observation, and brings us back to a consideration of these patterns and limits as invariably sad (but not tragic) and ultimately violent (though sometimes life-affirming) in a disconcertingly Foucauldian way[59] (the Panopticon? Who's in charge here? Who's surveilling whom?) – but on a societal scale, and not always discouragingly.
MH: Unlike formal archives, Google Cache rejects the notion and impetus for creating a permanent historical record of the web. Instead, when pages disappear, Google claims to delete 'dead' links as quickly as possible.[60] For now, however, Google Cache remains more theoretical than practical, as, by Google's own admission, there are only

---

56. Nancy Blachman and Jerry Peek, 'Cached Pages', Google Guide, http://www.googleguide.com/cached_pages.html.
57. John Battelle, *The Search: How Google and Its Rivals Rewrote the Rules of Business and Transformed Our Culture*, London: Nicholas Brealey Publishing 2005.
58. Jeffrey Beall argues this in 'How Google Uses Metadata to Improve Search Results', *The Serials Librarian* 59.1 (2010): 40-53.
59. A similar discussion about Foucault and society is found in Lynne Huffer and Elizabeth Wilson, 'Mad for Foucault: A Conversation', *Theory, Culture & Society* 27 (2010): 324-338.
60. Stefanie Olsen, 'Google Cache Raises Copyright Concerns', CNET News, 9 July 2003, http://news.cnet.com/2100-1038_3-1024234.html.

occasional clicks on the 'cache' button – and this for a search engine that gets in the order of a few billion hits each day.[61]

ML: So – we are in the process of exponentially generating and simultaneously eliminating our histories, though the evidence in the archives suggests that we ought to remain hopeful: there are traces after all, and we persist in trying to find and understand them. Right? This could mean that the action of collecting comments and searches – as you and others have done – kicks back against the totalizing or discouraging urge, or trajectory, and opens the door to hilarious, engaged, enjoyable. To say it more plainly, preferably without slipping into the trite, thinking and feeling histories and experiences of love and life – through popular culture, the formation of culture, the sharing of culture – are transformative. Even (perhaps especially) through the widely shared Google Suggest experience. How reaffirming to see so many hundreds of thousands of others who have asked your question before you. And yet, your own questions – and answers/responses – may be entirely different.

Big thank you to Andrea Zeffiro with help formatting footnotes and works cited for this piece.

References

Anderson, Benedict. *Imagined Communities*, London and New York: Verso, 2006 (1983).
Battelle, John. *The Search: How Google and Its Rivals Rewrote the Rules of Business and Transformed Our Culture,* London: Nicholas Brealey Publishing 2005.
Beall, Jeffrey. 'How Google Uses Metadata to Improve Search Results', *The Serials Librarian* 59.1 (2010): 40-530.
Bennett, Milton. 'Culture is Not Like an Iceberg', IDR Institute blog, 6 May 2013, http://www.idrinstitute.org/page.asp?menu1=14.
'Billy Graham', BrainyQuote.com, Xplore Inc, 24 December 2013, http://www.brainyquote.com/quotes/quotes/b/billygraha113622.html.
Blachman, Nancy and Jerry Peek, 'Cached Pages', Google Guide, http://www.googleguide.com/cached_pages.html.
'Death is Nothing at all', Poemhunter.com, 28 November 2004, http://www.poemhunter.com/poem/death-is-nothing-at-all.
Diaz, Jesus. 'Google Proves Humanity Is Sick and Sad Yet Absolutely Hilarious', Gizmodo.com, 2 December 2009, http://gizmodo.com/5152141/google-proves-humanity-is-sick-and-sad-yet-absolutely-hilarious.
'Ernest Hemingway', BrainyQuote.com, Xplore Inc, 24 December 2013, http://www.brainyquote.com/quotes/quotes/e/ernesthemi131094.html.
Fairchild, Mary. '"Love Is Patient, Love Is Kind" Bible Verse', About.com Christianity, http://christianity.about.com/od/prayersverses/qt/Love-Is-Patient-Love-Is-Kind.htm.
Fox, Vanessa. 'Google Realtime Search Goes Missing', Search Engine Land, 3 July 2011, http://searchengineland.com/google-realtime-search-goes-missing-84130.
Google, 'Our Products and Services', http://www.google.com/corporate/tech.html.
'Google Annual Search Statistics', 16 June 2013, http://www.statisticbrain.com/google-searches/.
Hogan, Mél. Crashing the Archive: A Research-Creation Intervention into the SAW Video Mediatheque, PhD thesis, Concordia University, 2012, http://spectrum.library.concordia.ca/973890.
_____. 'Google's Suggestive Archive', 25 June 2012, http://melhogan.com/website/google-sugges-

---

61. Olsen, 'Google Cache Raises Copyright Concerns'.

tions-archive-of-human-sense.

———. 'Show Me Your Desktop', 5 June 2012, http://melhogan.com/website/show-me-your-desktop.

———. 'People This 2012 Shit is Hype!' YouTube.com, 2 Sept 2010, http://www.youtube.com/watch?v=v6O6UqLnZql.

———. '#boulderflood', 15 Sept 2013, http://melhogan.com/website/sept-boulderflood/.

———. 'Comment Collection: "What is this 'PAY' word you speak of?"' 23 June 2010, http://melhogan.com/website/comment-collection-what-is-this-pay-word-you-speak-of/.

———. 'Comment Collection: "Les sources de quoi, chéri?"' 23 Feb 2011, http://melhogan.com/website/comment-collection-les-sources-de-quoi-cheri/.

Hogan, Mél and Mary Elizabeth Luka. 'Archiving ArtSpots with Mary Elizabeth Luka', *No More Potlucks*, Vol. 25 (January/February 2013).

Huffer, Lynne and Elizabeth Wilson. 'Mad for Foucault: A Conversation', *Theory, Culture & Society* 27 (2010): 324-338.

Lovink, Geert. 'Back from Gent: Notes On Memories of the Future', Net Critique blog, 26 June 2010, http://networkcultures.org/wpmu/geert/2010/06/26/back-from-gent-notes-on-memories-of-the-future.

Olsen, Stefanie. 'Google Cache Raises Copyright Concerns', *CNET News*, 9 July 2003, http://news.cnet.com/2100-1038_3-1024234.html.

Paine, Jake. 'Webbie "Savage Life 4Ever" Release Date, Trill Fam "Respect Is A Must Tour" Dates', Hip Hop DX, 27 June 2013, http://www.hiphopdx.com/index/news/id.24471/title.webbie-savage-life-4ever-release-date-trill-fam-respect-is-a-must-tour-dates.

'Pure Sadness: The Top 10 Google Searches', Geekologie.com, 12 December 2012, http://geekologie.com/2012/12/pure-sadness-the-top-10-google-searches.php.

Rhiannon, Alexis. 'Other Sad Google Searches: Twitter Hashtag Trending', Crushable.com, 14 August 2013, http://www.crushable.com/2013/08/14/other-stuff/sad-google-searches-twitter-hashtag-trending.

Ruhly, Sharon. *Orientations to Intercultural Communication*, Chicago: Science Research Associates, 1976.

Sullivan, Danny. 'What Is Real Time Search? Definitions & Players', Search Engine Land, 9 July 2009, http://searchengineland.com/what-is-real-time-search-definitions-players-22172.

Vaidhyanathan, Siva. *The Googlization of Everything (And Why We Should Worry)*, Berkley: University of California Press, 2011.

Winterson, Jeannette. *Written on the Body*, Toronto: Random House of Canada, 1992

Yoshimoto, Banana. *Kitchen*, trans. Megan Backus, New York: Washington Square Press/Simon & Schuster Inc., 1993 (1988).

Young, Nora. *The Virtual Self: How Our Digital Lives Are Altering the World Around Us*, Toronto: McClelland & Stewart, 2012.

Algorithming the Algorithm

Martina Mahnke and Emma Uprichard

Algorithming the Algorithm
¬
Martina Mahnke and Emma Uprichard

#hello

Imagine sailing across the ocean. The sun is shining, vastness all around you. And suddenly [BOOM] you've hit an invisible wall. Welcome to the Truman Show! Ever since Eli Pariser published his thoughts on a potential filter bubble,[1] this movie scenario seems to have become reality, just with slight changes: it's not the ocean, it's the internet we're talking about, and it's not a TV show producer, but algorithms that constitute a sort of invisible wall.[2] Building on this assumption, most research is trying to 'tame the algorithmic tiger'.[3] While this is a valuable and often inspiring approach, we would like to emphasize another side to the algorithmic everyday life. We argue that algorithms can instigate and facilitate imagination, creativity, and frivolity, while saying something that is simultaneously old and new, always almost repeating what was before but never quite returning. We show this by threading together stimulating quotes and screenshots from Google's autocomplete algorithms. In doing so, we invite the reader to re-explore Google's autocomplete algorithms in a creative, playful, and reflexive way, thereby rendering more visible some of the excitement and frivolity that comes from being and becoming part of the riddling rhythm of the algorithmic everyday life.

#warning

We've adopted an alternative textual style, which may annoy and confuse some readers, though hopefully also amuse and intrigue others. Therefore we keep this discussion reasonably short and deliberately provocative. However, we don't want to confuse or provoke so that nothing is heard. Our purpose is not to mess with the importance

---

1. Eli Pariser, *The Filter Bubble: What the Internet is Hiding from You,* London: Penguin Press, 2011.
2. Kevin Salvin, 'How Algorithms Shape Our World', TED Talks, July 2011, http://www.ted.com/talks/kevin_slavin_how_algorithms_shape_our_world.html; John Naughton, 'How Algorithms Secretly Shape the Way We Behave', *The Guardian,* 15 December 2012, http://www.guardian.co.uk/technology/2012/dec/16/networker-algorithms-john-naughton.
3. David Beer, 'Power Through the Algorithm? Participatory Web Cultures and the Technological Unconscious', *New Media & Society* 11 (September 2009): 985; Taina Bucher, 'Want to Be on the Top? Algorithmic Power and the Threat of Invisibility on Facebook', *New Media & Society* 14.7 (November 2012): 1164-1180; Tarleton Gillespie, 'Can an Algorithm Be Wrong? Twitter Trends, the Specter of Censorship, and Our Faith in the Algorithms Around Us', Culture Digitally blog, 19 October 2011, http://culture digitally.org/2011/10/can-an-algorithm-be-wrong/; Bernhard Rieder, 'Democratizing Search? From Critique to Society-oriented Design', in Konrad Becker and Felix Stalder (eds) *Deep Search. The Politics of Search beyond Google,* Innsbruck: Studienverlag, 2009, pp. 133-151; Bernhard Rieder. 'Networked Control: Search Engines and the Symmetry of Confidence', *International Review of Information Ethics* 3.1 (2005): 26-32; Christopher Steiner, *Automate This: How Algorithms Came to Rule Our World,* New York, NY: Portfolio/Penguin, 2012.

of academic prose for the sake of it. Instead, what we do is experimental and reflects some of the unexpected landings, spontaneity, and at times insanity of our algorithmically-linked travels into (new and old) media spaces.

Fig. 1. I Google, therefore I am.

#searching

Search engines in general, and Google in particular, have become entry points to the internet. We use Google to verify information, to verify credibility, to verify existence. Google seems to answer all of our questions. 'I google, therefore I am'? René Descartes tried to prove existence by radically doubting his own; now visibility through Google is used as proof. Google seems to be all-knowing and omnipresent. Is Google the new God? The 'Church of Google' seeks proof through scientific reasoning and concludes, 'We at the Church of Google believe the search engine Google is the closest humankind has ever come to directly experiencing an actual God'.[4] 'To google' has become today's synonym for searching the web, even though official language committees disfavor this trend. Sometimes it's hard to imagine what life would be without Google. What would we do? Use another search engine? Not care about information on the internet?

Trying to answer these, albeit hypothetical, questions leads us to the conclusion that Google is more than just a tool; it is a modern myth. But let's not forget, Google is still also 'just' a search engine. The development of search engines can be divided into three periods from a marketing perspective:[5] (1) the period of 'technological entrepreneurs' from 1994 until 1997, (2) the period of 'portals and vertical integration' from 1997 until 2001, and (3) the period of 'syndication and consolidation' starting in 2002,

---

4. Church of Google, http://www.thechurchofgoogle.org/.
5. Elizabeth Jane Van Couvering, *Search Engine Bias*, PhD diss., Department Media and Communications, London School of Economics and Political Science, London, 2009.

which still persists. Google introduced its radically new search algorithm in the second period in 1998.[6] Google's autocomplete function was launched 1 April 2009, and it's this autocomplete algorithm that we want to focus on in our discussion.

Our aim is not a detailed critique of what has already been written on the subject.[7] Instead, we want to offer an alternative way of thinking about search, to reflect some of 'jagged-jixie' involved when we casually surf, explore, and search the web, when we find (not) new material, (not) new friends, and (not) new colleagues – all the while speaking through and with the algorithm. We aim to contribute to current discussions about the social implications of algorithms. After all, algorithms are quintessentially social – they are socially constructed and take on meanings that are variable across time and space. Algorithms are full of ethical and political issues; they (dis)connect the (inter)connected, and they are let loose by the very few with the power and technical expertise to do so. So yes, we know and agree that algorithms are powerful and governing, as so much of the existing literature argues. However, algorithms can also instigate imagination, creativity, and frivolity, if we allow them to. And all of a sudden we might learn: their power is mutable, once we start playing around.

#perspectives
From a mathematical perspective, algorithms have been around for centuries. As Charbert summarizes in simple terms,[8] algorithms are recipes or step-by-step instructions. Algorithms were used by the Babylonians for deciding points of law, as well as by Latin teachers for teaching grammar. Today's computer algorithms are more complex processes, developed and translated into machine language by the fields of machine learning and computer intelligence. In 1950 in his 'game of imitation', Alan Turing, one of the pioneers in this field, raised this question for the first time: what if machines can think?[9] He theorized that if machines can imitate the communication of a human, they could be considered just as intelligent. While back then this speculation was a *gedankenexperiment*, it has now almost, depending on the perspective, become true. An ordinary user is not able to distinguish between machinery and human input anymore. Data journalism – semi-automated production of text out of statistical data – has taken over the simple text-producing routines of journalists. This 'algorithmic turn' can be seen in various areas in society. Even though we are not entirely determined by technology, we are definitely living in a world that is strongly driven by computational algorithmic technology. This development can most clearly be seen in the area of social media. While social media producers started with vague ideas and deficient business models, they now are allocated a great part of the internet, influencing our definition of what information is and how it should be distributed.

Computational processes are carried out through algorithms. The algorithms used in search engines are still a list of instructions, but they are not as strict as 'either-or' rules; most of the time, they fall into the category of intelligent algorithms, which means they learn and change over time. Typically, authors tend to represent the issue of algo-

---

6. Van Couvering, *Search Engine Bias*, p. 113.
7. A great reading list is available at http://governingalgorithms.org/resources/reading-list/.
8. Jean-Luc Chabert, *A History of Algorithms,* Berlin, Heidelberg: Springer, 1999.
9. Alan Turing, 'Computing Machinery and Intelligence', in: Paul A. Meyer (ed.) *Computer Media and Communication: A Reader,* Oxford: Oxford University Press, 1999, pp. 37-58.

rithms as a question of control: who has control over what and whom? This is a classic question of sovereignty, which introduces the notion of hierarchy. Thought of this way, algorithms can be frightening; they are surveilling, governing, and controlling. While exploring algorithms and Google's search algorithm from the perspective of power regimes is valuable and inspiring, we'd like to highlight another side of our algorithmic everyday life, namely what it means 'to find'. To discover something that may or may not have been searched. *Search and find need one another*; they come together and make castles in the digital sand, building layers upon layers of new configurations and algorithmic word towers. What we have found is that algorithms can say something that is simultaneously old and new, always almost repeating what was before, but never quite returning. Fast forward. Rewind. Google's autocomplete search algorithm is another way of searching and finding, re-imagining, creating, and playing with what is there already in the present and what will be in the future. In other words, autocomplete instigates and facilitates imagination, creativity, and frivolity.

#whatalgorithmsdo

Through their rule-based simplicity, algorithms enable a space, place, and time to re-do the old and new simultaneously, nonlinearly, in an awe-inspiring magical kaleidoscope. As Waldrop sums up beautifully:

> As we begin to understand complex systems, we begin to understand that we're part of an ever-changing, interlocking, non-linear, kaleidoscopic world. [...] The elements always stay the same, yet they're always rearranging themselves. So it's like a kaleidoscope: the world is a matter of patterns that change [and have continuity], that partly repeat, but never quite repeat, that are always new and different.[10]

Repeating and rearranging, threading and weaving, knitting the crochet macabre macramé world of the web. Searching and re-searching. Re-finding and de-re-finding. The new and the old. Growing and changing and not changing together. The invariable, invariant variety of patterns in the Googleland of the present. Past becomes the future of futures, time and time and time again. Again. Repeat. The dynamics of the algorithmic 'live' search engine ensure the patterned repetition and ever-morphing world.

Inputting, storing, processing, and outputting are the functions of our algorithms; this is all they can (currently) do. We embrace the algorithm and its rules-based logarithms; they are simple. If you are an algorithm, there is no ambiguity. You need to know exactly which step, which function, which action will be performed. Humans, on the other hand, introduce ambiguity, fuzziness, and confusion. The unambiguous algorithmic world combines with the lone surfer, who constantly flits from one thought to the next, confusing paths, laying new stones for those who follow, kicking up dust, masquerading as the present, multiplying the future, and re-clicking a new and emergent present. Masquerading at a ball, like a harlequin clown, juggling with hyperlinks and net-edges, working and erasing time all the time.

---

10. M. Mitchell Waldrop, *Complexity: The Emerging Science at the Edge of Order and Chaos,* New York: Simon and Schuster, 1992, p. 332.

It's not just fun and play. Algorithms have social implications. Donald Knuth,[11] Thomas Corman et al.,[12] Steven Skiena,[13] and many authors have shown that the relationship between algorithms and the social is complicated. But only sort of. There are so many ways to sort and search the social. Clustering and classifying. Machines learning patterns. Sorting this thing from that, in and out. This box, not that one. With those and without these. Sorting what cannot be sorted easily. Behind the 'black box' of search algorithms lies the need to sort out in order to search. Indeed, a search algorithm mostly comes down to how we measure and define difference and similarity, distance and proximity, how something is measured to be 'far' or 'near'. Scaling up and scaling down. Ordering disorder. Always and everywhere. This or that. In short: sorting is all about *matching* and *ranking*. Two items are matched against each other and displayed in a ranked (dis)order.

#diggingintothealgorithm
In order to dig into Google's autocomplete algorithm a little further, we took screenshots and combined them with citations. We joined co-authored emails and internet searches. To and from, as we both searched for the search. Piecing together the incoherent. Reflecting the process and the (con)text. Tracing and tracking, snatching and clipping. In Denmark and the U.K. The data reflects the autoethnographic approach taken. Participating and observing. Immersing. Taking notes. Memos. Comments. Getting lost and coming back. In order to think, reflect, and write. Understanding the internet as a *digging place* for archaeological excavation. And using the internet to dig through the autocompleted links.

>start [enter]

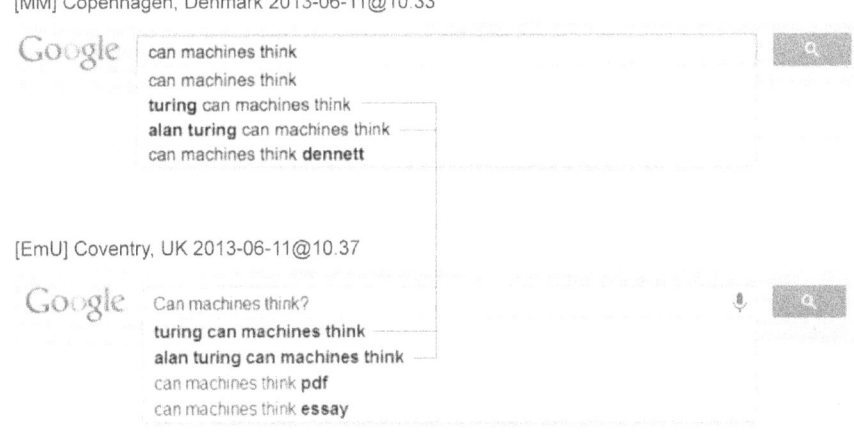

Fig. 2. Same but different.

---

11. Donald Knuth, *Fundamental Algorithms*, vol. 1 of *The Art of Computer Programming*, Boston: Addison-Wesley, 1997 (1968); Donald Knuth, *Sorting and Searching*, vol. 3 of *The Art of Computer Programming*, Boston: Addison-Wesley, 1993 (1973).
12. Thomas Corman et al., *Introduction to Algorithms*, Cambridge, MA: MIT Press, 2009.
13. Steven Skiena, *The Algorithm Design Manual*, London: Springer, 2008.

#thinkingmachines
What's the difference between human and machine? Is there a difference? Daniel Dennett [I'm feeling lucky ENTER] argues: 'It is that special inner light, that private way that is with you that nobody else can share, something that is forever outside the bounds of computer science.'[14] Boden noted in 1985: 'Artificial intelligence (AI) was conceived in the mid-1940s [...]. Since then, it has had some notable successes, enabling computers to perform – albeit in a very limited way – some of the tasks normally done by our minds.'[15] In the end isn't AI just a copycat copying what's already there? Trying to reach the original, just never quite getting there?

As can be seen in Figure 2, a quick search for 'Can machines think?', typed in a sloppy everyday way, not caring about upper and lower cases and question marks, in Denmark and the U.K., produces slightly similar, but still different autocomplete terms. Yet, in Figure 3 (see page 263) we notice it is not only that the autocompleted terms differ across countries, but also across time. That is to say, the same search terms used just 11 minutes apart make visible a different set of terms – some the same and some new. In contrast, the same search terms two days apart have no visible effect. While these outcomes raise concerns, they also trigger a whole other possible set of reactions. Indeed, it is tempting to immediately question the censoring and governing actions of the algorithms, which delimit and determine the outcomes of our searches. We want to suggest that it is precisely in the similarities and differences of Google's autocomplete that we are offered alternative ways of 'playing' with and against Google itself. Moreover, it is in making visible these different and similar affordances that Google's autocomplete algorithm becomes both a site and a mechanism whereby *imagination, creativity, and frivolity* produce accessibility.

#imagination
Imagination is a way of seeing, knowing, and learning; it asks us to look beyond what we take for granted.[16] Imagination premises openness. Imagination builds on top of the known. Imagination resides 'where perception, memory, idea generation, emotion, metaphor, and no doubt other labeled features of our lives, intersect and interact'.[17] The collected data shows that the actual list of words varies across time and space. The differences and similarities matter as much as they do not matter and simply echo Google's idea of relevance, trying to sense and predict the virtual waves of the digital seas between man and machine. Imagining a world without Google is now like remembering a world without computers. It is not the world we live in. What is for sure: other things will take over, replacing Google in a time to come. At the moment, however, our searches begin and end with Google's stamp.

---

14. Daniel Dennett, 'Can Machines Think?' In Christof Teuscher (ed.) *Alan Turing: Life and Legacy of a Great Thinker,* Berlin: Springer, 2004, p. 313.
15. Margaret A. Boden, 'The Social Impact of Thinking Machines' in Tom Forester (ed.) *The Information Technology Revolution,* Oxford: Basil Blackwell, 1985, pp. 95-103.
16. Kieran Egan, *Imagination in Teaching and Learning: The Middle School Years,* Chicago: The University of Chicago Press, 1992.
17. Robert Lake, *A Curriculum of Imagination in an Era of Standardization: An Imaginative Dialogue with Maxine Greene and Paulo Freire,* Charlotte, NC: Information Age Pub, 2013.

Creative Reflections

Fig. 3. Difference in time and space.

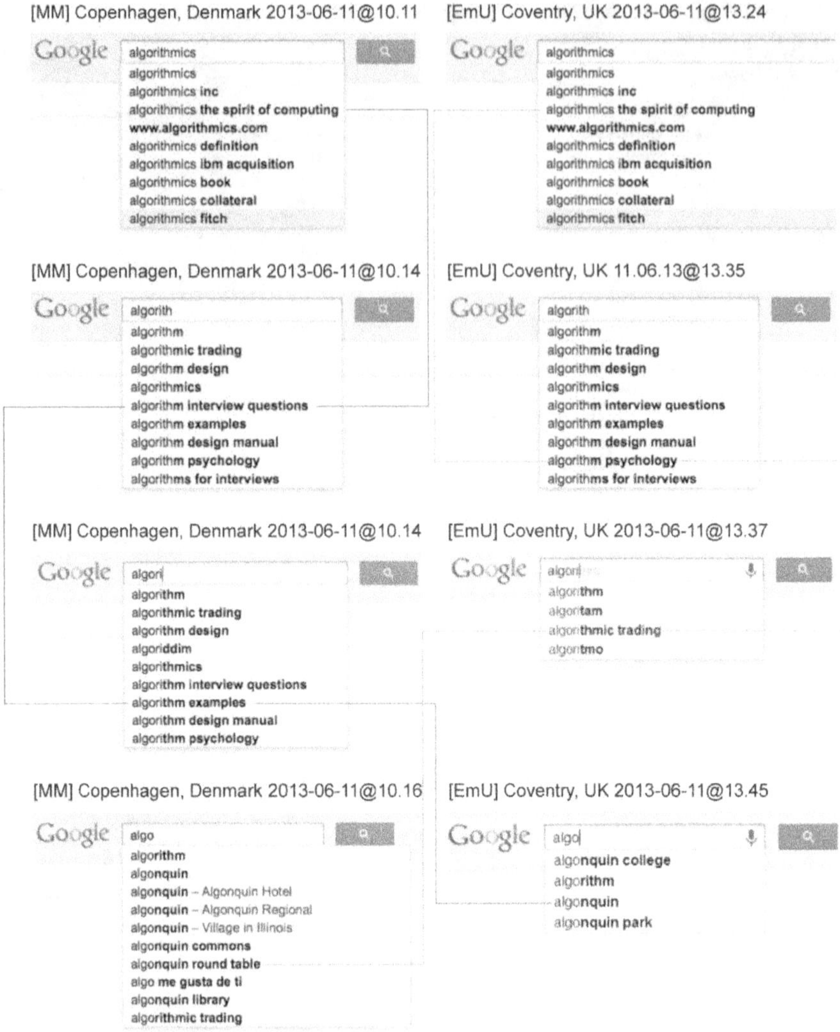

Fig. 4. Growing an 'imagination tree'.

>end [stop]

In Figure 4 (see page 264), for example, Google's autocomplete algorithm has started a new, imaginative story for us, where typing 'algo' with algorithm in mind led us to 'algonquin', a hotel. Autocomplete allows us to see, use, and re-invent. We might start nurturing an 'imagination tree'. Any number of stories might stem from Google's autocomplete terms when used and re-imagined creatively, and the stories might never have been imagined without Google giving us some words to play with in the first place.

But yes, Google also censors the unsearched. However, it's inevitable that we never know what we cannot know. Therefore, algorithms do have the capacity to reinforce what we already know; this can also mean reinforcing negative discourses. Baker and Potts, for example, suggest that racist, homophobic, and sexist stereotypes are reinforced through visible autocomplete words.[18] Imagination, however, may help to balance this out and let us find nuggets of word-worlds that we may not have previously considered. How can a search engine know what we do not know and may not want to know? In our data material, we find that Google U.K. tends to make fewer words visible than Google Denmark. Is it really Google, or, since the query is based on personal search, does it rather have something to do with our own search behavior? Are these really 'missing' words? Are they even hidden? Or just visible somewhere else? Then how might we find them? Did no one ask for them? Does no one care? The irony is that to answer these questions, we are pulled into the mystery of Google, once again. Searching for answers while Google has us trapped. Searching for the search to find the answer to the search sucks us back into an almost never-ending quest to find the answers to the questions we have never searched. However, this search also allows us to maintain a sense of creativity.

#creativity

Creativity is process. Creativity constitutes. To view Google's autocomplete creatively can help us learn and think in new ways. The initial conditions of our googled ideas vary across time and space, depending on which words float to the top (Figure 3). As Alexander suggests, 'there is a deep and important underlying structural correspondence between the pattern of a problem and the process of designing a physical form which answers that problem'.[19] And so too is the case here: the underlying structure of Google's autocomplete algorithm presents its own problem of form. That is to say, the physical form of the algorithm lies in part in its effects. Conversely these effects shape the algorithm, like a sculptor shape-shifting the clay he or she shapes, always morphing dialectically together, yet always with a little more control than the clay itself, which only becomes animated through the hands of the sculptor. Google's search enables us to find what we want to find, but those discoveries are also shaped by a massively abnormal curve that is constantly contorted by unpredictable word lists.

In turn, therefore, there is potential for maximizing our crowdsourcing capacity to shape Google's autocomplete in our favor. For example, what would happen if we collectively ceased to use Google for just one day? Alternatively, what if billions of users searched

---

18. Paul Baker and Amanda Potts, '"Why do white people have thin lips?" Google and the Perpetuation of Stereotypes via Auto-Complete Search Forms', *Critical Discourse Studies* 10.2 (2013): 187-204.
19. Christopher Alexander, *Note on the Synthesis of Form*, Cambridge, MA: Harvard University Press, 1964, p. 132.

'capitalism needs to change' or 'racism must be punished' at the same time? Given the recursivity built into Google's autocomplete algorithm, which is clearly sensitive to time and space, perhaps there is more we can do to change normative attitudes than we may have yet realized. Perhaps the capacity to act collectively towards a common good is by actively interacting with Google's autocomplete in ways that are similar to activist movements. If Google can *shape* our views, perhaps we can use Google to *change* our views?

#frivolity

> Frivolity is considered a harmless, unproductive activity outside the more structured activity of play. Huizinga (1950) in Homo Ludens notes that play is a 'free activity standing quite consciously outside of "ordinary" life as not being serious, but at the same time absorbing the player intensely and utterly.' Frivolity, on the other hand, is more transitory and generally without rules or order. [20]

In *The Archaeology of the Frivolous,* Jacques Derrida argues, among other things, that frivolity is always seen as 'bad' and 'dangerous' and that we can use it to disturb and deconstruct views that are taken for granted.[21] Indeed, one of the key points we want to make is that search algorithms need to be carefully looked at and looked after. We need to make sure that we know who is doing the looking and looking after. However, we want to emphasize that even though search algorithms tend to take on a life of their own once they are produced, put into action, and acted upon, they are no different to any other social construct. The power they are assigned, and the independence they are seen to take on, are both socially constructed. Their power is made to 'hold' in much the same way that statistical measures of significance are 'made' to hold through the social practices and institutions that reinstate them, as Desrosières argues in his excellent book, *The Politics of Large Numbers.*[22] Indeed, we go so far as to say that search algorithms are constructions just as are objects in science. As Collins and Pinch point out in their classic book, *The Golem: What You Should Know About Science,*[23] it is not science that is 'good' or 'bad'. Rather, what is done with and to the world in the name of 'science' is what can be judged as good or bad.

Perhaps, as we have suggested throughout, it is not Google's search algorithm that is problematic, despite its power. Instead, it is perhaps the things that we as individuals, and collectively as governments, may (or may not) do (and don't do) with Google which are problematic. In itself, the autocomplete algorithm may be seen as a Golem, following Collins and Pinch's logic. A mythological creature. A bit daft. Silly. Playful. Not good or bad. Just searching. Waiting for instructions on what to search for. In

---

20. Rodger A. Bates and Emily Fortner, 'The Social Construction of Frivolity', *The Journal of Professional and Public Sociology*, 5.1 (2013), http://digitalcommons.kennesaw.edu/jpps/vol5/iss1/5.
21. Jacques Derrida, *The Archeology of the Frivolous*, trans. J. Leavey Jr., Pittsburg: Duquesne University Press, 1973.
22. Alain Desrosières, *The Politics of Large Numbers: A History of Statistical Reasoning*, trans. Camille Naish, Cambridge, MA: Harvard University Press, 1998.
23. Harry Collins and Trevor Pinch, *The Golem: What You Should Know about Science,* Cambridge, U.K.: Cambridge University Press, 1998.

turn, therefore, we suggest that we can put Google's search algorithm to frivolous use to disrupt and disturb the ordinary words that inscribe and shape our world. Using Google's autocomplete to resist and confuse. After all, for every 'search', there needs to be a 'find' to discover something that may or may not have been searched. *Search and find need one another.*[24] Browsing and laughing through hyperlinks, giggling away at the joy of discovering and uncovering and recovering new spaces, new worlds, the unexpected. Using Google frivolously to make up new algorithmic fables, new tales, and new futures. Daily, mundanely. Juggling with hyperlinks and autocorrect. Everyday. Every day. 'Taming the algorithmic tiger' with a smile, with frivolity, creativity, and imaginary rhythms.

#lessonstolearn
'Ceci n'est pas une pipe' – 'this is not a pipe'. Magritte shows us that things are not always what they appear to be. We live in a world in which we rely heavily on information on the one hand, but, on the other, cannot validate it anymore through our own experiences. Hence, we gather information through various intermediaries such as Google's autocomplete algorithms. While in the era of print these intermediaries seemed definite and somehow understandable, this is not the case anymore. Let's face it: the internet – once thought of as a free information space – has become quite chaotic. Constant innovation within the area of digital technology and machine intelligence offers algorithmic answers to everyday information chaos. The concepts behind the algorithms are not easy to grasp, especially when businesses rely on the secrecy of those algorithms in order stay in business. This situation has created anxiety about what kind of information users receive. Mostly it is feared that when algorithms calculate their stream based on a set of rules that nobody knows, information becomes one-sided. We don't think this outcome will necessarily be the case: search algorithms are not solely based on the algorithm itself, but also on us as users and our search-and-find behavior. *Let's start accepting this state of things and stop surrendering*.

Searching the search is finding difference and similarity, change and stagnancy, always in time and space. Algorithms learn and change and repeat and remain the same too. Search algorithms govern and are visibly invisible; this much we already know. What we have done and need to do now is – *play creatively*. What Google gives us is the chance to play around. How boring would the world be if we always got the same results, whatever we did? This actually gives us the opportunity to be active. We're not running into a wall that always stays the same no matter what. Goodbye Google Truman Show! If we understand algorithms as mirrors, we can actively take on responsibility to create our own mirror image. We have never had that chance before. We have never been that kind of 'enabled citizen'. Let's stop measuring Google against some sort of mythical normative standard and start to think about how we can use Google creatively.

And importantly, we must not ignore the fun and delight and playfulness of the search. After all, search is duality. Search allows us to make sense of the world and ourselves in that world. Search is a verb. 'Searching' implies that the 'searcher' knows something about what they are looking for. Indeed, we might say that:

---

24. See #intro.

Search = Being curious.
       = Looking for answers.
       = Looking for the unknown.
       = Finding.
       = Finding the known.
       = Finding the unknown.
       = Finding questions.
       = Being confused.
       = Being surprised.
       = Being not surprised.
       = A social practice in different times but the same place.
       = A social practice at the same time but in different places.
       = A social practice that finds the same in different places in different times.
       = Searching for searches and finding searches.
       = Jack-in-a-box, always and never a surprise, predictably unpredictable.

#thestorybehind

The story started on Facebook in May 2013. Martina (author one) had set up a new Facebook page and invited friends to 'like' the page. Emma (author two) received such an invitation, not from Martina, as both authors didn't know each other, but instead from another of her Facebook friends. The invitation was to 'like' a page called 'Algorithmic Media Spaces', but the next day, Emma noticed that the name of the page had changed to 'Algorithmic Media'. Thinking that her friend had set up the page, Emma sent a silly message asking about the change of title (Figure 5). 'Algorithmic Media', alias Martina, replied and explained.

Fig. 5. Facebook conversation.

This is how algorithms brought us together, just as they bring so much of our world together, and they do so across time and space, everyday (Figure 6).

Fig. 6. How the authors are related in time and space.

#thanks

We'd like to thank Philipp Lenssen (http://outer-court.com) for kindly allowing us to use his image in the #searching section. We have titled it 'I Google, therefore I am'. It's not the original title. We further like to thank Miriam Rasch and René König for their editorial effort.

#references

Alexander, Christopher. *Note on the Synthesis of Form*, Cambridge, MA: Harvard University Press, 1964.

Baker, Paul and Amanda Potts. '"Why do white people have thin lips?" Google and the Perpetuation of Stereotypes via Auto-Complete Search Forms', *Critical Discourse Studies* 10.2 (2013): 187-204.

Bates, Rodger A. and Emily Fortner. 'The Social Construction of Frivolity', *The Journal of Professional and Public Sociology*, 5.1 (2013), http://digitalcommons.kennesaw.edu/jpps/vol5/iss1/5.

Beer, David. 'Power Through the Algorithm? Participatory Web Cultures and the Technological Unconscious', *New Media & Society* 11 (September 2009): 985-1002.

Boden, Margaret A. 'The Social Impact of Thinking Machines' in Tom Forester (ed.) *The Information Technology Revolution*, Oxford: Basil Blackwell, 1985, pp. 95-103.

Bucher, Taina. 'Want to Be on the Top? Algorithmic Power and the Threat of Invisibility on Facebook', *New Media & Society* 14.7 (November 2012): 1164-1180.

Chabert, Jean-Luc. *A History of Algorithms*, Berlin, Heidelberg: Springer, 1999.

Collins, Harry and Trevor Pinch. *The Golem: What You Should Know about Science*, Cambridge, U.K.: Cambridge University Press, 1998.

Corman, Thomas H., Charles E. Leiserson, Ronald L. Rivest, and Clifford Stein. *Introduction to Algorithms*, Cambridge MA: MIT Press

Dennett, Daniel. 'Can Machines Think?' in Christof Teuscher (ed.) *Alan Turing: Life and Legacy of a Great Thinker*, Berlin: Springer, 2004

Derrida, Jacques. *The Archeology of the Frivolous*, trans. J. Leavey Jr., Pittsburg: Duquesne University Press, 1973.

Desrosières, Alain. *The Politics of Large Numbers: A History of Statistical Reasoning*, trans. Camille Naish, Cambridge, MA: Harvard University Press, 1998.

Egan, Kieran. *Imagination in Teaching and Learning: The Middle School Years*, Chicago: The University of Chicago Press, 1992.

Gillespie, Tarleton. 'Can an Algorithm Be Wrong? Twitter Trends, the Specter of Censorship, and Our Faith in the Algorithms Around Us', Culture Digitally blog, 19 October 2011, http://culture digitally.org/2011/10/can-an-algorithm-be-wrong/.

Knuth, Donald. *Fundamental Algorithms*, vol. 1 of *The Art of Computer Programming*, Boston: Addison-Wesley, 1997 (1968).

____, *Sorting and Searching*, vol. 3 of *The Art of Computer Programming*, Boston: Addison-Wesley, 1993 (1973).

Lake, Robert. *A Curriculum of Imagination in an Era of Standardization: An Imaginative Dialogue with Maxine Greene and Paulo Freire*, Charlotte, NC: Information Age Pub, 2013.

Naughton, John. 'How Algorithms Secretly Shape the Way We Behave', *The Guardian*, 15 December 2012, http://www.guardian.co.uk/technology/2012/dec/16/networker-algorithms-john-naughton.

Pariser, Eli. *The Filter Bubble: What the Internet is Hiding from You*, London: Penguin Press, 2011.

Rieder, Bernhard. 'Democratizing Search? From Critique to Society-oriented Design', in Konrad Becker and Felix Stalder (eds) *Deep Search. The Politics of Search beyond Google*, Innsbruck: Studienverlag, 2009, pp. 133-151.

____. 'Networked Control: Search Engines and the Symmetry of Confidence', *International Review of Information Ethics* 3.1 (2005): 26-32.

Skiena, Steven. *The Algorithm Design Manual*, London: Springer, 2008.

Slavin, Kevin. 'How Algorithms Shape Our World', TED Talks, July 2011 http://www.ted.com/talks/kevin_slavin_how_algorithms_shape_our_world.html.

Steiner, Christopher. *Automate This: How Algorithms Came to Rule Our World*, New York, NY: Portfolio/Penguin, 2012.

Turing, Alan. 'Computing Machinery and Intelligence', in Paul A. Meyer (ed.) *Computer Media and Communication: A Reader*, Oxford: Oxford University Press, 1999, p. 37-58.

Van Couvering, Elizabeth Jane. *Search Engine Bias*, PhD diss., Department Media and Communications, London School of Economics and Political Science, London, U.K., 2009.

Waldrop, M. Mitchell. *Complexity: The Emerging Science at the Edge of Order and Chaos*, New York: Simon and Schuster, 1992.

Search-Art: The Narcissus Search Engine, Skateboarding, and Oranges

Phil Jones and Aharon Amir

Search-Art:
The Narcissus Search Engine, Skateboarding, and Oranges

֬

Phil Jones
and Aharon Amir

Artists Phil Jones[1] and Aharon Amir[2] created the Narcissus Search Engine for N.E.W.S. in 2009.[3] Narcissus searches a body of documents for matching keywords and shows them to the user in the normal manner. However it records when users click-through to see the results and will penalize results that appear too popular. Initially Narcissus will push a popular result down its ranking but, if the result continues to be clicked, will obscure it altogether for a time. Hidden results will eventually return to visibility if they are matched by enough searches while hidden.[4]

We think of Narcissus as a 'Search Art' practice. Narcissus will discover the 'shadow' data which would otherwise be ignored in favor of the popular. The way Narcissus operates – the Narcissus Opera in a sense – is a mediation focusing on the use of the positive feedback that leads to filter bubbles in so many contemporary internet services. It invites you to reflect, evolve, and question rather than seek entertainment or the security of the known and expected.

Narcissus is Phil and Aharon's first attempt at using search as a language, an aesthetic that is in and of itself a technology of the imagination, to be with and be skeptical of. Since Narcissus, Aharon has been developing an artistic practice of search in a number of different works that involve him searching both online and in physical spaces and engaging or recruiting others to join him.

The following dialogues are distilled from a conversation between Aharon and Phil discussing these works and the poetics or language of search itself. We hope the reader will get a sense that we are not giving an answer but are engaging in our own search

---

1. See, http://synaesmedia.net.
2. See, http://aharonic.net/blog/tag/search-art/, http://aharonic.net/blog/tag/search/. I'd like to apologize for the unintended authoritative tone I seem to have in the texts.
3. See, http://searchnarcissus.net/ and http://northeastwestsouth.net/.
4. The algorithm uses Complex Numbers for ranking. And penalization can push a result into the 'imaginary' zone where it will not appear at all.

for these questions, in which the reader is welcome to participate.[5] The full, unabridged transcriptions of the dialogues are available and searchable via Narcissus itself,[6] and the original recordings are also available.[7]

About Narcissus
Aharon Amir: I think Narcissus asks you to search within yourself how to imagine a search filter, by being confronted with a visibly changing result to the same query. This draws attention to the filter, and because it shows something you might have not seen previously, Narcissus has the capacity to make you imagine the results differently.

Phil Jones: Narcissus is about imposing a certain filter bubble.

AA: It's very up-front about it.

PJ: But it's not self-evident, if we didn't tell you. Or do we, via Narcissus, draw attention to the fact it's hiding things from the users? This seems like the classic problem in literature, how to make a boring character interesting to the reader. How do you make a strategy of subterfuge in an artwork into something that is visible?

AA: I think what you do, and this is one of the maybe traditional elements in Narcissus, is that it kind of gives you clues. To remain with your literature analogy, there are different clues given to you in a story that say what the writer is trying to convey. Narcissus speaks in the language of a search filter. You search and click the result, then next time it's not there or is in a different position. That's a language of search you learn to read.

PJ: OK. I suppose if you repeatedly search the same things, use search as a kind of backup of your own memory, then it would be more obvious. You'd keep 'forgetting' things.

AA: Remember when we talked about the Guinea in the pub? The coin. There was a question that the Guinea was called Guinea because gold came from Guinea in Africa.

PJ: People started Googling on their mobiles.

AA: Well, the sequence was: people first tried to mine their memories. Then they tried to search. And I was saying this is a typical difference between our generation and [my daughter's] because the younger generation goes: 'why do I need to mine my head?'

PJ: They'd dive into search faster, whereas we waited for our memory to fail.

AA: So we now remember differently. Sometimes all you recall is how to search for the thing. I'm looking for a film. No need to remember the name. All I need is to search something with vampires in 1964 in Rome.

---

5. See, http://arty.li/contacts.
6. See, http://arty.li/rawfiles.
7. See, https://archive.org/details/Soq06a.

PJ: I've got 'Last Man on Earth'.

AA: Yes, that's the film. You don't need to remember. Sometimes it's a question of remembering a term and where you searched for it. Whereas let's take something classic. Finding your key is an exact thing. There's just you and the key. You need to remember exactly where you put that key. With a phone it's different because it's connected; you don't need to remember where the phone is, you just need to find someone with the number of that phone, and they can call it.

PJ: Externalized memory. Interestingly, Google Mine wants to catalog all your stuff (including your keys?).[8] But to return to my earlier point, sometimes we aren't searching for the same thing as part of externalized memory but doing a one-off.

AA: Sometimes. However with Narcissus, the result would be the outcome of other people's searches, and maybe you wouldn't get the meaning of it. Just like you might read a book and miss out on certain things. In fact people read interesting stories several times because each time you discover different elements. Or pieces of music: if you get the idea of a piece of music the first time, that's pop music. You listen it to a few times, and then you don't listen again because it's not very interesting. Narcissus plays with the filter itself. It's being tongue-in-cheek without this pseudo-democratic 'you can have your choice'.

PJ: 'Pseudo-democratic'?

AA: When stuff tries to pretend that it doesn't have a filter, it gives you pseudo-choice. But Narcissus doesn't do that. It imagines a new kind of filter; this imagination helps you search the filter inside you. It questions the filter.

PJ: I agree it questions the filter. But it doesn't give you the option of eliminating the filter.

AA: It doesn't give you the false sense of eliminating the filter by making your own filter that isn't a filter but is actually a filter. It doesn't do that. Narcissus doesn't do this pseudo-shit.

Filter Bubbles
AA: I think 'Search Art', and Narcissus for a start, is interesting in that it's the beginning of a different way of imagining. By 'Search Art' we're saying, 'let's put it on steroids'. Let's do, 'how do we imagine stuff as a search?' We are learning to value the links, pointers, networks. We don't need to value the singular object, just like we don't need to value the imagination of the singular genius. We can imagine how we link with the world and produce meanings, in a more interdependent and co-operative way.

PJ: But doesn't relying on external search make us vulnerable? People doing the search for us can be manipulating; they start controlling what we see. We're address-

---

8. 'Google Mine', Google Operating System, 21 June 2013, http://googlesystem.blogspot.co.uk/2013/06/google-mine.html.

ing half of that problem in Narcissus – the innocent side effect of positive feedback loops that reward popularity. We're not addressing the more pernicious problems of, say, search engines that choose to censor the results as opposed to things that seem like a good idea but have unfortunate results.

AA: Could you elaborate?

PJ: The idea of positive feedback loops, let's say the PageRank algorithm or highlighting popular search results, was done for a 'good' reason, which is the idea that some results have a higher quality than others and that popularity was a good way of discovering high quality sources. It led to a different problem, which is that popularity isn't just quality. Popularity can also express popular prejudice. Popularity can be group-think and restrict creativity. So a search engine that promotes the things that are already popular ends up unfairly highlighting things that don't deserve it. That's one sort of problem. And that's the problem that Narcissus talks to.

There's an entirely different sort of problem which is that someone might think, for example, that people shouldn't know about documents on Wikileaks. The U.S. government then tells Google that people shouldn't be able to find that kind of stuff, and some of it might disappear from the index.

AA: That's a political question.

PJ: Exactly. That's not something we have addressed so far. But we could make a search engine and then deliberately censor some results and not show them. That's a different question. Both are kinds of filter bubbles and both are problematic, although they have a dynamic and character that's very different. Something that seems to be responsible for even more constraining of your search is the attempt to infer what you 'really want'.

Siri for example: it tries to infer what you're saying from your context. For instance: 'Because I know your position in time and place you are probably in the kitchen, and looking for chocolate cake recipes rather than ready-mades cakes.' Even Google used to be easier for the user to control. Then it began to give you more of what it wants to, rather than your query. The search is more and more a front. In the name of making it easier, they make more and more assumptions that increasingly narrow possibilities down based on their stereotype of you. That's a problem.

AA: Is it not a mirror of false dichotomy, made up of freedom and security?

PJ: Computers do something very problematic: they eliminate areas of uncertainty. When spying was done by people we could perhaps have security and freedom. People make judgments. The police ask, 'is he really causing a problem or is he just a bit noisy?' So they let you off. But when you have a computer, it doesn't do that!

AA: I kind of feel that as a sort of paranoia. You are guilty before anything else. Say Captcha: instead of learning that you are not a bot, it is predisposed to thinking you are a bot. So you are guilty before anything is proved. You are a bot unless proven otherwise, not innocent.

PJ: Computers don't have to do this. The programmers chose the whitelist approach rather than the blacklist.[9] But you cannot program a computer not to choose one option or the other.

AA: Don't some programmers decide to use one way over another?

PJ: Not all the internet is like that. Say, Facebook, they try a blacklist approach.

AA: With Facebook, they want you to mingle. 'Guilty unless proven otherwise' seems to be more prevalent. Would a distributed search engine such as YaCy be less susceptible,[10] I wonder?

PJ: If it's distributed then the policy would have to be public and agreed on by the participants. But the policy would still need to be mechanical. Look, I agree that this world of software creates this kind of paranoia. However, you're slightly diagnosing it wrong. What gives you that sense of rigidity is that the software forces you into one thing or the other. Not so much a bias towards guilt but the lack of room for open-endedness. That restrictiveness is also a source of security.

AA: Maybe there is a connection between technology's restrictiveness and a false sense of security. In terms of Narcissus, I think it's interesting that we put 'distributed' into the initial specifications,[11] precisely to question distribution over networks from the perspectives of search, visibility, and power. Like, we wanted to have different groups being able to search and influence each other's hidden data. However this element in Narcissus is yet to be implemented, perhaps because the technology is expensive? Why is that? Is it not a question of tradition, habits, and costs? Is centralized technology cheaper because imagining it this way is more prevalent? Do we go with what's well understood or what's 'secure'? I guess this is also where the bit about agreed upon policies come into play in Narcissus' question of network distribution.

That's a very interesting question I think, both in terms of the NSA and the fact that people will use technology not just because it makes them feel like they do stuff quicker, but because it makes them feel secure.

Search and Research
PJ: So are people scared of search? Is it about a sort of fear? We mustn't go off the 'beaten track' or we'll get lost and won't find what we're looking for.

AA: We don't know in terms of general people. But I'd say people tend towards research: 'I want to know who did this or that film.' Or why we call 'orange' an 'orange'. I think people limit themselves to a range of queries, rather than go on a 'search' that is open, where they say: 'Let's check out what we might bump into by colliding with elements'.

---

9. Wikipedia contributors, 'Whitelist', http://en.wikipedia.org/wiki/Whitelist, accessed 5 January 2014.
10. YaCy: http://arty.li/Zg3.
11. See, Phil Jones and Aharon Amir, Narcissus Search Engine, http://searchnarcissus.net/narcissus_pseudo_code.pdf.

A practical example: one of the search-art activities I did recently, at the 'Hack the Barbican' event in London[12] (HtB) was titled: 'How to Imagine Swapping Spaces Between Hackers in the Gallery and Residents of the Barbican'. I went to people with 'search in mind'. I tried to find a person or a few people with whom you might want to imagine how, what, and if this swapping of spaces can be done. And then to get talking and imagining together. I was very surprised that, without exception, people's reactions were to try to figure out for themselves what would happen. I had to say, 'look, actually it's a negotiation'.[13]

PJ: Sorry, what were you asking?

AA: How they could imagine together with other people or with an artist-resident what would mean the swapping of spaces. What each person did, instead of picking up with 'would you like to do a negotiation?' then saying 'I have a flat, you do music', they said 'I would like the end results of this process to be this.'

PJ: But they're talking to you, right? Not to the other person. How could they 'negotiate'?

AA: I was using myself as a link between people. So people kept coming to me with, 'No, I can't do that because I'm not going to just let anyone into my flat'. And I was like, 'this isn't the question, man! Why are you focused on the end rather than the linking process?'

PJ: But isn't that what they're accustomed to? Starting from the end-point and thinking backwards. So when you ask them, that's what they'll do. Until you ask them to start earlier and think forwards or sideways or something?

AA: Following an exchange with my ISP[14] (internet service provider), it became visible to me that what I really wanted to say is that searching has a different trajectory of sequences than researching or seeking. A search is from, rather than for, with, of something. I search from a term or idea – not for that term or idea. Indeed, it could be said that Google and the likes, by matching the query terms, are being narcissistic. Looking for similarities, reflections of the term. Is this a difference between language of research and search?

A Language of Search
PJ: You talk of 'giving as a search'. For example, there is a pedagogical technique where you give students an exercise to work out, with the assumption that they will learn more, understand things better, if they work it out for themselves rather than being told facts. Is this the same kind of thing?

AA: It's a step further. Instead of saying 'I know that one plus one equals two, while you don't', and I let you figure it out so you'll understand better, I'm saying, 'Let's see. Do I

---

12. See, http://hackthebarbican.org.
13. Aharon Amir, 'Hissbhgrb', 1 November 2013, http://aharonic.net/blog/hissbhgrb.
14. Aharon Amir, 'An ISP Story', 1 November 2013, http://aharonic.net/blog/an-isp-story.

remember how it was before one plus one equals two? Do I recall when I was searching?' Maybe I was in the jungle, thinking of the desert when this happened. Now the question is that for you, something else might happen, precisely because it is a search. No one has a clue how, what, or whether it will happen.

PJ: What if it hadn't been a search?

AA: If it wasn't a search, I'd give you more precise elements. Or, I'd think that the result of walking in the jungle, for example, will always be one plus one equals two.

PJ: Hang on! Are you saying that search is defined by the indeterminacy of the results you are going to get? Search means 'I'm doing something and I don't know what I am going to get'? Any activity that has no goals can be defined as search? I don't think that's what you want to say.

AA: Yes. I see your point... Well, first I think search is open-ended in the sense that you don't know. But there's more to it. Say I am in a new city, looking for a house – the Gaudi house. That is research, in my mind, because you have a certain goal. Search is not anything you happen to do.

PJ: What limits it?

AA: I think at the edges there are negotiations rather than limits. Limits project trajectory-like into a territory.[15] Edges are space-times, periods, places where we are goal-less. You have certain precise elements that maybe the artist develops – ingredients that, like molecules, like elements of an atom, are immanent for one another. Once they are together, they can be used as search. The atom had no idea it could be a bomb.

Narcissus search is perhaps an early, primitive sort of example of this approach, this language. You have certain ingredients – the algorithm, the database arrangement, the visualized layer, and the content – that can be taken separately into other works, ideas or projects, but together, they are required by each other to make this organism, searchnarcissus. In that sense they are both separate and immanent for one another. Together they make a search language based on degrees of invisibility that can be used, abused, and applied in ways we can't imagine. Like Japanese, Swahili, or Context. It can be in someone else's imagination – however unlike these other languages, Narcissus is 'Given as a Search' rather than stuff to imagine while being beholden to projected pre-conceptions.

PJ: Can we get up in the morning and say something like 'today I am not going to do any search'?

AA: To be honest I don't know. I think this links with the non-spectacle-yet-innate element. Perhaps we cannot live without doing search.

---

15. Aharon Amir, 'A Rhythmic Way to Imagine Territories? Or', 23 October 2013, http://aharonic.net/roo/a-rhythmic-way-to-imagine-territories-or/.

PJ: This seems to be becoming very abstract. 'Search' becomes another label, a general word for all these other things that we cannot help doing. Like 'existence'. It seems to cover everything.

AA: Well, no… I mean we say there is a difference between search and research.

PJ: But not between search and cleaning your teeth?

AA: No. I don't think that we do a search every time we clean our teeth. It's a sequence. Certain sequences and rhythms. Once we do that sequence, it becomes search. And we do that sequence very instinctively. But it's not everything we do.

PJ: That's why I am asking. There are times we do and don't. I'm trying to get the times we might not do search. Your original example, walking in the jungle, thinking of desert, getting one plus one equals.

AA: Well, yes. But walking in the jungle is not, in itself, a search. Doesn't mean or imply search. I think we are talking about a complex activity. Like a complex number.

PJ: Multi-dimensional.

AA: Even a simple search in Google is multi-dimensional. You need at least three actors. I call it a sequence. BTW, when you have a minute, watch this SharkWheel video?[16]

Skateboarding and Search
PJ: Yes, talking of wheels and surfaces, skateboarding. You were searching for the Gasworks Gallery.

AA: 'Searching for Gasworks Gallery[17] on the way to Furtherfield Gallery.'[18]

PJ: Do you think this is the same kind of work as in the Barbican?

AA: Well I didn't expect it, OK? I kind of bump into things rather than expect. There's always a collision, and what comes out of it. I can say, considering it beforehand, I thought, 'somebody is going to beat me up'. That didn't happen, but I did think this might be a possibility. Because I said: 'Look, I know where Gasworks is, and I'm not going there. I'm just wondering if you would know where it is.' It was basically asking if a person has a clue where Gasworks Gallery might be. And (initially) how many pushes of the skateboard I would have to do until I bump into someone else who has no idea where Gasworks Gallery is. I was asking them to speculate on that.

PJ: What do you mean by 'speculate'? Making a 'guess'?

---

16. See, http://sharkwheelskate.com.
17. See, http://gasworks.org.uk/, near Oval, South London.
18. See, http://furtherfield.org/, in North London.

AA: Yes, some sort of guesswork. It's almost random. Then I asked 'how many pushes' and some people gave me 100 pushes.

PJ: Why ask the number of pushes to the next person who doesn't know, rather than the number of pushes to get to the place?

AA: The focus of the search was the movement towards Furtherfield and between collision points. My interest in that was to have some sort of reflective critique of the Situationists, what I see as the conservative element in Situationism. The attempt to 'map', the attempt to see the situation as a whole. Rather than slowly building something without knowing what it is.

PJ: So it's a kind of 'anti-mapping'. A strategy for avoiding mapping? You're trying to find something that is unknowable or uncapturable inside the territory?

AA: 'Avoiding' implies wanting or is a logical maneuver. But this, I think, is something different. More a strand of collisions in a collider, with the collider being the opposing movements and questions. The people and questions – they are collision points. Strung together there is a certain rhythm. I'm trying to do something that mapping avoids: a 'pre-mapping' process. The issue with producing a map is that you can transfer it from one person to another. You can say, 'This is the map of where I've been, and if you want to go there, you can follow it'.

That skips the process. Prior to making the map, there was a search, and you encapsulated it in the map. That process of encapsulation is conservative. So that's why I was interested – not in Situationist 'drifting', because I know where I'm going – but in doing something that has a search in it. And the search happens between collision points along the way.

Initially I thought that the transferable elements would be the numbers of pushes across certain distances. As I was doing it, I realized that I was being conservative myself, so it evolved (because it's a search process itself) into 'what kind of pushes will I need to do?' And people looked at me like 'what do you mean?' [Laughs]

PJ: Well if they're not skateboarders they may not know the kinds of pushes.

Search and Spectacle
PJ: What is the connection between search and spectacle?

AA: The connection is giving something as a search, not as an answer. For Google, search is a theater. You think you are searching how to get from Brasilia to Rio. You search planes, buses, etc. But Google shows you hotels in Rio. Google's real financial interest is the information about you.

PJ: Why 'theater'?

AA: Because just like 'security', with Google things are not what they seem. It's not 'come and give us your details so we can push some ads'. It's: 'let's pretend you search while we observe you'. We need fake search bots to obscure the information they gather on a certain IP. (A kind of accelerationist[19] strategy, though I don't advocate accelerationism.)

PJ: 'Giving it as a search' seems like offering people the chance to pull things out rather than pushing to them. Is it like the difference between going to a restaurant with a set menu, and going to the supermarket where you can get the stuff off the shelves and make it yourself?

AA: One of the differences. It also happens to be stuff that we do innately. It's not even a talent that few have. We all do this. This is an interpretative activity. You see or hear something. And if I asked you what you saw or heard, you would give me your own version. That's one of the main differences between us and other animals.[20] That's why when apes use tools, an ape will see another ape using a stick to pick up ants and think, 'I can do that'. A human will look at it and say, 'how can I make it slightly different?' You 'imagine from' not 'imagine to'.

Search is talking that very language. Rather than giving it to you in a static way. (Even though we know it isn't static, so you will have to take away the bombastic-ness. It's like 'fucking hell, I'm giving you a headache'.)

PJ: So 'giving as search', whether it's our artwork (Narcissus) or Google, is actually keying into something that humans are doing all the time, that's perhaps ignored by other sorts of media that were always pushing something at you?

AA: I don't know about media – that's very big.

PJ: Well, spectacle is something that betrays that human need to be going and pulling, in favor of bombast or pushing?

AA: But not so much media as 'approach to the media'.

PJ: Someone could do a painting where you went in and found ambiguities?

AA: Allowing you to search rather than find what you wanted. Going back to Narcissus, it is a search in itself, it's never going to give you what is culturally desired. It's like the desire of the non-desired. That's what's interesting. I don't think this is medium-specific.

I want to say something else that I think is important. One of the difficulties with the Situationist critique of spectacle is precisely that we do spectacle not just for political reasons but also as an innate activity. If I want you to remember something or you want to remember something, one way of doing it is to make a spectacle of it. By putting something in a rhythm or rhyme or using a gun or some other power. But by making something a search, I'm losing the 'specificity'. I can't tell you 'this is

---

19. Ray Brassier, 'Accelerationism', http://moskvax.wordpress.com/2010/09/30/accelerationism-ray-brassier/. Also see TrackMeNot, https://cs.nyu.edu/trackmenot/.
20. The views are in relation to possible misreadings and interpretations of Michael Tomasello's book *The Cultural Origins of Human Cognition*, Cambridge, MA: Oxford University Press, 2000.

red' (and want you to remember 'this is red'). I'm being more humble. I don't know what is important. But I know this sequence is interesting. Well, I don't know if it's interesting to you.

PJ: The point for the Situationists was that *dérive*, drifting, was a strategy of resistance against the spectacle. For you, you're always talking about it as being something that's provided to us. One can present something 'as spectacle' or 'as search', but it's something the artist or society does to the others. This is different from the psychogeographic thing where drifting is something you take. Something you go and do. With Narcissus, we were talking about us as artists giving search to the viewer. When we talk about the *dérive* we're talking about someone going to a city and saying 'I will do my own drifting in the city'. Not that architects give us that.

AA: I take the drift itself as part of a larger sequence; a bunch of Situationists came up with the idea, you picked up on it and said, 'Hey, that's a good idea, I'll do drifting in Brasilia tomorrow'. In that sense it's similar to the sequence I'm talking about. There's no difference.

PJ: So, search is trying to recover something human in the face of the spectacle? I take the point that making a spectacle is itself a human thing, and not artificial or imposed on humans.

AA: Spectacle is a political thing. I accept the Situationist critique that says there is a capitalistic abuse of spectacle. Appropriating this desire that we have. I accept that. That's what happens. But I am saying that if you do drifting, let's not make a spectacle. This in itself has a difficulty – how do you transfer from one person to another? This is an innate thing for us. We share things. We say 'have you seen this?' or 'hey, I drifted yesterday, that was great fun.' This is the problem. How do I give you something similar to that? I'm your friend, I'd like to share it with you. How do I do that? The only way we know how to is through making a spectacle out of stuff – drifting included.

PJ: You faced this problem in your Firefly search.[21] You went to the gallery and searched and the question was how do you convey to people that they can search with you?

AA: This is the bane of my life. It's a question of how to share without the spectacle. Without putting a gun to someone's head.

PJ: Surely that's a very negative analogy. To compare making a performance for people with threatening to shoot them.

AA: Of course. But I think it's hard to disagree that there's an issue of power.

PJ: Between the performer and performed to?

AA: Even without the performance. Saying, 'I want you to remember this object or

---

21. Aharon Amir, 'How to Imagine Aesthetics of Living-Dead Fireflies', 30 March 2013, http://www.arty.li/firefly-aesthetics-search.

sculpture or whatever. So I want to make it in a way that you will feel in awe of it. That there is a power of it over you.' There's always a certain element of power with the spectacle. Maybe it's not a fundamental element, maybe it's arguable how important. But we agree it's there. For me it always feels like a gun to the head. Shakespeare's Macbeth or Duchamp's Urinal, they're results of searches. There was an element of searching and these are developments of these searches. So instead of putting myself in the center of the world, saying 'I have this fantastic idea', I attest that I'm not the center of the world.

PJ: Just say, 'This is what happened when I did search'?

Borders and Security
AA: Think of an airport. The security in airports is nothing but search. It drives people nuts! They have no idea who might have a bomb. They have no idea about anything. So they are going to search and search and search. They are going to build these machines and give people power to ask stupid questions. Like, when we came back from Israel: 'Where in London do you live?' 'Well we live in Brighton, it's south of London.' 'Ah! The north of England?' 'Yes,' we said.

PJ: They did that to try catching you out. Like Google, it's a theater. A pre-judgment.

AA: They search in special machines, special tables, special gloves, special tools to look for bombs, special rooms – all to search and search and search. Constant search. All they know is that they search, rather than what they search for.

PJ: Perhaps it is done to discourage people. In that sense, it works. It's an interesting use of search, not just to find stuff.

AA: Yes. In that sense it's a very theatrical piece. It's a sort of a show. But I always fly with a bomb on me.

PJ: HUH??!!

AA: Yes. I always carry oranges onboard planes. They let me do that, and oranges explode very easily.[22]

---

22. See, http://arty.li/ZgU.

References

Amir, Aharon. 'Hissbhgrb', 1 November 2013, http://aharonic.net/blog/hissbhgrb.
_____. How to Imagine Aesthetics of Living-Dead Fireflies', 30 March 2013, http://www.arty.li/firefly-aesthetics-search.
_____. 'An ISP Story', 1 November 2013, http://aharonic.net/blog/an-isp-story.
_____. 'A Rhythmic Way to Imagine Territories? Or', 23 October 2013, http://aharonic.net/roo/a-rhythmic-way-to-imagine-territories-or/.
Brassier, Ray. 'Accelerationism', http://moskvax.wordpress.com/2010/09/30/accelerationism-ray-brassier/.
'Google Mine', Google Operating System, 21 June 2013, http://googlesystem.blogspot.co.uk/2013/06/google-mine.html.
Jones, Phil and Aharon Amir. Narcissus Search Engine, http://searchnarcissus.net/narcissus_pseudo_code.pdf.
Tomasello, Michael. The Cultural Origins of Human Cognition, Cambridge, MA: Oxford University Press, 2000.
Wikipedia contributors. 'Whitelist', http://en.wikipedia.org/wiki/Whitelist, accessed 5 January 2014.

Appendices

¬

Society of the Query Conferences & Author Biographies

SOCIETY OF THE QUERY I
November 13-14, 2009, TrouwAmsterdam

FRYIDAY, NOVEMBER 13, 2009

10.15 – 12.30
Society of the Query
Moderator: Geert Lovink
Speakers: Yann Moulier Boutang (F), Matteo Pasquinelli (NL), Teresa Numerico (IT), David Gugerli (CH)

Book Presentation: *Deep Search. The Politics of Search Beyond Google* (Studienverlag & Transaction publishers, 2009)
Speaker: Konrad Becker

13.45 – 15.30
Digital Civil Rights
Moderator: Caroline Nevejan
Speakers: Joris van Hoboken (NL), Ippolita Collective (IT)

15.45 – 17.30
Alternative Search 1
Moderator: Eric Sieverts
Speakers: Matthew Fuller (UK), Cees Snoek (NL), Ingmar Weber (E)

SATURDAY, NOVEMBER 14, 2009

10.00 – 12.30
Art and the Engine
Moderator: Sabine Niederer
Speakers: Lev Manovich (USA), Daniel van der Velden (NL), Christophe Bruno (FR), Allessandro Ludovico (IT)

Flarf Performance
Ton van het Hof (NL)

13.45 – 15.30
Googlization
Introduction and moderation by Andrew Keen
Speakers: Siva Vaidhyanathan (US), Martin Feuz (CH), Esther Weltevrede (NL)

15.45 – 17.30
Alternative Search 2
Moderator: Richard Rogers
Speakers: Florian Cramer (NL), Antoine Isaac, Steven Pemberton (NL)

20.30 – 23.30
Evening Program
host: Michael Stevenson (NL)

SOCIETY OF THE QUERY II
November 7-8, 2013, OBA Amsterdam

THURSDAY, NOVEMBER 7, 2013

13.00 – 15.00
Google Domination
Moderator: René König
Speakers: Siva Vaidhyanathan (US), Astrid Mager (AT), Dirk Lewandowski (GE)

15.15 – 16.30
Search Across the Border
Moderator: Steven Pemberton
Speakers: Thomas Petzold (GE), Min Jiang (US), Payal Arora (NL)

16.30 – 17.30
The Art of Search
Moderator: Renée Ridgway
Speakers: Rebecca Lieberman (US), Anja Groten (DE), Isabelle Massu (FR), Rosa Menkman (NL)

FRIDAY, NOVEMBER 8, 2009

10.00 – 12.15
Reflections on Search
Moderation: Geert Lovink
Speakers: Kylie Jarett (IRE), Antoinette Rouvroy (BE), Anton Tantner (AT)

12.15 – 12.30
Book launch
The Dark Side of Google by Ippolita (IT)

13.30 – 15.15
Search in Context
Moderator: Jelte Timmer
Speakers: Simon Knight (UK), Sanne Koevoets (NL), Maarten Sprenger (NL)

15.45 – 17.30
The Filter Bubble Show
Moderator: Miriam Rasch
Speakers: Erik Borra (NL) and René König (GE), Pascal Jürgens (GE), Engin Bozdag (NL)

21.00 – 1.00
Party: I'm Feeling Lucky
Roest, Amsterdam

Author Biographies

Aharon Amir graduated from Brighton University's visual & performing arts, and continued to question and practice performance in digital and network environments. Through time Aharon's work moved from performative acts, to project making, and through to development of imagination and search technologies. Since late 80s, Aharon has presented in conferences and galleries (e.g., Conciousness-Reframed, Performance-Philosophy, Philadelphia ICA, Mediterranean Biennale); created and co-developed events and participation contexts (e.g., art and chat monthly, art-as-political-uselessnes ssymposium, future-of-production conference); co-created Narcissus (searchnarcissus.net) – award-winning search engine algorithm for dark data; developed events and projects with Interactive-TV, cultural websites, collaborative organisations, and educational organisations (e.g., Digi-hub, Lighthouse and Basekamp).

Vito Campanelli is a writer and a new media theorist. His main research interest is the technological imaginary. He is also a freelance curator of digital culture events and co-founder of MAO – Media & Arts Office. His essays on media art are regularly published in international journals. http://vitocampanelli.eu

Dave Crusoe is Director of Academic Success – Technology for The Boys & Girls Clubs of America, and is responsible for designing and implementing technology education programs in support of the Movement. Prior to this current role, he founded The Public Learning Media Laboratory, which produced tools and resources to teach digital literacy. He completed two degrees at the Harvard Graduate School of Education and, if nobody is listening, plays old-time banjo.

Angela Daly is a research fellow in Swinburne University of Technology's Institute for Social Research (Melbourne, Australia) and a PhD candidate in the Department of Law at the European University Institute (Florence, Italy) where she is finalizing a thesis on 'corporate dominance of online data flows'. Her research concerns the intersection of law and technology, and her contribution to this reader is based on a chapter of her PhD thesis providing a critical analysis of the U.S. and E.U. competition investigations into Google's online search and advertising business.

Vicențiu Dîngă is a Romanian new media researcher and journalist currently based in Amsterdam. He holds a Master's degree in New Media and Digital Culture (2013, University of Amsterdam) and has joined the Institute of Network Cultures in August 2013, where he assisted in the production of the Society of the Query conference and the MoneyLab program. In parallel, he is independently working in social media management and online marketing with various companies. In the past, he has worked as a contributing editor for several publications and as a project manager of one of the most important cultural cooperative platforms in Romania, where he was taking care of specialized projects and events.

Author Biographies

Martin Feuz is a PhD researcher at the Centre for Cultural Studies, Goldsmiths, University of London and lecturer in Interaction Design at Zurich University of the Arts. His research focuses on exploratory search and health information interactions and how such interactions can be meaningfully supported.

Ulrich Gehmann (Dipl.-Biol., lic. oec. HSG et MA History) is founder of the working group Formatting of Social Spaces at University of Karlsruhe and editor-in-chief of the journal *New Frontiers in Spatial Concepts*. http://ejournal.uvka.de/spatialconcepts

Olivier Glassey is a sociologist, senior lecturer and researcher at the Observatory Science, Policy and Society (OSPS) and at the Laboratory of Digital Cultures and Humanities (LaDHUL) at the University of Lausanne, Switzerland. He studies online mass collaboration and emergent collective behaviors in several domains (social norms, distributed production of knowledge, user driven innovation, open classification and video games). He is currently working on collective memory production, the materiality of online social interactions and the sociology of big data.

Richard Graham is a PhD candidate in English (with specialism in Digital Humanities) at the University of Exeter, England. His research topic focuses on the ways in which search engines change our conceptions of thought and knowledge. He also teaches modules in critical theory and literature at Exeter. Outside of academia, Richard uses his skills developed from his digital humanities research to build and maintain databases for local heritage and archival centres, most recently working on 16th Century minute books concerning the wool and cloth trade in Exeter. He blogs at http://richardnvgraham.blogspot.co.uk/ and tweets from @richardnvgraham.

Mél Hogan is Postdoctoral Fellow in Digital Curation at the University of Colorado – Boulder, CO. Her current research is at the intersection of media, archives and the environment. Her most recent publications revolve around media and ecological impacts, data storage centers, media archaeologies, queer and feminist design, and the politics of preservation. As a practitioner, aspects of these same issues are addressed through media arts interventions and research design projects. Hogan is also the art director of online and p.o.d. journal of arts and politics, nomorepotlucks.org; on the advisory board of the Fembot collective; a Faculty Fellow at the Media Archaeology Lab, and a research design consultant for mat3rial.com and archinodes.com. Hogan recently completed her mandate of 6 years on the administrative board of Studio XX.

Ippolita is an international collective for convivial research and writings. Investigations and workshop topics include: (reality) hacking, free software and philosophy and anthropology of technologies. As a heteronomous identity, Ippolita published 'Open Is Not Free' (2005, it); 'The Dark Side of Google' (2007; it-fr-es-en); 'In the Facebook Aquarium: The Resistible Rise of Anarcho-Capitalism (2012; it-es-fr). Ippolita's independent server provides their copyleft works, exploring the cutting edge 'technologies of domination' with their social effects. Forthcoming project: Algocracies. Or, how Masters of Clouds are becoming Gods. www.ippolita.net & info@ippolita.net

Kylie Jarrett is a lecturer in Multimedia at the Centre for Media Studies at the National University of Ireland, Maynooth, responsible for teaching modules on digital media.

Her research interest is critical analysis of commercial digital media, in particular those forms referred to as social media.. Her current research is focussed on applying feminist labour theories in understanding consumer labour in digital media contexts. She has recently published with colleagues a study of Google and the culture of search, and she has also published on YouTube and eBay. Her doctoral study investigated the discourse of consumer empowerment in the field of e-commerce, using semiotics and sociolinguistics to explore this representation.

Min Jiang is Associate Professor of Communication and Research Affiliate at the Center for Global Communication Studies, University of Pennsylvania. She teaches graduate and undergraduate courses in new media technology, global media and research methods. Her research focuses on the intersections of Chinese Internet technologies, politics and policies. Her work is highly interdisciplinary, blending new media studies, political communication, international communication, legal studies, and information science, focusing on Chinese digital technologies (search engines, microblogging), internet policies, social activism, and digital diplomacy. A recipient of over a dozen research grants, she was the first Research Fellow at UNC Charlotte's Center for Humanities, Technology, and Science, a faculty member of the 2009 Annenberg-Oxford Summer Institute and a finalist in 2009 Knight News Challenge. She received her Ph.D. in Communication from Purdue University in 2007. Prior to pursuing her doctor's degree in the U.S., she worked as an international news editor for BTV and CCTV as well as assistant to director for Kill Bill I in China.

Anna Jobin is a researcher at the Laboratory of Digital Cultures and Humanities (LaDHUL) at the University of Lausanne, Switzerland. She is interested in sociology, algorithms, and everything in between.

Phil Jones (http://synaesmedia.net/) is a programmer, digital artist and electronic musician. He plays with the Brasilia Laptop Orchestra (BSBLOrk) and organizes 'Lago Lounge', an electronic music meet-up. Phil also works on software for defining physical objects and machines that are suitable for fabricating with 3d printers or laser-cutters. (Recently exhibited in ObjectOriented II at the Galeria Espaço Piloto IdA/UnB, Brasilia.) Phil has collaborated with Aharon Amir for several years, co-creating the Narcissus Search Engine, co-organizing the monthly Art & Chat meetups in Brighton, and recently installing the BomBane's CommunityBox Gallery in a local cafe.

Simon Knight's research focuses on student's epistemic practices in information seeking. Following teaching high school philosophy and psychology, he completed his MA in philosophy of education exploring the implications of the 'extended mind' thesis for our understanding of knowledge and its assessment. That work particularly focussed on the Danish use of internet in examinations, asking the question 'Is Wikipedia a part of my extended mind?' He then completed an MPhil in Educational research, focussing on the epistemic dialogue children used in collaborative information seeking tasks. His PhD work at the U.K.'s Open University continues this line of research, applying learning analytic techniques to the exploration of epistemic dialogue and commitments in collaborative information seeking. He tweets @sjgknight and blogs at http://people.kmi.open.ac.uk/knight.

Author Biographies

René König is a sociologist researching at the Institute for Technology Assessment and Systems Analysis (ITAS), Karlsruhe Institute of Technology. He is interested in online knowledge hierarchies and he focuses on transformation processes in academia triggered by Web 2.0. He co-edited this volume and the Society of the Query #2 conference. Website: renekoenig.eu.

Dirk Lewandowski is a professor of information research and information retrieval at the Hamburg University of Applied Sciences. Prior to that, he worked as an independent consultant and as a part-time lecturer at the Heinrich-Heine-University Düsseldorf. His research interests are Web Information Retrieval and users' interaction with Web search engines.

Mary Elizabeth (M.E.) Luka is an award-winning documentary producer-director for television and digital media including as founder of CBC ArtSpots. As a Vanier Canada Graduate Scholar and doctoral candidate (ABD) wrapping up her doctoral work in Communication and Media at Concordia University, she probes the work of artists in relation to broadcasting and digital media. Deeply involved with the culture and education sectors as a strategic planning consultant including Canadian Public Arts Funders and Women in Film and Television-Atlantic, she is also a leadership volunteer with Arts Nova Scotia (founding Vice-Chair), Creative Nova Scotia Leadership Council and the NSCAD University Board of Governors.

Astrid Mager Dr. Phil, is a postdoctoral researcher at the Institute of Technology Assessement (ITA), Austrian Academy of Sciences, and a lecturer at the Department of Science and Technology Studies, University of Vienna. At present, she is leader of the project "Glocal Search. Search technology at the intersection of global capitalism and local socio-political cultures" (funded by the Jubiläumsfonds of the Oesterreichische Nationalbank (OeNB), project number 14702). Her theoretical background is in Science and Technology Studies (STS) and her primary research interests include internet and society, search engine politics, knowledge production, privacy, digital methods, and critical theory. Recent publications: "Technoscientific promotion and biofuel policy. How the press and search engines stage the biofuel controversy", in Media, Culture & Society, 2013 (together with Jenny Eklöf), "Algorithmic ideology. How capitalist society shapes search engines", in Information, Communication & Society, 2012, "Search engines matter: From educating users towards engaging with online health information practices, Policy & Internet, 2012. Visit http://www.astridmager.net, email: astrid.mager@oeaw.ac.at.

Martina Mahnke is a PhD Fellow at the University of Erfurt/Germany, currently visiting the Center for Communication and Computing at the University of Copenhagen/Denmark. Her research is located at the crossroad of communication and computer science and deals with the question of how algorithms and human are communicatively interrelated. In particular, she is interested in the underlying socio-technical dynamics of 'algorithmic media'.

Andrea Miconi teaches Media Studies and Sociology of Culture at IULM University, Milan, and The Network Society at the University of Lugano, Switzerland. He had been visiting lecturer at Communication & Arts School of Sao Paulo University, Brazil. His research is mainly focused on media history and critical Internet theory.

Jacob Ørmen is a PhD Fellow at the University of Copenhagen (Department of Media, Cognition and Communication). Jacob researches individuals' engagement with political news and their propensity to deliberate politics both face-to-face and through various media. The PhD is part of a wider research project on cross-media communication in the digital age called "Meaning across media – Cross-media communication and co-creation". Jacob is also interested in empirical methods (particularly newer digital forms), digital humanities and communication theory. He has background as a communication advisor and holds a MA in political science from Central European University as well as a BA in history from University of Copenhagen.

Miriam Rasch started working as a publication manager at the Institute of Network Cultures in June 2012. She holds a masters degree in Literary Studies (2002) and Philosophy (2005). Since graduating she worked as a (web) editor and from 2008 on as a programmer for the public lectures department at Utrecht University, Studium Generale. Next to that she worked as a lecturer for Liberal Arts and Sciences, and is teaching philosophy and media theory at the Media, Information and Communication department. She writes book reviews and guest posts for different websites and magazines; her personal blog can be found on miriamrasch.nl.

Martin Reiche is an audiovisual artist living and working in Berlin, Germany. http://www.martinreiche.com

Amanda Scardamaglia completed her LLB (Hons) and BA at The University of Melbourne before being admitted to practice as an Australian Legal Practitioner in the Supreme Court of Victoria. More recently, she completed her PhD at The University of Melbourne, entitled 'A History of Trade Mark Law: The Colonial Trade Mark Regime'. Her research is in the area of trade mark law, especially the historical development of trade mark law, as well as the use of trade marks in internet search and advertising.

Anton Tanter is lecturer at the Department of History at Universität Wien. His research interests include the history of intelligence/registry offices in Europe, house numbering, and new media in historical sciences. In 2004 he defended a dissertation about the history of the census and house numbering in the Habsburg monarchy that was published in 2007 as Ordnung der Häuser, Beschreibung der Seelen. Hausnummerierung und Seelenkonskription in der Habsburger-monarchie (=Wiener Schriften zur Geschichte der Neuzeit; 4). Innsbruck/Wien/Bozen: Studienverlag, 2007. www.tantner.net

Emma Uprichard is Associate Professor at the Centre for Interdisciplinary Methodologies at the University of Warwick. She is director of the Warwick Q-Step Centre for the advancement of quantitative methods in the social sciences. She is co-editor with David Byrne of four volumes on 'Cluster Analysis' (Sage, 2012). She is especially interested in developing new methods and methodologies relating to studying complex socio-spatial and temporal change. Her substantive research interests include: methods, time, childhood, food, and cities.

www.ingramcontent.com/pod-product-compliance
Lightning Source LLC
Chambersburg PA
CBHW071144160426
43196CB00011B/2002